THE GREAT NAME

ANCIENT EGYPTIAN ROYAL TITULARY

SBL

Society of Biblical Literature

Writings from the Ancient World

Theodore J. Lewis, General Editor

Associate Editors

Daniel Fleming
Martti Nissinen
William Schniedewind
Mark S. Smith
Emily Teeter
Theo P. J. van den Hout
Terry Wilfong

Number 33
The Great Name

THE GREAT NAME

Ancient Egyptian Royal Titulary

Ronald J. Leprohon

Edited by
Denise M. Doxey

Society of Biblical Literature
Atlanta

THE GREAT NAME

Ancient Egyptian Royal Titulary

Library of Congress Cataloging-in-Publication Data

The great name : ancient Egyptian royal titulary / edited by Ronald J. Leprohon.
pages cm. — (Writings from the ancient world ; Number 33)
Includes bibliographical references and index.
ISBN 978-1-58983-767-6 (hardcover binding : alk. paper) — ISBN 978-1-58983-735-5 (paper binding : alk. paper) — ISBN 978-1-58983-736-2 (electronic format) 1. Egypt—Kings and rulers—Titles. 2. Titles of honor and nobility—Egypt—History—To 1500. 3. Egypt—History—To 332 B.C. 4. Egypt—History—332-30 B.C. I. Leprohon, Ronald J.
DT83.G74 2013
932—dc23

2013004011

Printed on acid-free, recycled paper conforming to
ANSI /NISO Z39.48–1992 (R1997) and ISO 9706:1994
standards for paper permanence.

To the memory of

Bernard D. Leprohon
(July 4, 1922–July 10, 2012)

Diane O. Leprohon
(September 13, 1948–July 25, 2012)

C'est à votre tour de vous laisser parler d'amour

Contents

List of Figures ix

Series Editor's Foreword xi

Preface xiii

Chronological Table xv

Map of Egypt xvii

Abbreviations xix

I. Introduction 1

1. Intended Audience and Previous Work 2
2. Sources Used 3
3. Notes on the Translations 3
4. Names and Their Importance 5
5. The Five Names of the King 7
   - 5.1 Introductory Remarks 7
   - 5.2 Choosing and Proclaiming the Titulary 9
   - 5.3 The Horus Name 12
   - 5.4 The Two Ladies Name 13
   - 5.5 The Golden Horus Name 15
   - 5.6 The Throne Name 17
   - 5.7 The Birth Name 18

II. Early Dynastic Period 21

III. Old Kingdom 31

IV. First Intermediate Period 49

V. Middle Kingdom 54

VI. Second Intermediate Period 81

VII. New Kingdom 93

VIII. Third Intermediate Period 136

IX. Late Period 164

X. The Macedonian and Ptolemaic Dynasties 175

Appendix A. Index of Royal Names 189

Appendix B. Alphabetical List of Kings 231

Appendix C. Greek–Egyptian Equivalents of Royal Names 241

Bibliography 243

Indexes

Names of Kings 261

Deities 263

Personal Names 264

Place Names 265

Subjects 266

Sources 267

Concordances

Texts in *Urkunden* IV 269

Texts in Kitchen, *Ramesside Inscriptions* 269

List of Figures

Figure 1. Map of Egypt xvii
Figure 2. Fivefold Titulary of King Thutmose I (Eighteenth Dynasty) (redrawn by B. Ibronyi) 11
Figure 3. *Serekh* of King Djet (First Dynasty) (redrawn by B. Ibronyi) 14

Series Editor's Foreword

Writings from the Ancient World is designed to provide up-to-date, readable English translations of writings recovered from the ancient Near East.

The series is intended to serve the interests of general readers, students, and educators who wish to explore the ancient Near Eastern roots of Western civilization or to compare these earliest written expressions of human thought and activity with writings from other parts of the world. It should also be useful to scholars in the humanities or social sciences who need clear, reliable translations of ancient Near Eastern materials for comparative purposes. Specialists in particular areas of the ancient Near East who need access to texts in the scripts and languages of other areas will also find these translations helpful. Given the wide range of materials translated in the series, different volumes will appeal to different interests. However, these translations make available to all readers of English the world's earliest traditions as well as valuable sources of information on daily life, history, religion, and the like in the preclassical world.

The translators of the various volumes in this series are specialists in the particular languages and have based their work on the original sources and the most recent research. In their translations they attempt to convey as much as possible of the original texts in fluent, current English. In the introductions, notes, glossaries, maps, and chronological tables, they aim to provide the essential information for an appreciation of these ancient documents.

The ancient Near East reached from Egypt to Iran and, for the purposes of our volumes, ranged in time from the invention of writing (by 3000 B.C.E.) to the conquests of Alexander the Great (ca. 330 B.C.E.). The cultures represented within these limits include especially Egyptian, Sumerian, Babylonian, Assyrian, Hittite, Ugaritic, Aramean, Phoenician, and Israelite. It is hoped that Writings from the Ancient World will eventually produce translations from most of the many different genres attested in these cultures: letters (official and private), myths, diplomatic documents, hymns, law collections, monumental inscriptions, tales, and administrative records, to mention but a few.

Significant funding was made available by the Society of Biblical Literature for the preparation of this volume. In addition, those involved in preparing this volume have received financial and clerical assistance from their respective institutions. Were it not for these expressions of confidence in our work, the arduous tasks of preparation, translation, editing, and publication could not have been accomplished or even undertaken. It is the hope of all who have worked with the Writings from the Ancient World series that our translations will open up new horizons and deepen the humanity of all who read these volumes.

Theodore J. Lewis
The Johns Hopkins University

Preface

The genesis of this book goes back many years, when I asked myself what the name "Khufu" meant. King Khufu, sometimes referred to by his Greek name Cheops, is of course famous for being the builder of the Great Pyramid, and his name appears in countless writings on pharaonic Egypt. After parsing the various elements of the name and realizing that it meant "He protects me," with the divine name Khnum added in some instances of the name (giving the full name "Khnum, he protects me"), I developed an interest in ancient Egyptian names in general. The fact that pharaohs took on a series of additional names at their coronation also intrigued me. Thus was born the idea of translating the more than one thousand names found in this book.

The rendering of some names was fairly straightforward, while others offered different choices, all of which could be defended grammatically. At times, as explained in the introduction, I simply had to decide on a given rendering and not bother the reader with more than one choice. If I remember her wise counsel properly, the great popular historian Barbara Tuchman once wrote that scholars should never argue their evidence in front of their audience (*Practicing History: Selected Essays* [New York: Knopf, 1981]), as she preferred to lay out her story in a clear linear fashion. This is what I have opted to do on a number of occasions in this catalogue of names. It is my hope that the readers of this book will use it not only as a reference work but also as a springboard from which more work can be done on the topic.

I am grateful to Denise Doxey for accepting to take on the editing of this project. She made some rather good suggestions along the way, caught a number of silly—and at times humorous—mistakes, and generally made the manuscript much better all around. A great tip of the hat goes her way. I have also benefited from a number of conversations with my colleague Katja Goebs here at the University of Toronto. Her insightful comments forced me to rethink some of my renderings and my thinking about ancient Egyptian kingship in general; she also suggested a number of bibliographical items of which I was unaware. I also thank my student Vicky Murrell for helping to find the provenance and full references for many of the Ramesside Period additional names. Colleagues who helped along the way include Jim Allen, with whom I discussed the parsing of royal names; Aidan Dodson, who kindly sent me parts of his new book on the Third Intermediate Period before it was published; Elizabeth Frood, who helped with discussions on royal names in general; Salima Ikram, who shared some ideas about early dynastic kings; and Nigel Strudwick, for his friendship and constant encouragement. To them, and surely to others whom I am forgetting, I extend heartfelt thanks. Gratitude is also due to Ted Lewis, the series editor for Writings from the Ancient World, for his unfailing patience with my repeated promises to finish the manuscript within the next year. It has indeed taken me too long to finish this project. Above all, I cannot thank enough the two most important people in my life, my wife, Barbara Ibronyi, and my son, Thomas Leprohon, for providing me with love and laughter, and for putting up with the many mood swings that inevitably accompany the end of a project such as this. I also owe special gratitude to Barbara for copyediting my prose and for the artwork found in these pages.

The completion of this book was marred by the loss of two people. My father, my first hero and my role model, and my magnificent sister passed away within fifteen days of one another during the final push to finish the manuscript. To them I dedicate this book.

Chronological Table

The table is based on Clayton 1994 and all years are B.C.E. All dates prior to the mid-seventh century B.C.E. are approximate.

Early Dynastic Period	
Dynasty "0"	3150–3050
Dynasty 1	3050–2890
Dynasty 2	2890–2686
Old Kingdom	
Dynasty 3	2686–2613
Dynasty 4	2613–2498
Dynasty 5	2498–2345
Dynasty 6	2345–2181
Dynasty 8	2181–2161
First Intermediate Period	
Dynasties 9-10	2160–2040
Dynasty 11a	2134–2060
Middle Kingdom	
Dynasty 11b	2060–1991
Dynasty 12	1991–1782
Dynasty 13	1782–1650
Dynasty 14	?–1650
Second Intermediate Period	
Dynasty 15	1663–1555
Dynasty 16	1663–1555
Dynasty 17	1663–1570
New Kingdom	
Dynasty 18	1570–1293
Dynasty 19	1293–1185
Dynasty 20	1185–1070

Third Intermediate Period	
Dynasty 21	1069–945
Dynasty 22	945–712
Dynasty 23	818–712
Dynasty 24	727–715
Dynasty 25	747–656
Late Period	
Dynasty 26	664–525
Dynasty 27	525–404
Dynasty 28	404–399
Dynasty 29	399–380
Dynasty 30	380–343
Dynasty 31	343–332
Macedonian Dynasty	332–305
Ptolemaic Period	305–30

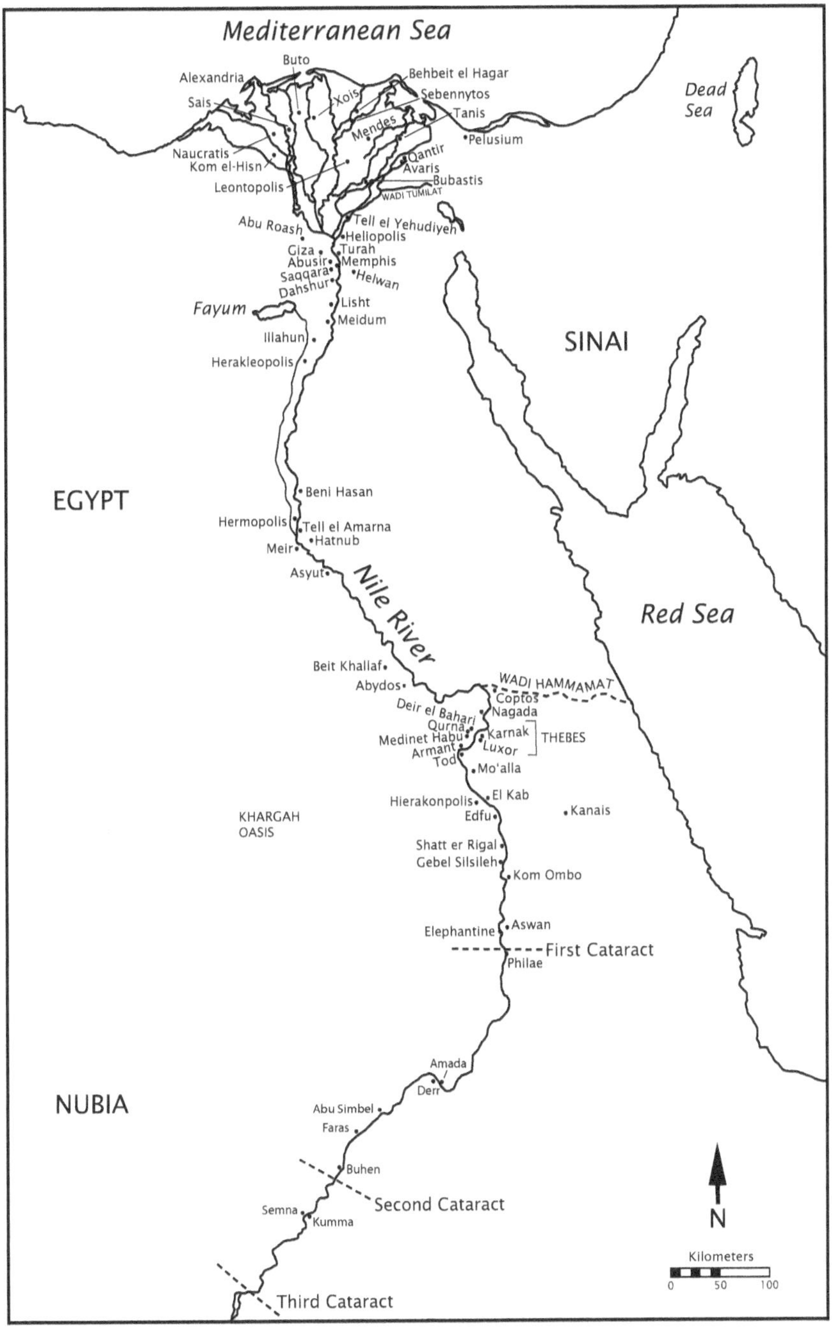

Figure 1. Map of Egypt (drawn by B. Ibronyi)

Abbreviations

ASAE	*Annales du Service des Antiquités de l'Egypte*
BACE	*Bulletin of the Australian Centre for Egyptology*
BASOR	*Bulletin of the American Schools of Oriental Research*
BdÉ	Bibliothèque d'Étude
BIFAO	*Bulletin de l'Institut Français d'Archéologie Orientale*
BiOr	*Bibliotheca Orientalis*
BMMA	*Bulletin of the Metropolitan Museum of Art*
BSEG	*Bulletin de la Société d'Égyptologie de Genève*
BSFE	*Bulletin de la Société Française d'Égyptologie*
CAJ	*Cambridge Archaeological Journal*
CdE	*Chronique d'Égypte*
CDME	Raymond O. Faulkner, *A Concise Dictionary of Middle Egyptian*. Oxford: Griffith Institute, 1962.
DE	*Discussions in Egyptology*
ENIM	*Égypte Nilotique et Méditerranéenne*
GM	*Göttinger Miszellen*
HÄB	Hildesheimer Ägyptologische Beiträge
IFAO	Institut Français d'Archéologie Orientale
JARCE	*Journal of the American Research Center in Egypt*
JEA	*Journal of Egyptian Archaeology*
JEGH	*Journal of Egyptian History*
JEOL	*Jaarbericht Ex Oriente Lux*
JNES	*Journal of Near Eastern Studies*
JSSEA	*Journal of the Society for the Study of Egyptian Antiquities*
KRI	Kenneth A. Kitchen, *Ramesside Inscriptions, Historical and Biographical*. 8 vols. Oxford: Blackwell, 1975–91.
LD	Richard Lepsius, *Denkmäler aus Ägypten und Äthiopien: nach den Zeichnungen der von Seiner Majestät dem Könige von Preussen Friedrich Wilhelm IV. nach diesen Ländern gesendeten und in den Jahren 1842–1845 ausgeführten wissenschaftlichen Expedition*. 12 vols. Berlin: Nicolaische Buchhandlung, 1849–59.
MÄS	Münchner Ägyptologische Studien

MDAIK	*Mitteilungen des Deutschen Archäologischen Instituts Abteilung Kairo*
MIFAO	Mémoires publiés par les membres de l'Institut Français d'Archéologie Orientale du Caire
MMJ	*Metropolitan Museum Journal*
OBO	Orbis Biblicus et Orientalis
OIP	Oriental Institute Publications
OLA	Orientalia Lovaniensia Analecta
OLZ	*Orientalistiche Literaturzeitung*
Or	*Orientalia*
PM	Bertha Porter and Rosalind L. B. Moss, with Ethel W. Burney and Jaromir Málek (from 1973). *Topographical Bibliography of Ancient Egyptian Hieroglyphic Texts, Reliefs and Paintings.* 7 vols. Oxford: Griffith Institute, 1927–52. 2nd ed., 1960–.
PSBA	*Proceedings of the Society of Biblical Archaeology*
RdE	*Revue d'Égyptologie*
SAOC	Studies in Ancient Oriental Civilizations
SAK	*Studien zur Altägyptischen Kultur*
Urk. IV	Kurt Sethe and Wolfgang Helck, *Urkunden der 18. Dynastie.* Leipzig: Hinrichs; Berlin: Akademie-Verlag, 1906–58.
Urk. VII	Kurt Sethe, *Historisch-Biographische Urkunden des Mittleren Reiches.* Leipzig: J. C. Hinrichs; Berlin: Akademie-Verlag, 1935.
Wb	A. Erman and H. Grapow, *Wörterbuch der aegyptischen Sprache.* 5 vols. Leipzig: J. C. Hinrichs, 1926–31. Reprinted 1971.
WZKM	*Wiener Zeitschrift für die Kunde des Morgenlandes*
ZÄS	*Zeitschrift für Ägyptische Sprache und Altertumskunde*

I

Introduction

> Besides, the king's name is a tower of strength,
> Which they upon the adverse part want.
> Shakespeare,
> *Richard III,* V, iii

The pharaoh is one of the most recognizable figures in ancient Egypt. As far back as the late Predynastic period, a ruler was easily identifiable in a pictorial composition by the fact that he was depicted on a larger scale than the other human figures around him.[1] Other symbols of authority were the regalia the king wore and the titulary he assumed at his coronation. At first consisting only of the so-called Horus name, the titulary was expanded over time to include other epithets chosen to represent the king's special relationship with the divine world. By the time of the Middle Kingdom (late twenty-first century B.C.E.), the full fivefold titulary was clearly established and kings henceforth used all five names regularly.

It is these names that the present volume will offer in transliteration and translation. The corpus will consist of all royal names from the so-called Dynasty "0" (thirty-second century B.C.E.) down to the last Ptolemaic ruler in the late first century B.C.E. The order in which they will be presented is Horus, Two Ladies, Golden Horus, Throne, and Birth names. Each entry will first offer a traditional scholarly transliteration (e.g., *wꜣḥ-ꜥnḫ*), using Gardiner's (1957a) simple method of transliteration, with which English-speaking scholars will be mostly familiar. Note that, as in the example given here, a phrase consisting of an adjective qualifying a noun (e.g., "enduring of life") will be hyphenated. Next will come an anglicized version of the transliteration in italics (e.g., *wah ankh*), for readers not familiar with the study of the ancient Egyptian language. These two sets of transliteration will be followed by a translation of the phrase. The corpus will not include the names of queens, even though some of these are written within cartouches, unless the queen is specifically believed to have ruled the

1. For an example from the Nagada IIIA1 period, see Darnell 2002, fig. on p. 10. See also Robins 2000, 21, 32–33.

country, for example, Queens Nitocris, Sobeknefru, Hatshepsut, Tawosret, and a few Ptolemaic queens.[2] Additionally, Nubian rulers will not be included, except those who actually ruled over Egypt, that is, what is referred to as Dynasty 25.[3] Because they would essentially constitute a separate study, the numerous epithets further describing the king have also been left out of this book.[4]

1. Intended Audience and Previous Work

This set of translations of ancient Egyptian royal names is aimed at specialists and nonspecialists alike. For the latter, the double set of transliterations offered will, it is hoped, make the entries easier to understand, and of course the translations are mostly intended for those who cannot read ancient Egyptian. The specialists will already have access to a number of publications dealing with the subject, although none of these presents as much material as the current volume. The standard collection of Egyptian royal names, given in hieroglyphic font, remains Henri Gauthier's *Le Livre des rois d'Égypte, recueil de titres et protocoles royaux* (the pertinent volumes for the present book are vols. 1–4 (1907, 1912, 1914, 1916), although this is fairly out of date[5] and Gauthier did not translate the names. A newer publication of royal names, offered in clear handwritten hieroglyphs and with transliteration, is Jürgen von Beckerath's *Handbuch der ägyptischen Königsnamen* (2nd ed., 1999). Although significantly more up-to-date and tremendously useful, the volume was written with specialists in mind, as the names are not translated. It must be added that the present book owes a great depth of gratitude to von Beckerath's work, since, unless otherwise indicated, the order of kings in most periods follows his own. Another book that must be cited is Michel Dessoudeix's wonderful *Chronique de l'Égypte ancienne: Les pharaons, leur règne, leurs contemporains* (2008). Dessoudeix presents not only the events from each king's reign, his building activities and burial site, the main officials from the period, and relevant bibliographies, but also a full set of names translated into French. Where the present book mainly differs from Dessoudeix's work is in the rendering of the kings' Throne names, as will be explained below. Two other relevant books are Stephen Quirke's *Who Were the Pharaohs? A History of Their Names with a List of Cartouches* (1990) and Peter Clayton's *Chronicle of the Pharaohs: The Reign-by-Reign Record of the Rulers and Dynas-*

2. The latter will be given additional numbers (e.g., "5a") within the dynasty. For a recent and useful study of queens' names, see Grajetzki 2005.

3. For Nubian rulers contemporary with early Middle Kingdom Egyptian kings, see Aufrère 1982, 64, 69; Postel 2004, 379–84; and Grajetzki 2006, 27–28. For the later Nubian monarchs who ruled from Napata, see especially Eide et al. 1994, 1996, 1998, 2000.

4. Aufrère (1982, 31–34) offers a number of examples; for the material from the New Kingdom on, see Grimal 1986.

5. In this respect, it is noteworthy to remember that Gauthier presented his Eighteenth Dynasty rulers a full decade before the discovery of Tutankhamun's tomb.

ties of Ancient Egypt (1994). The former contains a most useful history of the development of the royal titulary along with a number of names at the end, but again none of these is translated. Clayton's book is another masterful offering, but not all royal names are presented or translated.

2. Sources Used

The lists of royal names gathered by Gauthier and von Beckerath constitute the main sources for the names presented herein. These come mainly from material emanating from the royal workshops, whether official stelae, funerary monuments, inscriptions carved on temple walls, or obelisks added to the temple courtyards. A further source for ancient Egyptian royal names is King Lists compiled in later periods.[6] These must be used carefully, however, since in cases such as the Early Dynastic rulers, as much as seventeen centuries separated the original rulers from the Ramesside scribes who compiled the lists. For certain eras, such as the first two so-called Intermediate periods, the later King Lists are often the only extant evidence for a good number of rulers. In such cases—for example, the kings of Dynasty 3A presented below, none of whom is attested contemporaneously—the name will be followed by an asterisk and designated as "Later cartouche name." This will help distinguish those rulers attested in contemporary records from those known only from later lists.[7]

3. Notes on the Translations

The art of translating consists in deconstructing one code—in this case, the ancient Egyptian language—and reconstructing it into another, here, modern English. I have made every effort to render the names as faithfully as possible to the original. Hence, a two-word expression consisting of an adjective qualifying a noun will usually be rendered with the same word order as in the original phrase. Thus, the Horus name of King Intef II, *wꜣḥ–ꜥnḫ*, will be translated "enduring of life," with the phrase meaning "the one whose life is enduring." In cases where an English idiomatic expression exists, a more modern rendering will be offered. Thus, the phrase *nḫt–ꜥ*, lit. "strong of arm," used as part of a secondary Horus name of King Ramses III, will be translated as "strong-armed."

Readers will also note that Egyptian participles, which have the meaning of an English relative clause where the subject is the same as the antecedent (e.g., "one who loves")[8] will be rendered in the past tense ("one who loved"). The reason for this is that the participial forms of mutable verbs met in the phrases form-

6. Redford 1986.

7. See Baumgartel 1975, 28, for similar reservations about such lists compiled so long after the fact.

8. Gardiner 1957a, §353.

ing the royal titulary are never written in their "imperfective" form, where the last root of the verb is reduplicated, but only in their "perfective" (i.e., past tense) forms. Compare *mrr,* "one who loves," to *mr,* "one who loved."[9] One exception, which proves the point nicely, is the Throne name of Apries, where the participle is written in its imperfective form, thus giving us a present continuous form: *ḥʿʿ ib rʿ,* "One who (continually) rejoices over the mind of Re." The use of the past tense may have had something to do with the length of time between the king's accession at the death of his predecessor and his coronation, during which time the titulary was composed. When the new king's names were announced at his coronation, perhaps the sentiments expressed in the various epithets were already considered a *fait accompli.*

Names are notoriously difficult to translate, and sometimes I have made choices that will seem arbitrary. This dilemma is particularly revealed when certain verbal forms can be parsed either as Egyptian participles or relative forms. Both are rendered with English relative clauses, but the latter are distinguished from the former because the subject is different than the antecedent; compare "the woman who reads a book" to "a book (that) the woman is reading." In some cases, translating a particular phrase with a participle is the clear choice. One example is Mentuhotep III's Horus name, *sʿnḫ tꜣwy.f(y),* "the one who has sustained his Two Lands," in which the king was obviously said to be acting on behalf of his country. The same king's first Throne name is *sʿnḫ kꜣ rʿ,* which can be rendered as "the one who has sustained the ka of Re" or "the one whom the ka of Re has sustained." If one argues that the king was acting for the benefit of the god by making offerings in a temple, the verb *sʿnḫ,* "to live," could be parsed as a participle ("the one who has sustained the ka of Re"). If, however, one assumes that the god was acting on behalf of the king, then the verb form is to be parsed as a relative ("the one whom the ka of Re has sustained"). Because the second translation seems to be more in accord with what we know of the relationship between the king and the gods in ancient Egypt, it is the form selected in this book. In Mentuhotep III's case, an additional Throne name of the king perhaps makes the choice clearer; it reads *snfr kꜣ rʿ,* and I have rendered the phrase as "the one whom the ka of Re has made perfect," because it seems obvious that it is the god who is making the king "perfect."

Careful readers will also perceive what seem to be inconsistencies in the rendering of some words or phrases. The reasons for the changes are a wish on my part to be as idiomatic as possible in my renderings. For example, the noun *ib,* which is often translated as "heart," was actually the "mind" or even "intellect."[10] Thus, part of a secondary Two Ladies name of Ramses II, *mꜣi sḫm–ib,* lit. "the lion who is powerful of heart," is translated "stout-hearted lion" in the catalogue,

9. I owe this observation to an anonymous referee who read a draft of an article submitted to the *UCLA Encyclopedia of Egyptology* (Leprohon 2010b).

10. See, e.g., Bonhême and Forgeau 1988, 310.

while Sekhemib's Horus name, *sḫm–ib*, lit. "the one who is powerful of will," is rendered "the resolute one." Other inconsistencies will occur because of common spellings seen in most studies. For example, although the name of the primary god during the New Kingdom is transliterated as *imn* (*imen*) in these pages, it will be rendered as "Amun" throughout, unless it occurs in theophoric names such as Amenemhat or Amenhotep. Some kings, who are mostly known by their Greek names—for example, King Smendes or King Apries—will be presented with their Egyptian name first, followed by the more common Greek name in a bracket. Thus, the two preceding monarchs will be referred to as Nes-ba-neb-djed (Smendes) and Wahibre (Apries), respectively. An appendix of Greek names and their Egyptian equivalents is offered at the end of the book.

4. Names and Their Importance

Choosing a particular name was an especially symbolic act for an ancient Egyptian ruler, since names were so significant within the culture. After all, the original act of creation by the primeval god himself was inextricably linked to the act of naming the various entities he created.[11] Kings wished their names to "remain" (*mn*) and be "enduring" (*wꜣḥ*),[12] or for posterity to "give thanks to god" (*dwꜣ nṯr*) in their name.[13] A king could also make his name "perfect" (*nfr*) through "combat" (*ꜥḥꜣ*),[14] which cemented his reputation as a "brave warrior" (*ḳn*)[15] in "every country."[16] And that reputation could then be circulated by a court official who "established" (*smn*)[17] or "caused to live" (*sꜥnḫ*)[18] his lord's name. In fact, courtiers were urged to "fight" (*ꜥḥꜣ*) on behalf of their sovereign's name.[19] Kings were also mindful of former monarchs: for example, we find Amenhotep II "causing to live" (*sꜥnḫ*) the names of the Fourth Dynasty rulers Khufu and Khafre[20] as well as that of his own father Thutmose III.[21] This led to officials also "commemorating" (*dm*, lit. "pronouncing")[22] the names of former queens and royal children.

---

11. Cf. the Memphite Theology, col. 55, which reads: "The teeth and the lips in his mouth, which proclaimed the name of everything," and the demiurge "who created names" (*ḳmꜣ rnw*); on this, see Vernus 1980, col. 321, notes 3–4, with references.
12. *Urk.* IV, 366:15.
13. KRI I, 66:5.
14. KRI II, 79:6–9.
15. *Urk.* IV, 1710:7, 1752:11, and 1921:1.
16. Ibid., 1685:14, 1693:17.
17. Ibid., 1822:11.
18. Ibid., 1934:15.
19. Cairo Stela CG 20538, Verso 19. For an easily accessible version, see Lichtheim 1973, 128; see also Leprohon 2009, 283.
20. *Urk.* IV, 1283:3.
21. Ibid., 1295:7–8.
22. Ibid., 1778:3.

In turn, individuals wished their own names to "remain" (*mn*)[23] or be "permanent" (*rwd*)[24] in people's mouths, which led them to wish for posterity to "pronounce" (*dm*),[25] "invoke" (*nis*),[26] "remember" (*sḫ3*),[27] or simply "not forget" (*n smḫ*)[28] their name. This desire for their name to continue "existing" (*wn*)[29] or "not perish" (*n sk*)[30] would lead to their reputation (lit. their "name") being "perfect" (*nfr*)[31] or "blameless" (*twr*, lit. "clean"),[32] a success that could be achieved through what an official himself had "accomplished" (*m irt.n.f*),[33] resulting in having his name "advanced" (*sḫnt*) by the king.[34] Thus could an individual's name be "known" (*rḫ*) to the king,[35] which could lead to his being "greeted by name" (*nḏ-ḥr*) by his ruler.[36] This recognition enabled his name to be "great"(*ʿ3*) in "the Two Lands of Horus"[37] and "heard" (*sḏm*) in "Upper and Lower Egypt."[38] This correlation between reputation and position is nicely summed up in the epithet of one official, who claimed that he was "great in his name and important in his rank" (*wr m rn.f ʿ3 m sʿḥ.f*).[39] In the end, it was a family's duty to keep the memory of a deceased relative alive, as the ubiquitous phrase "to cause the name to live" (*sʿnḫ rn*) was applied to one's father,[40] mother,[41] or grandfather.[42] We even encounter a brother causing his sibling's name to live.[43]

Additionally, because ancient Egyptians believed that everything was animated with *bau*-power,[44] an energy believed to be divine intervention into the

23. Ibid., 1785:14, 1875:18.
24. Ibid., 1805:4.
25. Ibid., 1626:15, 1845:20.
26. Ibid., 1835:9, 1846:15.
27. Ibid., 1537:2.
28. Ibid., 1601:2.
29. Ibid., 1805:4.
30. Vernus 1976, 5–6.
31. *Urk.* IV, 1800:19, 1912:6.
32. Ibid., 1818:10.
33. Ibid., 2:5; on this theme, see also Schott 1969.
34. *Urk.* IV, 1410:4.
35. Doxey 1998, 332, 393.
36. Ibid., 374.
37. Ibid., 276.
38. Ibid., 332.
39. Fischer 1973, 20–21; Vernus 1980, col. 321, n. 15.
40. *Urk.* IV, 1446:18, 1504:8, 1641:19, 1808:11, 1913:20, 1919:3, etc. See also the epithet "one whose name was made in stone by his son" (Doxey 1998, 270).
41. *Urk.* IV, 1446:12.
42. Ibid., 1939:16 and 1950:12, where the bequests are made by the "son of his son" (*s3 n s3.f*).
43. Ibid., 1493:7.
44. Žabkar 1968, 48–50; Green 1980, 35 n. 6.

affairs of humans,[45] everyday objects were given names. The list of such named items runs from a well dug under the aegis of a king,[46] or the latter's chariot[47] and battleship.[48] Army divisions were named,[49] and even a besieging wall could be given an appellation compounded with the king's name.[50] Buildings were of course given names, whether they were temples[51] or fortresses on Egypt's frontiers.[52] Within those structures, the pylons,[53] gateways and doors,[54] and statues were named.[55]

5. The Five Names of the King

5.1. Introductory Remarks

Since the king was a human being who held a divine office as well as the link between his subjects and the gods, the royal court wished to express the essential features of this unique circumstance. One of the ways it accomplished this was by composing special epithets that the king assumed at his accession, which would serve as a brief statement of his qualities or of his relationship with the divine and the terrestrial world.

These epithets could consist of short phrases with a simple adjective qualifying a noun, such as "enduring of life" or "great of manifestations." More common were longer declarations in which an Egyptian participle, whether active or passive, was used alone ("the one who has united," or "the beloved one") or, more frequently, with a direct object ("the one who has seized all lands") or an adverbial phrase ("the one who has appeared in Thebes"). The Egyptian participle was also used by itself as a noun ("the one who is established," with the meaning of "the established one") followed by other nouns ("the perfect one of—i.e., belonging to—the ka of Re"). In the New Kingdom and Third Intermediate period,

45. Borghouts 1982.

46. KRI I, 66:11.

47. *Urk.* IV, 1302:3.

48. Ibid., 1297:7–8. Divine barques were also named; see, e.g., *Urk.* IV, 1652:12.

49. KRI II, 15:11–15. Although this is not unusual in a military context, it is noteworthy that the divisions were named after various gods.

50. *Urk.* IV, 661:6 and 1254:9, from Thutmose III's account of his siege of the city of Megiddo.

51. A few examples are found in *Urk.* IV, 1709:17 and 1710:7 (Luxor Temple); 1668:10 (temple of Montu, Karnak); 1252:7 (Thutmose III's Festival Hall, Karnak); 1655:2 and 1752:11 (temples of Soleb and Gebel Barkal, Nubia, respectively); 1250:16 and 1355:9 (Mortuary Temples of Thutmose III and Amenhotep II, respectively).

52. *Urk.* IV, 740:1, 1421:10.

53. Ibid., 1650:5.

54. Ibid., 1268:2; and Nims 1969, 70.

55. *Urk.* IV, 1405:19, 1554:2, 1741:1, 1758:10, and 1796:15.

when the titulary became more elaborate, a combination of such types of phrases would often be employed.

There was a long period of experimentation,[56] as new categories of names were created over time. First to appear was the Horus name, followed by the Golden Horus name halfway through the First Dynasty, in the reign of King Den. Next came a reference to "the one who belongs to Upper and Lower Egypt," and then a mention of the Two Ladies in the mid to late First Dynasty, in the reigns of Adjib and Semerkhet, respectively. The oval ring that contained the last two names of the king, and which was originally a simple circle, is first met in the reign of King Sanakht in the Third Dynasty.[57] Called *shen* in Egyptian, a word that means "to encircle," it was a symbol of the king's rule over all that the sun god encompassed and had both protective and solar associations.[58] This development of the titulary lasted until the Middle Kingdom, at which point the five names finally achieved their "canonical" form. No king from the Early Dynastic period and very few from the Old Kingdom bore all five names, and even the latter group did not necessarily present all of these in the order in which we expect to see them.[59]

It is also during this period that we first meet the designation of the royal titulary. A text now in Berlin and thought to be from the Fayum, dated to the reign of Amenemhat III, announced the king's coregency with his father Senwosret III.[60] The text is fragmentary, but one of the blocks reads /// *rn.f wr* [*n*(*y*)-*sw*]-*bỉt* [*n*(*y*)-*mꜣꜥt-rꜥ*] ///, "/// his Great Name, the Dual King [Nimaatre] ///."[61] The text would later be copied by Hatshepsut when proclaiming her putative coregency with her father Thutmose I.[62] Her version of that particular passage reads *rn.s wr n*(*y*)-*sw-bỉt mꜣꜥt-kꜣ-rꜥ dỉ ꜥnḫ*, "her Great Name, the Dual King [sic][63] Maatkare, given life."[64] An analysis of the phrase Great Name has shown that it can refer to each royal name separately as well as the full five names.[65] For the fuller list, the texts mostly used the term *nḫbt*, which could refer either to the Horus name

56. Because we sometimes tend to telescope time when dealing with ancient history, it is worth mentioning here that around four and a half centuries elapsed between the beginning of the First Dynasty and King Radjedef of the Fourth Dynasty, the first monarch to introduce the epithet "son of Re" in the royal titulary.

57. It is found on a fragmentary sealing from Beit Khallaf in Middle Egypt, for which see Garstang 1903, pl. 19:7; see also T. A. H. Wilkinson 2001, 208.

58. Baines 1995, 9.

59. For a list of the variations met in the order of the names, see Aufrère 1982, 22–26; see also Bonhême 1987, 5.

60. For discussions, see Murnane 1977, 228–29; and Leprohon 1980, 297–302.

61. Fragment 15803c; see Roeder 1913, 138.

62. *Urk.* IV, 261–62.

63. The phrase *n*(*y*)-*su-bỉt* is not written with a feminine form.

64. *Urk.* IV, 261:17.

65. Bonhême 1978, 360–68.

alone or actually stand for the complete titulary.[66] Other terms used to refer to the royal names were *rn mꜣꜥ*, "Real Name," found only in a text from the reign of Hatshepsut,[67] as well as the simple *rn*, "Name," which, like the Great Name, could refer to each individual name or the full titulary.[68]

5.2. Choosing and Proclaiming the Titulary

The logistics of choosing the four names taken at the coronation largely escape us, but a few texts give us a hint of the process. In an inscription carved on the exterior of the south wall of the chamber south of the main sanctuary at Karnak, Thutmose III claimed that it was none other than Amun-Re who had chosen his name: "[He[69] established] my appearances and set a titulary (*nḫbt*) for me himself."[70] Hatshepsut's Coronation Inscription gives us a more prosaic version of the events, as she declared that the learned men of the palace composed her titulary: "His Majesty[71] commanded that lector-priests (*ẖryw-ḥbt*) be brought in to inscribe her Great Names, (at the time) of receiving her titulary of Dual King."[72] The text goes on to say, "They then proclaimed her names of Dual King, since, indeed, the god had brought about (his) manifestations in their minds, exactly as he had done previously."[73] If the first quoted passage hints at divine revelation, the second rather implies divine *inspiration,* as the god's will made itself manifest in the priests' minds (*ib*).[74]

In the sources, the various names chosen for the new king were said to have been "created" (*ỉr*),[75] "assigned" (*wḏꜥ*),[76] "fixed" (*mn*),[77] "specified" (*nḫb*),[78] "given" (*rdỉ*),[79] "established" (*smn*),[80] or "consolidated" (*srwd*)[81] by the palace. The names could then be "sanctified" (*sḏsr*),[82] at which point they were ready to

66. Ibid., 350–60.
67. Ibid., 368–69.
68. Ibid., 369–74.
69. What precedes makes it clear that the pronoun refers to the god.
70. *Urk.* IV, 160:10–11; PM II, 106 (Room 24, no. 328, plan 12).
71. Hatshepsut's long-dead father, Thutmose I.
72. *Urk.* IV, 261: 2–4.
73. Ibid., 261: 11–13.
74. For the observation, see Bonhême 1987, 12.
75. *Urk.* IV, 80:11, 2118:11, 2123:16, etc.
76. KRI VI, 5:6.
77. *Urk.* IV, 383:12.
78. KRI VI, 7:7.
79. See PM II^2, 28 (45); and 508.
80. *Urk.* IV, 358:14, 383:12.
81. See PM II^2, 30 (68–69).
82. *Urk.* IV, 276:11.

be "recorded" (*wdn*),[83] "inscribed" (*mtn*),[84] "engraved" (*ḫti*),[85] "copied" (*spẖr*),[86] "written down" (*sš*),[87] and ultimately "displayed" (*wḥꜥ*).[88]

Once composed, the titulary had to be promulgated. If a single text can be said to bear witness to a consistent policy on the part of the crown, Thutmose I's announcement to his viceroy in Nubia gives us an idea of the sort of proclamation that must surely have been sent throughout the realm whenever a new king appeared on the throne (fig. 2):

> A royal decree to the King's Son and Overseer of Southern Countries, Turi.
>
> Now see here, this royal [decree] is brought to you to let you know that My Majesty—alive, sound, and healthy—has appeared as the Dual King upon the Horus-throne of the Living, without his like within earthly eternity.
>
> My titulary (*nḫbt*) has been drawn up as follows:
> The Horus "Victorious bull, beloved of Maat";
> He of the Two Ladies, "The one who has appeared by means of the uraeus, the one great-of-might";
> The Golden Horus, "The one perfect of years, who has sustained minds";
> The Dual King, Aakheperkare ("The great one is the manifestation of the ka of Re");
> The Son of Re, Thutmose, living forever and ever.
>
> Now, how you should have divine offerings presented to the gods of Elephantine, of the most southerly region, is in doing what is praised on behalf of the life, prosperity, and health of the Dual King Aakheperkare, who is given life.
>
> Likewise, how you should have the oath established is in the name of My Majesty—alive, sound, and healthy—born of the King's Mother, Seniseneb, who is in good health.
>
> This is a communication to let you know about it, as well as the fact that the Palace is safe and sound. Regnal Year 1, 3rd month of winter, day 21, the day of the feast of the coronation.[89]

---

83. Ibid., 160:11, 285:6.
84. KRI VI, 6:3.
85. KRI II, 586:11.
86. KRI III, 304:1.
87. *Urk.* IV, 252:3, 6.
88. KRI VI, 5:6. This list of verbs is found in the exhaustive catalogue collected by Bonhême 1978, 353–77.
89. *Urk.* IV, 80–81.

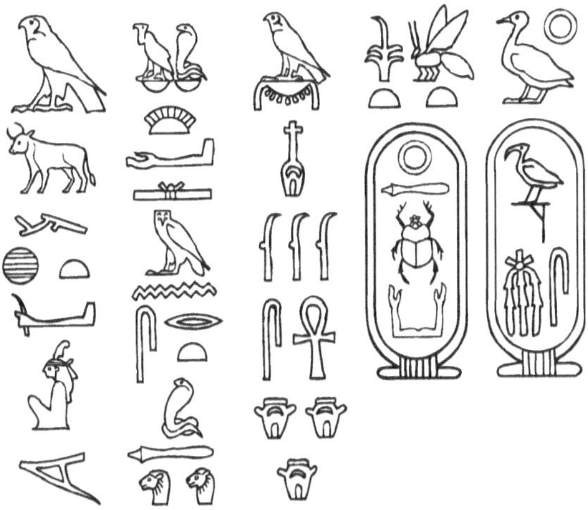

Figure 2. Fivefold Titulary of King Thutmose I (Eighteenth Dynasty) (redrawn by B. Ibronyi)

In this text, the king gives an unadorned[90] listing of his full titulary, with specific instructions on how to use the last two elements. The Throne name, with its solar associations,[91] was to be used for sacred matters, while the Birth name could suffice for mundane administrative affairs.[92]

The last sentence of Thutmose I's announcement also reveals the timing of such proclamations. This was the day of the coronation, with the titulary presumably composed during the period between the accession day and the official coronation.[93] This interval raises the question of how anticipatory the phrases used in the titulary were meant to be.[94] When examining a particular king's titulary, it is tempting to look at his accomplishments and see his titulary as a reflection of these, although the phrases were of course drawn up at the beginning of the reign. Nevertheless, given the time frame just mentioned for the composition of the titulary, it is possible that the court's knowledge of the situation facing

90. The original royal decree, most probably written in the hieratic script on papyrus, survives in two hieroglyphic copies engraved on stelae found at Buhen (Stelae Berlin 13725 and Cairo CG 34006/Buhen ST9, for which see PM VII, 141; and Klug 2002, 65–70, 503–4). It can safely be assumed that the scribe responsible for the stelae copied the original verbatim.

91. For the solar association of the Throne name, see Birkstam 1984.

92. Bonhême and Forgeau 1988, 313.

93. Gardiner 1953, 28; Bonhême 1987, 15–17.

94. Cabrol 2000, 178–79; Leprohon 2010b, 2–3.

the new king did, in fact, influence its creation. Thus, some of the phrases used in the titulary may indeed have reflected the king's position. The young crown prince Ramses participated in his father Sety I's campaigns,[95] so when the newly crowned Ramses II claimed to have "subdued foreign lands" and been "great of victories" in his original Two Ladies and Golden Horus names, respectively, he may have been stretching the truth somewhat, but he was not making the epithets up out of whole cloth. Similarly, Sety II's aggressive epithets, which proclaimed him to be "great of dread in all lands," who had "repelled the Nine Bows," may well have recalled the king's actions on the battlefield while he was still a crown prince.[96] In such matters, we must also distinguish the original titulary proclaimed at the coronation from additional phrases composed during the king's reign. The latter commemorated special events such as Sed festivals or were carved on newly erected temple walls, and could therefore very much demonstrate the state of affairs at the time. These additional names will be set apart from the original titulary in the catalogue presented herein.

5.3. The Horus Name

Given that the Horus name is the first specific designation of a ruler encountered at the end of the Predynastic period in Egypt, it is tempting to imagine the courts of these early chieftains exploiting what may already have been an ancient tale about a celestial falcon god named Horus and associating their leaders with this divine figure. The oral transmission of the tale is of course lost in the mist of time, but enough pictorial representations have survived to attest to its existence.

Images of animals had been used as symbols for the ruler far back into the Predynastic period,[97] but falcons especially were considered emblems of royalty.[98] Thus did the king become "the Horus." This assumption of a new name by the king may be reflected in a passage from the Pyramid Texts that reads: "King NN is a Great Falcon (*bik ꜥꜣ*) who is upon the ramparts (*znbw*) of the One-whose-name-is-hidden (*imn-rn*)."[99] The allusion to a hidden name possibly indicated that the designation by which the king was known was not actually his real name

95. Kitchen 1982, 24–25.

96. Kitchen 1987, 135–36.

97. Cf. the various animals on the verso of the late Predynastic Libyan Palette (Tiradritti 1999, 38) as well as the lion on the Battlefield Palette from the same date (Forman and Quirke 1996, 15). On early animal symbolism, see also T. A. H. Wilkinson 2000, 27–28.

98. For an early example from the late Nagada I period, see Baumgartel 1975, pl. 15:2; the previously mentioned Libyan Palette also shows a falcon alone and two falcons perched on standards. For other examples, see Kemp 2000, 221–23; T. A. H. Wilkinson 2000, 26 n. 19; and a Nagada IIIA 1 graffito from the Western Desert, for which see Darnell 2002, fig. on p. 10.

99. Spell 627B, §1778a, for which see Faulkner 1969, 260; and Allen 2005, 244. Compare the later Coffin Texts Spell 148, which is almost identical but specifies that the ramparts are part of a *ḥwt*-mansion; for a discussion, see Gilula 1982, 263.

but a distinctive epithet denoting his newfound authority.[100] Notwithstanding that the king himself was not a divine figure,[101] it is noteworthy that gods were said to be "many-named" (*ꜥšꜣ-rnw*),[102] reflecting their multiple attributes.[103] In that respect, it is interesting to see the many references to the king's "manifestations" (*ḫpr*/*ḫprw*) in the royal titulary of the Eighteenth Dynasty.[104]

If, as stated earlier, the court artists had decided to promote the king in a scene by depicting him on a larger scale, it is tempting to think that the same process went into the writing of his Horus name. This special name had to be easily recognizable in an artistic tableau, and hence it was written inside a particular hieroglyph called a *serekh,* a word that meant "to cause to know, to display."[105] The *serekh* (fig. 3) consisted of a vertical rectangle divided into two sections. The lower portion showed a patterned area representing a niched façade common in mud-brick architecture, while the upper part depicted a plan of the palace into which the king's name was inserted.[106] Atop the *serekh* was perched a falcon figure symbolizing the celestial god Horus, of whom the king was thought to be a representative on earth. Thus, the full image of the *serekh*-hieroglyph stood for the concept of the Horus-king residing within his palace. In the earlier periods of Egyptian history, the Horus name remained the primary manner of identifying the reigning monarch in writing.

5.4. The Two Ladies Name

Sometimes called the Nebty name from the word *nebty,* Egyptian for "two ladies," or "two mistresses,"[107] the Two Ladies name placed the king under the protection of the two goddesses Nekhbet and Wadjet. In pictorial representations, both goddesses rest on top of baskets, with the full composition writing out the

100. Gilula 1982, 263 n. 15; and R. H. Wilkinson 1985, 99.

101. An accessible summary of the question is found in O'Connor and Silverman 1995, xxiii–xxvi.

102. Vernus 1980, col. 324, n. 6.

103. Private individuals were also often given more than one name; see Vernus 1980, cols. 322–23, with many references; and Vernus 1986.

104. See, e.g., the Horus name of Ahmose (II); the Golden Horus name of Thutmose II; and the Throne names of Thutmose I, Thutmose II, Thutmose III, Amenhotep II, Thutmose IV, Amenhotep IV/Akhenaten, Nefer-neferu-aten, Tutankhamun, Ay, and Horemheb.

105. *Wb.* IV, 200, which, however, gives no example of the word dated prior to the Eighteenth Dynasty.

106. On the analogy of the false door, which may have been reinterpreted in the late Old Kingdom into having the main top panel representing a window into the home (Lacau 1967, a suggestion that has not won full approval), one wonders whether the same reinterpretation was applied to the *serekh,* which would then have made the top panel a window into the royal palace through which the king's name was seen.

107. The masculine word *neb,* written with the basket hieroglyph, is usually translated as "lord."

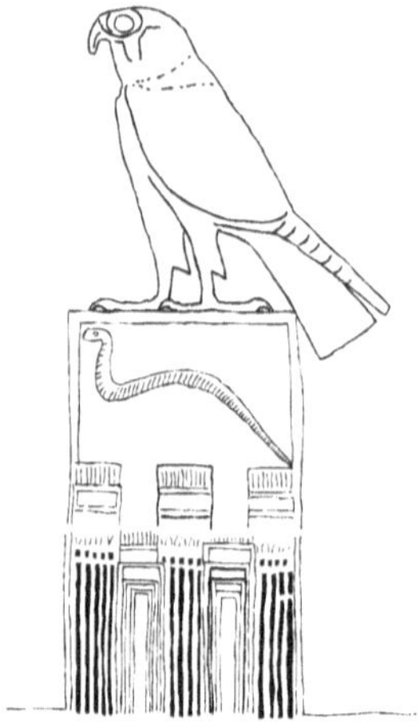

Figure 3. *Serekh* of King Djet (First Dynasty) (redrawn by B. Ibronyi)

phrase "the Two Ladies, Nekhbet and Wadjet." The vulture-shaped Nekhbet was the tutelary goddess of the city of El Kab in southern Upper Egypt, while the cobra goddess Wadjet was the guardian deity of the city of Buto in Lower Egypt. Both sites were significant in the Pre- and Early Dynastic periods. El Kab,[108] ancient *Nekheb,* was the capital city of the Third Upper Egyptian nome. It was situated on the east bank, across the river from Hierakonpolis, the important "City of the Falcon," the site where both the Scorpion Macehead and the Narmer Palette were found. The divine name Nekhbet means "the one (fem.) from Nekheb." Remains dating back to the Paleolithic have been found at El Kab and important cemeteries from the late Predynastic and Early Dynastic, as well as a temple from the latter date, have been found there. Buto,[109] ancient *Pe* and *Dep,* in the northwestern Delta close to the Mediterranean, was the capital city of the Sixth Lower Egyptian nome. The Greek name Buto comes from ancient Egyptian *Per-Wadjet,* "The Domain of Wadjet,"[110] reflecting the name of the goddess relevant for this study. Late Predynastic strata at the site show traditional Lower Egyptian pottery types gradually being replaced by Upper Egyptian ones, indicating a growing influence of the southern culture over that of the north in the late Prehistoric era.

This last fact has led scholars to reconsider the old simplistic model of an aggressive conquest of the north by the south, using the warlike scenes on the Narmer Palette and others as templates for the conquest.[111] Instead, the refer-

108. Hendrickx 1999 gives a useful overview of the site.

109. For an easily accessible review of the site, see von der Way 1999.

110. Baines and Málek 1980, 170.

111. For concise summaries of the difficulties of interpreting the archaeological evidence from this period, see Bard 2000, 61–65; and Köhler 2011, among others. Warfare as a method

ences to Upper and Lower Egypt in both the Two Ladies and Throne (sometimes referred to as the "Dual King" designation) names are now considered by many rather as symbolic allusions to the basic duality of the Egyptians' worldview, with the two different lands—the narrow valley of the south compared to the wide lush fields of the north—being complementary.[112] Indeed, although there were a number of competing polities in Upper Egypt, notably Hierakonpolis, Nagada, and Abydos, their northward march does not seem to find a comparable "kingdom" in the north, save perhaps for the site of Buto.[113] Whether such references to Upper and Lower Egyptian entities in the royal titulary reflected a subjugation of the north by the south, the fact remains that, as early as the First Dynasty, part of the titulary referred to two goddesses who represented important ancient sites from Upper and Lower Egypt, respectively. This must surely have demonstrated a wish on the part of the royal court to identify the king with the two parts of the country, both of which he was said to control.

The hieroglyphic group of the vulture and cobra resting atop baskets is first met early in the First Dynasty, in the reign of Aha.[114] Written beside the *serekh* containing the king's name, it is uncertain whether this was, in fact, meant to represent the king's Two Ladies name, or simply the name of the shrine inside which the signs are written.[115] Late in the First Dynasty, Semerkhet introduced the *nebty* element as part of his titulary, from which point the title was used fairly regularly.

5.5. The Golden Horus Name

The third name in the series is the most elusive.[116] The hieroglyph for "gold," a collar of beads with its ties hanging on each side, first appears as part of a king's titulary in the reign of Den (Dyn. 1:4), alongside of which is written the rearing cobra hieroglyph, rendering the epithet "the golden uraeus." The reign of Khaba (Dyn. 3:3) is the first to introduce the grouping of the falcon on a standard with the "gold" sign, to spell out the phrase "the golden falcon." In the Fourth Dynasty,

---

of conquest should not be dismissed altogether, however, as Darnell has made clear (2002, 17–19).

112. Quirke 1990, 10–11; von Beckerath 1999, 15–16; and T. A. H. Wilkinson 2001, 203–6.

113. Köhler 1995.

114. Tiradritti 1999, 42; conveniently illustrated in T. A. H. Wilkinson 2001, p. 204, fig. 6.5 (1). A veiled reference to a Two Ladies name may actually occur on the verso of the Narmer Palette, if one agrees with Barguet's suggestion (1951) that the balloon-shaped object on the last standard in the procession of standard-bearers, immediately behind the Wepwawet standard, represents the king's Two Ladies name. For a recent interpretation of the object, see Evans 2011.

115. Quirke 1990, 23; T. A. H. Wilkinson 2001, 203.

116. For a recent semiotic study on the Golden Horus name during the Old Kingdom, see Borrego Gallardo 2010.

the gold sign can be seen accompanied by one, two, or even three falcons, but it is only in the reign of Khafre that an additional epithet is added, to render the fuller "the golden falcon is powerful."[117] This has led to a proposal[118] that the title should be referred to as "The Gold" name, rather than the more traditional "Golden Horus" name. The suggestion certainly holds merit, but I have opted for the older designation in this book because, by the time of the Middle Kingdom, the title is consistently written with both the falcon and gold hieroglyphs followed by a short phrase,[119] which may suggest that it had been reinterpreted and was now understood as the "Horus of Gold."

The meaning of the title is also capable of different interpretations, not all of which are mutually exclusive. Because of its brilliance and immutability, gold was associated with solar symbolism and was also considered to be the material from which divine flesh was made. Thus, along with the "Horus" designation, the "Golden" part of the title signified the sun-filled daytime sky and also symbolized the permanence of the institution of kingship. This celestial reference, coupled with the earthly realm embodied by the Horus name, is wonderfully illustrated on an ivory comb from Abydos. This shows a *serekh* containing the name of King Djet (Dyn. 1:3) topped by the expected falcon figure. Over this composition, a falcon perched in a barque is ferried across the sky, represented by a bird's wings underneath the barque.[120]

It is also possible that an affiliation with the god Seth was understood in the Golden Horus name.[121] Seth was believed to have come from the town of Nagada, the Egyptian name of which was *Nubet,* "Gold Town."[122] Given the importance of the site of Nagada in the Predynastic period and the ancient Egyptians' dualistic views of the world, the presence of Horus in the early titulary of the king may have been balanced with that of Seth under the guise of the Golden Horus name. Given his fratricidal act as recounted in the sacred tales of ancient Egypt, perhaps a direct mention of Seth within the royal titulary was considered beyond the boundaries of decorum. Both gods were certainly well entrenched in royal iconography, as attested by the ubiquitous depiction where they are seen tying together the heraldic plants of Upper and Lower Egypt around the hieroglyphic sign for "unification,"[123] as well as the Ramesside statue where they are crowning

---

117. The variations are given in Aufrère 1982, 47–50.

118. Von Beckerath 1999, 17–20.

119. Cf. the previously mentioned fragment from the reign of Amenemhat III, which reads: "/// his name of gold, the Golden Horus 'Enduring of Life,'given life ///", for which see Roeder 1913, 138.

120. See Malek and Forman 1986, 35; and R. H. Wilkinson 1985, 102–3, and fig. 6.

121. So also T. A. H. Wilkinson 2001, 207, although the motif of Horus conquering Seth must surely be disregarded in this context.

122. Hart 1986, 194–95.

123. Conveniently illustrated in Kemp 2006, p. 70, fig. 20.

King Ramses III.[124] Given Seth's aggressive behavior within the divine realm, his suggested association with the Golden Horus name may help explain the belligerent phrases often seen in these royal names from the New Kingdom on.[125]

5.6. The Throne Name

Also referred to as the Praenomen or the Cartouche name, the Throne name was the last of the four names taken by the king at his accession. The Egyptian phrase *ni-su-bit* has often been translated as "King of Upper and Lower Egypt,"[126] but actually simply meant "the one who belongs to the sedge and the bee," the symbols of Upper and Lower Egypt, respectively. The first part of the title, *ni-su,* seems to have referred to the eternal institution of kingship itself. It was, in fact, the word for "king" in expressions like *per-nisu,* "palace" (lit. "house of the king"), *wedj-nisu,* "royal decree" (lit. "command of the king"), or *sa-nisu,* "crown prince" (lit. "son of the king").[127] The word *bit,* on the other hand, more properly referred to the ephemeral holder of the position.[128] In this way, both the divine and the mortal were referenced in the phrase, along with the obvious dual division of the northern and southern lands.[129] For these reasons, the translation "Dual King" is preferred today.[130]

The Horus Den (Dyn. 1:4) introduced the designation of *swty-bity,* "the one of the sedge and bee," in his titulary, but it was his successor Adjib who was the first to use the phrase along with an epithet. The Throne name was compounded with the name of the sun god Re in a few instances in the Fourth, Fifth, and Sixth Dynasties, after which the divine element became a regular part of the name. From the Middle Kingdom on, the Throne name would become the most important of the king's five names, and—perhaps because it was so readily identifiable within its cartouche—was the one mentioned when the king was referred to by only one name. The Throne name is also the one used in the later King Lists, where only a single cartouche is mentioned.

A few words must now be said about the translations of the Throne name found in this book. Given that it was compounded with the name of the sun god, it was long treated by scholars as a proclamation about the god himself. For example, Thutmose III's famous Throne name, *mn ḫpr rꜥ*, was usually interpreted as "The manifestation of Re is firm," taking the initial word as a predicate

124. R. H. Wilkinson 2003, 197.

125. Parent 1992; Meffre 2010, 228.

126. Following the translation on the Rosetta Stone; see Gardiner 1957a, 73.

127. Goedicke 1960, 17–36.

128. Thus, as Quirke has demonstrated (1986, 123–24), the ubiquitous title *ḫtmty bity* need not refer specifically to a "Treasurer of the King of Lower Egypt" but rather generally to a "Treasurer of the (current) king."

129. Shaw and Nicholson 1995, 153.

130. Quirke 1990, 11.

adjective in a nonverbal sentence.[131] Later, John Bennett quite rightly suggested that "one would expect the king to be the person referred to, not the god."[132] To achieve his rendering, he added the preposition *mi*, "like," in the phrase, assuming that the preposition had been left out for the sake of brevity.[133] His translation of Thutmose III's Throne name would therefore have read "Firm of manifestation (like) Re." More recently, Jürgen von Beckerath,[134] building on Rolf Krauss's work,[135] also wished to see the name as a statement of the king's relationship with the sun god.[136] By parsing the initial adjective as a nominal form ("the firm one," "the perfect one," and so on) and the rest of the epithet as a genitival phrase, he suggested rendering Thutmose III's Throne name as "The firm one of—i.e., belonging to—the manifestation of Re." This is the system I have followed. Additionally, since a number of personal names can simply consist of two juxtaposed nominal forms that are equated with each other,[137] I have rendered some of the names as "The great one is a manifestation of Re" (Throne name of Thutmose I).

5.7. The Birth Name

As the name used here implies, the Birth name, also called the Nomen, was the name given to the crown prince at birth, which was enclosed in a cartouche after his accession to the throne. The fact that it had always been the individual's name is underscored by a portion of Thutmose III's text detailing his titulary.[138] After the introductory passage, in which the king claims that the sun god himself had established his titulary, the segment that mentions his Birth name begins with an independent pronoun, which had a strong emphatic meaning,[139] thus: "I am (the one who is) his son . . . in this name of mine of 'son of Re' Thutmose."[140]

131. An ancient Egyptian nonverbal sentence is one in which the copula is left unexpressed.

132. Bennett 1965, 206.

133. Ibid., 207; Bennett's work was subsequently expanded by Iversen (1988), a suggestion refuted by Fischer (1989a).

134. Von Beckerath 1984, 27–31.

135. Krauss 1978, 122–32.

136. Followed by Baines 1995, 9.

137. Cf. names such as *i͗mn-pꜣy.i͗-i͗dnw*, "Amun is my representative (lit. 'deputy')" (Ranke 1935, 27:9); *i͗mn-pꜣy.i͗-ṯꜣw*, "Amun is my breath" (Ranke 1935, 27:10); *i͗mn-pꜣ-nfr*, "Amun is the perfect one" (Ranke 1935, 27:11); *i͗mn-nb-tꜣwy*, "Amun is the lord of the Two Lands" (Ranke 1935, 29:17); *ḥr-ḫw.f*, "Horus is his protection" (Ranke 1935, 250:11); as well as the theophoric names compounded with the expression *i͗r-di͗-s(w)/s(t)*, "God NN is the one who made him/her," such as Amen-irdis, Atum-irdis, Onuris-irdis, Ptah-irdis (Ranke 1935, 26:24–25, 51:21–22, 35:12, and 138:16–17, respectively), and the like.

138. *Urk.* IV, 160–61; see particularly Quirke 1990, 13.

139. As opposed to using the so-called "*m* of predication," a preposition that implied an acquired attribute; see Gardiner 1957a, §38.

140. *Urk.* IV, 161:9–12; for the interpretation, see Bonhême and Forgeau 1988, 308.

Since names tended to repeat themselves within a family and some royal names were subsequently used by other rulers, this is the name to which we add roman numerals to differentiate the various monarchs within a dynasty (e.g., Thutmose III and Ramses II). It should be noted, however, that this is a modern convention, one not used by the ancient Egyptians, who, as stated earlier, generally referred to their kings by their Throne names.

A preceding epithet, "the son of Re," first used in the Fourth Dynasty by Radjedef, was yet another way of establishing a direct link between the king and the sun god. Since Re was the supreme creator god, it is perhaps not surprising to see the king associated with him, since the king was thought to essentially re-create the world at his accession.[141]

141. Cf. Tutankhamun's Restoration Stela, line 5, where it is stated that the new king's accession meant that henceforth "*maat*-harmony is firmly [in its place]" and "the land is as it was at the First Occasion," that is, at the original moment of creation (= *Urk*. IV, 2026:18–19).

II

Early Dynastic Period

Dynasty "0" (3150–3050 B.C.E.)

The designation "Dynasty 0,"[1] in the Prehistoric period referred to as Nagada IIIb,[2] was first used by James E. Quibell to describe artefacts he discovered at Hierakonpolis whose archaeological context made it plain that they preceded those of the First Dynasty.[3] King Scorpion, whose famous macehead is now in the Ashmolean Museum, Oxford (no. AN1896–1908.E3632),[4] is a well-known example of such rulers. Another group, which also immediately precedes the First Dynasty, is firmly attested from the royal Cemetery B at Abydos.[5]

The three main Upper Egyptian centers of power at the time were Abydos, Nagada, and Hierakonpolis. As the rulers of these polities took part in the final stages of the unification of the country, they began to use symbols of power such as the *serekh* in the writing of their names to establish their authority.

Because there was not a single line of kings ruling from a given site, the term "dynasty" is actually inappropriate[6] but has been adopted here for purely practical reasons. The number and order of kings of Dynasty 0 are difficult to establish;[7] the rulers presented herein are the ones whose names are attested within *serekhs* and who can reasonably be designated as "kings." They will be presented in chronological order, from the oldest to the more recent, insofar as this can be established.

---

1. For a recent study of the period, see Raffaele 2003, and for its chronology, see Regulski 2008.
2. Kaiser 1957.
3. Quibell 1900, 5; see also Raffaele 2003, 105 n. 25.
4. Conveniently illustrated and discussed in Whitehouse 2009, 19–25.
5. Kaiser and Dreyer 1982.
6. See T. A. H. Wilkinson's cautious remarks (2001, 53).
7. This analysis is made even more difficult by the fact that some *serekhs* from the period are frustratingly empty, leaving the intended ruler anonymous; see, e.g., T. A. H. Wilkinson 1995, 206–7.

1. Iry-Hor[8]

Horus: *ỉry-ḥr* (*iry-hor*), The companion of Horus[9]

2. Ka[10]

Horus: *k3* (*ka*), The ka-life force[11]

3. Narmer[12]

Horus: *nʿr mr* (*nar mer*), The menacing catfish[13]

Another sequence of rulers is attested, whose archaeological context shows them to be contemporary with the Iry-Hor to Narmer sequence. Neither of these is attested at Abydos

4. Scorpion[14]

Horus: *srḳ* (*sereq*), The scorpion

---

8. Von Beckerath 1999, 36–37.

9. For this king, whom Petrie (1902, 4–5) had first identified as King Ro, "Utterance (of authority)," see Barta 1982. Darnell (2002, 14) points out that the designation of a king by a falcon alone is unattested before Iry-Hor. However, not all scholars agree that this individual was actually a king; see T. A. H. Wilkinson (1993), who reads the signs as marking the provenance of the objects on which they are carved.

10. Von Beckerath 1999, 36–37.

11. Because of the uncertainty of reading the sign, the name has also been read as *sḫn* (*sekhen*), "The one whom (Horus) has embraced." See Kaplony (1958, 56–57), who rendered the name as "The one who occupies (the palace)." The name Ka is generally accepted today; see Gilroy 2001, 69–70; Jiménez-Serrano 2001, 81 n. 4; Kahl 1994, 38–40; and Köhler and van den Brink 2002, 63.

12. Gauthier 1907, 1–3, 17–19; von Beckerath 1999, 36–37. Narmer is possibly the King Menes—Egyptian *mnỉ* (*meni*), "The established one"—of tradition, although some scholars equate the Horus Aha with Menes. See, lately, the discussion in Raffaele 2003, 106–7.

13. For the importance of the Nile catfish (*Clarias*)—a particularly powerful fish—at Hierakonpolis, see Ikram 2001; the name, which may seem strange at first, is thus most fitting for a ruler. On Narmer and the catfish, see also Takács 1997. Earlier, Godron (1949) had proposed a reading of *mry nʿr(ỉ)* (*mery nari*), "Beloved of (the god) Nari," which was adopted by Monnet Saleh (1986, 227 n. 1). However, it should be noted that Godron himself simply used the name Narmer in his more recent study of King Den (1990, passim). Barta (1969, 51–57) has proposed Nary, "The Horus who belongs to the Catfish god." Other suggestions have been made by Goedicke (1995), who rendered *nʿr mnḫ ḥr* (*nar menekh hor*) "The excellent fighter (of) Horus," while T. A. H. Wilkinson (2000, 24–26) and Ray (2003, 2004) have proposed *ḥr s3b* (*hor sab*), "Horus the dappled one." For other discussions and additional references, see also Gilroy 2001, 68–69; and Raffaele 2003, 110 n. 46.

14. Gauthier 1907, 33; von Beckerath 1999, 36–37. Although some scholars (e.g., Malek and Forman 1986, 29) deny the existence of this ruler, preferring to interpret the scorpion

5. Crocodile

Horus: *šny/šndt* (*sheny/shendet*), The crocodile[15]

A third line of rulers, and also contemporary with the Iry-Hor to Narmer sequence, is attested from their names written in *serekh*s found at various sites,[16] although no tombs have been found for these rulers.[17]

6. Hedju-Hor

Horus: *ḥḏw-ḥr* (*hedju-hor*), The maces (of?) Horus[18]

7. Ny-<Hor>

Horus: *n*(*y*)-<*ḥr*> (*ny*-<*hor*>), The one who belongs to <Horus>[19]

8. Haty-Hor

Horus: *ḥ3ty*-<*ḥr*> (*haty*-<*hor*>), The foremost <Horus>

9. Horwy

Horus: *ḥrwy* (*horwy*), The double falcon

10. Ny-Neith

Horus: *n*(*y*)-*nt* (*ny-net*), The one who belongs to (the goddess) Neith[20]

---

simply as a ceremonial image, the consensus remains that he was, in fact, king; see T. A. H. Wilkinson 2001, 56; Dreyer 1992a; H. S. Smith 1992, 244; and Darnell 2002, 14–19.

15. A ruler who is attested at the site of Tarkhan, north of the important prehistoric site of Gerza; he may be contemporary with the Horus Ka. For this king, see Dreyer 1992b and Köhler and van den Brink 2002, 70. Raffaele (2003, 114–15) proposes the reading *snd* (*sened*), "The Dreadful one."

16. For a useful list with discussion, see Raffaele 2003, 115–20. See also Dreyer 1998, 178–79, for other possible rulers, including a "King Elephant," for which see Darnell 2002, 17 n. 86.

17. T. A. H. Wilkinson (2001, 54–55) believes that most of these markings do not indicate personal names.

18. For the name, compare the various royal maceheads from this period as well as the mace held in Narmer's hand in the Smiting Motif scene on the recto of his famous palette. This ruler is attested at Turah and in the eastern Delta.

19. The falcon atop the *serekh* is to be read as part of the name; this ruler is attested at the sites of Turah and Buto.

20. An otherwise unattested ruler, whose name is found on a jar discovered at Helwan, and who may date to a time after the Horus Ka; see Köhler and van den Brink 2002, 65–67.

A few other rulers whose names have been discovered relatively recently can be listed.

11. Horus "A"

Horus: ꜥ (*a*), The (raised?) arm[21]

12. Horus "Pe"

Horus: *p* (?) (*pe*?), The (very) throne of Horus[22]

Dynasty 1 (3050–2890 B.C.E.)

The rulers of the next two dynasties, which are sometimes referred to as the Thinite period (from the Manethonian tradition that its kings came from This, near Abydos),[23] followed in the footsteps of their "Dynasty 0" predecessors. Establishing their capital city at the very northern end of Upper Egypt just before the Nile Valley fans out into a verdant Delta, they called their place of residence *ineb hedj,* "the White Wall," a site more commonly referred to by its Greek name, Memphis. The transition to a centralized government ruling over a vast area must have been challenging, as the new rulers needed to organize a bureaucracy to take care of the logistics of governing and presumably also had to placate a population accustomed to long-standing local practices. Perhaps this need to accommodate different religious traditions is reflected in some of the categories of royal names, which, as discussed in the introduction, took a number of regional divinities into consideration. The highly aggressive epithets taken by the kings of the First Dynasty, however, also make the gravity of the task quite apparent.

In the following catalogue, the entry for each king will give additional names from later sources—such as the Old Kingdom Cairo Annals,[24] the Abydos King List from the temple of Sety I,[25] the Royal Canon of Turin,[26] and the Saqqara King List from the tomb chapel of Tjunuroy,[27] with the last three dating to the Ramesside period—after the names attested from contemporary records.

21. Ikram 2004. The name may refer to the raised arm of a ruler in the smiting position.

22. Or perhaps Khenty-pe, "Foremost of the seat [i.e., the throne]." This ruler is sometimes simply referred to as "King B": see T. A. H. Wilkinson 1995 and 2001, p. 53, fig. 2.3, and Ikram 2004, 215.

23. Waddell 1940, 30–31.

24. Daressy 1916; Baud and Dobrev 1995, 26 n. 18. The text will be considered authentic, notwithstanding O'Mara's arguments (1986, 1999a, 1999b).

25. KRI I, 178; this will be referred to as "Abydos."

26. Gardiner 1957b, pl. 1; this will be referred to as "Turin."

27. KRI III, 481–82; this will be referred to as "Saqqara."

To distinguish these later designations from the contemporary attestations, the later names will be followed by an asterisk. Given that these Ramesside names were compiled so long after the fact, it is difficult to know whether the later compilers thought of them as Throne or Birth names; for such cases, I have adopted the term "Later cartouche name." The known burial places of the kings from this period are at Abydos.

1. Aha[28]

Horus: *ꜥḥꜣ* (*aha*), The fighter
Two Ladies: *mn* (*men*) The established one[29]
Later cartouche name: *tti* (*teti*)*, Teti[30]
Later cartouche name: *ity* (*ity*)*, The sovereign[31]

2. Djer[32]

Horus: *ḏr* (*djer*), The one who repulses (enemies)
Golden Horus: *n*(*y*)-*nbw* (*ny-nebu*)*, He who belongs to the Golden One[33]
Later cartouche name: *iti* (*iti*)*, The sovereign[34]

3. Djet/Wadjet[35]

Horus: *ḏt*/*wꜣḏt* (*djet*/*wadjet*),[36] The cobra
Later cartouche name: [*i*]*ty* ([*i*]*ty*)*, The sovereign[37]
Later cartouche name: *itꜣ* (*ita*)*, Ita[38]

---

28. Gauthier 1907, 3–4, 29–30; von Beckerath 1999, 38–39.

29. I have included this entry for the sake of completeness, but it is likely that the hieroglyphs of the vulture and the cobra may not actually be part of Aha's titulary. It has been suggested that the *men*-hieroglyph refers to the name of the shrine itself, which was called "The Two Ladies are Established"; see Quirke 1990, 23; and T. A. H. Wilkinson 2001, 203.

30. Abydos 2.

31. Turin 2,12.

32. Gauthier 1907, 5, 30–31; von Beckerath 1999, 38–39.

33. Daressy 1916, 163.

34. Abydos 3.

35. Gauthier 1907, 5, 31–32; von Beckerath 1999, 38–39.

36. For the name Wadjet, from a graffito in the Shatt er Rigal where the cobra *wꜣḏ*-sign is clear, see Legrain 1903, p. 221, fig. 7; and Vergote 1961.

37. Turin 2,15.

38. Abydos 4, presumably for Ity, as in the Turin Canon.

4. Den[39]

Horus: *dn* (*den*), The severer (of heads)[40]
Golden Horus: *iꜥrt nbw* (*iaret nebu*), The golden uraeus
Throne: *ḫꜣsty* (*khasety*), The highlander[41]
Later cartouche name: *spꜣty* (*sepaty*)*, He of the two districts[42]
Later cartouche name: *zmty* (*zemty*)*, The desert man[43]

5. Adjib[44]

Horus: *ꜥḏ-ib* (*adj ib*), Hale-hearted[45]
Throne: *mr(y) p biꜣi* (*mer pe biai*), The one who wished the eternal throne[46]
Later cartouche name: *mr(y) biꜣ p* (*mer(y) bia pe*)*, The eternally beloved of the throne (?)[47]
Later cartouche name: *mr(y) biꜣ pn* (*mer(y) bia pen*)*, The eternally beloved one (?)[48]
Later cartouche name: *mr(y) grg pn* (*mer gereg pen*)*, The beloved of this establishment[49]

6. Semerkhet[50]

Horus: *smr ḫt* (*semer khet*), Friend of the (divine) body (i.e., the Ennead)
Two Ladies: *iry-nbty* (*iry-nebty*), He who is connected to the Two Ladies[51]

---

39. Gauthier 1907, 6–9; von Beckerath 1999, 38–39. For King Den, see particularly Godron 1990. The king's name has been read a number of different ways, the most common of which are Dewen ("He who spreads [his (falcon's) wings]") or Udimu ("He who pours water"). For other variants, see Godron (1990, 11–17), who rightly opts for the reading Den, which he renders as "The slaughterer."

40. For the rendering "severer," see Meltzer 1972; the iconographic motif is well known from the first register on the verso of the Narmer Palette, where the king surveys two rows of decapitated enemies.

41. Godron (1990, 17–21) renders as "The foreigner," in reference to the king's military incursion into the Sinai; see also T. A. H. Wilkinson 2001, 206.

42. Abydos 5.

43. Turin 2,16.

44. Gauthier 1907, 9–11; von Beckerath 1999, 40–41. The first sign has also been read *ꜥnḏ*, giving the name *ꜥnḏ-ib* (*anedj-ib / Andjib*); see *Wb* I, 208.

45. Kaplony (1972, col. 63, n. 1) renders "Brave of heart," lit. "fat-hearted"; for *ꜥḏ*, see Kahl 2002, 96–100.

46. The name is preceded by the expression *swty-bity*, "He of the sedge and the bee." For the adjective *biꜣi*, see Kahl 2002, 137–38.

47. Abydos 6.

48. Saqqara 1.

49. Turin 2,17.

50. Gauthier 1907, 11–14; von Beckerath 1999, 40–41.

51. T. A. H. Wilkinson (2001, 207) suggests "The guardian of the Two Ladies."

Later cartouche name: *smsw* (*semsu*)*, The eldest[52]
Later cartouche name: *smsm* (*semsem*)*, The eldest[53]

7. Qaa[54]

Horus: *ḳ3-ʿ* (*qa-a*), (Whose) arm is raised[55]
Two Ladies 1: *ḳ3-ʿ* (*qa-a*), (Whose) arm is raised
Two Ladies 2: *sn* (*sen*), The one whom the Two Ladies have kissed.[56]
Two Ladies 3: *sḥtp* (*nbty*) (*sehetep nebty*), The one who has pacified the Two Ladies[57]
Later cartouche name: *ḳbḥ* (*qebeh*)*, The cool one[58]

Dynasty 2 (2890–2686 B.C.E.)

For unknown reasons, the first three kings of the Second Dynasty were buried at Saqqara, while the last two, like their First Dynasty predecessors, were buried at Abydos. Toward the end of the period, a disruption occurred, when King Peribsen unexplainably chose a "Seth name" rather than the traditional Horus name. This disturbance seems to have been resolved by a peacemaker, the Horus Khasekhem, who subsequently appeared as the "Horus and Seth Khasekhemwy." The exact nature of what has been dubbed the "Seth rebellion" may never be known.

The royal names from this period became slightly more developed as well as less aggressive and are associated with the divine more than was the case previously. Some of the kings repeated part of their Horus name in their Two Ladies name, indicating that, at this time, the titulary essentially remained an elaboration of a single concept.

1. Hetepsekhemwy[59]

Horus: *ḥtp sḫmy* (*hetep sekhemwy*), The two powers[60] are satisfied
Two Ladies: *ḥtp* (*hetep*), The Two Ladies are satisfied

---

52. Abydos 7; for the reading, see Gardiner 1943, 75.
53. Turin 2,18; the word *smsm* must have been meant for *smsw*.
54. Gauthier 1907, 14–15, 32; von Beckerath 1999, 40–41.
55. Cf. the Smiting King motif.
56. That is, have given him the breath of life; cf. the relief from Dahshur where King Snefru is kissed by a leonine goddess (easily accessible in Fakhry 1961, p. 82, fig. 46). This seems more likely than rendering the name as "equal" or "brother" (so T. A. H. Wilkinson 2001, 204), since an actual identification of the king with a divinity is less likely.
57. For references, see T. A. H. Wilkinson 2001, 204–5.
58. Abydos 8; Turin 2,19; and Saqqara 2.
59. Gauthier 1907, 37; von Beckerath 1999, 42–43.
60. Horus and Seth.

Later cartouche name: *bḏ3w* (*bedjau*)*, Bedjau[61]
Later cartouche name: *nṯri-b3w* (*netjeri-bau*)*, Divine of might[62]

2. Nebre[63]

Horus: *nb rʿ* (*neb ra*), My lord is the sun god[64]
Throne: *nbw nfr* (*nebu nefer*), The perfect golden one (?)
Later cartouche name: *k3 k3w* (*ka kau*)*, Bull of bulls[65]

3. Ninetjer[66]

Horus: *n*(*y*)-*nṯr* (*ni-netjer*), The one who belongs to the god
Two Ladies: *n*(*y*)-*nṯr* (*ni-netjer*), The one who belongs to the divinity of the Two Ladies
Golden Horus: *rn nbw* (*ren nebu*), The golden named one (lit. "name of gold")
Later cartouche name: *b3 n nṯr* (*ba en netjer*)*, The spirit of the god[67]

4. (Two Ladies) Weneg[68]

Horus: (remains unknown)[69]
Two Ladies: *wng* (*weneg*), The *weneg*-plant (a designation of the sun god)[70]
Later cartouche name: *w3ḏ-ns* (*wadj-nes*)*, Sturdy (lit. "hale") of tongue[71]

5. Sened*[72]

Birth: *snd* (*sened*)*, The frightful one[73]
Later cartouche name: *sndi* (*sendi*)*, The frightful one[74]

---

61. Abydos 9.

62. Turin 2,20 and Saqqara 3; von Beckerath (1999, 42 n. 2) suggests that this name may be a corruption of the previous *bḏ3w*. The name has also been read as *b3w nṯr* (*bau netjer*), "The (very) might of the god."

63. Gauthier 1907, 38; von Beckerath 1999, 42–43.

64. T. Schneider (1996, 258) suggests "Lord and sun god." The name could also be read *rʿ nb*(.*i*) (*ra nebi*), "Ra is my lord."

65. Abydos 10; Turin 2,21; and Saqqara 4.

66. Gauthier 1907, 20, 38–39; von Beckerath 1999, 42–43.

67. Abydos 11; Turin 2,22; and Saqqara 5.

68. Gauthier 1907, 20–21; von Beckerath 1999, 42–43.

69. See T. A. H. Wilkinson 2001, 87, and references there.

70. For the *weneg*-plant and its interpretation, see *Wb* I, 325:11, and Kahl 2002, 119. For the original reading of the name, see Grdseloff 1944, 291.

71. Abydos 12, Saqqara 6.

72. Gauthier 1907, 21–22; von Beckerath 1999, 42–43.

73. This Birth name is found on a few Dynasty 4 texts; for the references, see von Beckerath 1999, 42; and T. A. H. Wilkinson 2001, 88.

74. Abydos 13, Turin 2,24, and Saqqara 7.

6. Sekhemib[75]

Horus 1: *sḫm-ib* (*sekhem-ib*), The resolute one (lit. "Powerful of will")
Horus 2: *sḫm-ib pr.n m3ʿt* (*sekhem-ib per.en maat*), The resolute one, (for whom) Maat has come forth[76]
Two Ladies: *sḫm-ib pr.n m3ʿt* (*sekhem-ib per.en maat*), The resolute one of the Two Ladies, (for whom) Maat has come forth

7. Peribsen[77]

Seth name: *stḫ pr*(*w*) *ib.sn* (*per(u) ib.sen*), Seth, (for whom ?) their will has come forth[78]
Two Ladies: *pr ib.sn* (*per ib.sen*), (For whom) Their will has come forth
Throne: *pr ib.sn* (*per ib.sen*), (For whom) Their will has come forth

8. Khasekhem/Khasekhemwy[79]

Horus 1: *ḫʿ sḫm* (*kha sekhem*), The powerful one[80] has appeared
Horus/Seth 2: *ḫʿ sḫmy nbwy ḥtp*(*.w*) *im.f* (*kha sekhemwy nebwy hetep(u) im.ef*), The two powerful ones[81] have appeared, the two lords[82] being satisfied with him
Two Ladies 1: *ḫʿ sḫmy nbwy ḥtp*(*.w*) *im.f* (*kha sekhemwy nebwy hetep(u) im.ef*), The two powerful ones have appeared, the two lords being satisfied with him[83]
Two Ladies 2: *ḫʿ sḫmy nbw ḫt.sn* (*kha sekhemwy nebu khet.sen*), The two powerful ones have appeared, the golden one of their bodies
Later cartouche name: *ḏ3ḏ3y* (*djadjay*)*, The head-man (?)[84]
Later cartouche name: *bby*/*bbty* (*beby/bebty*)*, Beby/Bebty[85]

---

75. Gauthier 1907, 22–24, 40; von Beckerath 1999, 44–45. It is also possible that the Horus Sekhemib and the Seth Peribsen are one and the same king; see T. A. H. Wilkinson 2001, 90, and the references there.

76. Less likely, "The dwelling place of Maat"; for the Early Dynastic writing of *pr*, "house, dwelling," written without the stroke determinative, see Kahl 2002, 149.

77. Von Beckerath 1999, 44–45.

78. Less likely, "The dwelling place of their will."

79. Gauthier 1907, 34–36, 47–48; von Beckerath 1999, 44–45.

80. That is, Horus.

81. Horus and Seth; both animals appear on the top of the *serekh*.

82. Horus and Seth again.

83. If the two signs *nbwy* in the last phrase were placed in honorific transposition, this part of the name might read *ḥtp nbwy im.f*, "The two lords within him are satisfied."

84. Abydos 14; according to Kitchen (1993, 154), this refers to King Khasekhemwy.

85. Saqqara 11 and Turin 3,3, respectively.

9. Seneferka[86]

Horus: *snfr kꜣ* (*senefer ka*), The one whom a ka has made perfect[87]
Later cartouche name: *nfr kꜣ rꜥ* (*nefer ka ra*)*, The perfect one of the ka of Re[88]

Dynasty 2a

The Ramesside Lists add a number of kings in this group, although none of these rulers is actually attested in contemporary documents.

1. Neferkasokar*[89]

Later cartouche name: *nfr kꜣ skr* (*nefer ka seker*)*, The perfect one of the ka of Sokar[90]

2. "Hudjefa" (I)* (?)[91]

Later cartouche name: *ḥ(w) ḏfꜣ* (*hu djefa*)*, Hudjefa[92]

86. Gauthier 1907, 26; von Beckerath 1999, 44–45.
87. For this king, see lately Ryholt 2008.
88. Turin 2,25 and Saqqara 8.
89. Gauthier 1907, 27, 58–59; von Beckerath 1999, 44–45.
90. Turin 3,1 and Saqqara 9.
91. Von Beckerath 1999, 44–45.
92. Turin 3,2. Note that this king may not actually have existed; Goedicke (1956) has proposed that the entry in the Royal Canon of Turin simply contains the word *ḏfꜣ*, "missing, lacking," indicating a gap in the scribe's sources, thus effectively rendering a "King Lacuna."

III

Old Kingdom

Dynasty 3 (2686–2613 b.c.e.)

The period of Dynasties 3 to 8 is the so-called Pyramid Age, when astonishing technological and architectural advances allowed the building of these magnificent structures. By the time of the Third Dynasty, the problems besetting the end of the previous dynasty seemed to have been resolved and the palace could move on to governing the country. The crowning achievement of the age was the Step Pyramid at Saqqara, built for King Djoser by his architect Imhotep. Transforming the traditional media of mud brick and vegetation into stone, Imhotep was able to translate the older perishable architectural motifs into a design that could withstand time. The symbolism behind the shape of the stepped pyramid is explained in Pyramid Texts Spell 267, which reads: "A stairway to heaven is laid for him [the king], so that he may ascend on it to heaven." The Step Pyramid also bears witness to a highly functioning bureaucracy, which had the ability to muster the manpower needed to quarry the stone then transport it to the work site, and subsequently feed and house the workforce who built the pyramid at the burial site.

The titulary of this period largely follows the pattern set in the previous dynasty, with mostly short epithets describing the king's relationship to the divine world. This is especially marked with the use of the word *ẖt,* literally "body," which was also a designation of the "Corporation" of gods, that is, the divine Ennead, the primeval group of gods who preceded humanity in Egyptian theological thought. If this secondary meaning of the word is retained, the kingship was thus seen to be associated with the beginnings of time. Toward the end of the dynasty, King Qahedjet Huni could then claim to be "high of the White Crown" (*ḳ3 ḥḏt*), a powerful symbol of royalty.[1]

1. Goebs 1998.

1 Netjerikhet/Djoser*[2]

Horus: *nṯri-ḫt* (*netjeri-khet*), The one (whose) body is divine[3]
Two Ladies: *nṯri-ḫt* (*netjeri-khet*), The one (whose) body is divine
Later cartouche name: *ḏsr* (*djeser*)*, The sacred one[4]

2. Sekhemkhet[5]

Horus: *sḫm-ḫt* (*sekhem-khet*), The one (whose) body is powerful[6]
Two Ladies: *ḏsr nbty ʿnḫ.t(i)* (*djeser nebty ankh.t(i)*), The sacred one of the Two Ladies, (long) may you live[7]
Later cartouche name: *tti* (*teti*)*, Teti[8]
Later cartouche name: *ḏsr tti* (*djeser teti*)*, Teti is sacred[9]
Later cartouche name: *ḏsr ti* (*djeser ti*)*, Teti (?) is sacred[10]

3. Khaba[11]

Horus: *ḫʿ bꜣ* (*kha ba,*) The (very) appearance of a *ba*
Golden Horus: *bik nbw* (*bik nebu*), The golden falcon[12]

2. Gauthier 1907, 50–53; von Beckerath 1999, 48–49. For a recent study of the king's reign, see Baud 2007, where a discussion of his names is found on pp. 76–80.

3. Lit. "divine of body." Perhaps less likely, the name may mean "The divine one of the (divine) Corporation," with the last term in the name referring to the Ennead, for which see *Wb* III, 357:18 and Hannig 2006b, 1972.

4. The name Djoser, by which this king is better known, appears only in later records. It is attested as early as the Middle Kingdom in Pap. Westcar (1,14) and on a seated figure of Djoser dedicated by King Senwosret II in Karnak Temple (statue Berlin 7702, for which see Roeder 1913, 144; Wildung 2003, 75–76; and Baud 2007, 78–79). It is also known from the Ramesside Lists: Saqqara List (no. 12) offers the short moniker Djoser, while the Abydos List (no. 16) gives [///] *ḏsr-sꜣ* (/// *djeser sa*), "[///] Sacred of protection," and the Turin Canon (3,5) offers *ḏsr it* (?) (*djeser it*), "The sacred one and sovereign (?)." By the Ptolemaic period, the king was certainly known by the two names Netjerikhet and Djoser, as shown on the famous Famine Stela, for which see Barguet 1953; and Ritner 2003, 387.

5. Gauthier 1907, 55; von Beckerath 1999, 48–49. For a recent survey of this king, see Baud 2007, 36–40.

6. Lit. "powerful of body." Less likely, "The powerful one of the (divine) Corporation."

7. For an easily accessible drawing of the name, see T. A. H. Wilkinson 2001, p. 98, fig. 3.5; see also Kahl 1995, 134–35.

8. Abydos 17.

9. Saqqara 13.

10. Turin 3,6.

11. Gauthier 1907, 42; von Beckerath 1999, 50–51. For a recent survey of this king, see Baud 2007, 29–36.

12. This is the first attested use of the hieroglyphic group of the falcon on a standard over the "gold" sign; see Dobrev 1993, 193 n. 47; von Beckerath 1999, 18; and Baud 2007, 171.

4. Sanakht[13]

Horus: *s3 nḫt* (*sa nakht*), The powerful protector
Throne: *nb k3* (*neb ka*), Lord of the ka[14]

5. Qahedjet/Hui/Huni*[15]

Horus: *ḳ3-ḥḏt* (*qa-hedjet*), (Whose) White Crown is high[16]
Throne: *nsw ḥwi* (*nesu hui*), The smiting king[17]
Later cartouche name: *ḥwni* (*huni*)*, The smiter[18]

Dynasty 3a

Other kings may belong to Dynasty 3, hence the designation "Dynasty 3a" here.

1. Sedjes*[19]

Later cartouche name: *sḏs* (*sedjes*)*, "Broken (?)"[20]

---

13. Gauthier 1907, 48–49; von Beckerath 1999, 50–51. For a recent survey of this king, see Baud 2007, 18–21. The identification of the Horus Sanakht with King Nebka is ascertained by a fragmentary sealing from Beit Khallaf, north of Abydos; see T. A. H. Wilkinson 2001, 101–3; Baud 2007, 19–20, 41; and Ryholt 2008, 170. Both the Turin Canon (3,4) and the Abydos King List (no. 15) also give a cartouche name Nebka and place the king at the beginning of Dynasty 3, before Djoser; the presence of a royal name within a cartouche, however, should place him toward the end of the dynasty, as T. A. H. Wilkinson (2001, 101) points out.

14. Or perhaps simply "Possessor of a ka."

15. Gauthier 1907, 57–58; von Beckerath 1999, 48–51. For the possible equation of the Horus Qahedjet with King Huni, see Vandier 1968; Vercoutter 1992, 248; T. Schneider 1996, 351; T. A. H. Wilkinson 2001, 104–5; and Baud 2007, 41.

16. Lit. "High of the White Crown." For this Horus name, found on a stela dated stylistically to a time close to the end of Dynasty 3, see Vandier 1968; and Kahl 1995, 164–65. See also T. A. H. Wilkinson 2001, 104–5; and Baud 2007, 40–42.

17. Huni was the first king to enclose his Throne name in a cartouche; see Dobrev 1993, 193 n. 49.

18. Turin 3,8. The form *ḥwni*, by which this king is usually known, is simply a later variant of the contemporary name *nsw ḥwi*; cf. *Wb* III, 49:5–7. See Meltzer 1971; von Beckerath, 1999, 48 n. 8; and Baud 2007, 25–29.

19. Gauthier 1907, 57.

20. Abydos 18; the entry should perhaps read *sḏ sy*, (*sedj sy*), "It is broken," for which see Ryholt 2008, 164. This royal name is not attested anywhere else, and, like the following entry, may simply be an indication of a gap in the Ramesside scribe's records. Perhaps the word *sḏs* is meant for *sḏb*, "broken," for which see *Wb* IV, 381–82, and Hannig 2003, 1274–75.

2. "Hudjefa" (II)*[21]

Later cartouche name: *ḥ(w) ḏfꜣ* (*hu djefa*)*, "Lacuna"[22]

3. Neferkare (I)*

Later cartouche name: *nfr kꜣ rꜥ* (*nefer ka ra*)*, The perfect one of the ka of Re[23]

4. Nebkare*[24]

Later cartouche name: *nb kꜣ rꜥ* (*neb ka ra*)*, The possessor of the ka of Re[25]

Dynasty 4 (2613–2498 B.C.E.)

With the advent of King Snefru, who may have been related to Huni, the last ruler of the Third Dynasty, Egypt began a new phase of its history. With its centralized government fully established, it was able to undertake massive building projects to the glory of its rulers. Snefru himself built a pyramid at the site of Meidum and two others at Dahshur. The amount of stone quarried for these pyramids exceeds that of the Great Pyramid. Snefru was succeeded by his son Khufu (Greek Cheops), under whose reign the Great Pyramid was built on the limestone plateau at Giza, the last surviving one of the famed classical Seven Wonders of the World. This was followed by two additional pyramids at the site, those of Khafre and Menkaure. Never again would Egypt repeat such an extraordinary undertaking.

Names compounded with that of the sun god appeared a number of times during this period, such as Radjedef, Khafre, Baufre, and Menkaure, attesting to the growing importance of this divinity.[26] This importance is reflected also in the symbolism behind the shape of the pyramid, as Pyramid Texts Spell 523 reads, "Heaven has strengthened the rays of the sun for King NN, so that this King NN may lift himself up to heaven." The titularies of many of the Fourth Dynasty kings mostly elaborated upon a theme set out in the Horus name. Thus, Khufu began his titulary with the verb *mḏd,* "to adhere to, to follow," a theme he

21. Gauthier 1907, 54–55.

22. Turin 3,7. Like King "Hudjefa" of Dynasty 2, this ruler may not actually have existed, the name simply designating a gap in the Ramesside scribe's records.

23. That is, "The perfect one belonging to the ka of Re." The name is attested only in the Abydos List (no. 19) but not in contemporary records.

24. Gauthier 1907, 53–54; von Beckerath 1999, 48–49.

25. Saqqara 14. Like the preceding entry, this ruler is attested only in a later list, where he appears before Huni. A contemporary King Nebka(?) may in fact have existed; see Černý 1958; Dodson 1981; Kahl 1995, 202–3; T. A. H. Wilkinson 2001, 101–3; and Ryholt 2008, 170 and n. 34.

26. On the early cult of the sun god, see Quirke 2011. The Fourth Dynasty titulary has been discussed by Dobrev 1993.

continued in his Two Ladies name, "The one who has adhered to the Two Ladies" (*mḏd r nbty*). Kings Radjedef, Khafre, Menkaure, and Shepseskaf followed the same principle with the words *ḫpr*, "to manifest (oneself)"; *wsr*, "strong"; *kꜣ*, "bull"; and *šps*, "noble," respectively. For his part, Khafre continued his theme of being *wsr*, "strong," with a similar adjective, *sḫm*, "powerful," in his Golden Horus name.

1. Snefru[27]

Horus 1: *nb mꜣꜥt* (*neb maat*), Possessor of Maat
Horus 2: *nb mꜣꜥt snfr w*(*i*) (*neb maat senefer wi*), The lord of Maat has made me perfect
Two Ladies: *nb mꜣꜥt* (*neb maat*), Possessor of Maat
Golden Horus: *bik nbw* (*bik nebu*), Golden falcon[28]
Throne: *snfr w*(*i*) (*senefer wi*), <God N> has made me perfect[29]

2. Khufu (Cheops)[30]

Horus: *mḏdw* (*medjedu*), Who has been adhered to/followed[31]
Two Ladies: *mḏd r nbty* (*medjed er nebty*), Who has adhered to the Two Ladies
Golden Horus: *bikwy nbw* (*bikwy nebu*), The golden double falcon[32]
Throne, short form: *ḫw.f wi* (*khu.ef wi*), He protects me
Throne, full form: *ẖnmw ḫw.f wi* (*khnum khu.ef wi*), Khnum, he protects me[33]

3. Radjedef[34]

Horus: *ḫpr* (*kheper*), The one who has manifested (himself)

---

27. Gauthier 1907, 61–71; von Beckerath 1999, 52–53.

28. From this time on, the Golden Horus became a regular part of the royal titulary; see Dobrev 1993, 189.

29. If the term is not an abbreviated form of a theophoric name—as is the name of Snefru's son, Khufu—one could also simply render *snfrw*, "The one who has been made perfect," reading the form as an imperfective passive participle, for which see Edel 1955, § 638 f.

30. Gauthier 1907, 72–83; von Beckerath 1999, 52–53.

31. Reading as another passive participle, from "to follow, adhere to" (*Wb* II, 192: 3–5). Gardiner and Peet (1955, 58) and T. Schneider (1996, 149) prefer the meaning "to strike" for the verb *mḏd* (*Wb* II, 191: 14–17). I have opted for the former rendering because of the king's Two Ladies name. For the problem of interpreting the name, see Dobrev 1993, 188 n. 33; and Baud 1998, 18 n. 5.

32. Perhaps referring to Khufu and his father Snefru, for which see Dobrev 1993, 189–94.

33. This fuller name is the theophoric version of the abbreviated "personal"—and commonly used today— name of Khufu; see Dobrev 1993, 195 n. 55.

34. Gauthier 1907, 83–85; von Beckerath 1999, 52–53.

Two Ladies: *ḫpr m nbty* (*kheper em nebty*), Who has manifested (himself) by means of the Two Ladies
Golden Horus: *bikw* (*nṯrw*) *nbw* (*biku (netjeru) nebu*), The (divine) falcons are golden
Throne: *rꜥ ḏd.f* (*re djed.ef*), Re is his stability[35]

4. Khafre (Chephren)[36]

Horus: *wsr-ib* (*weser ib*), Strong-minded
Two Ladies: *wsr m nbty* (*weser em nebty*), Who is strong by means of the Two Ladies
Golden Horus: *sḫm bik nbw* (*sekhem bik nebu*), The golden falcon is powerful
Throne: *ḫꜥ.f rꜥ* (*kha.ef ra*), He appears (as) Re[37]

5. Baufre*

Later cartouche name: *bꜣw.f rꜥ* (*bau.ef ra*)*, His *bas* are those of Re[38]

6. Menkaure (Mycerinus)[39]

Horus: *kꜣ ḫt* (*ka khet*), The bull of the (divine) Corporation
Two Ladies: *kꜣ <m> nbty* (*ka <em> nebty*), The bull <by means of> the Two Ladies[40]
Golden Horus: *nṯri bik nbw* (*netjeri bik nebu*), The golden falcon is divine
Throne: *mn kꜣw rꜥ* (*men kau ra*), The established one of the kas of Re

35. I have opted for the reading Radjedef because of its later Greek form Rathotis (Waddell 1940, 102). A reading "Djedefre" would give us "Re endures," lit. "He endures, (namely) Re," but such a phrase would not refer to the king himself, which a name ought to do. It is also to be noted that Radjedef was the first to use the designation *sꜣ rꜥ*, "the son of Re," to introduce his Throne name.

36. Gauthier 1907, 86–94; von Beckerath 1999, 54–55.

37. If the name were to be patterned after that of his half-brother Radjedef, we should then read Ra-khaf, "Re is his (very) appearance," which would make very good sense, but I have opted for the customary "Khafre" because of the later Greek rendering Chephren.

38. This royal prince's name is surrounded by a cartouche in a Middle Kingdom graffito found in the Wadi Hammamat, which lists Kings Khufu, Radjedef, and Khafre, followed by the two names Hordjedef and Baufre, also written inside cartouches (see Drioton 1954); the name is also known from Pap. Westcar 4,17–18. It is not likely that Prince Baufre actually reigned as king; see Redford 1986, 25; Vercoutter 1992, 285–86; T. Schneider 1996, 134; and Baud 1999, 548, 631.

39. Gauthier 1907, 95–100; von Beckerath 1999, 54–55.

40. For this interpretation of the name, which can be compared to other Two Ladies names from the same dynasty, see Dobrev 1993, 188.

7. Shepseskaf[41]

Horus: *šps ẖt* (*shepes khet*), The noble one of the (divine) Corporation
Two Ladies: *šps <m> nbty* (*shepes <em> nebty*), The noble one <by means of> the Two Ladies
Golden Horus: (unknown)[42]
Throne: *špss k3.f* (*shepses ka.ef*), His ka is noble

Dynasty 5 (2498–2345 b.c.e.)

As with the passage from the Third to the Fourth Dynasty, this numbering of a new dynasty is purely conventional in that it follows Manetho's divisions.[43] The first king of the Fifth Dynasty, Userkaf, probably married into the preceding royal family. The influence of the sun god Re is ever more prominent at this period, as the royal pyramids at Abusir are significantly smaller than those at Giza, but the kings built sun temples as well at the site. The latter had open courtyards with short squat obelisks, a solar symbol of the sacred *benben* stone from Heliopolis. Also significant was the Saqqara pyramid of Unas, the last ruler of the dynasty, the interior walls of which were inscribed with the earliest occurrence of the Pyramid Texts. Although these equated the deceased king with the chthonic god of the dead Osiris, the frequent theme of the king ascending to the sky has made scholars believe that the Pyramid Texts were composed at Heliopolis, the main cult center of the sun god Re.

Foreign affairs began to take on more importance at this time, as many of the kings from this period are attested in Western Asia and Nubia; Sahure and Niuserre even sent expeditions as far away as the legendary land of Punt.

Politically speaking, this period saw the growing importance of nonroyal families, as the highest offices of the land were no longer automatically held by members of the royal family. Additionally, local provincial rulers, usually referred to by the Greek term "nomarchs," administered their territories from their own home base rather than from the capital city. This led to a gradual decentralization of the country and the creation of a powerful provincial nobility that the crown could no longer afford to ignore.

The titularies from this period follow one of two patterns. Kings Userkaf and Sahure imitated Djoser by simply repeating the same phrase in their Horus and Two Ladies names. Neferirkare and Niuserre, for their part, followed the pattern of the Fourth Dynasty, where the theme set out in the Horus name was further

41. Gauthier 1907, 101–3; von Beckerath 1999, 54–55. An additional king named Thamphthis, for whom no Egyptian sources are known, is sometimes added at the end of Dynasty 4; see von Beckerath 1999, 54 n. 5.

42. See Dobrev 1993, 189 n. 37.

43. Waddell 1940, 50–51.

elaborated upon in the Two Ladies name. This latter development extended to the Golden Horus names of Sahure, Nefer(ef)re, Djedkare, and Unas. Of note is that Neferirkare's titulary adopted the same two adjectives, "strong" (*wsr*) and "powerful" (*sḫm*), seen earlier in the titulary of Khafre.

It has been suggested[44] that a few of the Fifth Dynasty Birth names may simply be short forms of the Throne name. Thus, the Throne name Neferirkare became Kakai in his second cartouche name, Niuserre became Ini, and Menkauhor became Ikauhor. This most plausible suggestion may help explain certain rulers' Birth names, which seem to defy translation. Since the Throne name was given to the king at his coronation, this would imply that a moniker such as Kakai may not actually have been the king's Birth name. The designation "anthroponym" for this and other kings of the dynasty has been proposed for these second cartouches.[45]

The reader will notice that I have sometimes referred to a king either by his Birth name (Userkaf, Sahure, and Unas) or by his Throne name (Neferirkare, Shepseskare, Niuserre, etc.). This is purely for practical reasons, since these are the names by which these particular kings are usually known.

1. Userkaf[46]

Horus: *ỉr m3ʿt* (*ir maat*), The one who has accomplished Maat
Two Ladies: *ỉr m3ʿt* (*ir maat*), The one who has accomplished Maat
Golden Horus: *bỉk nbw nfr* (*bik nebu nefer*), The perfect golden falcon
Birth: *wsr k3.f* (*weser ka.ef*), His ka is strong

2. Sahure[47]

Horus: *nb ḫʿw* (*neb khau*), Possessor of appearances[48]
Two Ladies: *nb ḫʿw* (*neb khau*), Possessor of appearances
Golden Horus: *bỉkwy nbw* (*bikwy nebu*), The golden double falcon[49]
Birth: *s3ḥ w(ỉ) rʿ* (*sah w(i) ra*), Re has endowed me[50]

44. Scheele-Schweitzer 2007.
45. Ibid., 93.
46. Gauthier 1907, 105–8; von Beckerath 1999, 56–57.
47. Gauthier 1907, 109–13; von Beckerath 1999, 56–57.
48. Less likely, "Possessor of crowns."
49. If this interpretation of the name is correct, Sahure seems to be repeating Khufu's association of himself with his predecessor in his Golden Horus name; cf. Dobrev 1993, 190 n. 41.
50. For this meaning of *s3ḥ*, see *Wb* IV, 21:15–20; and Hannig 2006b, 2088.

3. Neferirkare (I)[51]

Horus: *wsr-ḫꜥw* (*weser khau*), Strong of appearances
Two Ladies 1: *ḫꜥ m nbty* (*kha em nebty*), Who has appeared by means of the Two Ladies
Two Ladies 2: *wsr-ḫꜥw nbty* (*weser khau nebty*), Strong of appearances <by means of> the Two Ladies
Golden Horus: *sḫmw nbw* (*sekhemu nebu*), The triple power[52]
Throne: *nfr ỉr kꜣ rꜥ* (*nefer ir ka ra*), The perfect one is the one whom the ka of Re has engendered (lit. "made")
Birth (?) name: *kꜣ kꜣ.ỉ* (*ka ka.i*), My ka is a (true) ka (?)

4. Shepseskare[53]

Horus: *sḫm ḫꜥw* (*sekhem khau*), Powerful of appearances
Two Ladies: unknown
Golden Horus: unknown
Throne: *špss kꜣ rꜥ* (*shepses ka ra*), The noble one of the ka of Re
Birth: *nṯr(ỉ) wsr* (*netjer weser*), The divine and strong one

5. Nefer(ef)re[54]

Horus: *nfr ḫꜥw* (*nefer khau*), Perfect of appearances
Two Ladies: *nfr m nbty* (*nefer em nebty*), Who is perfect by means of the Two Ladies
Golden Horus: *bỉk nbw nfr* (*bik nebu nefer*), The perfect golden falcon
Throne 1: *nfr rꜥ* (*nefer ra*), The (very) perfection of Re
Throne 2: *nfr.f rꜥ* (*nefer.ef ra*), He is perfect (in the manner of) Re[55]
Birth: *ỉzỉ* (*izi*), Izi[56]

---

51. Gauthier 1907, 116–19; von Beckerath 1999, 56–57.

52. Or perhaps literally "The three powers," referring to the first three kings of the dynasty, with the three *sekhem*-scepter hieroglyphs replacing the falcon sign in the name; see Dobrev 1993, 190 n. 41.

53. Gauthier 1907, 119; von Beckerath 1999, 56–57.

54. Gauthier 1907, 120–22; von Beckerath 1999, 58–59

55. The name *nfr.f rꜥ* is a contemporary reinterpretation of the original *nfr rꜥ;* see Verner 1985. The reading Renefer/Reneferef, with a meaning of "Re is perfect," which has also been proposed by Verner (1985), focuses on the sun god rather than on the king himself; hence my preference for the reading Nefer(ef)re.

56. The name may simply be another diminutive; see Scheele-Schweitzer 2007.

6. Niuserre[57]

Horus: *st-ỉb tꜣwy* (*set-ib tawy*), The favorite[58] of the Two Lands
Two Ladies: *st-ỉb nbty* (*set-ib nebty*), The favorite of the Two Ladies
Golden Horus: *bỉk nbw nṯrỉ* (*bik nebu netjeri*), The divine golden falcon
Throne: *n(y) wsr rʿ* (*ni weser ra)*, Who belongs to the power of Re
Birth (?): *ỉnỉ* (*ini*), Ini[59]

7. Menkauhor[60]

Horus: *mn-ḫʿw* (*men khau*), Established of appearances
Golden Horus: *bỉk nbw ḥḏ* (*bik nebu hedj*), The radiant golden falcon
Throne: *mn kꜣw ḥr* (*men kau hor*), The established one of the kas of Horus
Birth (?) 1: *ỉkꜣw ḥr* (*ikau hor*), Ikauhor
Birth (?) 2: *ỉkꜣw* (*ikau*), Ikau[61]

8. Djedkare[62]

Horus: *ḏd-ḫʿw* (*djed khau*), Enduring of appearances
Two Ladies: *ḏd-ḫʿw nbty* (*djed khau nebty*), Enduring of appearances <by means of?> the Two Ladies
Golden Horus: *bỉk nbw ḏd* (*bik nebu djed*), The enduring golden falcon
Throne 1: *ḏd kꜣ rʿ* (*djed ka ra)*, The enduring one of the ka of Re
Throne 2: *ḏd kꜣ ḥr* (*djed ka hor*), The enduring one of the ka of Horus
Birth: *ỉzzỉ* (*izezi*), Izezi[63]

9. Unas[64]

Horus: *wꜣḏ tꜣwy* (*wadj tawy*), The sturdy one of the Two Lands

---

57. Gauthier 1907, 124–29; von Beckerath 1999, 58–59.

58. Lit. "the place of the heart."

59. One might suggest "The delayed one" (*CDME*, 23), perhaps referring to a baby whose birth was overdue. Alternatively, perhaps the name means something like "The (one with the bushy?) eyebrows" (*CDME*, 23). Perhaps simpler, the name may be a nickname of Niuserre; see Scheele-Schweitzer 2007.

60. Gauthier 1907, 130–32; von Beckerath 1999, 58–59.

61. The name Ikau was simply an abbreviation of the fuller name Ikauhor (Gauthier 1907, 123; von Beckerath 1999, 58); the latter was itself derived from the Throne name Menkauhor (Edel 1960, 79–80; and Fischer 1989a, 23 n. 6), which may again mean that the name was not actually the king's Birth name.

62. Gauthier 1907, 133–38; von Beckerath 1999, 60–61.

63. The name, which could simply be a diminutive, may be derived from the imperative verb *iz*, "go!" (*Wb* I, 126:8–16), an expression possibly uttered by a midwife at the time of the birth.

64. Gauthier 1907, 138–42; von Beckerath 1999, 60–61. Unas's titulary is discussed by Aufrère (1982, 52–53), who has suggested an unattested Throne name *Wadjkare.

Two Ladies: *wꜣḏ m nbty* (*wadj em nebty*), The one who is sturdy by means of the Two Ladies
Golden Horus: *bik nbw wꜣḏ* (*bik nebu wadj*), The sturdy golden falcon
Birth: *wnis* (*wenis*), Unas[65]

Dynasty 6 (2345–2181)

Since there is a possibility that King Teti was Unas's son-in-law, the transition from one dynasty to another may again be purely artificial and due to Manetho's numbering system.[66] There certainly was no interruption in the bureaucracy, as two of Teti's viziers, Mehu and Kagemni, had begun their careers in the late Fifth Dynasty. Another Manethonian tradition is that of Teti being assassinated, but there are no contemporary records corroborating this crime.[67] One source from the period, the autobiography of Weni the Elder from Abydos, does, however, mention a disturbance within the royal palace and his involvement in a trial of an unnamed queen.[68]

Royal activities continued in western Asia, but the crown's attention seemed to have shifted south to Nubia. A number of texts of high officials from Elephantine speak of their travels in Lower Nubia. Among these is the Overseer of Upper Egypt Harkhuf, whose texts show the growing power of a single ruler in Upper Nubia near the Third Cataract.[69] Within the country, an upsurge in local autonomy forced some of the kings into marriage alliances with powerful provincial families.

Largely conforming to the tradition used by the preceding dynasties, the titulary of the Sixth Dynasty kings repeats the main theme of the Horus name with variations in their other names. Thus, Teti was the Horus *sḥtp tꜣwy,* "the one who satisfied the Two Lands," and the Two Ladies *sḥtp nbty,* "the one who satisfied the Two Ladies," while Pepy I was the Horus *mry tꜣwy,* "the beloved of the Two Lands" and the Two Ladies *mry ẖt nbty,* "the beloved of the Two Ladies' bodies." Of note is the first Throne name of Pepy I, *nfr zꜣ ḥr,* "Perfect is the protection of Horus," a rare example of a nonsolar theophoric designation in a Throne name.[70]

65. If, as suggested by Scheele-Schweitzer (2007, 93–94), the name is read *wn is,* that is, the verb followed by a strengthening particle, the name might perhaps mean something like "The one who truly exists," lit. "who exists indeed."

66. Waddell 1940, 52–53.

67. For an interesting if highly conjectural treatment of this question, see Kanawati 2003.

68. Strudwick 2005, 353–54. On this official and the important rediscovery of his funerary complex, see Richards 2002, 2010, and Forthcoming.

69. Strudwick 2005, 330–31.

70. Dobrev 1993, 196 n. 57.

1. Teti[71]

Horus: *sḥtp tꜣwy* (*sehetep tawy*), The one who has satisfied the Two Lands
Two Ladies: *sḥtp nbty* (*sehetep nebty*), The one who has satisfied the Two Ladies
Golden Horus: *smꜣ* (*sema*), The uniter
Throne: (unknown)[72]
Birth: *tti* (*teti*), Teti[73]

2. Userkare (I)[74]

Horus: (unknown)
Two Ladies: (unknown)
Golden Horus: (unknown)
Throne/Birth (?): *wsr kꜣ rꜥ* (*weser ka ra*), The strong one belonging to the ka of Re

3. Pepy I[75]

Horus: *mry tꜣwy* (*mery tawy*), Beloved of the Two Lands
Two Ladies: *mry ẖt nbty* (*mery khet nebty*), Beloved of the Two Ladies' bodies
Golden Horus: *bikw nbw* (*biku nebu*), The triple falcons are golden[76]
Throne 1: *nfr zꜣ ḥr* (*nefer za hor*), Perfect is the protection of Horus[77]
Throne 2: *mry rꜥ* (*mery ra*), Beloved of Re
Birth: *ppy* (*pepy*), Pepy[78]

---

71. Gauthier 1907, 146–50; von Beckerath 1999, 62–63.

72. See Aufrère (1982, 53–54), who, on the analogy of Pepy I, has proposed an unattested Throne name of *Sehetepre for Teti.

73. Some examples of the name show the epithet *sꜣ rꜥ*, "the son of Re," written within the cartouche and preceding the name Teti.

74. Gauthier 1907, 145; von Beckerath 1999, 62–63. On this obscure king, who probably reigned for a short period of time between Teti and Pepy I, see Baud and Dobrev 1995, 59–63, and Baud 1999, 625, and the references given there. His memory lived on, as he is also attested in the Ramesside Abydos List (no. 35) between the two aforementioned rulers. His identification with the King Iti mentioned in two graffiti in the Wadi Hammamat (Couyat and Montet 1913, nos. 168, 169) is highly speculative; see Baud and Dobrev 1995, 60 and n. 95.

75. Gauthier 1907, 150–62; von Beckerath 1999, 62–63.

76. Perhaps referring to himself and his two predecessors; see Dobrev 1993, 190 n. 41. Compare the Golden Horus names of Khufu and Sahure.

77. With the mention of Horus here, the king is presumably referring to himself. This earlier Throne name of Pepy I is known from graffiti at Hatnub and at Tomas in Nubia (for the latter text, see Strudwick 2005, 150). Dobrev (1993, 196 n. 57) has noted that this is a rare example of a nonsolar theophoric Throne name.

78. As with King Teti, some instances show the epithet *sꜣ rꜥ*, "the son of Re," written within the cartouche. For the transliteration of the name, see Fischer 1989b.

4. Merenre (I)[79]

Horus: *ʿnḫ ḫʿw* (*ankh khau*), (Whose) appearances are (very much) alive
Two Ladies: *ʿnḫ ḫʿw nbty* (*ankh khau nebty*), (The one for whom) The appearances of the Two Ladies are alive
Golden Horus: *bikwy nbw* (*bikwy nebu*), The golden double falcon
Throne: *mr.n rʿ* (*mer.en ra*), The one whom Re has loved
Birth: *nmty m z3.f* (*nemty em za.ef*), (The god) Nemty is his protection

5. Pepy II[80]

Horus: *nṯri-ḫʿw* (*netjeri khau*), Divine of appearances
Two Ladies: *nṯri-ḫʿw nbty* (*netjeri khau nebty*), The divine one of the appearances of the Two Ladies
Golden Horus: *bik nbw sḫm* (*bik nebu sekhem*), The powerful golden falcon
Throne: *nfr k3 rʿ* (*nefer ka ra*), The perfect one of the ka of Re
Birth 1: *ppy* (*pepy*), Pepy[81]

6. Merenre II[82]

Horus: unknown (?)
Two Ladies: unknown (?)
Golden Horus: unknown (?)
Throne: *mr.n rʿ* [*nmty?*] *m z3.f* (*mer.en ra [nemty?] em za.ef*), The one whom Re has loved, [Nemty][83] is his protection
Birth: *nmty m z3.f* (*nemty em za.ef*), (The god) Nemty is his protection

7. Queen Neith-iqeret (Nitocris*)[84]

Birth: *nt iḳrt* (*net iqeret*)*, (The goddess) Neith is excellent[85]

---

79. Gauthier 1907, 163–68; von Beckerath 1999, 62–63.

80. Gauthier 1907, 169–76; von Beckerath 1999, 64–65.

81. As with Kings Teti and Pepy I, the epithet *s3 rʿ* can sometimes precede the name within the cartouche.

82. Gauthier 1907, 176; von Beckerath 1999, 64–65.

83. Von Beckerath (1999, p. 64, n. 3) has suggested reading the sign in the Abydos List (no. 39) as *ḏf3*, "lacuna," but this presumably indicates a missing divine name *nmty*.

84. Gauthier 1907, 177–78; von Beckerath 1999, 64–65.

85. Turin 4,7. As the asterisk indicates, this queen is not actually attested in contemporary documents; for a survey of the reign, see Coche-Zivie 1972, 119–32; and the remarks in Baud 1999, 631.

Dynasty 8 (2181–2161 B.C.E.)

Following the overly long reign of Pepy II, a series of ephemeral rulers, the memory of whom was sometimes confused in later King Lists, reigned for a generation or so. Manetho's Seventh Dynasty, which he described as "70 kings of Memphis, who reigned for 70 days,"[86] does not actually exist.[87] Few of the kings ascribed to an Eighth Dynasty, who are also said by Manetho to have continued ruling from Memphis,[88] are attested in contemporary records.

The order of kings in this section largely follows that of von Beckerath.[89] I have opted to first list the names as presented in the Abydos King List numbers 40–56,[90] here numbered 1 to 17. The Turin Canon's entries in col. 4,8 to 4,13[91] coincide with Abydos numbers 51 to 56.[92] Some of the cartouches in the Abydos List contain two names, which may reflect a Throne as well as a Birth name. As with previous rulers for whom contemporary records are missing, the entries will be referred to as "Later cartouche name" and will be followed by an asterisk. After the catalogue from the Abydos List will come eight rulers who are attested contemporaneously. They will be referred to as Dynasty 8a.

The titularies chosen by these ephemeral kings were largely borrowed from the kings of the Old Kingdom, whose names would have been easily attested in the Memphite area.

1. Netjerikare*[93]

Later cartouche name: *nṯri k3 rˁ* (*netjeri ka ra)*,* The divine one of the ka of Re

2. Menkare*[94]

Later cartouche name: *mn k3 rˁ* (*men ka ra*),* The established one of the ka of Re

3. Neferkare (II)*[95]

Later cartouche name: *nfr k3 rˁ* (*nefer ka ra)*,* The perfect one of the ka of Re

86. Waddell 1940, 56–57.
87. Redford 1986, 238.
88. Waddell 1940, 58–59.
89. Von Beckerath 1999, 66–71.
90. KRI I, 178:11–179:1.
91. KRI II, 832:3–8.
92. Von Beckerath 1962, 145.
93. Abydos 40; Gauthier 1907, 180; von Beckerath 1999, 66–67.
94. Abydos 41; Gauthier 1907, 181; von Beckerath 1999, 66–67.
95. Abydos 42; Gauthier 1907, 181; von Beckerath 1999, 66–67.

4. Neferkare Nebi[96]

Throne: *nfr k3 rꜥ* (*nefer ka ra)*, The perfect one of the ka of Re.
Birth: *nby* (*neby*), Who belongs to <his> lord

5. Djedkare Shemay*[97]

Later cartouche name: *ḏd k3 rꜥ* (*djed ka ra)*,* The enduring one of the ka of Re
Second later cartouche name: *šm3y* (*shemay*),* The foreigner[98]

6. Neferkare Khendu*[99]

Later cartouche name: *nfr k3 rꜥ* (*nefer ka ra)*,*The perfect one of the ka of Re
Second later cartouche name: *ẖndw* (*khendu*),*The wanderer

7. Merenhor*[100]

Later cartouche name: *mr*(*y*) *n ḥr* (*mer(y) en hor*),* Beloved of Horus

8. Neferkamin*[101]

Later cartouche name: *nfr k3 mnw* (*nefer ka menu*),* The perfect one of the ka of (the god) Min[102]

96. Abydos 43 gives both names Neferkare and Nebi in the single cartouche; Gauthier 1907, 182–84; von Beckerath 1999, 66–67. The word "lord" presumably refers to a divine master. The king's name is attested contemporaneously from that of his pyramid, *ḏd-ꜥnḫ-nfr-k3-rꜥ* (*djed-ankh-nefer-ka-re*), "Neferkare is stable and alive," from a fragmentary stela found in one of the rooms belonging to Queen Iput at Saqqara (Jéquier 1933, 53).

97. As with the previous ruler, both names Djedkare and Shemay are given in a single cartouche in Abydos 44; Gauthier 1907, 184; von Beckerath 1999, 66–67.

98. Perhaps also "the nomad," for which see T. Schneider 1998, 25, and the references there.

99. Abydos 45 gives both names in the single cartouche; Gauthier 1907, 185; von Beckerath 1999, 66–67.

100. Abydos 46; Gauthier 1907, 185–86; von Beckerath 1999, 66–67.

101. Von Beckerath 1999, 66–67.

102. For the reading of the sign as the Min emblem (Gardiner Sign List R 22), as opposed to the door bolt sign (Gardiner Sign List S 29), see von Beckerath 1999, 66 n. 5. The divine emblem sign was subsequently misread by the Ramesside scribe (Abydos 47 [Gauthier 1907, 186]) as the door bolt, which gives the name Seneferka, "The one who makes the ka of Re perfect" (e.g., Gardiner 1961, 437). The designation "Later cartouche name" for this king comes from von Beckerath's suggestion (1999, 66 n. 5) that the gold plaque that contains the name, along with the next king's (cf. Gardiner 1961, 437 n. 4), is not contemporary.

9. NIKARE*[103]

Later cartouche name: *n(y)-k3 rˁ* (*ny-ka ra)*,* Who belongs to the ka of Re

10. NEFERKARE TERERU[104]

Throne: *nfr k3 rˁ* (*nefer ka ra)*, The perfect one of the ka of Re
Birth: *trrw* (*tereru*), The respected one (?)

11. NEFERKAHOR*[105]

Later cartouche name: *nfr k3 ḥr* (*nefer ka hor*),* The perfect one of the ka of Horus

12. NEFERKARE PEPYSENBU*[106]

Later cartouche name: *nfr k3 rˁ* (*nefer ka ra)*,* The perfect one of the ka of Re
Second later cartouche name: *ppy snb*(*.w*) (*pepy senbu*),* Pepy is healthy

13. NEFERKAMIN ANU*[107]

Later cartouche name: *nfr k3 mnw* (*nefer ka menu*),* The perfect one of the ka of Min
Second later cartouche name: *ˁnw* (*anu*),* The beautiful one[108]

14. QAKARE IBI I[109]

Throne: *ḳ3 k3 rˁ* (*qa ka ra)*, The exalted (lit. "high") one of the ka of Re
Birth: *ỉbỉ* (*ibi*), The kid (lit. "the young goat")

---

103. Abydos 48; Gauthier 1907, 187; von Beckerath 1999, 66–67.

104. The name is found on a scarab, for which see Petrie 1917, p. x and pl. 10, no.7.10. See also Abydos 49, which gives both names in the single cartouche; Gauthier 1907, 188; von Beckerath 1999, 68–69.

105. Abydos 50; Gauthier 1907, 188; von Beckerath 1999, 68–69.

106. Abydos 51; Turin (4,8) only writes the name as *nfr-ḥ3t* but adds the epithet *šri*, "The younger," to the name; Gauthier 1907, 189; von Beckerath 1999, 68–69.

107. As with the previous king named Neferkamin (8:8), the Ramesside scribe (Abydos 52) read the name as Seneferka; the other Ramesside scribe (Turin 4,9) simply offers the name "Nefer." See Gauthier 1907, 190; von Beckerath 1999, 68–69.

108. Here one is tempted to render the full name as Neferkamin the Fair.

109. Turin (4,10) only gives the Birth name Ibi. This king is known from an unfinished pyramid at South Saqqara, for which see Jéquier 1935; and von Beckerath 1962, 141, 144. Abydos 53, which gives only the Throne name, offers the plural *k3w* (*kau*), ". . . the kas of Re." Gauthier 1907, 190; von Beckerath 1999, 68–69.

15. Neferkaure[110]

Horus: *ḫꜥ* [*bꜣw*] (*kha [bau]*), The (very) appearance of power[111]
Throne: *nfr kꜣw rꜥ* (*nefer kau ra)*, The perfect one of the kas of Re

16. Neferkauhor Khuwihapi[112]

Horus: *nṯri-bꜣw* (*netjeri bau*), Divine of might
Throne: *nfr kꜣw ḥr* (*nefer kau hor*), The perfect one of the kas of Horus[113]
Birth: *ḫw wi ḥꜥpy* (*khu wi hapy*), (The Nile god) Hapy protects me

17. Neferirkare II*[114]

Later cartouche name: *nfr ir kꜣ rꜥ* (*nefer ir ka ra)*,* The perfect one is the one whom the ka of Re has engendered[115]

Dynasty 8a–attested names[116]

1. Sekhemkare[117]

Throne: *sḫm kꜣ rꜥ* (*sekhem ka ra)*, The powerful one of the ka of Re

2. Wadjkare[118]

Horus: *dmḏ ib tꜣwy* (*demedj ib tawy*), Who has united (lit. "assembled") the will (lit. "mind") of the Two Lands
Throne: *wꜣḏ kꜣ rꜥ* (*wadj ka ra)*, The flourishing one of the ka of Re

---

110. Abydos 54, which gives only the Throne name; Gauthier 1907, 190; von Beckerath 1999, 68–69.

111. The name is known from Coptos Decree (h), for which see Hayes 1946, 5, 11–13, 20.

112. Abydos 55, which gives only the Throne name; Gauthier 1907, 190; von Beckerath 1999, 68–69.

113. The name is known from Coptos Decrees (j) to (q), for which see Hayes 1946, 5–6, 19–20; and von Beckerath 1962, 144.

114. Abydos 56; Gauthier 1907, 191; von Beckerath 1999, 68–69.

115. This ruler is sometimes identified with the Horus Demedj-ib-tawy; see W. S. Smith 1971, 995; and, tentatively, Kitchen 1993, 155.

116. For the names of Dynasty 8a, see von Beckerath 1999, 70–71.

117. Attested on a fragmentary piece of papyrus from Elephantine (Pap. Berlin 10523), for which see Möller 1911, pl. 5, 6/9 and X/XV. The first sign, which is probably the *sekhem*-scepter, could also be read as the *ankh*-sign, which would give the name *ankh ka re,* "The living one is the (very) ka of Re."

118. Attested in Coptos Decree (r), for which see Hayes 1946, 6, 20.

3. Iti[119]

Throne: *ỉty* (*ity*), Iti

4. Imhotep[120]

Throne: *ỉỉ m ḥtp* (*ii em hetep*), The one who has come in peace

5. Hotep[121]

Throne: /// *rʿ* (/// *ra*), /// of Re ///
Birth: *ḥtp* (*hetep*), The one who is at peace

6. Khui[122]

Birth: *ḫw wỉ* (*khu wi*), The one who protects me[123]

7. Isu[124]

Birth: *ỉsw* (*isu*), The ancient one (?)

8. Iytjenu[125]

Birth: *ỉy ṯnw* (*iy tjenu*), The one who has come (already) distinguished

---

119. Known from two graffiti left in the Wadi Hammamat (nos. 168 and 169, for which see Couyat and Montet 1913, 94); the latter text gives the name of the king's pyramid as *mr bꜣw-ỉtỉ* (*mer bau iti*), "The pyramid of the *ba*-power of Iti."

120. Known from a graffito left in the Wadi Hammamat (no. 206, for which see Couyat and Montet 1913, 103), which details an expedition undertaken on behalf of an "Imhotep," whose name is written in a cartouche; see also Gauthier 1907, 143.

121. This name may simply be a short form of the previous one; see von Beckerath 1999, p. 70, n. 3.

122. The name, written in a cartouche, is found on a fragmentary limestone relief from Middle Egypt near Dara, a site on the west bank of the Nile between Meir and Asyut, for which see Kamal 1912, 132–33. A pyramid found nearby may well belong to this king (cf. Fakhry 1961, 202–4) but the attribution cannot be proven; see Grajetzki 2006, 7–8.

123. The name may be a shortened form of a theophoric name, "<God X> is the one who protects me."

124. From a graffito found in the Gebel Silsileh area, written by the King's Son and Chief Lector-priest Isu-ankhu ("Isu is alive"), where the element "Isu" of the compound name is written in a cartouche; see Weigall 1908, 110.

125. The royal name comes from the basiliphoric name of a woman called Zat-Iytjenu ("The daughter of <King> Iytjenu") on an Eighth Dynasty stela found at Saqqara; like the previous entry, the element "Iytjenu" of the compound name is written in a cartouche; see Fischer 1963, 36, and pl. 6.

IV

First Intermediate Period

Dynasties 9–10a (2160–2040 b.c.e.)[1]

Following the accelerating decentralization of the country after the Sixth Dynasty, the nomarchs of the twentieth Upper Egyptian nome in their home base of Neni-Nesu (Greek Herakleopolis) declared themselves heirs to the Horus throne. This line, which is ignored by the compilers of the Abydos List, was assigned two different figures by Manetho in his numbering of dynasties,[2] but is actually the same family and, in fact, is treated as such in the Turin Canon.[3] Hence they are grouped together here. It is likely that the Tenth Dynasty ruled only Lower and Middle Egypt and was contemporary with the early Eleventh Dynasty.

Only five kings of this Herakleopolitan dynasty are known from contemporary monuments: Neferkare, Nebkaure Khety, Meryibre Khety, Merykare, and Wahkare Khety. There are no properly attested traces of these kings south of Asyut. As with the previous kings who are not attested in contemporary records but only in later King Lists, their names will be followed by an asterisk.

The phrase *kꜣ rꜥ*, "the ka of Re," seen in a number of the titularies from this period harks back to Pepy II's Throne name Neferkare, indicating the new rulers' wish to emulate their venerable predecessors. Similarly, Meryibre Khety's use of the phrase *mry ib tꜣwy*, "beloved of the mind of the Two Lands," in his Horus and Two Ladies names recalls the Horus name of Pepy I, *mry tꜣwy*, "beloved of the Two Lands." King Khety's use of the same epithet in his first two names is also a repetition of an Old Kingdom practice.

1. For the first nine kings in this section, see von Beckerath 1999, 72–73.
2. Waddell 1940, 60–63.
3. Columns 4,18 to 5,9 (= KRI II, 832:13–833:11); see Málek 1982, 105.

1. [Khety I]*[4]

Birth: *ẖty* (*khety*),* The one belonging to the divine corporation[5]

2. ///// (name missing in the Turin List [4,19])

3. Neferkare (III)[6]

Throne: *nfr k3 rꜥ* (*nefer ka ra*), The perfect one of the ka of Re

4. Khety II*[7]

Birth: *ẖty* (*khety*),* Khety

5. Senen ////*[8]

Cartouche: *snn////* (*senen///*),* The (very) likeness [of ? ///]

6. [Khety III]*[9]

Birth: [*ẖty s3? nfr k3 rꜥ*] ([*khety sa nefer ka ra]*),* [Khety's son(?), Neferkare]

7. [Khety IV]*[10]

Throne and birth: *mry* /// [*ẖty*] (*mery /// [khety]*),* Beloved of /// [Khety]

8. Shed ////*[11]

Birth: *šd* /// (*shed///*),* The savior ///

---

4. Although the name is missing in the Turin Canon (col. 4,18), Manetho's Ninth Dynasty consisted of "nineteen kings of Herakleopolis," the first of whom was a "King Achthoes" (Waddell 1940, 60–61). Hence, it is possible that the missing name in Turin 4,18 was a King Khety, as the original Egyptian name read, who is numbered as the First here. The name Achthoes is sometimes rendered as Akhtoy in history books.

5. For the term *ẖt* meaning "the (divine) Corporation," referring to the Ennead, see *Wb* III, 357:18 and Hannig 2006b, 1972.

6. Turin 4,20. The name may be attested in the caption accompanying a fishing scene in the tomb of the nomarch Ankhtyfy at Mo'alla (see Vandier 1950, text 16:18, and pp. 36, 263; and Gomaà 1980, 32–33), although the identification of the name written there as Ka-nefer-Re with our King Neferkare is not beyond doubt (Franke 2001, 528).

7. Turin 4,21.

8. Turin 4,22.

9. Turin 4,23, although the actual entry in the Turin Canon is missing today; for the reconstruction, see von Beckerath 1966, 18–19.

10. Turin 4,24.

11. Turin 4,25.

9. Hu ////*[12]

Birth: *ḥ /// (h[u?]///)*,* The smiter (?) ///

Dynasties 9–10b (2160–2020 b.c.e.)[13]

The following kings, here labeled "Dynasties 9–10 b" are attested in contemporary records, although their specific order is difficult to establish.

1. Wahkare Khety (V)[14]

Throne: *w3ḥ k3 rˁ* (*wah ka ra*), The enduring one of the ka of Re
Birth: *ẖty* (*khety*), The one belonging to the divine corporation

2. Mery ///[15]

Birth: *mry ///* (*mery ///*), Beloved of [divine name]

3. Khety (VI)[16]

Throne and Birth: *s//// rˁ ẖty* (*se//// ra khety*), Who ////[17] Re, Khety

4. Nebkaure Khety (VII)[18]

Throne: *n-sw-bity nb k3w rˁ ˁnḫ ḏt* (*nesu bity neb kau ra ankh djet*), The Dual King "The possessor of the kas of Re," living forever
Birth; *ẖty* (*khety*), Khety[19]

---

12. Turin (4,26) gives only the first letter of the word; hence, my reconstruction of the name is purely conjectural. There are nine more entries in the Turin Canon (5,1 to 5,9), which belong to this period but the names are destroyed today.

13. For the six kings in this section, see von Beckerath 1999, 74–75.

14. Known from a coffin (Cairo CG 28088) usurped in the Twelfth Dynasty, for which see Allen 1976; Gauthier 1907, 205–6.

15. From a graffito in the travertine (Egyptian alabaster) quarries at the site of Hatnub, southeast of Tell el-Amarna (= Anthes 1928, pl. 7, no. IX).

16. The cartouche is found in the same quarry as the preceding entry (= Anthes 1928, pl. 6, no. X).

17. The word, a noun or a verb, is unreadable.

18. This king is known from two sources: a red jasper weight from the Wadi Tumilat (Petrie 1906, 32, pl. 33:4; Petrie 1917, 13, pl. X, no. 9.2), from which the divine element "Re" is missing in the name; and the famous story of the Eloquent Peasant (= texts B1 104 [= Pap. Berlin 3023] and R 17.1 [Pap. Berlin 10499], for which see Parkinson 1991, 19), where the divine name "Re" is written in the cartouche; Gauthier 1907, 206.

19. Note that both Throne and Birth names are written on the seal, with the element "The

5. Meryibre Khety (VIII)[20]

Horus: *mry ib t3wy* (*mery ib tawy*), Beloved of the mind of the Two Lands
Two Ladies: *mry ib t3wy* (*mery ib tawy*), Beloved of the mind of the Two Lands[21]
Golden Horus: *mry* (?) (*mery* ?), The beloved one
Throne: *mry ib rꜥ* (*mery ib ra*), The beloved one of the mind of Re
Birth: *ẖty* (*khety*), Khety

6. Merykare[22]

Throne: *mry k3 rꜥ* (*mery ka ra*), The beloved one of the ka of Re

Dynasty 11a (2134–2060 b.c.e.)

In the south of Egypt, the rulers of a family from Thebes challenged the supremacy of the Herakleopolitans by putting their own names in cartouches and adopting Horus names. Various local nomarchs declared their allegiance to one or the other faction and a civil war ensued.

The first four rulers of Dynasty 11[23] were contemporary with Dynasty 10, which is why I have split the dynasty in two, Dynasties 11a and 11b, and included the first group in the First Intermediate period. It has been suggested[24] that these early Eleventh Dynasty monarchs chose only Horus names in order to emulate the rulers of the Early Dynastic period, perhaps because they saw themselves as inaugurating a new phase of Egyptian history.

From this dynasty on, the royal names[25] are well attested in contemporary records, hence, in most cases, there will be no need to indicate the provenance of the name.

Dual King" immediately preceding the name Khety. Because of the frequency of the proper name "Khety" in this dynasty, I have opted to present the latter as a Birth name.

20. The titulary of this king is known in full from a broken ebony staff found in a tomb at Meir (Kamal 1910) and partially from a small copper vessel now in the Louvre (Maspero 1891, 429–31); on the latter piece, the Horus name is abbreviated to *mry ib* while the Golden Horus name is absent.

21. The Two Ladies names is known from the previously mentioned staff as well as a fragmentary inlaid ivory chest from Lisht, where the end of the cobra over the basket hieroglyphs are clear immediately before the *mry ib t3wy* elements (Hayes 1953, 143, fig. 86). Henceforth, the Two Ladies name becomes a regular part of the royal titulary; see von Beckerath 1999, 74 n. 6.

22. King Merykare is well known for the instructions written by his father on his behalf (Tobin 2003, 152–65, 570–72), as well as a number of other attestations, including later references to the funerary cult attached to his pyramid (von Beckerath 1980); Gauthier 1907, 209–10.

23. The dynasty has been thoroughly studied by Postel (2004).

24. Aufrère 1982, 46–47.

25. For the list, see von Beckerath 1999, 76–81.

1. Mentuhotep I[26]

Later Horus name: *tp ꜥ* (*tepy a*),* "The ancestor"[27]
Birth: *it-nṯrw mnṯw-ḥtp(.w) ꜥꜣ mry sṯt nbt ꜣbw* (*it netjeru mentu hotep aa, mery Satet nebet Abu*), The God's Father[28] Mentuhotep ("Montu is satisfied") the Great, beloved of Satet, mistress of Elephantine[29]

2. Intef I[30]

Horus: *shr tꜣwy* (*seher tawy*), Who has made the Two Lands content
Birth: *in it.f* (*in it.ef*), The one whom his father has brought forth[31]

3. Intef II[32]

Horus: *wꜣḥ-ꜥnḫ* (*wah ankh*), Enduring of life
Birth: *sꜣ rꜥ in it.f ꜥꜣ* (*sa ra in it.ef aa*), The son of Re, Intef ("The one whom his father has brought forth") the Great

4. Intef III[33]

Horus: *nḫt nb tp-nfr* (*nakht neb tep-nefer*), The possessor of a perfect beginning is victorious[34]
Birth: *sꜣ rꜥ in it.f* (*sa ra in it.ef*), The son of Re Intef

26. Ibid., 76–77.

27. Lit. "The one (who came) before." This Horus name is a New Kingdom fabrication, found in the Karnak List (*Urk.* IV, 608:14; and see Postel 2004, 46).

28. A priestly title, for which see Ward 1982, 69–70; Jones 2000, 1:345; and Postel 2004, 48–53.

29. The additional epithets are written within the cartouche; the statue comes from the sanctuary of Heqaib on the island of Elephantine, which explains the reference to the goddess Satet; see Postel 2004, 303.

30. Gauthier 1907, 204–5; von Beckerath 1999,76–77. The name "Intef" is sometimes rendered "Inyotef"; the latter name reflects the Coptic word for father, ⲉⲓⲱⲧ.

31. At Tod, in a chapel erected by Mentuhotep II, the epithet *sꜣ rꜥ* (*sa ra*), "The son of Re," is added within the cartouche; see Postel 2003, 409, fig, 3.

32. Gauthier 1907, 225–27; von Beckerath 1999, 76–77.

33. Gauthier 1907, 227; von Beckerath 1999, 76–77.

34. Or perhaps "The victorious one is the possessor of a perfect beginning." A stela in the Metropolitan Museum of Art (14.2.6), for which Clère and Vandier 1948, p. 18, §22, abbreviates the name to *nb tp-nfr*, "The possessor of a perfect beginning." For the rendering of *nḫt* as "victorious" in the context of a royal titulary, see Galán 1995, 42–44.

V

Middle Kingdom

Dynasty 11b (2060–1991 b.c.e.)

Around the middle of the twenty-first century b.c.e., King Mentuhotep II defeated the Herakleopolitans and ended the civil war. To indicate the various stages of his reign, he changed his titulary a number of times.[1] The three stages of this process are labeled (a), (b), and (c) in the list. The first set of names comes from early in his reign, when he called himself the Horus *sꜥnḫ ib tꜣwy*, "The one who has sustained the mind of the Two Lands." By his fourteenth regnal year, this was changed to the Horus and Two Ladies *nṯri ḥḏt*, "The one whose White Crown is divine." The third set of names came some time before Regnal Year 39, a date possibly corresponding to his victory over the Herakleopolitan forces, when he claimed to be the Horus and Two Ladies *smꜣ tꜣwy*, "The uniter of the Two Lands."[2] Mentuhotep II was certainly considered to be the inaugurator of a new era by the later New Kingdom Egyptians.[3]

The royal names from this period are mostly well attested in contemporary records.[4] There will, therefore, be no need to indicate the provenance of the name. If the first part of the dynasty harked back to the Early Dynastic period, the second group decidedly looked back to the halcyon days of the Old Kingdom by repeating and elaborating the concept chosen for the Horus name.[5] Thus, Mentuhotep III used the expression *sꜥnḫ tꜣwy.f(y)*, "The one who has sustained his Two Lands" in his Horus and Two Ladies names, while being the Dual King *sꜥnḫ kꜣ rꜥ*, "The one whom the ka of Re has sustained." Similarly, Mentuhotep IV was the Horus and Two Ladies *nb tꜣwy*, "The lord of the Two Lands," a phrase expanded in his Throne name of *nb tꜣwy rꜥ*, "The possessor of the Two Lands of Re." An additional elaboration was to take the word *nb*, "lord," of his first two names and transform it into the adjective *nbw*, "golden," for his Golden Horus

1. Mentuhotep II's titulary has been investigated by Gardiner (1956), Habachi (1963), Dieter Arnold (1969), and in Postel's thorough study (2004, 131–244).

2. It has also been suggested that his third set of names was composed for his jubilee festival around year 30; see Vandersleyen 1995, 20–22; and Postel 2004, 131.

3. See Leprohon 2010a, 9 n. 10, and the references there.

4. For the names, see von Beckerath 1999, 78–81.

5. Aufrère 1982, 51.

name, *nbw nṯrw*, "The golden one of the gods." Also noteworthy is how these last two kings repeatedly used the theme of "the Two Lands" in their titulary, as if to underscore the fact of a newly reunited country.

5A. Mentuhotep II (A)[6]

Horus: *sꜥnḫ ib tꜣwy* (*sankh ib tawy*), The one who has sustained[7] the mind of the Two Lands
Birth: *sꜣ rꜥ mnṯw ḥtp(.w)* (*sa ra mentu hetpu*), The son of Re,[8] Montu is satisfied

5B. Mentuhotep II (B)[9]

Horus: *nṯri-ḥḏt* (*netjeri hedjet*), The one whose White Crown is divine[10]
Two Ladies: *nṯri-ḥḏt* (*netjeri hedjet*), The one whose White Crown is divine
Throne: *nb ḥpt rꜥ* (*neb hepet ra*), The possessor of the steering oar of Re[11]
Birth: *sꜣ rꜥ mnṯw ḥtp(.w)* (*sa ra mentu hetpu*), The son of Re, Montu is satisfied

5C. Mentuhotep II (C)

Horus: *smꜣ tꜣwy* (*sema tawy*), The uniter of the Two Lands
Two Ladies: *smꜣ tꜣwy* (*sema tawy*), The uniter of the Two Lands
Golden Horus: *ḳꜣ-šwty* (*qa shuty*), High of plumes[12]
Throne: *nb ḥpt rꜥ* (*neb hepet ra*), The possessor of the steering oar of Re
Birth: *mnṯw ḥtp(w)* (*mentu hetep*), Montu is satisfied

6. Mentuhotep III[13]

Horus: *sꜥnḫ tꜣwy.f(y)* (*sankh tawy.f(y)*), The one who has sustained his Two Lands
Two Ladies: *sꜥnḫ tꜣwy.f(y)* (*sankh tawy.f(y)*), The one who has sustained his Two Lands
Golden Horus 1: *ḥtp(w)* (*hetep*), The one who is satisfied[14]

---

6. Gauthier 1907, 228; von Beckerath 1999, 78–79.
7. Lit. "caused to live."
8. The epithet is written within the cartouche.
9. Gauthier 1907, 228–37; von Beckerath 1999, 78–79.
10. Lit. "Divine of the White Crown"; one could also render "The divine one of the White Crown."
11. For a discussion of the solar connection in the name, see Postel 2003, 204–6; the Throne name can also be found in the Turin Canon, col. 5,16.
12. The name is noteworthy, given an epithet added to the Horus name in the so-called Chapel of the Princesses at Deir el-Bahari, *nṯr dm pt m šwty.f(y)*, "The divine one who pierces the sky with this two plumes," for which see Postel 2004, 138, 322, and the references there.
13. Gauthier 1907, 243–46; von Beckerath 1999, 80–81.
14. It is difficult to establish whether Mentuhotep III held the two different Golden Horus names concurrently or successively; for a discussion, see Postel 2004, 257–58.

Golden Horus 2: *sḫm* (*sekhem*), The one who is powerful[15]
Throne 1: *sꜥnḫ kꜣ rꜥ* (*sankh ka ra*), The one whom the ka of Re has sustained[16]
Throne 2: *snfr kꜣ rꜥ* (*senefer ka ra*),* The one whom the ka of Re has made perfect[17]
Birth: *mnṯw ḥtp*(*w*) (*mentu hetep*), Montu is satisfied

7. Mentuhotep IV[18]

Horus: *nb tꜣwy* (*neb tawy*), The lord of the Two Lands
Two Ladies: *nb tꜣwy* (*neb tawy*), The lord of the Two Lands
Golden Horus: *nbw nṯrw* (*nebu netjeru*), The golden one of the gods
Throne: *nb tꜣwy rꜥ* (*neb tawy ra*), The possessor (or "lord") of the Two Lands of Re
Birth: *mnṯw ḥtp*(*w*) (*mentu hetep*), Montu is satisfied

Dynasty 12 (1991–1782 b.c.e.)

It is difficult to establish the ease of the transition from the Eleventh to the Twelfth Dynasty. If Amenemhat I, who may have been the vizier under Mentuhotep IV, had to fight remaining pockets of resistance to maintain his throne,[19] the continuity of the high officials between the two dynasties would seem to negate the need for a complete purge on his part.[20] The move of the capital city from Thebes down to Itj-tawy—short for Amenemhat-Itj-tawy, "Amenemhat seizes the Two Lands"—near modern-day Lisht, may suggest a need for the new family to remove itself from the Theban establishment. Perhaps a relocation near the old Memphite capital would also rekindle memories of the glorious days prior to the civil war. The compiler of the Turin Canon was certainly aware of a new group of rulers at this point, as col. 5,19 reads "[Kings of the Resi]dence of Itj-tawy," followed by entries for the eight rulers of the Twelfth Dynasty, which is then summarized in col. 6,3, with the following: "*Total*:[21] Kings of the Residence [of Itj-tawy]: eight [kings], totaling (lit. "making") 213 years, 1 month, 17 days."[22]

---

15. The sign could also be read as *mnḫ*, "the potent one," as von Beckerath 1999, 80–81, has proposed.
16. This Throne name can also be found in Turin 5,17.
17. This is a later Throne name found in the Karnak List (Gauthier 1907, 247–48; *Urk*. IV, 609:15); the variation is simply due to an error on the part of the scribe who drew up the list.
18. Gauthier 1907, 222–25; von Beckerath 1999, 80–81.
19. See Leprohon 1996, 167 and n. 10, and the references there.
20. Postel 2004, 266–67.
21. The word is written in red ink to mark a transition in the text.
22. KRI II, 834:16.

The new king announced a new beginning with his titulary,[23] as he declared that he had "propitiated the mind of the Two Lands" (*sḥtp ỉb t3wy*) with his first Horus name, then inaugurated a renaissance of sorts with a second Horus name, "The one who has repeated births" (*wḥm mswt*). His son Senwosret I would reassure his subjects that his father's legacy would continue, as he proclaimed himself the Horus "who has lived the (re)birth" (*ʿnḫ mswt*). Their successors would continue to elaborate on their predecessors' titularies, as one king after another would create new names to fit his own position within the historical period.[24]

The external policy of the Twelfth Dynasty remained peaceful toward western Asia, as trade missions were exchanged between the two regions, and the turquoise mines of the Sinai were exploited to their fullest. The crown cast its eye toward the south, however, as a number of military campaigns were waged against Lower Nubia, with its abundant gold supplies. The result was the annexation of the region up to the Second Cataract by the end of the period, with huge fortresses built between Elephantine and Semna to help protect the king's commercial interests.

Internally, the palace could not ignore the independence of the local nomarchs of Middle and Upper Egypt—the sources are mostly silent on Lower Egypt—and the king had to tread carefully with his provincial rulers. By the end of the dynasty, Senwosret III had reorganized the administration of the country, dividing it into three subdivisions called *warets.* This greatly diminished the power of the nomarchs, but whether they were actually removed from office at the time is still under debate.

By the Middle Kingdom, the full canonical fivefold titulary had been established and, except for periods of royal decline, would be used henceforth. The reign of Senwosret II also ushered in a new development, as he chose a new phrase for each one of his names.[25]

1A. AMENEMHAT I (A)[26]

Horus: *sḥtp ỉb t3wy* (*sehetep ib tawy*), The one who has propitiated the mind of the Two Lands

Two Ladies: *sḥtp ỉb t3wy* (*sehetep ib tawy*), The one who has propitiated the mind of the Two Lands

Golden Horus: *sm3* (*sema*), The uniter[27]

Throne: *sḥtp ỉb rʿ* (*sehetep ib ra*), The one who has propitiated the mind of Re

Birth: *ỉmn m ḥ3t* (*imen em hat*), Amun is at the forefront

---

23. For Amenemhat I's titulary, see also Berman 1985, 3–10.

24. For a study of the Twelfth Dynasty titulary, see Leprohon 1996.

25. Aufrère 1982, 54–55.

26. Gauthier 1907, 253–65; von Beckerath 1999, 82–83. Amenemhat I's titulary has been discussed by Berman (1985, 3–10) and Postel (2004, 279–91).

27. Lit. "the one who has united."

1B. AMENEMHAT I (B)[28]

Horus: *wḥm mswt* (*wehem mesut*), The one who has repeated births[29]
Two Ladies: *wḥm mswt* (*wehem mesut*), The one who has repeated births
Golden Horus: *wḥm mswt* (*wehem mesut*), The one who has repeated births[30]
Throne: *sḥtp ib rʿ* (*sehetep ib ra*), The one who has propitiated the mind of Re
Birth: *imn m ḥ3t* (*imen em hat*), Amun is at the forefront

2. SENWOSRET I[31]

Horus: *ʿnḫ mswt* (*ankh mesut*), The one who has lived the (re)birth[32]
Two Ladies: *ʿnḫ mswt* (*ankh mesut*), The one who has lived the (re)birth
Golden Horus: *ʿnḫ mswt* (*ankh mesut*), The one who has lived the (re)birth
Throne: *ḫpr k3 rʿ* (*kheper ka ra*), The (very) manifestation of the ka of Re
Birth: *s n wsrt* (*s*[33] *en wosret*), The man belonging to (the goddess) Wosret

3. AMENEMHAT II[34]

Horus: *ḥkn m m3ʿt* (*heken em maat*), The one who has been acclaimed by[35] Maat
Two Ladies: *ḥkn m m3ʿt* (*heken em maat*), The one who has been acclaimed by Maat
Golden Horus 1: *m3ʿ-ḫrw* (*maa kheru*), Righteous of voice
Golden Horus 2: *m3ʿ-ḫrw m nb* [*t3wy?*] (*maa kheru em neb* [*tawy*]), Righteous of voice as the Lord of [the Two Lands?][36]

---

28. This new set of names taken by Amenemhat I may have coincided with his move from Thebes north to Itj-tawy, modern-day Lisht, near the ancient capital city of Memphis; on this move, see especially Do. Arnold 1991.

29. An expression often referred to as a "Renaissance." Note that I have retained the traditional translation of *mswt* as "births," *contra* Baines's suggested "manifestations" (1986).

30. From a contemporary graffito left in the quarries of the Wadi Hammamat (= Hammamat 199, Couyat and Montet 1913, 100–102). A later text in the tomb of Khnumhotep II at Beni Hasan, from the reign of Senwosret II (*Urk.* VII, 26:20), simply renders the Golden Horus name as *mswt*, which may be an abbreviated form of the fuller name.

31. Gauthier 1907, 265–84; von Beckerath 1999, 82–83. For a study of the reign of Senwosret I, see Obsomer 1995. The name Senwosret (Greek Sesostris) was rendered "Usertesen" in older publications.

32. The phrase refers to his father Amenemhat I's political renaissance.

33. Sometimes transliterated *zi;* the Egyptian word is only one letter, which can be rendered *s* or, in its earlier form, *z*.

34. Gauthier 1907, 284–94; von Beckerath 1999, 84–85.

35. Lit. "by means of."

36. This additional phrase, part of which is broken, is found at the top of the cornice of stela Leiden V 4, for which see Simpson 1974, pl. 30; for easily accessible translations of the stela, see Lichtheim 1988, 75–77; and Obsomer 1995, 535–39.

Throne: *nbw kȝw rꜥ* (*nebu kau ra*), The golden one of the kas[37] of Re
Birth: *ỉmn m ḥȝt* (*imen em hat*), Amun is at the forefront

4. Senwosret II[38]

Horus: *sšm tȝwy* (*seshem tawy*), The one who has guided[39] the Two Lands
Two Ladies: *sḫꜥ mȝꜥt* (*sekha maat*), The one who has caused Maat to appear[40]
Golden Horus: *ḥtp nṯrw* (*hetep netjeru*), (With whom) the gods are satisfied
Throne: *ḫꜥ ḫpr rꜥ* (*kha kheper ra*), The (very) appearance of the manifestation of Re
Birth: *s n wsrt* (*s en wosret*), The man belonging to (the goddess) Wosret

5. Senwosret III[41]

Horus: *nṯri-ḫprw* (*netjeri kheperu*), Divine of manifestations
Two Ladies: *nṯri-mswt* (*netjeri mesut*), Divine of births
Golden Horus: *ḫpr* (*kheper*), The one who has manifested (himself)
Throne: *ḫꜥ kȝw rꜥ* (*kha kau ra*), The (very) appearance of the kas of Re
Birth: *s n wsrt* (*s en wosret*), The man belonging to (the goddess) Wosret

6. Amenemhat III[42]

Horus: *ꜥȝ-bȝw* (*aa bau*), Great of might
Two Ladies: *ỉṯ ỉwꜥt tȝwy* (*itj iwat tawy*), The one who has seized the inheritance of the Two Lands
Golden Horus: *wȝḥ-ꜥnḫ* (*wah ankh*), Enduring of life
Throne: *n(y) mȝꜥt rꜥ* (*ni maat ra*),[43] The one who belongs to the Maat of Re
Birth: *ỉmn m ḥȝt* (*imen em hat*), Amun is at the forefront

7. Amenemhat IV[44]

Horus: *ḫpr ḫprw* (*kheper kheperu*), The (very) manifestation of manifestations

---

37. The scribe of the Saqqara List (entry no. 42) wrote the word "ka" in the singular (KRI III, 481:10).

38. Gauthier 1907, 295–301; von Beckerath 1999, 84–85.

39. Or "the planner of"; see Leprohon 2010b, 4.

40. Both von Beckerath (1999, 84–85) and Dessoudeix (2008, 152) give an abbreviated form of Amenemhat II's Horus name without the noun "maat," citing de Morgan 1894, 24, no. 165, but the *maat*-hieroglyph is clear in LD II, 123d.

41. Gauthier 1907, 302–16; von Beckerath 1999, 84–85. For a study of the reign of Senwosret III, see Delia 1980.

42. Gauthier 1907, 319–37; von Beckerath 1999, 86–87. For a study of the reign of Amenemhat III, see Leprohon 1980.

43. For this reading, which is widely accepted, see Edel 1972.

44. Gauthier 1907, 338–41; von Beckerath 1999, 86–87.

Two Ladies: *sḥb t3wy* (*seheb tawy*), The one who has made the Two Lands festive
Golden Horus: *sḫm nṯrw* (*sekhem netjeru*), The powerful one of the gods
Throne: *m3ʿ-ḫrw rʿ* (*maa kheru ra*), The righteous one[45] of Re
Birth: *imn m ḥ3t* (*imen em hat*), Amun is at the forefront

8. (Queen) Sobeknefru[46]

Horus: *mryt rʿ* (*meryt ra*), The one beloved[47] of Re
Two Ladies: *s3t sḫm nbt t3wy* (*sat sekhem nebet tawy*), The daughter of the powerful one[48] is (now) Mistress of the Two Lands
Golden Horus: *ḏdt-ḫʿw* (*djedet khau*), Stable (fem.) of appearances
Throne: *k3 sbk rʿ* (*ka sobek ra*), The (very) ka of (the god) Sobek-Re
Birth: *sbk nfrw* (*sobek nefru*), Sobek is perfect

Dynasty 13 (1782–1650 b.c.e.)

The long and prosperous reign of Amenemhat III was followed by the short reigns of the last two members of that illustrious family. What came next was a series of ephemeral kings still ruling from Itj-tawy at first, but whose relationships and order of succession are difficult to establish.[49] It seems clear that a number of the rulers were not of royal blood and did not all belong to the same family, although they are given the designation of Dynasty 13. The order of the names presented here largely follows the one found in Ryholt.[50] As before, the names not attested in contemporary records will be followed by an asterisk.

A number of the kings from this period patterned their names after more illustrious rulers.[51] At the beginning of the dynasty, a few monarchs are called Amenemhat or Ameny (an abbreviation of the former name) perhaps recalling the great Amenemhat III. Another source of names from farther back in time seems to have been the Eleventh Dynasty, as Amenemhat VI called himself the Horus *shr t3wy*, "The one who has pleased the Two Lands," following Intef I's own Horus name. Amenemhat VI also used the phrase *sʿnḫ ib rʿ*, "The one whom the mind of Re has sustained," for his Throne name, presumably patterning himself after Mentuhotep II's first Horus name of *sʿnḫ ib t3wy*, "The one who has

45. Lit. "true of voice."

46. Gauthier 1907, 341–43; von Beckerath 1999, 86–87. For a study of the reign, see Pignattari 2008. I have opted for reading the name as Sobeknefru, as opposed to Nefrusobek, because of its later Greek version, Scemiophris (Waddell 1940, 68–69).

47. The passive participle, here used as a noun, is in its feminine form.

48. Referring to her father Amenemhat III.

49. See, e.g., McCormack 2010.

50. Ryholt 1997a.

51. Dautzenberg 1997b, 43.

sustained the mind of the Two Lands."[52] Perhaps because the Thirteenth Dynasty kings were aware of their precarious position as monarchs, Amenemhat VI's Throne name underscores the close relationship between the king and the sun god, as a number of them used causative verbal forms to express the god's benefactions. Thus were kings "made to flourish" (*swꜣḏ*), "endowed" (*sḏfꜣ*), "made potent" (*smnḫ*), "sustained" (*sꜥnḫ*), or "made to rule" (*sḥḳꜣ*) by the ka of Re.[53]

1. Sobekhotep I[54]

Horus: *mnḫ- ///* (*menekh ///*), Potent of ///
Two Ladies: none attested
Golden Horus: *ꜥnḫ nṯrw* (*ankh netjeru*), The (very) life of the gods
Throne: *sḫm rꜥ ḫw tꜣwy* (*sekhem ra khu tawy*), The powerful one of Re is the protection of the Two Lands
Birth: *imn-m-ḥꜣt <sꜣ> sbk ḥtp(w)* (*imen em hat <sa> sobek hetep(u)*), Amenemhat's son, Sobekhotep ("Sobek is satisfied")

2. Senbef[55]

Horus: *mḥ ib tꜣwy* (*meh ib tawy*), The confidante (lit. "who fills the heart") of the Two Lands
Two Ladies: *iṯ sḫm.f* (*itj sekhem.ef*), The one who has seized his power
Golden Horus: none attested
Throne: *sḫm kꜣ rꜥ* (*sekhem ka ra*), The powerful one of the ka of Re
Birth: *imn-m-ḥꜣt <sꜣ> snb.f* (*imen em hat <sa> seneb.ef*), Amenemhat's son, Senbef

3. Nerkare[56]

Horus: none attested
Two Ladies: none attested
Golden Horus: none attested
Throne: *nr kꜣ rꜥ* (*ner ka ra*), The feared one is the (very) ka of Re
Birth: none attested

52. See the remarks by McCormack 2010, 376.
53. Kings Sewadjkare (13:11), Amenemhat VII (13:20), Imy-ra Mesha (13:23), Sewadjtu (13:35), and Sankhptah (13:55), respectively. See the remarks by Redford 1995, 158.
54. Gauthier 1912, 14–16; von Beckerath 1999, 92–93.
55. Gauthier 1912, 11; von Beckerath 1999, 88–89.
56. Gauthier 1912, 96; von Beckerath 1999, 106–7. For a rebuttal of L. Gabolde's suggestion (1990) that Nerkare did not exist, see Ryholt 1997a, 318, 337.

4. Amenemhat V[57]

Horus: none attested
Two Ladies: none attested
Golden Horus: none attested
Throne: *sḫm kꜣ rꜥ* (*sekhem ka ra*), The powerful one of the ka of Re
Birth: *ỉmn-m-ḥꜣt* (*imen em hat*), Amun is at the forefront

5. Qemau[58]

Horus: none attested
Two Ladies: none attested
Golden Horus: none attested
Throne: none attested
Birth: *ỉmny* (*sꜣ*) *ḳmꜣw* (*imeny (sa) qemau*), Ameny's[59] son, Qemau ("the begotten one")[60]

6. Sa-Hornedjheritef[61]

Horus: none attested
Two Ladies: none attested
Golden Horus: none attested
Throne: *<s>ḥtp ỉb rꜥ* (*<se>hetep ib ra*), The one who has propitiated the mind of Re
Birth: *ḳmꜣw sꜣ-ḥr-nḏ-ḥr-ỉt.f* (*qemau sa-hor-nedj-her-it.ef*), Qemau's son "Son-of-Horus is the protector of his father"[62]

7. Iufni*[63]

Horus: none attested
Two Ladies: none attested
Golden Horus: none attested
Throne: none attested
Birth: *ỉw.f n.ỉ* (*iu.ef en.i*), He belongs to me

---

57. Von Beckerath 1999, 88–89.
58. Von Beckerath 1999, 102–3.
59. The previous king, Amenemhat V.
60. Lit. "the created one." For the reading Qemau instead of Aamu, "the Asiatic," see von Beckerath 1999, 102 n. 3.
61. Gauthier 1912, 92; von Beckerath 1999, 90–91.
62. For further comments on the inclusion of the *sꜣ*-prefix in the king's name, see Dodson 2000, col. 50, n. 1.
63. Gauthier 1912, 7; von Beckerath 1999, 90–91.

8. Amenemhat VI[64]

Horus: *shr tꜣwy* (*seher tawy*), The one who has pleased the Two Lands
Two Ladies: *sḫm-ḫꜥw* (*sekhem khau*), Powerful of appearances
Golden Horus: *ḥkꜣ mꜣꜥt* (*heqa maat*), The ruler of Maat[65]
Throne: *sꜥnḫ ib rꜥ* (*sankh ib ra*), The one whom the mind of Re has sustained
Birth: *imny* (*sꜣ*) *in-it.f* (*sꜣ*) *imn-m-ḥꜣt* (*imeny (sa) in-it.ef (sa) imen-em-hat*), Amenemhat, (son of) Intef, (son of) Ameny[66]

9. Nebnun[67]

Horus: none attested
Two Ladies: none attested
Golden Horus: none attested
Throne: *smn kꜣ rꜥ* (*semen ka ra*), The one whom the ka of Re has established
Birth: *nb nnw* (*neb nenu*), (My) lord is Nun[68]

10. Sehetepibre[69]

Horus: *swsḫ tꜣwy* (*sewesekh tawy*), The one who has widened the Two Lands
Two Ladies: none attested
Golden Horus: none attested
Throne: *sḥtp ib rꜥ* (*sehetep ib ra*), The one who has propitiated the mind of Re
Birth: none attested

11. Sewadjkare (I)*[70]

Horus name: none attested
Two Ladies: none attested
Golden Horus: none attested
Throne: *swꜣḏ kꜣ rꜥ* (*sewadj ka ra*), The one whom the ka of Re has made flourish
Birth: none attested

12. Nedjemibre*[71]

Horus name: none attested

---

64. Gauthier 1912, 8–10; von Beckerath 1999, 90–91.
65. Or perhaps "The one who rules (through) Maat."
66. For a recently published block of Amenemhat VI, see Schmitt 2004.
67. Gauthier 1912, 10; von Beckerath 1999, 90–91.
68. The primordial god who symbolized the primeval water of the beginning of time.
69. Von Beckerath 1999, 88–89.
70. Ibid., 90–91.
71. Gauthier 1912, 11–12; von Beckerath 1999, 90–91.

Two Ladies: none attested
Golden Horus: none attested
Throne: *nḏm ỉb rʿ* (*nedjem ib ra*), The pleasant one of the mind of Re
Birth: none attested

13. Sobekhotep II[72]

Horus name: *smꜣ tꜣwy* (*sema tawy*), The one who has united the Two Lands
Two Ladies: *ḏd-ḫʿw* (*djed khau*), Stable of appearances
Golden Horus: *kꜣw nṯrw* (*kau netjeru*), (Possessor of?) The kas of the gods[73]
Throne: *ḫʿ ʿnḫ rʿ* (*kha ankh ra*), The living appearance of Re
Birth: *sbk ḥtp*(*w*) (*sobek hetep(u)*), Sobek is satisfied

14. Reniseneb[74]

Horus name: none attested
Two Ladies: none attested
Golden Horus: none attested
Throne: none attested
Birth: *rn.ỉ snb*(*w*) (*ren.i seneb(u)*), My name is healthy[75]

15. Hor (I)[76]

Horus: *ḥtp ỉb tꜣwy* (*hetep ib tawy*), The mind of the Two Lands is satisfied[77]
Two Ladies: *nfr-ḫʿw* (*nefer khau*), Perfect of appearances
Golden Horus: *nfr nṯrw* (*nefer netjeru*), The perfect one of the gods
Throne: *ꜣw-ỉb rʿ* (*au ib ra*), The (very) joy (lit. "expanded of heart") of Re
Birth: *ḥr* (*hor*), Horus[78]

16. Sekhemre Khutawy[79]

Horus: *ḫʿ-bꜣw* (*kha bau*), The glorious appearance of might
Two Ladies: *wḥm ḏd* (*wehem djed*), The one who has repeated stability
Golden Horus: *ʿnḫ-rnpwt* (*ankh renput*), (Fully) Alive of years

---

72. Gauthier 1912, 40–41; von Beckerath 1999, 90–91.
73. Unless the word *kꜣw* stands for "sustenance" here.
74. Gauthier 1912, 13; von Beckerath 1999, 92–93.
75. On King Reniseneb, see also Ryholt 1997b.
76. Gauthier 1907, 317–19; von Beckerath 1999, 92–93.
77. Perhaps for <*s*>*ḥtp ỉb tꜣwy*, "Who has propitiated the mind of the Two Lands."
78. The name can also be written with its accompanying title in the cartouche: *sꜣ rʿ ḥr*, "The son of Re, Horus"; see von Beckerath 1999, 93 (E3). For a more recent discussion of the position of this king within the late Middle Kingdom, see Aufrère 2001.
79. Von Beckerath 1999, 88–89

Throne: *sḫm rꜥ ḫw tꜣwy* (*sekhem ra khu tawy*), The powerful one of Re is the protection of the Two Lands
Birth: none attested

17. [User]kare (II)[80]

Horus: *ḏd-ḫprw* (*djed kheperu*), Stable of manifestations
Two Ladies: *ḏd-msw*(*t*) (*djed mesu(t)*), Stable of births
Golden Horus: *bik ꜥꜣ* /// (*bik aa* ///), Great falcon ///
Throne: [*wsr*] *kꜣ rꜥ* (*[weser] ka ra*), [The strong one of] the ka of Re
Birth: [///]*i* <*sꜣ*> *ḥr* (*[///]-i* <*sa*> *hor*), ////-i (son of) Hor

18. Seb/Sab (?)

Horus: none attested
Two Ladies: none attested
Golden Horus: none attested
Throne: none attested
Birth: *s*<*ꜣ?*>*b* (*s*<*a*>*b*), The jackal (?)[81]

19. Kay[82]

Horus: none attested
Two Ladies: none attested
Golden Horus: none attested
Throne: none attested
Birth: *kꜣy* (*kay*), The one who belongs to the ka

20. Amenemhat VII[83]

Horus: *ḥry-tp tꜣwy* (*hery tep tawy*), The chieftain of the Two Lands
Two Ladies: *nṯri-bꜣw* (*netjeri bau*), Divine of might
Golden Horus: *ꜥꜣ-pḥty* (*aa pehty*), Great of strength
Throne: *sḏfꜣ kꜣ rꜥ* (*sedjefa ka ra*), The one whom the ka of Re has endowed
Birth: *kꜣy* <*sꜣ*> *imn-m-ḥꜣt* (*kay* <*sa*> *imen em hat*), Kay's <son>, Amenemhat ("Amun is in front")

80. See Ryholt 1997a, 217.
81. This king is only attested as filiation in the name of the next king, his son Kay; see Ryholt 1997a, 219.
82. Ibid., 218–19.
83. Gauthier 1912, 93; von Beckerath 1999, 92–93.

21. Wegaf[84]

Horus: *sḫm nṯrw* (*sekhem netjeru*), The might of the gods
Two Ladies: *ḫʿ b3w* (*kha bau*), The glorious appearance of might
Golden Horus: *mry* [*t3wy*] (*mery [tawy]*), Beloved of [the Two Lands]
Throne: *ḫw t3wy rʿ* (*khu tawy ra*), The protector of the Two Lands of (?) Re
Birth: *wg3.f* (*wega.ef*), May he chew (?)[85]

22. Khendjer[86]

Horus: [///] *ʿnḫ*, ([///] *ankh*), /// alive ///
Two Ladies: *w3ḥ-mswt* (*wah mesut*), Enduring of birth
Golden Horus: none attested
Throne: *wsr k3 rʿ* (*weser ka ra*), The strong one of the ka of Re
Birth: *ḫnḏr* (*khendjer*), The wild boar[87]

23. Imy-ra Mesha[88]

Horus: none attested
Two Ladies: none attested
Golden Horus: none attested
Throne: *smnḫ k3 rʿ* (*semenekh ka ra*), The one whom the ka of Re has made potent
Birth: *ỉmy-r mšʿ* (*imy-er mesha*), The General (lit. "Overseer of the army")

24. Intef IV[89]

Horus: none attested
Two Ladies: none attested
Golden Horus: none attested
Throne: *sḥtp k3 rʿ* (*sehetep ka ra*), The one who has propitiated the ka of Re
Birth: *ỉn ỉt.f* (*in it.ef*), Intef ("The one whose father has brought forth")

25. Seth[90]

Horus: none attested

---

84. Gauthier 1912, 2–3; von Beckerath 1999, 88–89.
85. For the name, see Ryholt 1997a, 219.
86. Gauthier 1912, 138–39; von Beckerath 1999, 94–95.
87. A Semitic name, for which see Ryholt 1997a, 220–21.
88. Gauthier 1912, 17–18; von Beckerath 1999, 94–95.
89. Von Beckerath 1999, 94–95. Note that here, *contra* Ryholt 1997a, 73 and 342, I number this king as the fourth Intef, following the three kings named Intef of the Eleventh Dynasty; see also Dessoudeix 2008, 169; and Allen 2010, 7.
90. Von Beckerath 1999, 94–95.

Two Ladies: none attested
Golden Horus: none attested
Throne: [*mr?*] *ib rʿ* (*[mer?] ib ra*), The one whom the mind of Re has loved
Birth: *stẖ* (*seth*), Seth

26. Sobekhotep III[91]

Horus: *ẖw tȝwy* (*khu tawy*), The protector of the Two Lands
Two Ladies: *ḫʿ m sḫm.f* (*kha em sekhem.ef*), The one who has appeared through his power
Golden Horus: *ḥtp ḥr mȝʿt* (*hetep her maat*), Contented with Maat
Throne: *sḫm rʿ swȝḏ tȝwy* (*sekhem ra, sewadj tawy*), The (very) power of Re, who has made the Two Lands flourish
Birth: *sbk ḥtp*(*w*) (*sobek hetep(u)*), Sobek is satisfied

27. Neferhotep I[92]

Horus: *grg tȝwy* (*gereg tawy*), The founder of the Two Lands
Two Ladies: *wp mȝʿt* (*wep maat*), The one who has inaugurated[93] Maat
Golden Horus: *mn-mrwt* (*men merut*), Enduring of love
Throne: *ḫʿ sḫm rʿ* (*kha sekhem ra*), The (very) appearance of the power of Re
Birth: *nfr ḥtp* (*nefer hetep*), The beautiful/perfect one is satisfied

28. Sahathor[94]

Horus: none attested
Two Ladies: none attested
Golden Horus: none attested
Throne: *mn wȝḏ rʿ* (*men wadj ra*), The established and flourishing one of Re
Birth: *sȝ ḥt-ḥr* (*sa hut-hor*), Son of Hathor[95]

29. Sobekhotep IV[96]

Horus: *ʿnḫ ib tȝwy* (*ankh ib tawy*), The (very) life of the heart of the Two Lands
Two Ladies: *wȝḏ-ḫʿw* (*wadj khau*), Flourishing of appearances
Golden Horus: *wsr-bȝw* (*weser bau*), Rich in might
Throne: *ḫʿ nfr rʿ* (*kha nefer ra*), The (very) appearance of the perfection of Re

91. Gauthier 1912, 19–22; von Beckerath 1999, 94–95.
92. Gauthier 1912, 22–30; von Beckerath 1999, 96–97.
93. Or perhaps "discerned."
94. Gauthier 1912, 31; von Beckerath 1999, 96–97.
95. It has also been suggested that this "King's Son" never actually reigned as king; see Davies 1998.
96. Gauthier 1912, 31–38; von Beckerath 1999, 96–97.

Birth: *sbk ḥtp*(*w*) (*sobek hetep(u)*), Sobek is satisfied

30. Sobekhotep V[97]

Horus: none attested
Two Ladies: none attested
Golden Horus: none attested
Throne: *mr ḥtp rꜥ* (*mer hetep ra*), The one whom the peace of Re has appreciated (lit. "loved")
Birth: *sbk ḥtp*(*w*) (*sobek hetep(u)*), Sobek is satisfied

31. Sobekhotep VI[98]

Horus: none attested
Two Ladies: none attested
Golden Horus: none attested
Throne: *ḫꜥ ḥtp rꜥ* (*kha hetep ra*), The (very) appearance of the peace of Re
Birth: *sbk ḥtp*(*w*) (*sobek hetep(u)*), Sobek is satisfied

32. Ib-iau[99]

Horus: none attested
Two Ladies: none attested
Golden Horus: none attested
Throne: *wꜣḥ ib rꜥ* (*wah ib ra*), The enduring one is the (very) mind of Re
Birth: *ib iꜥ*(*w*) (*ib iau*), The quiet one (lit. "whose heart/mind is washed")

33. Iy[100]

Horus: none attested
Two Ladies: none attested
Golden Horus: none attested

97. Gauthier 1912, 90–91; von Beckerath 1999, 98–99.
98. Gauthier 1912, 42; von Beckerath 1999, 96–97.
99. Gauthier 1912, 43–44; von Beckerath 1999, 96–97.
100. Gauthier 1912, 44–45; von Beckerath 1999, 98–99.

Throne: *mr nfr rꜥ* (*mer nefer ra*), The one whom the perfection of Re has loved
Birth: *ỉy* (*iy*), "Hey!"[101]

34. Ini (I)[102]

Horus: none attested
Two Ladies: none attested
Golden Horus: none attested
Throne: *mr ḥtp rꜥ* (*mer hetep ra*), The one whom the peace of Re has appreciated (lit. "loved")
Birth: *ỉn.ỉ* (*in.i*), The one whom I[103] have brought forth

35. Sewadjtu[104]

Horus: none attested
Two Ladies: none attested
Golden Horus: none attested
Throne and Birth names: *sꜥnḫ.n rꜥ swꜣḏ.tw* (*sankh.en ra, sewadj.tu*), The one whom Re has sustained (when?) <He> was made to flourish

36. Ined*[105]

Horus: none attested
Two Ladies: none attested
Golden Horus: none attested
Throne: *mry sḫm rꜥ* (*mery sekhem ra*), The beloved one of the power of Re
Birth: *ỉnd* (*ined*), The sad one

37. Hori*[106]

Horus: none attested
Two Ladies: none attested
Golden Horus: none attested
Throne: *swꜣḏ kꜣ rꜥ* (*sewadj ka ra*), The one whom the ka of Re has made flourish
Birth: *ḥrỉ* (*hori*), Hori ("Who belongs to Horus")

101. An interjection (*Wb* I, 36).
102. Gauthier 1912, 45–46; von Beckerath 1999, 98–99.
103. Perhaps these words were said by the father at the birth. Compare the name Intef, "The one whom his father has brought forth."
104. Gauthier 1912, 46; von Beckerath 1999, 98–99.
105. Gauthier 1912, 47; von Beckerath 1999, 98–99.
106. Gauthier 1912, 47; von Beckerath 1999, 98–99.

38. Sobekhotep VII[107]

Horus: none attested
Two Ladies: none attested
Golden Horus: none attested
Throne: *mry k3w rʿ* (*mery kau ra*), Beloved of the kas of Re
Birth: *sbk ḥtp*(*w*) (*sobek hetep(u)*), Sobek is satisfied

39–45. Seven names lost[108]

46. Mer[///]re*

Throne: *mr /// rʿ* (*mer /// ra*), The beloved one of /// of Re[109]

47. Merkheperre[110]

Horus: none attested
Two Ladies: none attested
Golden Horus: none attested
Throne: *mr*(*y*) *ḫpr rʿ* (*mer(y) kheper ra*), The beloved one of the manifestation of Re[111]
Birth: none attested

48. Merka[re]*[112]

Horus: none attested
Two Ladies: none attested
Golden Horus: none attested
Throne: *mr*(*y*) *k3* [*rʿ*] (*mer(y) ka [ra]*), The beloved one of the ka of Re[113]
Birth: none attested

49. One name lost[114]

50. Mentuhotep V[115]

Horus: none attested

107. Gauthier 1912, 49; von Beckerath 1999, 98–99.
108. Turin 8,9–15.
109. Turin 8,16.
110. Gauthier 1912, 48; von Beckerath 1999, 100–101.
111. Turin 8,17.
112. Gauthier 1912, 48; von Beckerath 1999, 100–101.
113. Turin 8,18.
114. Turin 8,19.
115. Von Beckerath 1999, 104–5.

Two Ladies: none attested
Golden Horus: none attested
Throne: *swḏꜥ rꜥ* (*sewedja ra*), The one whom Re has made a judge[116]
Birth: *mnṯw ḥtp* (*mentju hetep*), Montu is satisfied

51. [///]-Mesra*

Throne: [///] *ms rꜥ* (*/// mes ra*), The one whom Re bore (?)[117]

52. Ibi II*[118]

Horus: none attested
Two Ladies: none attested
Golden Horus: none attested
Throne: [///] *mꜣꜥt rꜥ* (*/// maat ra*), The truth of Re is ///
Birth: *ỉbỉ* (*ibi*), The kid (lit. "young goat")[119]

53. Hor II*[120]

Horus: none attested
Two Ladies: none attested
Golden Horus: none attested
Throne: /// *wbn rꜥ* (*/// weben ra*), Re's shining is ///
Birth: *ḥr* (*hor*), Horus

54. Se /// kare*[121]

Horus: none attested
Two Ladies: none attested
Golden Horus: none attested
Throne: *s/// kꜣ rꜥ* (*se/// ka ra*), The one who makes the ka of Re ////
Birth: none attested

55. Sankhptah[122]

Horus: none attested
Two Ladies: none attested

116. The reading of the name is uncertain.
117. Turin 8,21.
118. Von Beckerath 1999, 100–101.
119. Turin 8,22.
120. Von Beckerath 1999, 100–101.
121. Ibid.
122. Ibid., 106–7.

Golden Horus: none attested
Throne: *sḥḳꜣ.n rꜥ* (*seheqa.en ra*), The one whom Re has made a ruler
Birth: *sꜥnḫ ptḥ* (*sankh ptah*), The one whom Ptah sustains

56. [///] Re*[123]

Horus: none attested
Two Ladies: none attested
Golden Horus: none attested
Throne: [///] *rꜥ* (*///] ra*), /// Re ////
Birth: none attested

57. Se [///] Re*[124]

Horus: none attested
Two Ladies: none attested
Golden Horus: none attested
Throne: *s*[///] *rꜥ* (*se[///].en ra*), The one whom Re has ////
Birth: none attested

Dynasty 13a

Additional names of Thirteenth Dynasty kings who cannot be placed with any certainty

1. Ini II[125]

Horus: none attested
Two Ladies: none attested
Golden Horus: none attested
Throne: *mry šps rꜥ* (*mery shepes ra*), Beloved of the grandeur of Re
Birth: *ini* (*ini*), The delayed one

2. Neferhotep II[126]

Horus: none attested
Two Ladies: none attested
Golden Horus: none attested
Throne: *mry sḫm rꜥ* (*mery sekhem ra*), The beloved one of the power of Re
Birth: *nfr ḥtp* (*nefer hetep*), The beautiful/perfect one is satisfied

---

123. Turin 8,26.
124. Turin 8,27.
125. Von Beckerath 1999, 104–5.
126. Gauthier 1912, 65; von Beckerath 1999, 98–99.

3. Senebmiu[127]

Horus: none attested
Two Ladies: none attested
Golden Horus: none attested
Throne: *sw3ḥ.n rʿ* (*sewah.en ra*), The one whom Re has made enduring
Birth: *snb mi iw* (*seneb mi iu*), Healthy like one who has arrived

4. Sekhaenre[128]

Horus: none attested
Two Ladies: none attested
Golden Horus: none attested
Throne: *sẖʿ.n rʿ* (*sekha.en ra*), The one whom Re has caused to appear[129]
Birth: none attested

Three additional kings who most probably belong to the Thirteenth Dynasty[130]

5. Horus Merytawy

Horus: *mry t3wy* (*mery tawy*), Beloved of the Two Lands
Two Ladies: none attested
Golden Horus: none attested
Throne: none attested
Birth: none attested

6. Two Ladies Userkhau

Horus: none attested
Two Ladies: *wsr-ẖʿw* (*weser khau*), Strong of appearances
Golden Horus: none attested
Throne: none attested
Birth: none attested

7. Sekhaenptah

Horus: none attested
Two Ladies: none attested
Golden Horus: *sẖʿ.n ptḥ* (*sekha.en ptah*), The one whom Ptah has caused to appear/be crowned
Throne: none attested
Birth: none attested

127. Gauthier 1912, 53–54; von Beckerath 1999, 100–101.
128. Gauthier 1912, 210; von Beckerath 1999, 100–101.
129. Perhaps meaning "crowned."
130. See Ryholt 1997a, 404–5.

Dynasty 14 (?–1650 B.C.E.)

The following are minor rulers from the northeastern part of the Delta who were probably contemporary with Dynasty 13—hence their inclusion in the Middle Kingdom section of the book. The order of the names again largely follows Ryholt's numbering, including his new placement of some of the fragments from the Turin Canon.[131] Most of the names numbered 7 to 51 below are attested only in the Turin Canon; these will again be followed by asterisks. They are found in the Turin Canon's col. 9,2 to 9,28 (with the entries in 9,14–15 now lost) and col. 10,7 to 10,15 (with the entries in 10,10–12 lost today). The last five entries, col. 10,16 to 10,20, also are lost. Ryholt's renumbering of the Turin Canon's col. 9,2 to 9,28 corresponds to Gardiner's old col. 8,2 to 8,27 and col. 9, frag. 123;[132] and Ryholt's col. 10,7 to 10,15 corresponds to Gardiner's col. 9,7 to 9,16.[133]

Since most of these rulers are known only from their Throne or Birth names, this section will dispense with the entire list of royal names and will give only the known occurrences of the names. For the rendering of the Semitic names, I have relied on T. Schneider's study of the period (1998).

1. Yakob-mu[134]

Throne: *sḫꜥ.n rꜥ* (*sekha.en ra*), The one whom Re caused to appear[135]
Birth: *yꜣ-k-b-mw* (*yakeb mu*), "(the goddess) Aya is a rock"[136]

2. Iamu[137]

Throne: *nbw wsr rꜥ* (*nebu weser ra*), The golden one is the strength of Re
Birth: *yꜥ-mw* (*ya-mu*), "Where is the uncle?"[138]

3. Qareh[139]

Throne: *ḫꜥ wsr rꜥ* (*kha weser ra*), The (very) appearance of the strength of Re
Birth: *ḳꜣ-r-ḥ* (*qareh*), The bald one[140]

131. Ryholt 1997a, 94–99.
132. Gardiner 1957b, pl. 3; KRI II, 838:6–839:15 and 841:2–3.
133. Gardiner 1957b, pl. 3; KRI II, 840:3–5 and 840:13–15.
134. Von Beckerath 1999, 118–19.
135. Or perhaps simply "crowned."
136. T. Schneider 1998, 130–31.
137. Von Beckerath 1999, 118–19.
138. T. Schneider 1998, 126–27.
139. Von Beckerath 1999, 120–21.
140. For this king, whose name was previously read as Qar, see Ryholt 1997a, 101.

4. Aamu[141]

Throne: *ꜥꜣ ḥtp rꜥ* (*aa hetep ra*), The great one is the (very) peace of Re
Birth: *ꜥꜣ-mw* (*aa mu*), "The Asiatic" (?)

5. Sheshi[142]

Throne: *mꜣꜥ ib rꜥ* (*maa ib ra*), The righteous one is the heart of Re
Birth: *š-š-i* (*sheshi*), Sheshi[143]

6. Nehsy[144]

Throne: *ꜥꜣ sḥ rꜥ* (*aa seh ra*), The great one of the shrine of Re
Birth: *nḥsy* (*nehsy*), The Nubian

7. Khakherure*[145]

Throne: *ḫꜥ ḫrw rꜥ* (*kha kheru ra*), The (very) appearance of the voice of Re[146]

8. Nebfaure*[147]

Throne: *nb fꜣw rꜥ* (*neb fau ra*), The possessor of the splendor of Re

9. Sehebre*[148]

Throne: *sḥb rꜥ* (*seheb ra*), The one who has made Re festive[149]

10. Merdjefare*[150]

Throne: *mr ḏfꜣ rꜥ* (*mer djefa ra*), The one whom Re's bounty has loved

---

141. Gauthier 1907, 211.
142. Gauthier 1907, 206–7; von Beckerath 1999, 116–17.
143. T. Schneider (1998, 141) suggests that this is a nickname.
144. Gauthier 1912, 54–55; von Beckerath 1999, 108–9.
145. Gauthier 1912, 56; von Beckerath 1999, 108–9.
146. King Khakherure's name was entered as *ḫꜥ tit rꜥ* (*kha tit ra*), "The (very) appearance of the image of Re," in Turin 9,2, with the copyist reading the *ḫrw*-oar sign as a *ti*-pestle sign; see KRI II, 838:6.
147. Gauthier 1912, 56; von Beckerath 1999, 108–09.
148. Gauthier 1912, 57; von Beckerath 1999, 108–9.
149. Or perhaps "The one whom Re has made festive."
150. Gauthier 1912, 58; von Beckerath 1999, 108–9.

11. SEWADJKARE (II)*[151]

Throne: *sw3ḏ k3 rʿ* (*sewadj ka ra*), The one whom the ka of Re has made thrive

12. NEBDJEFARE*[152]

Throne: *nb ḏf3 rʿ* (*neb djefa ra*), The possessor of Re's bounty

13. WEBENRE I*[153]

Throne: *wbn rʿ* (*weben ra*), The (very) rising of Re

14. NAME LOST[154]

15. /// DJEFARE*[155]

Throne: */// ḏf3 rʿ* (*/// djefa ra*), The one whom Re's bounty ///

16. /// WEBENRE II*[156]

Throne: */// wbn rʿ* (*/// weben ra*), //// the rising of Re

17. AWIBRE*[157]

Throne: *3w-ib rʿ* (*au ib ra*), The (very) joy of Re

18. HERIBRE*[158]

Throne: *ḥr ib rʿ* (*her ib ra*), Who has pleased Re's mind

19. NEBSENRE[159]

Birth: *nb.sn rʿ* (*neb.sen ra*), Their lord is Re

20–21. TWO NAMES LOST[160]

151. Gauthier 1912, 58; von Beckerath 1999, 108–9.
152. Gauthier 1912, 58; von Beckerath 1999, 108–9.
153. Gauthier 1912, 59; von Beckerath 1999, 108–9.
154. Turin 9,9.
155. Gauthier 1912, 59; von Beckerath 1999, 108–9.
156. Gauthier 1912, 60; von Beckerath 1999, 108–9.
157. Gauthier 1912, 60; von Beckerath 1999, 108–9.
158. Gauthier 1912, 60; von Beckerath 1999, 108–9.
159. Gauthier 1912, 61; von Beckerath 1999, 108–9.
160. The entry in Turin 9,14 reads "lacuna," while 9,15 is lost.

22. SEKHEPERENRE[161]

Throne: *sḫpr.n rꜥ (sekheper.en ra)*, The one whom Re has brought into being

23. DJEDKHERURE*[162]

Throne: *ḏd ḫrw rꜥ (djed kheru ra)*, The enduring one of the voice of Re

24. SANKHIBRE*[163]

Throne: *sꜥnḫ ib rꜥ (sankh ib ra)*, The one whom the mind of Re has sustained

25. NEFERTUM /// RE*[164]

Throne: *nfrtm /// rꜥ (nefertum /// ra)*, Re is the /// of Nefertum (?)[165]

26. SEKHEM /// RE*[166]

Throne: *sḫm /// rꜥ (sekhem /// ra)*, The powerful one of the //// of Re

27. KAKEMRE*[167]

Throne: *kꜣ km{t} rꜥ (ka kem{et} ra)*, The black[168] bull of Re

28. NEFERIBRE*[169]

Throne: *nfr ib rꜥ (nefer ib ra)*, The perfect one is the (very) mind of Re

29. I /// RE*[170]

Birth: *i /// rꜥ (i /// ra)*, I /// Re

161. Gauthier 1912, 61; von Beckerath 1999, 110–11.
162. Gauthier 1912, 62; von Beckerath 1999, 110–11.
163. Gauthier 1912, 62; von Beckerath 1999, 110–11.
164. Gauthier 1912, 62; von Beckerath 1999, 110–11.
165. The divine representation of the primeval lotus blossom, from which the sun god emerged. Von Beckerath (1999, 110–11), suggests adding the word *kꜣ* after the divine name Nefertum (followed by Dessoudeix 2008, 217), which could mean "Nefertum is the ka of Re," but such a name would hardly seem to refer to the current king.
166. Gauthier 1912, 62; von Beckerath 1999, 110–11.
167. Gauthier 1912, 63; von Beckerath 1999, 110–11.
168. The feminine ending on the adjective is simply a Late Egyptian writing of the word and can be discounted.
169. Gauthier 1912, 63; von Beckerath 1999, 110–11.
170. Gauthier 1912, 63; von Beckerath 1999, 110–11.

30. Khakare*[171]

Throne: *ḫꜥ kꜣ rꜥ* (*kha ka ra*), The (very) appearance of the ka of Re

31. Aakare*[172]

Throne: *ꜥꜣ kꜣ rꜥ* (*aa ka ra*), The great one of the ka of Re

32. Hepu*[173]

Throne: *smn.n rꜥ* (*semen.en ra*), The one whom Re has established
Birth: *ḥpw* (*hepu*), The runner[174]

33. Anati*[175]

Throne: *ḏd kꜣ rꜥ* (*djed ka ra*), The enduring one of the ka of Re
Birth: *ꜥꜣ-nꜣ-ti* (*aa-na-ti*), Anati[176]

34. Bebnem*[177]

Throne: /// *kꜣ rꜥ* (/// *ka ra*), The /// of the ka of Re
Birth: *b-b-n-m* (*bebnem*), Bebnem[178]

35–42. Eight names lost[179]

43. Senefer /// re*[180]

Throne: *snfr* /// *rꜥ* (*senefer* /// *ra*), Whom the /// of Re has made perfect

44. Men /// re*[181]

Throne: *mn* /// *rꜥ* (*men* /// *ra*), The established one of /// of Re

---

171. Gauthier 1912, 64; von Beckerath 1999, 110–11.

172. Gauthier 1912, 64, where the name is read *nḏ(?)-kꜣ-rꜥ;* von Beckerath 1999, 110–11, who reads the name *ꜥnḫ-kꜣ-rꜥ*.

173. Gauthier 1912, 64; von Beckerath 1999, 110–11.

174. Or, less likely, "the oar."

175. Von Beckerath 1999, 110–11.

176. For the name, see Ryholt 1997a,100.

177. Von Beckerath 1999, 110–11.

178. For the name, see Ryholt 1997a,100.

179. Turin 9,29–10,6.

180. Turin 10,7; von Beckerath 1999, 112–13.

181. Turin 10,8; von Beckerath (1999, 112–13 [14d]) suggests the name *mn* -[*ib*]-*rꜥ* (*men [ib] ra*), "The established one belonging to the mind of Re."

45. Djed /// Re*[182]

Throne: *ḏd /// rꜥ* (*djed /// ra*), The enduring one of the //// of Re

46–48. Three names lost[183]

49. Inek*[184]

Birth: *ỉn-k* (*in-ek*), Inek

50. I-neb ///[185]

Birth: *ỉ nb ///* (*i neb ///*), O the lord /// (?)

51. Ip-///*[186]

Birth: *ỉp ///* (*ip ///*), Ip ///[187]

52–56. Five names lost[188]

Dynasty 14a

Six kings with Semitic names whose position in the dynasty cannot be ascertained[189]

1. Nuya

Birth: *nu-ya*

2. Sheneh

Birth: *š-n-ḥ*

---

182. Turin 10,9; von Beckerath 1999, 112–13.
183. Turin 10,10–12.
184. Turin 10,13; Gauthier 1912, 69; von Beckerath 1999, 120–21; perhaps for *ỉnḳ*, "The one who has united <the Two Lands>."
185. Turin 10,14; von Beckerath 1999, 120–21.
186. Turin 10,15; Gauthier 1912, 69; von Beckerath 1999, 120–21.
187. Perhaps for "Apophis ///." See Ryholt 1997a, 381.
188. Turin 10,16–20.
189. Ryholt 1997a, 381–82.

3. Shenshek

Birth: *š-n-š-k* (*shenshek*), "The rescuer" (?)[190]

4. Wadjed[191]

Birth: *w3ḏd*

5. Khamure

Birth: *ḫ*ʿ-*mw-r*ʿ

6. Yakub-her[192]

Throne: *mr wsr r*ʿ (*mer weser ra*), The beloved one of the strength of Re
Birth: *y*ʿ-*kb-hr* (*ya-keb-her*), "(the god) Haddad protects"[193]

---

190. For the suggested rendering, see T. Schneider 1998, 140–41.
191. Von Beckerath 1999, 120–21.
192. Ibid., 116–17.
193. For the rendering, see T. Schneider 1998, 131.

VI

Second Intermediate Period

Dynasty 15 (1663–1555 b.c.e.)

Around the middle of the seventeenth century b.c.e., Egypt suffered a humiliating foreign occupation of the northeastern part of the country. The invaders from western Asia are commonly known as the Hyksos, a term derived from the Egyptian expression *heqa khasut,* "Ruler of Foreign Lands," a phrase the first three Hyksos rulers used in their own titulary. The old model of a sudden and violent invasion, an impression mostly derived from later New Kingdom propagandistic texts,[1] has been revised in the light of recent archaeological work. The latter has shown already existing settlements of Asiatics in the eastern Delta, into which the Hyksos kings integrated, eventually ruling from the city of Avaris, modern-day Tell el-Debaa.[2] In the south, the ruler of Upper Nubia took advantage of the weakening Egyptian power and seized Lower Nubia. From his stronghold at the site of Kerma at the Third Cataract, he may even have attempted an incursion into Upper Egypt.[3]

Perhaps in recognition of his foreign origins, Khyan included the plural word *t3w,* "lands," in his Horus name *ỉnḳ t3w,* "the one who has embraced the lands." His successor Apophis may have felt secure enough to claim that he had "pacified the Two Lands" (*sḥtp t3wy*) in his own Horus name. However, both kings did acknowledge the Egyptian sun god in their various Throne names.

1. Semqen[4]

Title and name: *ḥḳ3 ḫ3swt s-m-ḳ-n* (*heqa khasut semqen*), The Ruler of Foreign Lands Semqen ("He is my gift")[5]

1. For discussions of these, see Redford 1970 and 1997.
2. For an easily accessible description of the site, see Bietak 1999.
3. Davies 2003.
4. Von Beckerath 1999, 116–17.
5. For the rendering, see T. Schneider 1998, 137–38. The attribution of this king to the Fifteenth Dynasty is uncertain; see Ryholt 1997a, 383.

2. Aper-anati[6]

Title and name: *ḥḳ3 ḫ3swt ʿpr-ʿn-ti* (*heqa khasut aper-an-ti*), The Ruler of Foreign Lands Aper-anati ("the crew of [the goddess] Anat")[7]

3. Seker-her[8]

Two Ladies: *wʿf pḏwt* (*waf pedjut*), The one who has subdued the Nine Bows
Golden Horus: *ir t3š.f* (*ir tash.ef*), The one who has made his (own) border
Title and birth (?) name: *ḥḳ3 ḫ3swt sk-r-hr* (*heqa khasut sek-er-her*), The Ruler of Foreign Lands Seker-her[9]

4. Khyan[10]

Horus: *inḳ t3w* (*ineq tau*), The one who has embraced the lands
Throne: *swsr.n rʿ* (*seweser.en ra*), The one whom Re has made strong
Birth: *ḫy3n* (*khyan*), Khyan

5. Apepi (Apophis)[11]

Horus: *sḥtp t3wy* (*sehetep tawy*), The one who has pacified the Two Lands
Throne 1: *ʿ3 ḳn.n rʿ* (*aa qen.en ra*), The great one, whom Re has made brave
Throne 2: *ʿ3 wsr rʿ* (*aa weser ra*), The great one, whom Re has made strong
Title and birth name: *ḥḳ3 n ḥwt-wʿrt ipp* (*heqa en hut-waret, ipep*), The ruler of Avaris, Apophis

6. Khamudi[12]

Throne: *ḥtp ib rʿ* (*hetep ib ra*), The satisfied one of the mind of Re
Birth: *ḫ(3)mwdi* (*khamudi*), Khamudi

Dynasty 16 (1663–1555 b.c.e.)

The nature of the Sixteenth Dynasty is not well understood; it may, in fact, be wholly artificial, and simply due to Manetho's numbering system.[13] Using the entries in the Turin Canon's col. 11,1 to 11,14, with the names in 11,10 to 11,15 lost

6. Von Beckerath 1999, 116–17.
7. For a discussion of the name, see T. Schneider 1998, 133.
8. Von Beckerath 1999, 116–17.
9. For a discussion of the name, see T. Schneider 1998, 40–43.
10. Gauthier 1912, 135–37; von Beckerath 1999, 114–15.
11. Gauthier 1912, 139–43; von Beckerath 1999, 114–15.
12. Von Beckerath 1999, 114–15.
13. Waddell 1940, 92–93.

today,[14] Ryholt has reconstructed this group as a collection of Upper Egyptian rulers contemporary with the Hyksos kings of the Fifteenth Dynasty.[15]

For their Throne names, a number of these kings used the expression *sḫm rꜥ*, "the powerful one of Re," followed by a participle completed by the phrase "the Two Lands." Thus they claimed to have "solidified" (*smn*, lit. "made firm"), "strengthened" (*swsr*), and "sustained" (*sꜥnḫ*) the Two Lands.[16] King Sekhem-reshedwaset would ultimately be contented with having "rescued Thebes" (*šd wꜣst*).[17]

1. Name Lost[18]

2. Djehuty[19]

Horus: *iṯ m nḫtw* (*itj em nakhtu*), The one who has seized through victories[20]
Two Ladies: /// *ḏḥwty* (/// *djehuty*), /// Thoth
Golden Horus: *wsr-ḫꜥw* (*weser khau*), Strong of appearances
Throne: *sḫm rꜥ smn tꜣwy* (*sekhem ra, semen tawy*), The powerful one of Re, who has made the Two Lands firm
Birth: *ḏḥwty* (*djehuty*), (the god) Thoth[21]

3. Sobekhotep VIII[22]

Horus: none attested
Two Ladies: none attested
Golden Horus: none attested
Throne: *sḫm rꜥ swsr tꜣwy* (*sekhem ra, seweser tawy*), The powerful one of Re, who has strengthened the Two Lands
Birth: *sbk ḥtp(w)* (*sobek hetep(u)*), Sobek is satisfied

---

14. KRI II, 842:9–843:6.
15. Ryholt 1997a, 151–59.
16. Kings Djehuty (16:2), Sobekhotep VIII (16:3), and Neferhotep III (16:4), respectively.
17. For a discussion of the names of some of the kings from this period, see Dautzenberg 1997b.
18. Turin 10,31; see Ryholt 1997a, 388.
19. Gauthier 1912, 85; von Beckerath 1999, 126–27.
20. Or perhaps "as a brave one."
21. "Djehuty" could be an abbreviation of a common theophoric name such as Djehutymes ("Thutmose"), Dhejutynefer, Dhejutyhotep, or the like.
22. Gauthier 1912, 78; von Beckerath 1999, 104–5.

4. Neferhotep III Iykhernofret[23]

Horus: *wꜣḏ-ḫꜥw* (*wadj khau*), Flourishing of appearances
Two Ladies: *ꜥꜣ-pḥty* (*aa pehty*), Great of might
Golden Horus: *mn ///* (*men ///*), Established of ///
Throne: *sḫm rꜥ sꜥnḫ tꜣwy* (*sekhem ra, sankh tawy*), The powerful one of Re, who has sustained the Two Lands
Birth: *nfr ḥtp ỉỉ ḫr nfrt* (*nefer hetep, ii kher nefret*), The beautiful/perfect one is satisfied, the one who has come bearing happiness[24]

5. Mentuhotep VI[25]

Horus: *hr nṯrw* (?) (*her netjeru*), The one who has pleased the gods[26]
Two Ladies: none attested
Golden Horus: none attested
Throne: *sꜥnḫ.n rꜥ* (*sankh.en ra*), The one whom Re has sustained[27]
Birth: *mnṯw ḥtp*(*w*) (*mentju hetp(u)*), Mentuhotep ("[the god] Montu is satisfied")

6. Nebiryerau I[28]

Horus: *swꜣḏ tꜣwy* (*sewadj tawy*), The one who has made the Two Lands flourish
Two Ladies: *nṯri-ḫprw* (*netjeri kheperu*), Divine of manifestations
Golden Horus: *nfr-ḫꜥw* (*nefer khau*), Perfect of appearances
Throne: *swꜣḏ.n rꜥ* (*sewadj.en ra*), The one whom Re has made flourish
Birth 1: *nb ỉry r ꜣw* (*nb iry er au*), The possessor of all[29]
Birth 2: *nb ỉry* <*r*> *ꜣw rꜥ* (*nb iry* <*er*> *au ra*), The possessor of all (the things of) Re[30]

7. Nebiryerau II*[31]

Horus: none attested
Two Ladies: none attested
Golden Horus: none attested
Throne: none attested

---

23. Von Beckerath 1999, 102–3.
24. The latter name may simply be an epithet attached to the original name.
25. Von Beckerath 1999, 126–27.
26. For the Horus name, see Ryholt 1997a, 389.
27. For the verb *sꜥnḫ*, see Ryholt 1997a, 389 n. 2, contra the rendering in KRI II, 842:12 (Turin 11,4); see also von Beckerath 1999, 126 n. 2.
28. Gauthier 1912, 78; von Beckerath 1999, 126–27.
29. Lit. "what pertains to the length (of time or space)."
30. The additional divine name is found in Turin 11,5, for which see KRI II, 842:13.
31. Turin 11,6 (= KRI II, 842:14); Gauthier 1912, 79; von Beckerath 1999, 126–27.

Birth: *nb ỉry <r> ꜣw rꜥ* (*nb iry <e>r au ra*), The possessor of all (the things of) Re

8. Semenenre[32]

Horus: none attested
Two Ladies: none attested
Golden Horus: none attested
Throne: *smn.n rꜥ* (*semen.en ra*), The one whom Re has made firm
Birth: none attested

9. Bebiankh[33]

Horus: none attested
Two Ladies: none attested
Golden Horus: none attested
Throne: *swsr.n rꜥ* (*seweser.en ra*), The one whom Re has made strong
Birth: *bbỉ ꜥnḫ*(*w*) (*bebi ankh(u)*), Bebi is alive

10. Sekhemreshedwaset*[34]

Horus: none attested
Two Ladies: none attested
Golden Horus: none attested
Throne: *sḫm rꜥ šd wꜣst* (*sekhem ra shed waset*), The powerful one of Re, who has rescued Thebes

11–15. Five names lost[35]

Dynasty 16a

Five kings whose position in Dynasty 16 are difficult to ascertain

1. Dedumose I[36]

Horus: *wꜣḏ-ḫꜥw* (*wadj khau*), Flourishing of appearances
Two Ladies: *šd tꜣwy* (*shed tawy*), The one who has rescued the Two Lands
Golden Horus: *ỉn ḥtp* (*in hetep*), The one who has brought peace

---

32. Von Beckerath 1999, 126–27.
33. Ibid.
34. Turin 11,9 (= KRI II, 843:1); von Beckerath 1999, 128–29.
35. Turin 11,10–15.
36. Von Beckerath 1999, 100–101.

Throne: *ḏd ḥtp rʿ* (*djed hetep ra*), The stable one of the peace of Re
Birth: *ddw msw* (*dedu mesu*), The one (whose) birth has been granted

2. Dedumose II[37]

Horus: none attested
Two Ladies: none attested
Golden Horus: none attested
Throne: *ḏd nfr rʿ* (*djed nefer ra*), The stable one of the perfection of Re
Birth: *ddw msw* (*dedu mesu*), The one (whose) birth has been granted

3. Montuemsaf[38]

Horus: none attested
Two Ladies: none attested
Golden Horus: none attested
Throne: *ḏd ʿnḫ rʿ* (*djed ankh ra*), The firm one belonging to the life of Re
Birth: *mntw m s3.f* (*mentu em sa.ef*), Montu is his protection

4. Mentuhotep VII[39]

Horus: none attested
Two Ladies: none attested
Golden Horus: none attested
Throne: *mr(y) ʿnḫ rʿ* (*mer(y) ankh ra*), The beloved one of the life of Re
Birth: *mnṯw ḥtp* (*mentju hetep*), Montu is satisfied

5. Senwosret IV[40]

Horus: *wḥm ʿnḫ* (*wehem ankh*), The one who has repeated life
Two Ladies: *sʿnḫ t3wy* (*sankh tawy*), The one who has sustained the Two Lands
Golden Horus: *nfr-ḫʿw* (*nefer khau*), Perfect of appearances
Throne: *snfr ib rʿ* (*senefer ib ra*), The one whom Re's mind has made perfect
Birth: *s n wsrt* (*s en wosret*), The man belonging to (the goddess) Wosret

Dynasty 17 (1663–1570 b.c.e.)

The first rulers of the Seventeenth Dynasty seem to have been simple vassals of the Hyksos. First establishing their position in Upper Egypt, they next set

37. Gauthier 1912, 50–51; von Beckerath 1999, 100–101.
38. Gauthier 1912, 53; von Beckerath 1999, 102–3.
39. Gauthier 1912, 247; von Beckerath 1999, 102–3.
40. Gauthier 1912, 66–67; von Beckerath 1999, 102–3.

upon expanding their territory northward to Abydos. The last kings felt powerful enough to challenge the Hyksos supremacy and entered on an explicitly aggressive campaign against the foreign invaders. The mummy of Seqenenre Tao is certainly a grim witness to this military adventure, as his badly mangled body shows numerous wounds, some of them caused by Asiatic weapons.[41] His successor, Kamose, led his army north all the way to the Hyksos capital in the Delta but did not live to see the final liberation of the country by his kinsman Ahmose.

The new Theban rulers looked back to an ancient line from that city. King Rahotep (17:20) called himself the Horus *wꜣḥ-ꜥnḫ*, "enduring of life," recalling Intef II's own Horus name, and Kamose (17:28) claimed to be the Golden Horus *shr tꜣwy*, "the one who has pleased the Two Lands," calling to mind Intef I's Horus name. Also considering themselves as the heirs of the Thirteenth Dynasty, the last rulers of which had moved to Thebes, the Seventeenth Dynasty kings emulated the titulary of some of the better-known monarchs of that dynasty. The previously mentioned epithet *sḫm rꜥ*, "the powerful one of Re," had been used by Sobekhotep I (13:1), Sekhemre Khutawy (13:16), Sobekhotep III (13:26), and Neferhotep I (13:27) in their Throne names. This would now be part of the Throne names of Kings Wepwawetemsaf (17:17), Pantjeny (17:18), Rahotep (17:20), Sobekemsaf I (17:21), Intef V (17:22), Intef VII (17:24), and Sobekemsaf II (17:25).

During the war, Kings Senakhtenre Ahmose (I) (17:26) and Seqenenre Tao (17:27) felt secure enough to claim that Re had made them "victorious" (*snḫt*) and "brave" (*sḳn*), respectively. Finally, Kamose asserted in his own titulary that he had "provisioned" (*sḏfꜣ*) and "pleased" (*shr*) the Two Lands. For part of his Throne name, he would choose *ḫpr rꜥ*, "the manifestation of Re," a phrase that would occur numerous times in the next dynasty.

As with the dynasties immediately preceding them, the succession of the early kings of the Seventeenth Dynasty is difficult to establish. I have opted to follow D. Ben-Tor et al.[42] and James Allen[43] in assigning Ryholt's "Abydos Dynasty"[44] to the beginning of the Seventeenth Dynasty.[45] This comprises entries 17:1 to 17:16 in the present list, with only five names from this list actually preserved today. Again following Ben-Tor,[46] I have then placed the next three entries, 17:17 to 17:19, before the better-attested kings of the Seventeenth Dynasty. The overall numbering of this particular dynasty is therefore purely for convenience. Readers looking for a particular king may consult Appendix B to find where he appears in the present list.

41. See lately Ikram and Dodson 1998, 117–18.

42. Ben-Tor et al. 1999, 49.

43. Allen 2010, 4.

44. Ryholt 1997a, 392.

45. See also Dodson 2000, 51.

46. Ben-Tor et al. 1999, 52.

1. User /// re (I)*

Throne: *wsr /// rꜥ* (*weser /// ra*), The powerful one //// of Re[47]

2. User /// re (II)*

Throne: *wsr /// rꜥ* (*weser /// ra*), The powerful one //// of Re[48]

3–10. Eight names lost[49]

11. /// hebre (I)*

Throne: /// *ḥb rꜥ* (/// *heb ra*), [Who makes the /// of?] Re festive[50]

12–14. Three names lost.[51]

15. /// heb (?)-re (II)*

Throne: /// *ḥb rꜥ* (/// *heb ra*), [Who makes the /// of?] Re festive[52]

16. /// webenre (III)*[53]

Throne: /// *wbn rꜥ* (/// *weben ra*), /// the rising of Re ///[54]

17. Wepwawetemsaf[55]

Horus: none attested
Two Ladies: none attested
Golden Horus: none attested
Throne: *sḫm rꜥ nfr-ḫꜥw* (*sekhem ra, nefer khau*), The powerful one of Re is perfect of appearances
Birth: *wp-wꜣwt m sꜣ.f* (*wepwawet em sa.ef*), Wepwawet is his protection

47. Turin 11,16 (= KRI II, 843:8).
48. Turin 11,17 (= KRI II, 843:9).
49. Turin 11,18–25 (= KRI II, 843).
50. Turin 11,26 (= KRI II, 843:2).
51. Turin 11,27–29.
52. Turin 11,30.
53. Gauthier 1912, 52.
54. Turin 11,31.
55. Gauthier 1912, 70–71; von Beckerath 1999, 104–5.

18. Pantjeny[56]

Horus: none attested
Two Ladies: none attested
Golden Horus: none attested
Throne: *sḫm rꜤ ḫw tꜣwy* (*sekhem ra khu tawy*), The powerful one of Re is the protection of the Two Lands
Birth: *p(ꜣ) n ṯni* (*pa en tjeny*), Pantjeny ("The man of Thinis")[57]

19. Senaaib[58]

Horus: *swꜣḏ tꜣwy* (*sewadj tawy*), Who has made the Two Lands flourish
Two Ladies: none attested
Golden Horus: none attested
Throne: *mn ḫꜤw rꜤ* (*men khau ra*), The established one is (like) the appearances of Re
Birth: *snꜤꜤ ib* (*senaa ib*), The soother (lit. "who has made the heart smooth")

20. Rahotep[59]

Horus: *wꜣḥ-Ꜥnḫ* (*wah ankh*), Enduring of life
Two Ladies: *wsr-rnpwt* (*weser renput*), Rich in years
Golden Horus: *wꜣḏ* /// (*wadj*///), Flourishing of /////
Throne: *sḫm rꜤ wꜣḥ ḫꜤw* (*sekhem ra, wah khau*), The powerful one of Re is enduring of appearances
Birth: *rꜤ ḥtp(w)* (*ra hetep(u)*), Re is satisfied

21. Sobekemsaf I[60]

Horus: none attested
Two Ladies: none attested
Golden Horus: none attested
Throne: *sḫm rꜤ šd tꜣwy* (*sekhem ra shed tawy*), The powerful one of Re is the one who has rescued the Two Lands
Birth: *sbk m sꜣ.f* (*sobek em sa.ef*), Sobek is his protection

22. Intef V[61]

Horus: *wp mꜣꜤt* (*wep maat*), The one who has discerned Maat

56. Von Beckerath 1999, 88–89.
57. See Ryholt 1997a, 316 and 392; and Allen in Ben-Tor et al. 1999, 52.
58. Gauthier 1912, 67–68; von Beckerath 1999, 104–5.
59. Gauthier 1912, 88–90; von Beckerath 1999, 124–25.
60. Gauthier 1912, 74–78; von Beckerath 1999, 128–29.
61. Gauthier 1907, 219–21; von Beckerath 1999, 128–29.

Two Ladies: none attested
Golden Horus: none attested
Throne: *sḫm rʿ wp mꜣʿt* (*sekhem ra wep maat*), The powerful one of Re is the one who has discerned Maat
Birth: *in it.f ʿꜣ* (*in it.ef aa*), Intef ("the one whom his father brought forth") the Great[62]

23. Intef VI[63]

Horus 1: *nfr-ḫprw* (*nefer kheperu*), Perfect of manifestations
Horus 2: *ḫpr ḫprw* (*kheper kheperu*), The (very) manifestation of manifestations
Two Ladies: *hr ḥr nst.f* (*her her neset.ef*) Pleased with his throne
Golden Horus: /// *nṯrw* (/// *netjeru*), /// of the gods ////
Throne: *nbw ḫpr rʿ* (*nebu kheper ra*), The golden one is the (very) manifestation of Re
Birth 1: *in it.f* (*in it.ef*), Intef
Birth 2: *in it.f nḫt*(*w*) (*in it.ef nakht(u)*), Intef the Victorious

24. Intef VII[64]

Horus: none attested
Two Ladies: none attested
Golden Horus: none attested
Throne: *sḫm rʿ hr ḥr mꜣʿt* (*sekhem ra her her maat*), The powerful one of Re, who is pleased with Maat
Birth: *in it.f ʿꜣ* (*in it.ef aa*), Intef the Great

25. Sobekemsaf II[65]

Horus: *ḥtp nṯrw* (*hetep netjeru*), The one with whom the gods are satisfied[66]
Two Ladies: *ʿšꜣ*(ꜣ)-*ḫprw* (*ash(a) kheperu*), Numerous of manifestations
Golden Horus: *ink tꜣwy* (*ineq tawy*), The one who has embraced the Two Lands
Throne: *sḫm rʿ wꜣḏ-ḫʿw* (*sekhem ra, wadj khau*), The powerful one of Re is flourishing of appearances
Birth: *sbk m sꜣ.f* (*sobek em sa.ef*), Sobek is his protection

62. Or "the Elder."
63. Gauthier 1907, 238–42, 246; von Beckerath 1999, 124–25.
64. Von Beckerath 1999, 128–29.
65. Gauthier 1912, 71–73; von Beckerath 1999, 124–25.
66. Perhaps less likely, "The one who has satisfied the gods."

26. Senakhtenre Ahmose (I)[67]

Horus: *mry mꜣꜥt* (*mery maat*), The one who is beloved of Maat
Two Ladies: none attested
Golden Horus: none attested
Throne: *snḫt.n rꜥ* (*senakht.en ra*), The one whom Re has made victorious
Birth: *iꜥḥ ms*(*w*) *(iah mes(u)),* Iah (= the moon god) is born[68]

27. Seqenenre Tao[69]

Horus: *ḫꜥ m wꜣst* (*kha em waset*), The one who has appeared in Thebes
Two Ladies: none attested
Golden Horus: none attested
Throne: *sḳn.n rꜥ* (*seqen.en ra*), The one whom Re has made brave
Birth 1: *ḏḥwty ꜥꜣ*(.*w*) (*djehuty aa(u)*), Thoth is great[70]
Birth 2: *ḏḥwty ꜥꜣ*(.*w*) *ḳn* (*djehuty aa(u) qen*), Tao ("Thoth is great") the Brave

28. Kamose[71]

Horus 1: *ḫꜥ ḥr nst.f* (*kha her neset.ef*), The one who has appeared on his throne
Horus 2: *nfr ḫꜣb tꜣwy* (*nefer khab tawy*), The perfect one is the sickle of the Two Lands[72]
Horus 3: *sḏfꜣ tꜣwy* (*sedjefa tawy*), The one who has provisioned the Two Lands
Two Ladies: *wḥm mnw* (*wehem menu*), Who has renewed (lit. "repeated") monuments
Golden Horus: *shr tꜣwy* (*seher tawy*), The one who has pleased the Two Lands
Throne: *wꜣḏ ḫpr rꜥ* (*wadj kheper ra*), The flourishing one is the manifestation of Re
Birth: *kꜣ ms*(*w*) (*ka mes(u)*), Kamose ("The bull is born")
Birth: *kꜣ ms*(*w*) *nḫt*(*w*) (*ka mes(u) nakht(u)*), Kamose the victorious

---

67. The older references to a King Tao (I) are found in Gauthier 1912, 168–69; and von Beckerath 1999, 128–29. For the recent discovery of the king's Horus and Birth names on a lintel from the southern area of the temple of Ptah at Karnak, see Biston-Moulin 2012.

68. Such theophoric names as "God X is born" are thought to refer to the birthdays of the gods in question; see Gardiner 1936, 192.

69. Gauthier 1912, 156–61; von Beckerath 1999, 128–31. With the discovery of the previous king's Birth name as Ahmose, there is no need to number King Seqenenre Tao as "Tao the Second."

70. For the reading Djehuty (Thoth), which is written with the bread-loaf hieroglyph and has thus occasioned the rendering of the king's name as Taa or Tao, see Parlebas 1975.

71. Gauthier 1912, 165–67; von Beckerath 1999, 130–31.

72. Or perhaps "the one who has curbed the Two Lands"; see Leprohon 2010a, 12 n. 36.

Dynasty 17a

One king, whose position in the dynasty is difficult to ascertain

1. Nebmaatre[73]

Horus: none attested
Two Ladies: none attested
Golden Horus: none attested
Throne: *nb mꜣꜥt rꜥ* (*neb maat ra*), The possessor of the truth of Re
Birth: none attested

73. Gauthier 1912, 51; von Beckerath 1999, 118–19; and Ryholt 1997a, 400.

VII

New Kingdom

Dynasty 18 (1570–1293 b.c.e.)

Even though King Ahmose (II) was part of the previous royal family, his complete victory over the Hyksos anciently earned him the honor of being considered the inaugurator of the new era we call the New Kingdom.[1] Flush with victory, the Egyptians embarked on their greatest adventure yet. First turning to the south, they secured Lower and Upper Nubia, going as far up as the Fifth Cataract. Once this was accomplished, they cast their eye to the northeast. Still stinging from the occupation and perhaps feeling that the best defense was a good offense, the Egyptians set about creating a buffer zone between themselves and the mightiest military power in the ancient Near East at the time, the kingdom of Mitanni in modern-day northern Syria and southern Turkey. Successive military campaigns under Kings Thutmose I and Thutmose III gave Egypt control of the seaports of the eastern Mediterranean and of the trade routes in the southern Levant. This, coupled with their access to the gold mines of Nubia and the products of East Africa, made Egypt immensely wealthy and ushered in an age of opulence greater than it had ever seen.

This so-called Age of Empire is the Egypt most people know: the warrior kings Thutmose I, his grandson Thutmose III, and the latter's son and successor Amenhotep II; the great queen Hatshepsut, who dared to defy the male-dominated institution of kingship and installed herself on the throne when she deemed her nephew, the newly crowned Thutmose III, too young to rule; Amenhotep III, in whose reign Egypt was at its most prosperous and gold was said to be "more plentiful than dirt";[2] the iconoclastic Amenhotep IV, who changed his name to Akhenaten and challenged the religious establishment of his time; and of course the boy-king Tutankhamun, whose nearly intact tomb was discovered by Howard Carter in 1922. Thutmose III is also the king under whose reign the term *per-aa*, "the Great House," from which we get the word "pharaoh," was first used to designate the ruling monarch.[3]

1. See Leprohon 2010a, 9 n. 10, and the references there.

2. Amarna Letter EA 20, from King Tushratta of Mitanni to Pharaoh, for which see Moran 1992, 48; O'Connor and Cline 1998, 258; and Cabrol 2000, 294.

3. Found in a title of an official named Dedi, who was a *ḥry n pꜣ sꜣw n pr-ꜥꜣ ꜥnḫ(.w)*

Early in the dynasty, the kings' titularies[4] emulated celebrated predecessors whose cartouches would presumably have been available to them from monuments left at Karnak Temple. Thus, Ahmose's Two Ladies name, *twt mswt,* "The (very) image of (re)birth," was patterned after Amenemhat I's second Horus name, *wḥm mswt,* "The one who has repeated births"; the borrowing may not have been a coincidence, as Ahmose, who ushered in a new era, adapted an epithet chosen long ago by an inaugurator in his own right. Similarly, Amenhotep I's Throne name, *ḏsr kꜣ rꜥ,* "The sacred one of the ka of Re," may have been fashioned after Senwosret I's Throne name of *ḫpr kꜣ rꜥ,* "The (very) manifestation of the ka of Re;" the earlier king's titulary would have been easily visible to a new Theban monarch from his White Chapel at Karnak.[5] Well into the dynasty, kings adapted their more immediate predecessors' titularies. Thus was Thutmose I's Throne name *ꜥꜣ ḫpr kꜣ rꜥ,* "The great one is the manifestation of the ka of Re,"—itself a reworking of Senwosret I's Throne name—transformed into *ꜥꜣ ḫpr n rꜥ,* "The great one is the manifestation of Re," by his son Thutmose II for his own Throne name. Even the great iconoclast Akhenaten borrowed the motif of *nsyt*-kingship for his Two Ladies name from his grandfather Thutmose IV's own Two Ladies name.

The Eighteenth Dynasty monarchs also introduced a number of elements that would be used for centuries afterward in royal titularies. Amenhotep I was the first to call himself a "bull" in his Horus name, but it was his successor Thutmose I who began his Horus name with the expression *kꜣ nḫt,* "The victorious bull." This epithet would be used in Horus names well into the Twenty-Second Dynasty. Another innovation on his part was the doubling of epithets in the various elements of the titulary. He was the Horus "Victorious bull, who was beloved of Maat," the Two Ladies "The one who has appeared by means of the serpent goddess, the one great of might," and so on. Apart from a few periods that consciously imitated older patterns, this pairing of phrases would continue to be used by most kings henceforth.

Notwithstanding that Eighteenth Dynasty pharaohs were mostly content with wishes for their own well-being within their titulary,[6] another innovation of this period was the use of fairly belligerent epithets.[7] At the beginning of the dynasty, Ahmose (II) had been content with being the Golden Horus *ṯs tꜣwy,* "The one who has bound the Two Lands," proclaiming his victory over the Hyksos. Following this, Amenhotep I would first claim to have "subdued the lands"

wḏꜣ(.w) snb(.w), "Supervisor of the regiments of Pharaoh, alive, sound, and healthy" (= *Urk.* IV, 995:11).

4. For a study of the royal titulary of the Eighteenth Dynasty, see Leprohon 2010a. See also Dautzenberg 1997a, 37–39.

5. Lacau and Chevrier 1956, 1965.

6. See Leprohon 2010a, 36–38.

7. Unless otherwise indicated, the epithets are from the original titulary of the king mentioned.

(*wꜥf tꜣw*), Thutmose I would go further and "seize all lands" (*iṯ tꜣw nbw*),[8] and Thutmose III would then be "pleased with (his) victories" (*hr ḥr nḫtw*).[9] His son Amenhotep II would claim to have "seized by means of his power in all lands" (*iṯ m sḫm.f m tꜣw nbw*), and his own son Thutmose IV then bragged of "repelling the Nine Bows" (*dr pḏwt 9*). Amenhotep III, who had inherited a stable country from military victories going back to his great-grandfather's time as well as from his father's diplomatic alliances,[10] nevertheless trumpeted the fact that he would "strike down the Asiatics" (*ḥwi sṯtyw*). After him, the Amarna adventure mostly meant that Tutankhamun needed to "pacify the gods" (*sḥtp nṯrw*) and "keep the Two Lands quiet" (*sgrḥ tꜣwy*). Whether this was hyperbole or not, the palace's propagandistic message seems fairly clear at this point in time. Indeed, for all his military titles before he became king, Horemheb's titulary mostly consists of phrases that "re-created the Two Lands" (*sḫpr tꜣwy*) and honored Amun-Re by being "great of marvels in Ipet-sut," that is, Karnak Temple (*wr-biꜣwt m ipt swt*). What is noteworthy about this list of aggressive epithets is how few enemies are specifically identified. Apart from the generic Nine Bows,[11] only a few Asiatic peoples are named, and at that, solely by Amenhotep III. The latter wished to strike down the Setjetiu in his original Golden Horus name, then singled out the Iuntiu and Mentiu-bedouin in subsequent epithets composed for later monuments. The same king also mentioned Tjehenu-Libyans once, in the temple of Soleb in Nubia; the location of the epithet may help explain the reference to an African tribe. Indeed, absent from these lists of execrated enemies is any mention of Nubians, almost as if the palace considered that particular territory's conquest a *fait accompli,* which need not bother Pharaoh anymore.

Yet another innovation of Eighteenth Dynasty kings was the addition of short epithets to the cartouches, which made additional statements about divine actions taken for the benefit of the king.

Except for a few rulers at the beginning and end of the dynasty, kings from this period composed new names for special occasions such as the erection of obelisks in temples, to commemorate their Sed festival, or to inscribe on temple walls. In such cases, the original set of names taken at the coronation will first be presented, followed by the later names. Epithets added to the Throne and Birth names will also be presented after each entry.

1. Ahmose (II)[12]

Horus: *ꜥꜣ-ḫprw* (*aa kheperu*), Great of manifestations

8. A Two Ladies name from an obelisk at Karnak Temple.

9. A Golden Horus name from an obelisk at Karnak Temple.

10. Bryan 1991, 336–47.

11. Used by Thutmose I, Thutmose III, Thutmose IV, and Amenhotep III. For these symbolic enemies of Egypt, see especially Uphill 1965–66; and Valbelle 1990.

12. Gauthier 1912, 175–96; von Beckerath 1999, 132–33. With the recent discovery of

Horus 2: *k3 m w3st* (*ka em waset*), Bull in Thebes[13]
Two Ladies: *twt mswt* (*tut mesut*), The (very) image of (re-)birth
Golden Horus: *ṯs t3wy* (*tjez tawy*), The one who has bound the Two Lands
Throne: *nb pḥty rʿ* (*neb pehty ra*), The possessor of the might of Re
Birth: *iʿḥ ms*(*w*) (*iah mes(u)*), Iah (= the moon god) is born

Epithet added to the Throne name:

ḥk3 t3wy (*heqa tawy*), Ruler of the Two Lands[14]

Epithet added to the Birth name:

ḥk3 t3wy (*heqa tawy*), Ruler of the Two Lands

2. Amenhotep I[15]

Horus: *k3 wʿf t3w* (*ka waf tau*), Bull who has subdued the lands
Two Ladies: *ʿ3-nrw* (*aa neru*), Great of dread
Golden Horus: *w3ḥ-rnpwt* (*wah renput*), Enduring of years
Throne: *ḏsr k3 rʿ* (*djeser ka ra*), The sacred one of the ka of Re
Birth: *imn ḥtp*(*w*) (*imen hetpu*), Amun is satisfied

3. Thutmose I[16]

Original titulary

Horus: *k3 nḫt mry m3ʿt* (*ka nakht mery maat*), Victorious[17] bull, beloved of Maat
Two Ladies: *ḫʿ m nsrt ʿ3 -pḥty* (*kha em nesret, aa pehty*), The one who has appeared by means of the serpent goddess,[18] the one great of might

---

King Senakhtenre Ahmose I (Dynasty 17:26), the founder of the Eighteenth Dynasty must now be referred to as "Ahmose the Second."

13. Found on the so-called Donation Stela from the Tetisheri pyramid at Abydos (CG 34002), for which see Klug 2002, 15–21. The name change probably coincided with the expulsion of the Hyksos; see Leprohon 2010a, 11 n. 21, and the references there.

14. See Harvey (2007), who proposed this as a possible earlier name of King Ahmose. Although a King Heqatawy does not appear on any formal record, the occurrence of the phrase *s3 rʿ ḥk3 t3wy di ʿnḫ ḏt*, "The son of Re Heqatawy, given life forever"—with the name Heqatawy written within a cartouche—on a funerary cone of the High Priest of Amun and Overseer of Seal-bearers Djehuty along with the instance of the phrase *nṯr nfr nb pḥty rʿ di ʿnḫ ḏt*, "The good god Nebpehtyre, given life forever," on a different funerary cone belonging to the same high official is certainly noteworthy; for the funerary cones, see Harvey 2007, 345, figs. 4 and 5, and the references there.

15. Gauthier 1912, 197–212; von Beckerath 1999, 132–33. His titulary has been discussed in Schmitz 1978, 4–7.

16. Gauthier 1912, 212–27; von Beckerath 1999, 132–35. Thutmoses I's titulary has been discussed in Bonhême and Forgeau 1988, 313–14.

17. For this rendering of *nḫt*, see Galán 1995, 42–44.

18. This could represent the goddesses Sekhmet, Tefnet, or Hathor; see *Wb* II, 320:2–5.

Golden Horus: *nfr-rnpwt sꜥnḫ ibw* (*nefer renput, sankh ibu*), The one perfect of years, who has sustained minds
Throne: *ꜥꜣ ḫpr kꜣ rꜥ* (*aa kheper ka ra*), The great one is the manifestation of the ka of Re
Birth: *ḏḥwty ms*(*w*) (*djehuty mes(u)*), Thoth is born

Names added on an obelisk set up before the Fourth Pylon at Karnak Temple to commemorate the king's Sed festival:[19]

Horus 2: *kꜣ nḫt n rꜥ* (*ka nakht en ra*), The victorious bull of Re (south side)
Horus 3: *mry rꜥ ḫꜥ m ḥḏt* (*mery ra, kha em hedjet*), The one beloved of Re, who has appeared in the White Crown (north side)
Two Ladies 2: *iṯ tꜣw nbw* (*itj tau nebu*), Who has seized all lands (south side)
Two Ladies 3: *dwꜣ itmw ḫꜥ-ḫꜥw* (*dua itemu, kha khau*), Who worships Atum, radiant of appearances (north side)
Golden Horus 2: *ḥwi pḏwt-9* (*hui pedjut-9*), Who has struck down the Nine Bows (south side)
Golden Horus 3: *ꜥꜣ-pḥty wsr-ḫpš wꜣḏ-rnpwt m ḥwt-ꜥꜣt mꜣꜥt* (*aa pehty weser khepesh wadj renput em hut-aat maat*), Great of strength and strong-armed,[20] enduring of years in the temple[21] of Maat (north side)

Epithets added to the Throne name. The first four epithets come from the aforementioned obelisk.

ir.n rꜥ (*ir en ra*), Whom Re has made
stp.n rꜥ (*setep en ra*), Chosen by Re
tit imn (*tit imen*), The (very) image of Amun
mr.n rꜥ (*mer en ra*), Whom Re has loved
sꜥꜣ.n rꜥ (*saa.en ra*), Whom Re has made great[22]

Epithets added to the Birth name, again from the Karnak obelisk:

ḫꜥ mi rꜥ (*kha mi ra*), Who has appeared like Re
ḫꜥ nfrw (*kha nefru*), Who has appeared perfectly

4. Thutmose II[23]

Horus: *kꜣ nḫt wsr-pḥty* (*ka nakht weser pehty*), Victorious bull, strong of might
Two Ladies: *nṯri-nsyt* (*netjeri nesyt*), Divine of kingship

19. *Urk.* IV, 92–94; PM II, 78–80. On this obelisk, which faced west, see especially Gundlach 1979; and Bell 1985, 289 and n. 214. The front and back (west and east sides, respectively) of the obelisk held the king's regular titulary.
20. Lit. "powerful of arm."
21. Lit. "the Great Estate."
22. From a tomb at Hierakonpolis (*Urk.* IV, 135).
23. Gauthier 1912, 227–36; von Beckerath 1999, 134–35.

Golden Horus: *sḫm-ḫprw* (*sekhem kheperu*), Powerful of manifestations
Throne: *ꜥꜣ ḫpr n rꜥ* (*aa kheper en ra*), The great one is the manifestation of Re
Birth: *ḏḥwty ms*(*w*) (*djehuty mes(u)*), Thoth is born

An epithet added posthumously to the Birth name:

nḏty rꜥ (*nedjty ra*), Protector of Re[24]

5A. Thutmose III (A)[25]

From Regnal Year 1 to 22:[26]

Horus: *kꜣ nḫt ḫꜥ m wꜣst* (*ka nakht kha em waset*), The victorious bull who has appeared in Thebes
Two Ladies: *wꜣḥ-nsyt* (*wah nesyt*), Enduring of kingship
Golden Horus: *ḏsr-ḫꜥw* (*djeser khau*), Sacred of appearances
Throne name 1: *mn ḫpr rꜥ* (*men kheper ra*), The established one of the manifestation of Re
Birth: *ḏḥwty ms*(*w*) (*djehuty mes(u)*), Thoth is born

Additional name mostly used during the period of coregency between Thutmose III and Hatshepsut:[27]

Throne name 2: *mn ḫpr kꜣ rꜥ* (*men kheper ka ra*), The established one of the manifestation of the ka of Re[28]

6. Hatshepsut[29]

Horus: *wsrt-kꜣw* (*weseret kau*), Powerful of kas
Two Ladies: *wꜣḏt-rnpwt* (*wadjet renput*), Flourishing of years
Golden Horus: *nṯrt-ḫꜥw* (*netjeret khau*), Divine of appearances
Throne: *mꜣꜥt kꜣ rꜥ* (*maat ka ra*), The true one of the ka of Re
Birth: *ḫnmt ỉmn ḥꜣt špswt* (*khnemet imen, hat shepsut*), United with Amun, foremost of noble women

24. From a temple at Kumma in Nubia (LD III, 59a).

25. Gauthier 1912, 253–75; von Beckerath 1999, 136–39. For a study of the reign, see Cline and O'Connor 2006.

26. This first set of names was composed at the young king's accession and was also subsequently used through the coregency with Queen Hatshepsut.

27. On this coregency, see Maruéjol 2007.

28. On this particular designation, see Bell 1985, 257 n. 20.

29. Gauthier 1912, 236–52; von Beckerath 1999, 134–35. On Hatshepsut's titulary, see particularly Graefe 1995; Robins 1999; and Callender 2002, 34–37.

5B. Thutmose III (b)

From Regnal Year 22, after the death of Hatshepsut. The earlier names were used, to which additions were made:

Horus: *k3 nḫt ḫʿ m w3st* (*ka nakht kha em waset*), The victorious bull who has appeared in Thebes

Two Ladies: *w3ḥ-nsyt mi rʿ m pt* (*wah nesyt, mi ra em pet*), Enduring of kingship like Re in heaven

Golden Horus: *ḏsr-ḫʿw sḫm-pḥty* (*djeser khau, sekhem pehty*), Sacred of appearances and powerful of might

Throne: *mn ḫpr rʿ* (*men kheper ra*), The established one of the manifestation of Re

Birth: *ḏḥwty ms*(*w*) (*djehuty mes*(*u*)), Thoth is born

Additional names composed for the obelisks erected at the temples of Karnak and Heliopolis to celebrate the king's Sed Festivals.[30] The provenance of the names will be indicated by (K) and (H) for Karnak and Heliopolis, respectively.

Horus 2: *mry rʿ ḳ3-ḥḏt* (*mery ra, qa-hedjet*), Beloved of Re, (whose) White Crown is high (K)

Horus 3: *k3 nḫt mry rʿ* (*ka nakht mery ra*), Victorious bull, beloved of Re (K)

Horus 4: *k3 nḫt ḥʿ m m3ʿt* (*ka nakht ha em maat*), Victorious bull, who has rejoiced in Maat (K)

Horus 5: *mry rʿ* (*mery ra*), Beloved of Re (H)

Horus 6: *ḳ3-ḥḏt mry rʿ* (*qa-hedjet, mery ra*), (Whose) White Crown is high, beloved of Re (H)

Horus 7: *k3 nḫt ḫʿ m m3ʿt* (*ka nakht kha em maat*), Victorious bull, who has appeared in Truth (H)

Two Ladies 2: *sḫʿ m3ʿt mry t3wy* (*sekha maat, mery tawy*), Who has made Maat appear, beloved of the Two Lands (K)

Two Ladies 3: *ʿ3-šfyt m t3w nbw* (*aa shefyt, em tau nebu*), Great of majesty in all lands (K)

Additional names composed for the Sed Festival:

Two Ladies 4: *šsp ʿnḫ n itmw ḫpr m ḫpri ḥtp b3w iwnw ḥr m3ʿt.f* (*shesep ankh en itemu, kheper em khepri, hetep bau iunu her maat.ef*), Living image of Atum who has appeared as Khepri,[31] with whose offerings the Souls of Heliopolis are satisfied[32]

---

30. For references, see Leprohon 2010a, 25. For Thutmose III's Karnak obelisks, see also Blyth 2006, 86–88; as with Thutmose I's obelisk, the front of the obelisks held the king's regular titulary.

31. The early morning sun god.

32. *Urk.* IV, 600:5–6.

Golden Horus 2: *hr ḥr nḫtw* (*her her nakhtu*), Pleased with (his) victories (K)
Golden Horus 3: *ꜥꜣ-ḫpš ḥwi pḏwt 9* (*aa khepesh, hui pedjut 9*), The one great of strength who has struck down the Nine Bows (K)
Golden Horus 4: *hr ḥr nḫtw ḥwi ḥkꜣw ḫꜣswt pḥw sw* (*her her nakhtu, hui heqau khasut pehu su*), Pleased with (his) victories, the one who has struck down the rulers of the foreign lands who approached him (H)
Golden Horus 5: *sꜥr mꜣꜥt sḥtp rꜥ* (*sar maat, sehetep ra*), Who has elevated Maat and satisfied Re[33]

Epithets added to the Throne name from the king's twenty-second year onward, after the death of Hatshepsut:

iwꜥ rꜥ (*iwa ra*), The heir of Re
ir.n rꜥ (*ir.en ra*), Whom Ra made
mr.n rꜥ (*mer.en ra*), Whom Re has loved
stp.n rꜥ (*setep.en ra*), Whom Ra chose
sꜥꜣ.n rꜥ (*saa.en ra*), Whom Re has made great
nb ḫpš (*neb khepesh*), Possessor of a strong arm
nḫt ḫpš (*nakht khepesh*), The mighty-armed one
tit rꜥ (*tit ra*), The (very) image of Ra

Epithets added to the Birth name, also from the king's twenty-second year onward:

nfr-ḫprw (*nefer kheperu*), Perfect of manifestations
smꜣ-ḫprw (*sema kheperu*), United of manifestations
ḥkꜣ mꜣꜥt (*heqa maat*), Ruler of Maat
ḥkꜣ iwnw (*heqa iunu*), Ruler of Heliopolis
ḥkꜣ nṯri (*heqa netjeri*), Divine ruler
ḥkꜣ wꜣst (*heqa waset*), Ruler of Thebes
sꜣ itmw n ḫt.f ms.n n.f nbt iwnt (*sa itemu en khet.ef, mes.en en.ef nebet-iunet*), The bodily son of Atum, whom Nebet-iunet[34] bore for him (i.e., Atum)

7. Amenhotep II[35]

Original titulary

Horus: *kꜣ nḫt wr-pḥty* (*ka nakht wer pehty*), Victorious bull, great of might

33. Ibid., 600:8.
34. Lit. "the mistress of Dendera," i.e., the goddess Hathor.
35. Gauthier 1912, 276–90; von Beckerath 1999, 138–39. For a study of the reign, see Der Manuelian 1987.

Two Ladies: *wsr-f3w sḫꜥ m w3st* (*weser fau, sekha em waset*), Rich in splendor, who has been made to appear[36] in Thebes
Golden Horus: *iṯ m sḫm.f m t3w nbw* (*itj em sekhem.ef em tau nebu*), Who has seized by means of his strong arm in all lands
Throne: *ꜥ3 ḫprw rꜥ* (*aa kheperu ra*), The great one of the manifestations of Re
Birth: *imn ḥtp(.w)* (*imen hetpu*), Amun is satisfied

Additional names found on a graffito from Turah (Horus 2) and on various objects:

Horus 2: *k3 nḫt ꜥ3-pḥty* (*ka nakht aa pehty*), Victorious bull, great of might
Horus 3: *k3 nḫt spd-ꜥbwy* (*ka nakht seped abwy*), Victorious bull, sharp of horns
Horus 4: *k3 nḫt sḫm-pḥty* (*ka nakht sekhem pehty*), Victorious bull, powerful of might
Two Ladies 2: *ḫꜥ-ḫꜥw m ipt-swt* (*kha khau em ipet-sut*), Radiant of crowns in Ipet-sut[37]

Epithets added to the Birth name:

nṯr ḥk3 iwnw (*netjer heqa iunu*), God and ruler of Heliopolis
ḥk3 iwnw (*heqa iunu*), Ruler of Heliopolis
nṯr ḥk3 w3st (*netjer heqa waset*), God and ruler of Thebes[38]
ḥk3 w3st (*heqa waset*), Ruler of Thebes

8. Thutmose IV[39]

Original titulary:

Horus: *k3 nḫt twt-ḫꜥw* (*ka nakht tut khau*), Victorious bull, the (very) image of appearances
Two Ladies: *dd-nsyt mi itmw* (*djed nesyt mi itemu*), Stable of kingship like Atum
Golden Horus: *wsr-ḫpš dr pḏwt 9* (*weser khepesh, der pedjut 9*), The one great of strength who has repelled the Nine Bows
Throne: *mn ḫprw rꜥ* (*men kheperu ra*), The established one of the manifestations of Re
Birth: *ḏḥwty ms(w)* (*djehuty mes(u)*), Thoth is born

---

36. Perhaps a reference to the coronation itself.
37. Karnak Temple.
38. An additional epithet, *nsw ḥk3 w3st*, "King and ruler of Thebes," found in von Beckerath 1999, 138–39 (E7), is to be stricken. See Zayed 1985, pls. 1–2; and Der Manuelian 1987, 81, where the *nṯr*-sign ("God") is clear.
39. Gauthier 1912, 290–305; von Beckerath 1999, 138–41. For a study of the reign of Thutmose IV, see Bryan 1991.

Additional names found on an offering table from the Memphite area:

Horus 2: *k3 nḫt mry w3st* (*ka nakht mery waset*), Victorious bull, beloved of Thebes[40]
Two Ladies 2: *sḫm-ḫʿw m t3w nbw* (*sekhem khau em tau nebu*), Powerful of appearances in all lands
Golden Horus 2: *ḏd- ///// mi* [*ḥr*]*-3ḫty* (*djed ///////// mi [her]-akhty*), Enduring //// like [Hor]-akhty

Epithets added to the Throne name:

mr n rʿ (*mer en ra*), Beloved of Re
ir.n rʿ (*ir.en ra*), Whom Re has made
stp.n rʿ (*setep.en ra*), Whom Re has chosen
ḥk3 m3ʿt (*heqa maat*), Ruler of Maat

Epithet added to the Birth name:

ḫʿ-ḫʿw (*kha khau*), Radiant of crowns

9. Amenhotep III[41]

Original titulary

Horus: *k3 nḫt ḫʿ m m3ʿt* (*ka nakht kha em maat*), The victorious bull who has appeared in Truth
Two Ladies: *smn hpw sgrḥ t3wy* (*semen hepu, segereh tawy*), Who has established laws and pacified the Two Lands
Golden Horus: *ʿ3-ḫpš ḥwi sṯtyw* (*aa khepesh, hui setjetiu*), The great-of-strength one who has struck down the Asiatics
Throne: *nb m3ʿt rʿ* (*neb maat ra*), The possessor of the Maat of Re
Birth: *imn ḥtp(.w)* (*imen hetpu*), Amun is satisfied

Additional names

Temple of Soleb, Nubia[42]

Horus 2: *k3 nḫt sḫm-f3w* (*ka nakht sekhem fau*), The victorious bull powerful of splendor
Horus 3: *w3ḥ-rnpwt ʿš3-ḥbw* (*wah renput, asha hebu*), Enduring of years and numerous of festivals

40. A third Horus name mentioned by von Beckerath 1999, 138–39 (H3), *k3 nḫt s3 itmw*, "The victorious bull and son of Atum," from a small votive stela found at Memphis, is not contemporary; see Bryan 1991, 157; and Leprohon 2010a, 29 n. 142.

41. Gauthier 1912, 306–42; von Beckerath 1999, 140–43. For studies on the reign, see Schade-Busch 1992; O'Connor and Cline 1998; Cabrol 2000; and Kozloff 2012.

42. Erected for the king's first Sed festival; for the names found here, see LD III, 83.

Horus 4: *wṯs ḥḏt mry iwnw* (*wetjes hedjet, mery iunu*), Who has raised the White Crown, the beloved one of Heliopolis

Two Ladies 2: *smn hpw ṯs tꜣwy* (*semen hepu, tjes tawy*), Who has established laws and raised up the Two Lands

Golden Horus 2: *ḥwi mntyw dr ṯḥnw* (*hui mentiu, der tjehenu*), Who has struck down the bedouin and repelled the Tjehenu-Libyans

Golden Horus 3: *ṯḥn-ḫprw wr-biꜣwt* (*tjehen kheperu, wer biaut*), Dazzling of manifestations and great of wonders

Golden Horus 4: *ḥfnw-ḥbw mity rꜥ* (*hefenu hebu, mity ra*), Immeasurable of festivals, the (very) likeness of Re

Southern Colossus of Memnon, Western Thebes[43]

Horus 5: *kꜣ nḫt ḥkꜣ ḥkꜣw* (*ka nakht heqa heqau*), The victorious bull and ruler of rulers

Two Ladies 3: *wr-mnw r ḏꜣt pḥty.f* (*wer menu er djat pehty.ef*), Great of monuments so as to extend his strength

Golden Horus 5: *sꜥꜣ ḥwt.f nt ḏt* (*saa hut.ef net djet*), Who has magnified[44] his temple of eternity[45]

Granite sphinx, Temple of Mut, Karnak[46]

Two Ladies 4: *ꜥꜣ-nrw ḥr ḫꜣst nbt* (*aa neru her khaset nebet*), Great of dread in every foreign land

Golden Horus 6: *kꜣ n nsww dr pḏwt 9* (*ka en nesu, der pedjut 9*), The bull of kings who has repelled the Nine Bows

Golden Horus 7: *ptpt iwntyw iṯ tꜣ.sn* (*petpet iuntiu, itj ta.sen*), Who has trampled Asiatics and seized their land

Luxor Temple

Two Ladies 5: *smn hpw mi nb wꜣst* (*semen hepu mi neb waset*), Who has established laws like the lord of Thebes

White faience lid, Karnak[47]

Horus 6: *tit rꜥ ḫnty tꜣwy* (*tit ra, khenty tawy*), The (very) image of Re, who is at the head of the Two Lands

---

43. *Urk.* IV, 1746.

44. Lit. "made great."

45. Presumably a reference to the king's mortuary temple, in front of which the Colossi stood.

46. *Urk.* IV, 1747.

47. Ibid., 1748–49. The box, of which only the lid survives today, was possibly made for the king's first Sed festival; see Hayes 1948, 276.

Two Ladies 6: *ṯḥn-ḫʿw wr-šfyt* (*tjehen khau, wer shefyt*), Dazzling of appearances and great of majesty
Golden Horus 8: *wꜣḏ-kꜣw nfr-rnpwt nb ḥbw-sd* (*wadj kau, nefer renput, neb hebu sed*), Sturdy of sustenance, perfect of years, and lord[48] of Sed festivals

Epithets added to the Throne name:

tỉt rʿ (*tit ra*), The (very) image of Re
tỉt ỉmn (*tit imen*), The (very) image of Amun
šsp.n ỉtmw (*shesep en itemu*), Whom Atum has chosen
stp.n rʿ (*setep en ra*), Whom Re has chosen
ỉwʿ rʿ (*iwa ra*), The heir of Re
ỉr.n rʿ (*ir en ra*), Whom Re has made
mr.n rʿ (*mer en ra*), Whom Re has loved
sꜣ rʿ (*sa ra*), The son of Re

Epithets added to the Birth name:

ḥḳꜣ wꜣst (*heqa waset*), Ruler of Thebes
nṯr ḥḳꜣ wꜣst (*netjer, heqa waset*), The god and ruler of Thebes
ḥḳꜣ wꜣst ỉwʿ rʿ (*heqa waset, iwa ra*), Ruler of Thebes and heir of Re

10. Amenhotep IV/Akhenaten[49]

a. Regnal Years 1 to 5

Horus: *kꜣ nḫt ḳꜣ-šwty* (*ka nakht qa shuty*), Victorious bull, high of plumes
Two Ladies: *wr-nsyt m ỉpt swt* (*wer nesyt em ipet sut*), Great of kingship in Ipet-sut (i.e. Karnak Temple)
Golden Horus: *wṯs-ḫʿw m ỉwnw šmʿw* (*wetjes khau em iunu shemau*), Elevated of appearances[50] in southern Heliopolis (i.e., Thebes)
Throne: *nfr ḫprw rʿ wʿ n rʿ* (*nefer kheperu ra, wa en ra*), The perfect one of the manifestations of Re, the unique one of Re
Birth: *ỉmn ḥtp(w)* (*imen hetp(u)*), Amun is satisfied

Epithet added to the Birth name:

nṯr ḥḳꜣ wꜣst ʿꜣ m ʿḥʿw.f (*netjer, heqa waset, aa em ahau.ef*),
The god and ruler of Thebes, great in respect of his lifetime

b. Regnal Years 5 to 17

Horus: *mry ỉtn* (*mery iten*), Beloved of Aten

48. Lit. "possessor."
49. Gauthier 1912, 343–61; von Beckerath 1999, 142–43.
50. Or "crowns."

Two Ladies: *wr-nsyt m 3ḫt-itn* (*wer nesyt em akhet iten*), Great of kingship in Akhetaten ("The Horizon-of-Aten")[51]

Golden Horus: *wṯs rn n itn* (*wetjes ren en iten*), Who has elevated the Aten's name[52]

Throne: *nfr ḫprw rˁ wˁ n rˁ* (*nefer kheperu ra, wa en ra*), The perfect one of the manifestations of Re, the unique one of Re

Secondary "Birth name": *3ḫ n itn* (*akh en aten*), The one who is beneficial to the Aten

11. Nefer-neferu-aten[53]

Throne: *ˁnḫ ḫprw rˁ* (*ankh kheperu ra*), The (very) life of the manifestations of Re
Birth: *nfr nfrw itn* (*nefer neferu iten*), Perfect is the perfection of Aten

Epithets added to the Throne name:

mry wˁ n rˁ (*mery wa-en-ra*), Beloved of Wa-en-Ra (i.e., King Akhenaten)
mry nfr ḫprw rˁ (*mery nefer-kheperu-ra*), Beloved of Nefer-kheperu-Ra (i.e., Akhenaten again)

Epithets added to the Birth name:

mry wˁ n rˁ (*mery wa-en-ra*), Beloved of Wa-en-Ra
mry 3ḫ n itn (*mery akh-en-iten*), Beloved of Akhenaten

12. Smenkhkare[54]

Horus: none known
Two Ladies: none known
Golden Horus: none known
Throne and Birth names: *smnḫ k3 rˁ ḏsr-ḫprw* (*semenekh ka ra, djeser kheperu*), Whom the ka of Re has made potent, sacred of manifestations[55]

---

51. Modern-day Tell el Amarna.

52. Or perhaps "Elevated of name for the Aten," which is closer to the king's original Golden Horus name. Akhenaten certainly raised the profile of the Aten sun disk during his reign.

53. This enigmatic royal figure, some of whose names appear in feminine form (von Beckerath 1999, 142–43), may or may not be the famous Queen Nefertiti; for a useful recent study of this much-debated period, see M. Gabolde 1998, and Murnane's subsequent judicious remarks (2001).

54. Gauthier 1912, 362–64; von Beckerath 1999, 144–45.

55. Both names are written within the same cartouche.

13. TUTANKHAMUN[56]

Original titulary

Horus: *k3 nḫt twt mswt* (*ka nakht tut mesut*), Victorious bull, the (very) image of (re-)birth
Two Ladies: *nfr-hpw sgrḥ t3wy* (*nefer hepu, segereh tawy*), Perfect of laws, who has quieted down the Two Lands
Golden Horus: *wṯs-ḫꜥw sḥtp nṯrw* (*wetjes khau, sehetep netjeru*), Elevated of appearances, who has satisfied the gods
Throne: *nb ḫprw rꜥ* (*neb kheperu ra*), The possessor of the manifestations of Re
Birth 1: *twt ꜥnḫ itn* (*tut ankh aten*), The living image of Aten
Two Ladies 2: *nfr-hpw sgrḥ t3wy sḥtp nṯrw nbw* (*nefer hepu, segereh tawy, sehetep netjeru nebu*), Perfect of laws, who has quieted down the Two Lands and pacified all the gods[57]
Two Ladies 3: *wr ꜥḥ imn* (*wer ah imen*), The great one of the palace of Amun[58]
Golden Horus 2: *wṯs ḫꜥw it.f rꜥ* (*wetjes khau it.ef ra*), Who has elevated the appearances of his father Re[59]
Secondary "Birth name": *twt ꜥnḫ imn ḥk3 iwnw šmꜥw* (*tut ankh imen, heqa iunu shemau*), The living image of Amun, ruler of Southern Heliopolis[60]

Epithet added to the Throne name:

ḥk3 m3ꜥt (*heqa maat*), Ruler of Maat

14. AY[61]

Horus: *k3 nḫt ṯhn-ḫꜥw* (*ka nakht tjehen khau*), Victorious bull, dazzling of appearances
Two Ladies: *sḫm-pḥty dr sttyw* (*sekhem pehty, der setetiu*), Powerful of might, who has repelled the Asiatics
Golden Horus: *ḥk3 m3ꜥt sḫpr t3wy* (*heqa maat, sekheper tawy*), The ruler of Maat, who has created the Two Lands
Throne: *ḫpr ḫprw rꜥ ir m3ꜥt* (*kheper kheperu ra, ir maat*), The (very) manifestation of the manifestations of Re, who has accomplished Maat

56. Gauthier 1912, 365–73; von Beckerath 1999, 144–45.

57. *Urk*. IV, 2033. From a stela usurped by Horemheb found on the north side of the Seventh Pylon at Karnak; see Legrain 1903, 10.

58. On a wooden cubit found at Illahun; see Petrie 1891, pl. 24:12. Note that the references to the last two texts have been reversed in von Beckerath 1999, 144.

59. *Urk*. IV, 2044. From a statue found at Faras in Nubia.

60. This name was taken by the young king after his repudiation of his father Akhenaten's religious revolution.

61. Gauthier 1912, 374–80; von Beckerath 1999, 146–47. For a discussion of Ay's titulary, see Schaden 1978, 217–22.

Birth: *it nṯr iy* (*it netjer iy*), The god's father Ay[62]
Horus 2: *k3 nḫt ṯḥn-ḫprw* (*ka nakht tjehen kheperu*), Victorious bull, dazzling of manifestations[63]

Epithet added to the Birth name:

nṯr ḥḳ3 w3st (*netjer, heqa waset*), The divine one and ruler of Thebes

15. Horemheb[64]

Horus: *k3 nḫt spd-sḫrw* (*ka nakht seped sekheru*), The victorious bull, who is clever of plans
Two Ladies: *wr-bi3wt m ipt swt* (*wer biaut em ipet sut*), Great of marvels in Ipet-sut
Golden Horus: *hr ḥr m3ꜥt sḫpr t3wy* (*her her maat, sekheper tawy*), Pleased with Maat, who (re)-created the Two Lands
Throne: *ḏsr ḫprw rꜥ* (*djeser kheperu ra*), The sacred one of the manifestations of Re
Birth: *ḥr m ḥb* (*hor em heb*), Horus is festive (lit. "in holiday")

Epithets added to the Throne name:

stp.n rꜥ (*setep en ra*), Whom Re chose
ḥḳ3 m3ꜥt (*heqa maat*), Ruler of Maat

Epithet added to the Birth name:

mr.n imn (*mer.en imen*), Whom Amun has loved

Dynasty 19 (1293–1185 B.C.E.)

The first ruler of the Nineteenth Dynasty was Ramses I, who may have served as coregent under his predecessor Horemheb.[65] The new military family originated in the north and ruled from their new capital city called Per-Ramses ("House of Ramses"), modern-day Qantir in the eastern Delta.[66] The earlier part of the so-called Ramesside period was spent reestablishing Egypt's prestige in the Levant, with King Sety I and his son Ramses II campaigning actively against the kingdom of the Hittites, who were challenging Egypt's supremacy.[67] Although the famous

62. The name may simply be the interjection "hey" or the vocative "O!"
63. From his tomb in the Valley of the Kings; see LD III 113a.
64. Gauthier 1912, 381–96; von Beckerath 1999, 146–47. For a discussion of Horemheb's titulary, see Hari 1964, 212, 248, and 296.
65. Cf. his title *idnw n ḥm.f m šmꜥw t3 mḥw*, "Deputy of His Majesty in Upper and Lower Egypt," one of many titles on a statue found at the tenth pylon at Karnak Temple (= *Urk.* IV, 2175:14).
66. For an easily accessible overview of the site, see Pusch and Herold 1999.
67. For a review of the early military struggles of the Nineteenth Dynasty, see especially Murnane 1990.

battle of Kadesh in Ramses II's fifth year was essentially a draw, propagandistic texts trumpeted the young king's bravery on the battlefield. By Ramses II's twenty-first year, the Hittite king Hattusilis III felt threatened enough by his eastern neighbor Assyria that he initiated a peace treaty with Egypt. The alliance was cemented by two marriages between Hittite princesses and the pharaoh. His son and successor Merenptah suffered the first threat of invasion from the west. He glorified his victory against a coalition of Libyans and "Peoples of the Sea" in a long text; a coda mentioning defeated enemies in the Levant has earned this text the nickname of "The Israel Stela," for its first attestation of that toponym in history.

Ramses II's long reign afforded him time to be a great builder, and few sites escaped his architects' attention. He built extensively in Egypt and Nubia, or simply appropriated previous kings' monuments, and many of the additions to his titulary come from such activities.

Ramses I was content with a simple titulary,[68] patterning himself after the first king of the Eighteenth Dynasty, Ahmose (II). Where the latter had been the Dual King *nb pḥty rꜥ,* "The possessor of the might of Re," Ramses I was now *mn pḥty rꜥ,* "The established one of the might of Re." He also kept his titulary simple, much as earlier kings had done. Sety I also imitated previous monarchs, as he expanded Thutmose III's Horus name to become the Horus *kꜣ nḫt ḫꜥ m wꜣst sꜥnḫ tꜣwy,* "The victorious bull who has appeared in Thebes and sustained the Two Lands." He used another part of Thutmose III's titulary by transforming the latter's Throne name *mn ḫpr rꜥ* to *mn mꜣꜥt rꜥ,* "The established one belonging to the Maat of Re." As a ruler who felt he was beginning a new era, Sety I also borrowed from another inaugurator, refashioning Amenemhat I's phrase *wḥm mswt* into the Two Ladies *wḥm mswt sḫm-ḫpš dr pḏwt 9,* "The one who has repeated births, the strong-armed one who has repelled the Nine Bows." Ramses II also borrowed from a famous predecessor, the great conqueror Thutmose I, whose Horus name, *kꜣ nḫt mry mꜣꜥt,* "Victorious bull, beloved of Maat," he appropriated. He was the first to claim to be the *mk kmt,* "Protector of Egypt," in an original titulary, a phrase that would be used by a number of Ramesside kings after him, and his Throne name, *wsr mꜣꜥt rꜥ,* "The strong one belonging to the Maat of Re"—which may have been influenced by his father's Throne name of *mn mꜣꜥt rꜥ*—would almost become *de rigueur* with later monarchs. Merenptah adapted his father's Horus name to become *kꜣ nḫt ḥꜥ m mꜣꜥt,* "The victorious bull who has rejoiced in Maat." As his father's thirteenth son, who presumably saw his older brothers predecease him, Merenptah's Two Ladies name is noteworthy because it specifically mentions a Libyan tribe, suggesting that he and the Palace were well aware of the threat coming from the west. Thus did he assure his subjects that he would be "The lord of fear and the one great of majesty" (*nb snḏ*

68. For a study of the Nineteenth Dynasty titularies, see Kitchen 1987. See also Dautzenberg 1997a, 39–42.

ꜥ3-šfyt) in his Golden Horus name. The other Nineteenth Dynasty kings would then follow the aggressive phraseology they knew from their forebears.

Merenptah's mention of the Temehu-Libyans is noteworthy, as yet again very few ethnic groups were singled out in the series of belligerent phrases. Apart from the generic "foreign lands" (*ḫ3swt*)[69] and the traditional Nine Bows,[70] the only peoples specifically named are when Sety I wished to repel (*ḏr*) the Mentiu-bedouin and Ramses II claimed to have shattered (*sḏ*) the Setjetiu-Asiatics.

As with the Eighteenth Dynasty titularies, the original set of names will be presented, followed by additional names composed for special occasions or monuments. In the cases where there is only one set of names, for example, Ramses I and Tawosret, these will be presented without additional comments.

1. Ramses I[71]

Horus: *k3 nḫt w3ḏ-nsyt* (*ka nakht wadj nesyt*), Victorious bull, flourishing of kingship
Two Ladies: *ḫꜥ m nsw mi itmw* (*kha em nesu mi itemu*), Who has appeared as king like Atum
Golden Horus: *smn m3ꜥt ḫt t3wy* (*semen maat khet tawy*), Who has established Maat throughout the Two Lands
Throne: *mn pḥty rꜥ* (*men pehty ra*), The established one of the might of Re
Birth: *rꜥ ms sw* (*ra mes su*), Re is the one who bore him[72]

Epithets added to the Throne name:

ḥk3 m3ꜥt (*heqa maat*), Ruler of Maat
tit rꜥ (*tit ra*), The (very) image of Re

Epithet added to the Birth name:

ḥk3 m3ꜥt (*heqa maat*), Ruler of Maat

2. Sety I[73]

Original titulary

Horus: *k3 nḫt ḫꜥ m w3st sꜥnḫ t3wy* (*ka nakht kha em waset, sankh tawy*), The victorious bull who has appeared in Thebes and sustained the Two Lands

69. Used in various phrases by Sety I, Ramses II, Merenptah, and Tawosret.

70. Used by Sety I, Ramses II, and Merenptah.

71. Gauthier 1914, 2–9; von Beckerath 1999, 148–49.

72. For the rendering of this particular name containing the verb *ms*, "to bear," see Gardiner 1936, 192.

73. Gauthier 1914, 10–33; von Beckerath 1999, 148–53. For a study of the king's titulary, see Gundlach 2003; for the reign, see Brand 2000.

Two Ladies: *wḥm mswt sḫm-ḫpš dr pḏwt 9* (*wehem mesut, sekhem khepesh, der pedjut 9*), Renewing births, the strong-armed one who has repelled the Nine Bows

Golden Horus: *wḥm ḫꜥw wsr-pḏwt m tꜣw nbw* (*wehem khau, weser pedjut em tau nebu*), Who has repeated appearances, strong of troops in all lands

Throne: *mn mꜣꜥt rꜥ* (*men maat ra*), The established one belonging to the Maat of Re

Birth: *stḫy* (*sethy*), The one who belongs to (the god) Seth

Additional names

Barque Stand, Avaris[74]

Horus 2: *kꜣ nḫt mry rꜥ* (*ka nakht mery ra*), Victorious bull, beloved of Re

Two Ladies 2: *mn-mnw m ḥwt-ꜥꜣt mꜣꜥt* (*men menu em hut-aat maat*), Enduring of monuments in the Great Mansion of Maat

Golden Horus 2: *ꜣḫ n itw.f sḳꜣ pr.sn* (*akh en itu.ef, seqa per.sen*), The one beneficial to his fathers, who has exalted[75] their temples

Obelisk, Heliopolis[76]

Horus 3: *kꜣ nḫt dr ḫꜣswt m nḫtw.f* (*ka nakht der khasut em nakhtu.ef*), The victorious bull who has repelled foreign lands with his victories (main text, south face)

Horus 4: *kꜣ nḫt mry rꜥ mꜣꜥt* (*ka nakht mery ra maat*), Victorious bull, beloved of Re and Maat (main text, west face)

Horus 5: *kꜣ nḫt ḥtp ḥr mꜣꜥt* (*ka nakht hetep her maat*), The victorious bull who is satisfied with Maat (main text, north face)

Horus 6: *kꜣ nḫt mitt mnṯw* (*ka nakht mitet mentju*), The victorious bull and the (very) likeness of Montu[77] (base scene. west face)

Horus 7: *kꜣ nḫt sꜣ itmw* (*ka nakht sa itemu*), The victorious bull and the son of Atum (base scene, north face)

Two Ladies 3: *mn-mnw ḏt nḥḥ* (*men menu djet neheh*), Enduring of monuments forever and ever (main text, south face)

Two Ladies 4: *wꜥf ḫꜣswt dr mntyw* (*waf khasut, der mentiu*), Who has subdued the foreign lands and repelled the bedouin (main text, west face)

74. KRI I, 232–34; the quartzite stand, erected in the area of Khatâna-Qantir, is dedicated to the god Seth. The names are found on the right side of the upper register of text, from a scene showing the king tying the symbols of Upper and Lower Egypt together; see Habachi 1974, 97, fig. 2.

75. Lit. "made high."

76. KRI I, 118–20; PM VII, 409 (2). The east face of the obelisk was inscribed for Ramses II.

77. The Theban war god.

Two Ladies 5: *mnṯw n t3 mk kmt* (*mentju en ta mek kemet*), Montu of the land, the protector of Egypt (main text, north face)

Golden Horus 3: *sḥtp rʿ m mrrt.f* (*sehetep ra em merret.ef*), Who pleases Re with whatever he (i.e., Re) wishes[78] (main text, south face)

Golden Horus 4: *mr.n rʿ sʿ3 k3.f* (*mer.en ra, saa ka.ef*), Whom Re has loved, who has magnified[79] his ka (main text, west face)

Golden Horus 5: *sḫm nṯri ir.n ḫpri* (*sekhem netjeri, ir.en khepri*), Divine power, whom Khepri has begotten (main text, north face)

Temple, Kanais[80]

Horus 8: *k3 nḫt ḫʿ m ḥḏt mry rʿ* (*ka nakht kha em hedjet, mery ra*), The victorious bull who has appeared in the White Crown, the beloved of Re

Horus 9: *k3 nḫt ʿ3-šfyt mry rʿ* (*ka nakht aa shefyt, mery ra*), The victorious bull, great of majesty and beloved of Re

Horus 10: *k3 nḫt ḳ3-ḥḏt mry m3ʿt* (*ka nakht qa hedjet, mery maat*), Victorious bull, (whose) White Crown is high, the beloved of Maat

Abydos, Great Temple

Horus 11: *k3 nḫt sḫpr t3wy* (*ka nakht sekheper tawy*), The victorious bull who has created the Two Lands[81]

Horus 12: *k3 nḫt sḫm-pḥty* (*ka nakht sekhem pehty*), Victorious bull, powerful of might[82]

Horus 13: *k3 nḫt ʿ3-ḫpš* (*ka nakht aa khepesh*), Victorious bull, great of strong arm[83]

Horus 14: *k3 nḫt ḫʿ-ḫʿw* (*ka nakht kha khau*), Victorious bull, the (very) appearance of appearances[84]

Abydos, Great Temple, Seven Chapels

For the sake of completeness, and at the risk of introducing repetition, I have opted here to give all the names carved on the walls of each chapel, to give a bet-

---

78. So also Kitchen 1993, 99. Note that both von Beckerath (1999, 150) and Dessoudeix (2008, 333) read *sḥtp m rʿ mrr itw.f*, "Who pleases as Re, the one whom his fathers love." I read the transposition of the owl (*m*) and sun disk (*rʿ*) signs as purely graphic, and the writing of the feminine (to express the neuter) participle with the plural strokes is fairly common.

79. Lit. "made great."

80. KRI I, 70–71; Kanais is in the Wadi Mia, Eastern Desert, east of Edfu. As is often the case, the king's original titulary is found on the temple's main texts; the additional names given here were carved on the pillars in the main hall; see KRI I, 71:14 and the plan in PM VII, 322.

81. KRI I, 134:12.

82. Ibid., 185:8.

83. Ibid., 185:10.

84. Ibid., 185:12.

ter idea of the original intent of the authors of the texts. As can be seen, the names are sometimes not composed anew, but simply borrowed from other elements, for example, the original Two Ladies or Golden Horus names will be the source for a new Horus name.[85]

1. King's chapel[86]
a. Horus *kꜣ nḫt ḫꜥ m wꜣst sꜥnḫ tꜣwy* (*ka nakht kha em waset, sankh tawy*), The victorious bull who has appeared in Thebes and sustained the Two Lands
b. Horus *kꜣ nḫt wḥm mswt* (*ka nakht wehem mesut*), The victorious bull who has renewed births
c. Horus *kꜣ nḫt sḫm-ḫpš* (*ka nakht sekhem khepesh*), The victorious bull and strong-armed one
d. Horus [*kꜣ nḫt wḥm*] *ḫꜥw* (*[ka nakht wehem] khau*), The victorious bull who has repeated appearances
e. Horus ////

2. Chapel of Ptah[87]
a. Horus *kꜣ nḫt* [*ḫꜥ m wꜣst sꜥnḫ tꜣwy*] (*ka nakht [kha em waset, sankh tawy]*), The victorious bull [who has appeared in Thebes and sustained the Two Lands][88]
b. Horus *kꜣ nḫt* [*wḥm mswt*] *sḫm-ḫpš* (*ka nakht [wehem mesut] sekhem khepesh*), The victorious bull [who has renewed births], the strong-armed one
c. Horus *kꜣ nḫt wḥm ḫꜥw* <*dr*> *pḏwt 9* (*ka nakht wehem khau,* <*der*> *pedjut 9*), The victorious bull who has repeated appearances and <repelled> the Nine Bows
d. Horus *kꜣ nḫt wsr-pḏwt* (*ka nakht weser pedjut*), The victorious bull, strong of troops
e. Horus *kꜣ nḫt wꜣḥ-nsyt* (*ka nakht wah nesyt*), The victorious bull, enduring of kingship

3. Chapel of Re-Harakhty[89]
a. [Horus *kꜣ nḫt ḫꜥ m wꜣst sꜥnḫ tꜣwy*] ([*ka nakht kha em waset, sankh tawy]*), [The victorious bull who has appeared in Thebes and sustained the Two Lands]
b. Horus [*kꜣ nḫt*] *mry* [*rꜥ?*], (*[ka nakht mery [ra?]*), [The victorious bull], beloved of [Re?][90]

---

85. Ibid., 147–62.

86. Ibid., 147–49.

87. Ibid., 149–50.

88. Destroyed but can be reconstructed because the original name appears in every first instance in these chapels.

89. KRI I, 151–52.

90. This is Kitchen's suggested reconstruction (1993, 127), which would be expected in a chapel dedicated to Re-Harakhty, especially given the two following divine names.

c. Horus [*k3 nḫt*] *s3 ḫpri* (*[ka nakht], sa khepri*), Victorious bull, the son of Khepri[91]
d. Horus *k3 nḫt tit rꜥ itmw* (*ka nakht tit ra itmu*), Victorious bull, the (very) image of Re-Atum[92]
e. Horus *k3 nḫt ir.n rꜥ* (*ka nakht ir.en ra*), Victorious bull, begotten of Re

4. Chapel of Amun:[93]
a. Horus *k3 nḫt ḫꜥ m w3st sꜥnḫ t3wy* (*ka nakht kha em waset, sankh tawy*), The victorious bull who has appeared in Thebes and sustained the Two Lands
b. Horus *k3 nḫt s3 imn* (*ka nakht sa imen*), The victorious bull and son of Amun
c. Horus *k3 nḫt tit imn* (*ka nakht tit imen*), The victorious bull and the (very) image of Amun
d. Horus *k3 nḫt stp. n imn* (*ka nakht setep.en imen*), Victorious bull, whom Amun has chosen
e. Horus *k3 nḫt mr.n imn* (*ka nakht mer.en imen*), Victorious bull, whom Amun has loved

5. Chapel of Osiris[94]
a. [Horus *k3 nḫt ḫꜥ m w3st sꜥnḫ*] *t3wy* ([*ka nakht kha em waset, sankh] tawy*), [The victorious bull who has appeared in Thebes and sustained] the Two Lands
b. [Horus *k3 nḫt wḥm*] *mswt* ([*ka nakht wehem] mesut*), [The victorious bull who has renewed] births
c. [Horus *k3 nḫt wḥm ḫꜥw*] ([*ka nakht wehem khau]*), [The victorious bull who has repeated appearances]
d. [Horus *k3 nḫt s3 wsir*] ([*ka nakht sa wesir]*), [The victorious bull and son of Osiris]
e. Horus *k3 nḫt ///* (*ka nakht ///*), The victorious bull and ///

6. Chapel of Isis[95]
a. Horus *k3 nḫt ḫꜥ m w3st sꜥnḫ t3wy* (*ka nakht kha em waset, sankh tawy*), The victorious bull who has appeared in Thebes and sustained the Two Lands
b. Horus *k3 nḫt wḥm mswt* (*ka nakht wehem mesut*), The victorious bull who has renewed births
c. Horus *k3 nḫt wḥm ḫꜥw* (*ka nakht wehem khau*), The victorious bull who has repeated appearances
d. Horus *k3 nḫt s3 wsir* (*ka nakht sa wesir*), The victorious bull and son of Osiris
e. Horus *k3 nḫt nḏty rꜥ* (*ka nakht nedjty ra*), The victorious bull and protector of Re

91. The early morning manifestation of the sun god.
92. The evening manifestation of the sun god.
93. KRI I, 153–54.
94. Ibid., 154–57.
95. Ibid., 157–59.

7. Chapel of Horus[96]

a. Horus *k3 nḫt ḫꜥ m w3st sꜥnḫ t3wy* (*ka nakht kha em waset, sankh tawy*), The victorious bull who has appeared in Thebes and sustained the Two Lands

b. Horus *k3 nḫt wḥm mswt* (*ka nakht wehem mesut*), The victorious bull who has renewed births

c. Horus *k3 nḫt wḥm ḫꜥw* (*ka nakht wehem khau*), The victorious bull who has repeated appearances

d. Horus *k3 nḫt wsr-k3w* (*ka nakht weser kau*), The victorious bull, who is strong of kas

e. Horus *k3 nḫt wr-nsyt* (*ka nakht wer nesyt*), The victorious bull, who is great of kingship

Chapel of Horus, Ceiling Dedication

Horus *k3 nḫt ḫꜥ m ḥḏt* (*ka nakht kha em hedjet*), The victorious bull who has appeared in the White Crown

Golden Horus *nfr-rnpwt sꜥnḫ t3wy* (*nefer renput, sankh tawy*), Perfect of years, who has sustained the Two Lands

Epithets added to the throne name:

iwꜥw (n) rꜥ (*iwau (en) ra*), The heir of Re
ir.n rꜥ (*ir.en ra*), Whom Re engendered
mr.n rꜥ (*mer.en ra*), Whom Re has loved
ḥk3 iwnw (*heqa iunu*), Ruler of Heliopolis
ḥk3 w3st (*heqa waset*), Ruler of Thebes
ḥk3 m3ꜥt (*heqa maat*), Ruler of Maat
ḥk3 t3wy (*heqa tawy*), Ruler of the Two Lands
stp.n rꜥ (*setep.en ra*), Whom Re has chosen
tit rꜥ (*tit ra*), The (very) image of Re

Epithets added to the Birth name:

mry n ptḥ (*mery en ptah*), Beloved of Ptah
mry n imn (*mery en imen*), Beloved of Amun

3. Ramses II[97]

Original titulary

Horus: *k3 nḫt mry m3ꜥt* (*ka nakht mery maat*), Victorious bull, beloved of Maat

Two Ladies: *mk kmt wꜥf ḫ3swt* (*mek kemet, waf khasut*), The protector of Egypt, who has subdued the foreign lands

96. Ibid., 159–62.

97. Gauthier 1914, 33–113; von Beckerath 1999, 152–57.

Golden Horus: *wsr-rnpwt ꜥꜣ-nḫtw* (*weser renput, aa nakhtu*), Rich in years and great of victories

Throne: *wsr mꜣꜥt rꜥ* (*weser*[98] *maat ra*), The strong one belonging to the Maat of Re

Birth: *rꜥ ms sw* (*ra mes su*), Re is the one who bore him

Additionally, a shortened form of the Birth name appears occasionally: *s-sw* (*se-su*)

Additional names

The occurrences of further names composed for Ramses II's titulary on a multitude of monuments are too numerous to list individually by provenance.[99] The names will therefore be presented in the order in which they would appear in a dictionary of ancient Egyptian. The major monuments from which these additional names come are the twenty-six obelisks from Tanis,[100] a lintel from Memphis,[101] the king's temple at Abydos,[102] the two obelisks[103] and the pylon[104] from Luxor Temple, statuary from the "Karnak Cachette,"[105] a text containing a blessing of Ptah from various sites,[106] and material from some of the king's Nubian temples.[107]

Horus names

Horus 2: *wr-ḥbw-sd mi tꜣ-ṯnn* (*wer hebu sed mi ta-tjenen*), Great of Sed festivals like Ta-tjenen (Miscellaneous monuments, Memphis, KRI III, 111:14)

Horus 3: *nb ḥbw-sd mi tꜣ-ṯnn* (*neb hebu sed mi ta-tjenen*), Possessor of Sed festivals like Ta-tjenen (Musturud, Delta, KRI II, 469:11)

Horus 4: *kꜣ n rꜥ sḫm* (*ka en ra, sekhem*), The bull of Re, the powerful one (Tanis obelisk, KRI II, 420:13)

Horus 5: *kꜣ nḫt ꜥꜣ-šfyt* (*ka nakht aa shefyt*), Victorious bull, great of majesty (Tanis obelisk, KRI II, 424:5)

Horus 6: *kꜣ nḫt ꜥḥꜣ ḥr ḫpš.f* (*ka nakht aha her khepesh.ef*), Victorious bull, who has fought with his strong arm/sword (Luxor obelisk, KRI II, 603:2)

Horus 7: *kꜣ nḫt wꜥf ḫꜣswt* (*ka nakht waf khasut*), Victorious bull, who has subdued the foreign lands (Abu Simbel, KRI II, 259:11)

98. This is also rendered as "User."

99. And note that some names appear on a number of monuments from different sites.

100. KRI II, 408–28.

101. KRI III, 111.

102. KRI II, 547–48 for the two occurrences listed here.

103. Ibid., 598–605.

104. Ibid., 605–6.

105. Ibid., 586–91.

106. Ibid., 258–81.

107. For example, a stela from Abu Simbel (KRI II, 259) and texts from the temple of Derr (KRI II, 738–46).

Horus 8: *k3 nḫt wr-pḥty* (*ka nakht wer pehty*), Victorious bull, great of might (Tanis obelisk, KRI II, 424:3)

Horus 9: *k3 nḫt wr-nḫtw ꜥḥ3 ḥr ḫpš.f* (*ka nakht wer nakhtu, aha her khepesh.ef*), Victorious bull, great of victories, who fought with his strong arm/sword (Luxor obelisk, KRI II, 603:14)

Horus 10: *k3 nḫt wr-ḥbw-sd* (*ka nakht wer hebu sed*), Victorious bull, great of Sed festivals (Herakleopolis statue, KRI II, 501:5)

Horus 11: *k3 nḫt wr-ḥbw-sd mry t3wy* (*ka nakht wer hebu sed, mery tawy*), Victorious bull, great of Sed festivals and beloved of the Two Lands (Luxor obelisk, KRI II, 603:16)

Horus 12: *k3 nḫt wsr-pḥty* (*ka nakht weser pehty*), Victorious bull, strong of might (Tanis obelisk, KRI II, 411:14)

Horus 13: *k3 nḫt wsr-m3ꜥt* (*ka nakht weser maat*), Victorious bull, strong of Maat (Abydos Temple, KRI II, 546–47)

Horus 14: *k3 nḫt wsr-rnpwt* (*ka nakht weser renput*), Victorious bull, rich in years (Tanis obelisk, KRI II, 408:14)

Horus 15: *k3 nḫt wsr-ḫpš* (*ka nakht weser khepesh*), Victorious bull, strong of effectiveness/sword (Abydos Temple, KRI II, 548:6)

Horus 16: *k3 nḫt wṯs m3ꜥt* (*ka nakht wetjes maat*), Victorious bull, who has upheld[108] Maat (Abydos Temple, KRI II, 547:13)

Horus 17: *k3 nḫt mn-ib sḫm-pḥty* (*ka nakht men ib, sekhem pehty*), Victorious bull, decisive[109] and powerful of might (Luxor obelisk, KRI II, 599:5)

Horus 18: *k3 nḫt mry ptḥ* (*ka nakht mery ptah*), Victorious bull, beloved of Ptah (Tanis obelisk, KRI II, 409:13)

Horus 19: *k3 nḫt mry m3ꜥt nb ḥb*(*w*)*-sd mi it.f ptḥ-t3-ṯnn* (*ka nakht mery maat, neb hebu sed mi it.ef ptah-ta- tjenen*), Victorious bull, beloved of Maat, possessor of Sed festivals like his father Ptah-ta-tjenen (passim)[110]

Horus 20: *k3 nḫt mry mwt.f ḥwt-ḥr* (*ka nakht mery mut.ef hut-hor*), Victorious bull, beloved of his mother Hathor (Hathor Temple, Deir el Medina, KRI II, 703:3)

Horus 21: *k3 nḫt mry mntw* (*ka nakht mery montu*), Victorious bull, beloved of Montu (Tanis obelisk, KRI II, 413:5)

Horus 22: *k3 nḫt mry rꜥ* (*ka nakht mery ra*), Victorious bull, beloved of Re (passim)

Horus 23: *k3 nḫt mry rꜥ ptpt ḫ3swt nb*(*w*)*t ḫr ṯbwt.f* (*ka nakht mery ra, petpet khasut neb(u)t kher tjebut.ef*), Victorious bull, beloved of Re, who has trampled all the foreign countries under his sandals (Tanis stela, KRI II, 294:10)

108. Lit. "lifted up."

109. Lit. "firm-minded."

110. Name composed for the king's Sed festival, after his thirtieth regnal year.

Horus 24: *k3 nḫt mry stḫ* (*ka nakht mery setekh*), Victorious bull, beloved of Seth (Tanis obelisk, KRI II, 424:13)
Horus 25: *k3 nḫt n rʿ sḏ sṯtyw* (*ka nakht en ra, sedj setjetyu*), Victorious bull of Re, who has shattered the Asiatics (Luxor obelisk, KRI II, 602:15)
Horus 26: *k3 nḫt nb t3wy* (*ka nakht neb tawy*), Victorious bull and lord of the Two Lands (KRI II, 844:10)[111]
Horus 27: *k3 nḫt ḥʿ ḥr m3ʿt* (*ka nakht ha her maat*), Victorious bull, who has rejoiced over Maat (Karnak Cachette, KRI II, 586:9)
Horus 28: *k3 nḫt ḥwi t3 nb* (*ka nakht hui ta neb*), Victorious bull who has struck every land (Tanis obelisk, KRI II, 424:6)
Horus 29: *k3 nḫt ḫʿ m w3st sʿnḫ t3wy* (*ka nakht kha em waset, sankh tawy*), Victorious bull who has appeared in Thebes and sustained the Two Lands (Mortuary Temple of Sety I, Qurnah, KRI II, 641:6)
Horus 30: *k3 nḫt s3 ỉmn* (*ka nakht sa imen*), Victorious bull, son of Amun (Luxor pylon, KRI II, 605:4)
Horus 31: *k3 nḫt s3 ỉtmw* (*ka nakht sa itemu*), Victorious bull, son of Atum (Tanis obelisk, KRI II, 424:3)
Horus 32: *k3 nḫt s3 ptḥ* (*ka nakht sa ptah*), Victorious bull, son of Ptah (Tanis obelisk, KRI II, 410:12)
Horus 33: *k3 nḫt s3 ḫpri* (*ka nakht sa khepri*), Victorious bull, son of Khepri (Tanis obelisk, KRI II, 412:4)
Horus 34: *k3 nḫt s3 t3-ṯnn* (*ka nakht sa ta-tjenen*), Victorious bull, son of Ta-tjenen (Heliopolis obelisk, KRI II, 479:15)
Horus 35: *k3 nḫt spd-ʿbwy* (*ka nakht seped abwy*), Victorious bull, sharp-horned (Tanis obelisk, KRI II, 409:15)
Horus 36: *k3 nḫt sḫm-pḥty* (*ka nakht sekhem pehty*), Victorious bull, powerful of might (Tanis obelisk, KRI II, 409:9)
Horus 37: *k3 nḫt sḳ3 w3st* (*ka nakht seqa waset*), Victorious bull, who has exalted[112] Thebes (Luxor Temple, KRI II, 605:11)
Horus 38: *k3 nḫt sḏ sṯtyw* (*ka nakht sedj setjetyu*), Victorious bull who has shattered the Asiatics (Luxor Temple, KRI II, 605:15)
Horus 39: *k3 nḫt ḳ3-ḥḏt* (*ka nakht qa hedjet*), Victorious bull, (whose) White Crown is high (Tanis obelisk, KRI II, 424:6)
Horus 40: *k3 nḫt k3 n ḥk3w* (*ka nakht ka en heqau*), Victorious bull, bull of the rulers (Tanis obelisk, KRI II, 415:12)
Horus 41: *k3 nḫt twt ḫʿw* (*ka nakht tut khau*), Victorious bull, the (very) image of appearances (Bentresh Stela, KRI II, 284:14)

111. From a statue of the king's mother, now in the Vatican Museum, who is said to be "Mother of the victorious bull . . ."

112. Lit. "raised up."

Horus 42: *k3 nḫt ṯs t3wy* (*ka nakht tjes tawy*), Victorious bull who has governed[113] the Two Lands (Tanis obelisk, KRI II, 420:9)

Two Ladies names

Two Ladies 2: *ꜥḥ3 n ḥḥw m3i sḫm-ib* (*aha en hehu, mai sekhem-ib*), Who has fought for millions, a stout-hearted lion (Luxor obelisk, KRI II, 602:15)

Two Ladies 3: *ꜥḥ3 ḥr ḫpš.f mk mšꜥw.f* (*aha her khepesh.ef, mek meshau.ef*), Who has fought with his sword/strong arm, the protector of his armies (Luxor pylon, KRI II, 605:15)

Two Ladies 4: *wr-pḥty mi s3 nwt* (*wer pehty mi sa nut*), Great of might like the son of Nut (Derr temple, Nubia, KRI II, 740:5)

Two Ladies 5: *wr-mnw m pr ḫnmw* (*wer menu em per khnemu*), Great of monuments in the temple of Khnum (Elephantine block, KRI II, 716:2)

Two Ladies 6: *wr-šfyt mk kmt* (*wer shefyt, mek kemet*), Great of majesty, the protector of Egypt (Luxor obelisk, KRI II, 599:5)

Two Ladies 7: *mry 3ḫ n it.f* (*mery akh en it.ef*), The beloved one, who is beneficial to his father (Luxor pylon, KRI II, 352:13, 605:4)

Two Ladies 8: *nb t3wy* (*neb tawy*), Lord of the Two Lands (Ptah temple, Memphis, KRI II, 488:7)

Two Ladies 9: *mk kmt wꜥf ḫ3swt rꜥ ms nṯrw grg t3wy* (*mek kemet, waf khasut, ra mes netjeru, gereg tawy*), Protector of Egypt, who has subdued foreign lands, a Re whom the gods have borne, the founder of the Two Lands (passim)

Two Ladies 10: *ḥꜥ ḥr m3ꜥt mi 3ḫty* (*ha her maat mi akhty*), Who has rejoiced in Maat like the One of the Two Horizons (Luxor obelisk, KRI II, 599:8)

Two Ladies 11: *smnḫ mnw m ipt-rsy(t) n it.f imn di sw ḥr nst.f* (*semenekh menu em ipet-resy(t) en it.ef imen di su her neset.ef*), Who has made monuments splendid[114] in Ipet-Resyt (i.e., Luxor Temple) for his father Amun, who put him on his throne (Luxor pylon, KRI II, 605:11)

Two Ladies 12: *sḫr pḥw sw in pḥwy t3* (*sekher pehu su in pehwy ta*), Who has felled those who attacked[115] him and who has captured the ends of the earth (Luxor, west obelisk, KRI II, 603:2)

Two Ladies 13: *šsp nṯri n ḫpri* (*shesep netjeri en khepri*), The divine image of Khepri (Karnak Cachette, KRI II, 586:9)[116]

Two Ladies 14: *ḏd-nsyt mi itmw* (*djed nesyt mi itemu*), Stable of kingship like Atum (Bentresh Stela, KRI II, 284:14)

113. For the meaning of the verb *ṯs* in this context, see Grimal 1986, 342 n. 1127.

114. Or perhaps "who has embellished monuments."

115. Lit. "reached."

116. This is also the name found on the famous seated statue of Ramses II now in the Turin Museum (no. 1380), KRI II, 590:15.

Golden Horus names

Golden Horus 2: *di kmt m ršwt m šnyt.f imyw m ḥʿʿ m mrwt.f* (*di kemet em reshwet em shenyt.ef, imyu em haa em merut.ef*), Who caused Egypt to delight in his company;[117] those who are in it continually rejoice because of love of him[118]

Golden Horus 3: *ʿ3-ḫpš mry t3wy* (*aa khepesh, mery tawy*), Great of effectiveness, beloved of the Two Lands (Karnak Cachette, KRI II, 586:10)

Golden Horus 4: *wʿf bštw* (*waf beshtu*), Who has subdued the rebellious ones (Derr temple, Nubia, KRI II, 740:2)

Golden Horus 5: *wʿf ḫ3swt dr bštw* (*waf khasut, der beshtu*), Who has subdued foreign countries and repelled the rebellious ones (Luxor obelisk, KRI II, 599:5–6)

Golden Horus 6: *wr-f3wt sḫm-pḥty* (*wer fawet, sekhem pehty*), Great of splendor and powerful of strength (Luxor obelisk, KRI II, 603:2–3)

Golden Horus 7: *wr-nḫtw ḥr ḫ3st nbt* (*wer nakhtu her khaset nebet*), Great of victories in every foreign country (Luxor obelisk, KRI II, 602:16)

Golden Horus 8: *wḫ3 mi imy w3st* (*wekha, mi imy waset*), A (veritable) pillar,[119] like the one who is in Thebes (Luxor obelisk, KRI II, 599:3)

Golden Horus 9: *wsr-rnpwt ʿ3-nsyt mi itmw ity ms nṯrw sḫpr t3wy* (*weser renput, aa nesyt mi itemu, ity, mes netjeru, sekheper tawy*), Rich in years and great of kingship like Atum, the sovereign whom the gods fashioned, the one who has fostered the Two Lands (South Girdle Wall, Karnak, KRI II, 583:4)

Golden Horus 10: *wsr-ḫpš* (*weser khepesh*), Strong of might (Derr temple, Nubia, KRI II, 740:6)

Golden Horus 11: *wsr-ḫpš mry t3wy* (*weser khepesh, mery tawy*), Strong of might, beloved of the Two Lands (Luxor obelisk, KRI II, 599:8; and Luxor pylon, KRI II, 352:13)

Golden Horus 12: *wsr-ḫpš dr pḏwt 9* (*weser khepesh, der pedjut 9*), The one great of strength, who has repelled the Nine Bows (Bentresh Stela, KRI II, 284:14)

Golden Horus 13: *ḥḥy 3ḫwt n ms sw* (*hehy akhut en mes su*), Who seeks benefits for the one who bore him (Luxor pylon, KRI II, 605:12)

Golden Horus 14: *sḫm-ḫpš dr pḏwt 9* (*sekehm khepesh, der pedjut 9*), The powerful of arm/sword, who has repelled the Nine Bows (Luxor pylon, KRI II, 605:15–16)

117. Lit. "to be in joy in his entourage."

118. An additional phrase occasionally added to the original Golden Horus name.

119. For *wḫ3* comparing the king to a pillar, i.e., a support for the sky, see Grimal 1986, 240 and n. 758.

Epithets added to the Throne name:

iwꜥw rꜥ (*iwau ra*), The heir of Re
mry rꜥ (*mery ra*), Beloved of Re
nb ḫpš (*neb khepesh*), Possessor of a strong arm/sword
ḥḳꜣ wꜣst (*heqa waset*), Ruler of Thebes
stp n rꜥ (*setep en ra*), Chosen by Re
stp n rꜥ pḥty mi mnṯw (*setep en ra, pehty mi mentju*), Chosen by Re, the strong one like Montu
tit rꜥ (*tit ra*), The (very) image of Re

Epithets added to the Birth name:

wr-mnw (*wer menu*), Great of monuments
mry imn (*mery imen*), Beloved of Amun
mrwty mi itmw (*meruty mi itemu*), The beloved one, like Atum
nṯri ḥḳꜣ iwnw (*netjeri, heqa iunu*), the divine one and ruler of Heliopolis

4. Merenptah/Merneptah[120]

Original titulary

Horus: *kꜣ nḫt ḥꜥ m mꜣꜥt* (*ka nakht ha em maat*), Victorious bull, who has rejoiced in Maat
Two Ladies: *ir bꜣw r tꜣ n tmḥw* (*ir bau er ta en temehu*), Who has exercised[121] power against the land of the Temehu[122]
Golden Horus: *nb snḏ ꜥꜣ-šfyt* (*neb senedj, aa shefyt*), Lord of fear and great of majesty
Throne: *bꜣ n rꜥ* (*ba en ra*), The (very) spirit of Re
Birth: *mry n ptḥ ḥtp-ḥr mꜣꜥt* (*mery en ptah, hetep her maat*), Beloved of Ptah, satisfied with Maat

Additional names

Horus
A phrase often added to the original Horus name:
Horus 2: *ḥnk sw n rꜥ m ḫrt-hrw* (*henek su en ra em kheret-heru*), (Victorious bull, who has rejoiced in Maat), Who offers it[123] to Re in the course of every day (passim)

---

120. Gauthier 1914, 113–26; von Beckerath 1999, 156–59. The titulary has been discussed in Iskander 2002, 247–58.
121. Lit. "done, accomplished."
122. A Libyan tribe.
123. Maat.

Heliopolis obelisk[124]

Horus 3: *b3 n rˁ dt itmw* (*ba en ra, djet itemu*), The spirit of Re and (the very) body of Atum (face 1)

Horus 4: *ḥtp ḥr m3ˁt mi t3-ṯnn* (*hetep her maat mi ta-tjenen*), Satisfied with Maat, like Ta-tjenen (face 1)

Horus 5: *nḏ ḥr it.f mity m3ˁt* (*nedj her it.ef, mity maat*), Protector of his father, the likeness of Maat (face 2)

Horus 6: *k3 nḫt pr m rˁ* (*ka nakht per em ra*), Victorious bull, who has emerged from[125] Re (face 4)

Memphis palace[126]

Horus 7: *k3 nḫt dr pḏwt 9* (*ka nakht der pedjut 9*), Victorious bull who has repelled the Nine Bows (lintel, KRI IV, 54:11)

Horus 8: *nb ḥbw ḫˁw* (*neb hebu khau*), Possessor of Appearance Festivals[127] (doorway into pillared hall, KRI IV, 54:14)

Horus 9: *k3 nḫt nsw t3wy* (*ka nakht nesu tawy*), Victorious bull and king of the Two Lands (side door, KRI IV, 54:16)

Horus 10: *k3 nḫt s3 rˁ* (*ka nakht sa ra*), Victorious bull, the son of Re (side door, KRI IV, 55:1)

Various sites

Horus 11: *k3 nḫt 3ḫ n itmw* (*ka nakht akh en itemu*), Victorious bull, beneficial to Atum (dyad from Kafr Matbûl [near Xois], KRI IV, 50:13)

Horus 12: *k3 nḫt s3 imn* (*ka nakht sa imen*), Victorious bull, the son of Amun (Tanis statue, KRI IV, 43:9)

Horus 13: *k3 nḫt m3i ḥbn.n.f* (*ka nakht mai heben.en.ef*), Victorious bull, a lion who has triumphed (Amada Temple, Nubia, KRI IV, 1:8)

Two Ladies

Two Ladies 2: *ḫˁ mi ptḥ m ḫnw ḥfnw r smn hpw nfrw m-ḫt idbwy* (*kha mi ptah em khenu hefnu er semen hepu neferu em-khet idebwy*), Who has appeared like Ptah amidst hundreds of thousands in order to establish the perfect laws throughout the Two Banks (passim)

124. Found at the site of Qaha, in the south-central Delta; for the text, see KRI IV, 31:1–13. One of the faces of the obelisk had been cut away; it is possible that this now-destroyed side contained the original Horus name of the king. See Daressy 1920; Sourouzian 1989, no. 16, pp. 60–61, pl. 11a; and Iskander 2002, 161, no. 3.5.3.

125. Or "as."

126. For the texts, see KRI IV, 54–55.

127. Or "possessor of festivals and crowns."

Two phrases added to the previous Two Ladies name

Two Ladies 3: *ỉr m ꜥwy.f(y)* (*ir em awy.fy*), Who has acted with his arms (Temple at Memphis, KRI IV, 53:12)

Two Ladies 4: *ỉty wsr-ḫꜥw wr-bỉꜣwt* (*ity, weser khau, wer biaut*), The sovereign who is rich in appearances and great of marvels (Temple of Sety I, Qurnah, KRI IV, 66:1)

Two Ladies 5: *ꜥꜣ-pḥty wr-nḫtw* (*aa pehty, wer nakhtu*), Great of might and important of victories (Temple of Amada, KRI IV, 1:8)

Golden Horus

Golden Horus 2: *snḫt kmt dr pḏwt 9 r dỉt ḥtp nṯrw m mr.sn* (*senakht kemet, der pedjut 9 er dit hetep netjeru em mer.sen*), Who has strengthened Egypt and repelled the Nine Bows in order to satisfy the gods[128] with what they love/ wish for (passim)

Epithets added to the Throne name:

mry ỉmn (*mery imen*), Beloved of Amun
mry nṯrw (*mery netjeru*), Beloved of the gods

5. Sety II[129]

Original titulary

Horus: *kꜣ nḫt wr-pḥty* (*ka nakht wer pehty*), Victorious bull, great of might

Two Ladies: *nḫt-ḫpš dr pḏwt 9* (*nakht khepesh, der pedjut 9*), The strong-armed one who has repelled the Nine Bows

Golden Horus: *ꜥꜣ-nrw m tꜣw nbw* (*aa neru em tau nebu*), Great of dread in all lands

Throne: *wsr ḫprw rꜥ* (*weser kheperu ra*), The strong one of the manifestations of Ra

Birth: *stḫy* (*sethy*), The one who belongs to Seth

Additional names

Horus 2: *kꜣ nḫt mry rꜥ* (*ka nakht mery ra*), Victorious bull, beloved of Re

Horus 3: *kꜣ nḫt mk kmt* (*ka nakht mek kemet*), The victorious bull and protector of Egypt

Two Ladies 2: *sḫm ḫpš dr pḏwt 9* (*sekhem khepesh, der pedjut 9*), Powerful of arm/sword, who has repelled the Nine Bows

128. Lit. "cause the gods to be satisfied."

129. Gauthier 1914, 130–39; von Beckerath 1999, 158–61. For a discussion of Sety II's evolving—and fairly derivative—titulary, see Kitchen 1987, 135–36.

Two Ladies 3: *mk kmt wꜥf ḫꜣswt* (*mek kemet, waf khasut*), The protector of Egypt who has subdued foreign countries

Golden Horus 2: *ꜥꜣ-nḫtw m tꜣw nbw* (*aa nakhtu em tau nebu*), Great of victories in all lands

Epithets added to the Throne name:

mry imn (*mery imen*), Beloved of Amun
mr.n imn (*mer.en imen*), Whom Amun has loved
mry stḫ (*mery seth*), Beloved of Seth
stp. n rꜥ (*setep.en ra*), Whom Re has chosen

Epithet added to the Birth name:

mry n ptḥ (*mery en ptah*), Beloved of Ptah

6. Amenmesse[130]

Original titulary

Horus: *kꜣ nḫt mry mꜣꜥt smn tꜣwy* (*ka nakht mery maat, semen tawy*), Victorious bull, beloved of Maat, who has perpetuated[131] the Two Lands

Two Ladies: *wr-biꜣwt m ipt-swt* (*wer biawt em ipet-sut*), Great of marvels in Ipet-sut (i.e., Karnak Temple)

Golden Horus: *ꜥꜣ-ḫpš sꜥꜣ wꜣst n ms sw* (*aa khepesh, saa waset en mes su*), The one great of might, who has magnified[132] Thebes for the one who bore him[133]

Throne: *mn mi rꜥ stp n rꜥ mry imn* (*men mi ra, setep en ra, mery imen*), Established like Re, chosen by Re and beloved of Amun

Birth: *imn ms sw mry rꜥ ḥkꜣ wꜣst* (*imen mes su, mery ra, heqa waset*), Amun is the one who bore him, the beloved of Re and Ruler of Thebes

Additionally, a shortened form of the Birth name appears, *msy* (*mesy*), The one who was born

Additional names[134]

Horus 2: *wr-pḥty mi imn* (*wer pehty mi imen*), Great of strength like Amun

130. Gauthier 1914, 127–30; von Beckerath 1999, 158–59.

131. Lit. "made firm."

132. Lit. "made great."

133. For the name, which adds to von Beckerath's entry (1999, 158–59), see Hardwick 2006.

134. Both of the following names are from a stela from the temple of Sety I at Qurnah, and usurped by Merenptah-Siptah; see LD III, 201c, and KRI IV, 196:9, with the latter giving only the first of these two names.

Horus 3: *nb ḥbw-sd mi tꜣ-ṯnn* (*neb hebu sed mi ta-tjenen*), Possessor of Sed festivals like Ta-tjenen

7. Siptah[135]

Original titulary

Horus: *kꜣ nḫt mry ḥꜥpy sꜥnḫ tꜣ nb m kꜣ.f rꜥ-nb* (*ka nakht mery hapy, sankh ta neb em ka.ef ra neb*), Victorious bull, beloved of Hapy,[136] who has sustained every land by means of his ka[137] daily

Two Ladies: *sꜥꜣ iwnw ḳꜣb ꜥꜣbt di mꜣꜥt n rꜥ m ḫrt-hrw* (*saa iunu, qab aabet, di maat en ra em kheret heru*), Who has magnified Heliopolis, doubled the offerings, and presented Maat to Re every day

Golden Horus: *//// mi it.f rꜥ ity sꜥnḫ ibw n rḫyt di kmt m <r>š<wt?>* (*///// mi it.ef ra, ity, sankh ibu en rekhyet, di kemet em reshwet(?)*), //// like his father Re, the sovereign who has sustained the common folks' hearts, and brought joy to Egypt[138]

Throne: *sḫꜥ.n rꜥ* (*sekha.en ra*), Whom Re has caused to appear[139]

Birth: *sꜣ ptḥ* (*sa ptah*), The son of Ptah

Additional names

Horus 2: *kꜣ nḫt wr-pḥty* (*ka nakht wer pehty*), The victorious bull, great of might[140]

Throne 2: *ꜣḫ n rꜥ stp.n rꜥ* (*akh en ra, setep.en ra*), Beneficial to Re, whom Re chose[141]

Epithets added to the Throne name:

mry imn (*mery imen*), Beloved of Amun
stp.n rꜥ (*setep.en ra*), Whom Re chose

Epithet added to the Birth name:

mr.n ptḥ (*mer.en ptah*), Whom Ptah has loved

---

135. Gauthier 1914, 140–45; von Beckerath 1999, 160–63.

136. The Nile flood.

137. Or perhaps "provisions."

138. Lit. "put Egypt in joy"; for the reconstruction, cf. the additional phrase added to Ramses II's original Golden Horus name.

139. Perhaps meaning "crowned."

140. One of the names in his tomb in the Valley of the Kings (no. 47), KRI IV, 347:13.

141. From his tomb again (KRI IV, 347:13), as well as from Buhen temple, Nubia (KRI IV, 348–49).

8. Tawosret[142]

Original titulary

Horus: *k3 nḫt mry(t) m3ʿt nb(t) ʿn m nsw mi itmw* (*ka nakht mery(t) maat, neb(et) an em nesu mi itemu*), Victorious bull, beloved of Maat and possessor of beauty as king like Atum
Two Ladies: *grg(t) kmt wʿf(t) ḫ3swt* (*gereg(et) kemet, waf(et) khasut*), Who has founded Egypt and subdued[143] foreign countries
Golden Horus: not known
Throne: *s3t rʿ* (*sat ra*), Daughter of Re
Birth: *t3 wsrt* (*ta wosret*), The one (fem.) who belongs to (the goddess) Wosret[144]

Epithets added to the Throne name:

mry(t) n imn (*mery(t) en imen*), Beloved (fem.) of Amun
[*ḥnwt*] *t3-mry* (*[henut] ta-mery*), [Mistress of] the Beloved Land (i.e., Egypt)

Epithets added to the Birth name:

mr(t) n mwt (*mere(t) en mut*), Beloved of Mut
stp n mwt (*setep en mut*), Chosen by Mut

Dynasty 20 (1185–1070 b.c.e.)

The Twentieth Dynasty began after a tumultuous period at the end of the previous dynasty, and it is not known how King Sethnakht came to the throne. His successor, Ramses III, was faced with finishing the task begun by Merenptah when he had to repulse a number of invasions from the west and the northeast. The narratives of his campaigns, accompanied by vivid representations of a major battle on land and at sea in his eighth year, are fairly unsurpassed. Ramses III was the last ruler of any significance in this period, at the end of which Egypt was in true decline and beset by internal problems. The trials of the men who robbed the royal tombs in the Valley of the Kings and the surrounding areas during the reign of Ramses XI epitomize the state of affairs at the time.[145] At the very end of the dynasty, the viceroy of Nubia, who had rebelled against the throne but been repelled from Thebes, fled south, seizing the Nubian territory away from

142. Gauthier 1914, 145–48; von Beckerath 1999, 162–63. For studies on this queen, see R. H. Wilkinson 2011, 2012.
143. Of note is that neither participle is written in its feminine form.
144. Or perhaps simply "The powerful one," written in the feminine.
145. Aptly summarized in Vernus 1993.

Egypt's control. The loss of the Nubian gold mines would have severe repercussions on Egypt's economy.

The titularies of this period are mostly derivative of the preceding dynasty's. These were at times outright borrowings, such as the previously mentioned Throne name of Ramses II, which was appropriated by Ramses III, IV, V, VII, and VIII, or Sethnakht's Horus name, which was the same as Sety II's. Sethnakht also adapted Sety II's Throne name *wsr ḫprw rꜥ* into *wsr ḫꜥw rꜥ*, "The strong one of the appearances of Re." As the first of his line, Sethnakht may have also consciously borrowed from another inaugurator, when he transformed Ahmose II's Throne name, *nb pḥty rꜥ*, into his Horus name, *kꜣ nḫt wr-pḥty*, "The victorious bull, great of might." Ramses III used Ramses I's Horus name, transforming his predecessor's *kꜣ nḫt wꜣḏ-nsyt* into *kꜣ nḫt ꜥꜣ-nsyt*, "Victorious bull, great of kingship," while simply borrowing Ramses II's Throne name, to which he added epithets to distinguish his cartouches from those of his illustrious forebear.

Given the battles he fought, it is not surprising that Ramses III named specific enemies in some of the phrases composed for his Mortuary Temple at Medinet Habu. Vanquished were the Temehu- and Tjehenu-Libyans as well as the Setetiu- and Fenkhu-Asiatics. No other king mentioned any foreign people specifically, preferring to simply trumpet their military successes against the traditional Nine Bows.[146]

1. Sethnakht[147]

Original titulary

Horus: *kꜣ nḫt wr-pḥty* (*ka nakht wer pehty*), Victorious bull, great of might
Two Ladies: *twt ḫꜥw mỉ tꜣ-ṯnn* (*tut-khau mi ta-tjenen*) The (very) image of appearances like Ta-tjenen
Golden Horus: *sḫm-ḫpš dr rḳyw.f* (*sekhem khepesh, der reqyu.ef*), Powerful of effectiveness, who has subdued his enemies
Throne: *wsr ḫꜥw rꜥ* (*weser khau ra*), The strong one of the appearances of Re
Birth: *stẖ nḫt*(*.w*) (*seth nakht(u)*), Seth is strong[148]

Additional name

Golden Horus 2: <*ḥwỉ*> *pḏwt 9 ꜥn m nsyt* (<*hui*> *pedjut 9, an em nesyt*), <Who has struck> the Nine Bows, beautiful in kingship[149]

---

146. Mentioned by Sethnakht, Ramses III, IV, VII, and IX.
147. Gauthier 1914, 152–56; von Beckerath 1999, 164–65.
148. Or perhaps also "Seth the Victorious"; see Dessoudeix 2008, 382.
149. Stela from the Sinai (Gardiner and Peet 1955, no. 271, p. 186, pl. 73; see KRIV, 7 for an accurate copy, contra von Beckerath 1999, 165; and Dessoudeix 2008, 382). In this respect, it is noteworthy to see a nonroyal text offering a different titulary for the king.

Epithets added to the Throne name:

mry imn (*mery imen*), Beloved of Amun
stp n rꜥ (*setep en ra*), Whom Re chose

Epithets added to the Birth name:

mry rꜥ (*mery ra*), Beloved of Re
mrr imn (*merrer imen*), Whom Amun loves
mrr imn-rꜥ (*merrer imen-ra*), Whom Amun-Re loves

2. Ramses III[150]

Original titulary

Horus: *kꜣ nḫt ꜥꜣ-nsyt* (*ka nakht aa nesyt*), Victorious bull, great of kingship
Two Ladies: *wr-ḥbw-sd mi tꜣ-ṯnn* (*wer hebu-sed mi ta-tjenen*) Great of Sed festivals, like Ta-tjenen
Golden Horus: *wsr-rnpwt mi itmw* (*weser renput mi itemu*), Rich in years like Atum[151]
Throne: *wsr mꜣꜥt rꜥ* (*weser maat ra*), The strong one of the Maat of Re
Birth: *rꜥ ms sw* (*ra mes su*), Re is the one who bore him

Additional Horus names from Medinet Habu[152]

Horus 2: *kꜣ pḥty sḫm-ḫpš nḫt-ꜥ nb nrw m tꜣw ḫꜣswt fnḫw tmḥw* (*ka pehty, sekhem khepesh, nakht-a, neb neru em tau khasut fenkhu temehu*), Powerful bull, potent of sword, strong-armed, lord of dread in the lowlands and the highlands of the Fenkhu-Asiatics and the Temehu-Libyans[153]
Horus 3: *kꜣ nḫt mꜣi pḥty nḫt-ꜥ nb ḫpš ḥꜣḳ sttiw* (*ka nakht mai pehty, nakht a, neb khepesh, haq setetiu*), Victorious bull and powerful lion, strong-armed, the lord of strength who has captured the Asiatics[154]
Horus 4: *kꜣ nḫt mnḫ-mnw sḥtp nb-r-ḏr m nꜣy.f ꜣḫwt* (*ka nakht menekh menu, sehetep neb-er-djer em nay.ef akhut*), Victorious bull, splendid of monuments, who has satisfied the Lord of All[155] with his benefactions[156]
Horus 5: *kꜣ nḫt swsḫ kmt wsr-ḫpš nḫt-ꜥ smꜣ ṯḥnw* (*ka nakht sewesekh kemet, weser khepesh, nakht a, sema tjehenu*), The victorious bull who has widened (the

---

150. Gauthier 1914, 156–78; von Beckerath 1999, 164–67. For a discussion of Ramses III's titulary, see Grandet 1993, 52–53.

151. To the original name, the king sometimes added additional phrases: *ity mk kmt wꜥf ḫꜣswt* (*ity, mek kemet, waf khasut*), "the sovereign who has protected Egypt and subdued foreign countries." See Kitchen 1987, 137 n. 4.

152. From the First and Second Courts of the Great Temple.

153. From the southern end of the First Court, KRI V, 49:14.

154. From the western end of the First Court, exterior of the Second Pylon, KRI V, 37:10.

155. A designation of the god Re.

156. From the eastern end of the Second Court, KRI V, 314:8.

boundaries of) Egypt, the one powerful of sword and strong of arm who has slaughtered the Libyans[157]

Horus 6: *k3 nḫt-ʿ dm ḥnwty mn-ib wr-pḥty ḥr b3wy n ḳnw* (*ka nakht-a, dem henuty, men ib, wer pehty her bawy en qenu*), The strong-armed bull who has sharpened (his) two horns, decisive[158] and great of strength on the battlefield of bravery[159]

Horus 7: *ʿš3-mnw* (*asha menu*), With many monuments[160]

Horus 8: *sḫm-pḥty hd ḥfnw dḫ n3 pḥw sw dmḏ* (*ḫr*) *ṯbwy.f* (*y*) (*sekhem pehty, hed hefnu, dekh na pehu su, demedj (kher) tjebwy.fy*), Powerful of strength, who has attacked hundreds of thousands, overthrown those who have attacked him, and gathered (them) (under) his sandals[161]

Various monuments found outside the Royal Palace

Horus 9: *ʿn ḥr srḫ mi s3 3st* (*an her serekh mi sa aset*), Beautiful on the throne like the son of Isis[162]

Horus 10: *bity wr-mnw wr-bi3wt mḥ ipt-swt ḥr rn.f* (*bity, wer menu, wer biaut, meh ipet-sut her ren.ef*), The king of Lower Egypt,[163] great of monuments and great of wonders, who has filled Ipet-sut with his renown[164]

Horus 11: *nb ʿḥʿw mi it.f rʿ* (*neb ahau mi it.ef ra*), Lord of a lifetime like his father Re[165]

Horus 12: *s3 imn* (*sa imen*), Son of Amun[166]

Horus 13: *sʿ3 ḫʿw mi 3ḫty wbn.f ʿnḫ rḫyt* (*saa khau mi akhty weben.ef, ankh rekhyet*), Who has magnified[167] (his) appearances like the One of the Two Horizons when he rises, the (very) life of the *rekhyet*-people[168]

Horus 14: *nb ḥbw-sd mi t3-ṯnn* (*neb hebu-sed mi ta-tjenen*), Possessor of Sed festivals like Ta-tjenen[169]

Horus 15: *ṯḥn-ḫʿw* (*tjehen-khau*), Dazzling of appearances[170]

---

157. From the northern end of the Second Court, KRI V, 20:14.
158. Lit. "strong-minded."
159. From the northern end of the Second Court, KRI V, 315:11.
160. Lit. "the one of many monuments." From the eastern end of the Second Court, KRI V, 316:6.
161. From the exterior north wall of the Second Court, KRI V, 30:14.
162. Hölscher 1941, pl. 32 (a).
163. Or perhaps simply "The reigning king," as suggested in the introduction; see Quirke 1986, 123–24.
164. Lit. "name." Hölscher 1941, pl. 32 (a).
165. Ibid., pl. 32 (a).
166. Ibid.
167. Lit. "made great."
168. Hölscher 1941, pl. 32 (a).
169. Ibid., pl. 35 (b).
170. Ibid.

From Karnak

Horus 16: *ꜥn n nsw mi itmw mr.tw.f ꜣb.tw.f mi ḥm n rꜥ* (*an en nesu mi itemu, mer.tu.ef ab.tu.ef mi hem en ra*), Beautiful as king like Atum, he is loved and wished for like the majesty of Re[171]

Two Ladies

Two Ladies 2: *wsr-pḥty mi it.f mntw sksk pḏwt 9 dr m tꜣ.sn* (*weser pehty mi it.ef mentju, seksek pedjut 9, der em ta.sen*), Powerful of strength like his father Montu, who has annihilated the Nine Bows and repelled (them) in their (own) countries[172]

Two Ladies 3: *ir mꜣꜥt n psḏt sḥb rꜣ.w-pr rꜥ nb* (*ir maat en pesdjet, seheb rau-per ra neb*), Who has accomplished Maat for the Ennead and made (their) temples festive daily[173]

Two Ladies 4: [*wr-ḥbw-sd mi tꜣ-ṯnn*] *ptpt tḥnw m iwnw ḥr st.sn* ([*wer hebu-sed mi ta-tjenen,*] *petpet tjehenu em iunu her set.sen*), [Great of Sed festivals like Ta-tjenen,] who has trampled the Tehenu-Libyans into piles (of corpses) right there and then[174]

Golden Horus

Golden Horus 2: *wsr-rnpwt mi itmw ity mk kmt wꜥf ḫꜣswt* (*weser renput mi itemu, ity mek kemet, waf khasut*), Rich in years like Atum, the sovereign and protector of Egypt, who has subdued the foreign countries (Decree of Blessing of Ptah, KRI II, 262:8)

Golden Horus 3: *nṯri m pr.f m ḫt swḥt iḳrt sbḳt n ḥr-ꜣḫty* (*netjeri em per.ef em khet suhet iqeret sebqet en hor-akhty*), Divine as soon as[175] he emerged from the womb, the excellent and precious egg of Harakhty[176]

Golden Horus 4: *ꜥn tnr/ṯl m msw nṯrw nṯrywt ḳꜣb ꜥꜣbt.sn* (*an tener/tjel em mesu netjeru ntjeriut qab aabet.sen*), Beautiful and mighty, as the (very) progeny of gods and goddesses, who has doubled their offerings[177]

Golden Horus 5: *ḳn nb ḫpš ir tꜣš r mr.f m-sꜣ ḫftyw.f* (*qen neb khepesh ir tash er mer.ef em-sa kheftiu.ef*), The brave one, possessor of a strong arm, who has made (his) border as he wished, on the back of[178] his enemies[179]

171. From Ramses III's temple in the precinct of Mut, KRIV, 289:3.

172. From the western end of the First Court, exterior of the Second Pylon, KRI V, 37:10–11.

173. From the eastern end of the Second Court, KRI V, 314:8–9.

174. Lit. "in their places." From the northern end of the Second Court, KRI V, 20:14–15.

175. Lit. "when."

176. From the western end of the First Court, exterior of the Second Pylon, KRI V, 37:11.

177. From the eastern end of the Second Court, KRI V, 314:9.

178. Lit. "behind."

179. From the northern end of the Second Court, KRI V, 20:15–16.

Epithet added to the Throne name:

mry ỉmn (*mery imen*), Beloved of Amun

Epithet added to the Birth name:

ḥḳ3 ỉwnw (*heqa iunu*), Ruler of Heliopolis

3. Ramses IV[180]

Horus: *k3 nḫt ʿnḫ m m3ʿt nb ḥbw-sd mỉ ỉt.f ptḥ-t3-ṯnn* (*ka nakht ankh em maat neb hebu-sed mi it.ef ptah-ta-tjenen*), The victorious bull who lives on Maat, and lord of Sed festivals like his father Ptah-Ta-tjenen[181]

Two Ladies: *mk kmt wʿf pḏwt 9* (*mek kemet waf pedjut 9*), The protector of Egypt who has subdued the Nine Bows

Golden Horus: *wsr-rnpwt wr-nḫtw ỉty ms nṯrw sḫpr t3wy* (*weser renput, wer nakhtu, ity, mes netjeru, sekheper tawy*), Rich of years and great of victories, the sovereign whom the gods bore, who has created[182] the Two Lands[183]

Throne 1: *wsr m3ʿt rʿ* (*weser maat ra*), The strong one belonging to the Maat of Re

Throne 2: *ḥḳ3 m3ʿt rʿ* (*heqa maat ra*), The ruler of the Maat of Re[184]

Birth: *rʿ ms sw* (*ra mes su*), Re is the one who bore him

Epithets added to the Throne name:

stp. n ỉmn (*setep.en imen*), Whom Amun chose
stp. n ptḥ (*setep.en ptah*), Whom Ptah chose
stp. n rʿ (*setep.en ra*), Whom Re chose

Epithets added to the Birth name:

m3ʿty (*maaty*), The rightful one
ḥḳ3 m3ʿt mry ỉmn (*heqa maat, mery imen*), Ruler of Maat and beloved of Amun
stp.n ỉmn (*setep.en imen*), Whom Amun chose
stp.n ptḥ (*setep.en ptah*), Whom Ptah chose
stp.n rʿ (*setep.en ra*), Whom Re chose

---

180. Gauthier 1914, 178–90; von Beckerath 1999, 166–69. For a study of the titulary of Ramses IV, see Peden 1994, 14–15.

181. A short form of the name simply reads "The victorious bull who lives on Maat."

182. Lit. "caused to occur."

183. The phrases "the sovereign whom the gods bore, who has created the Two Lands" are additional.

184. From Regnal Year 2 on.

4. Ramses V[185]

Horus: *k3 nḫt mn-m3ʿt* (*ka nakht men maat*), Victorious bull, enduring of Maat
Two Ladies: not known
Golden Horus: *wsr-rnpwt mi itmw* (*weser renput mi itemu*), Rich in years like Atum
Throne: *wsr m3ʿt rʿ* (*weser maat ra*), The strong one belonging to the Maat of Re
Birth: *rʿ ms sw imn ḥr ḫpš.f* (*ra mes su, imen her khepesh.ef*), Re is the one who bore him, Amun is upon his strong arm

Epithet added to the Throne name:

sḫpr.n rʿ (*sekheper en ra*), The one whom Re has created

Epithet added to the Birth name:

mry imn (*mery imen*), Beloved of Amun

5. Ramses VI[186]

Horus: *k3 nḫt ʿ3-nḫtw sʿnḫ t3wy* (*ka nakht aa nakhtu, sankh tawy*), The victorious bull great of victories, who has sustained the Two Lands[187]
Two Ladies: *wsr-ḫpš hd ḥfnw* (*weser khepesh, hed hefnu*), The one great of strength who has attacked hundreds of thousands
Golden Horus: *wsr-rnpwt mi t3-ṯnn* (*weser renput mi ta-tjenen*), Rich in years like Ta-tjenen[188]
Throne: *nb m3ʿt rʿ* (*neb maat ra*), The possessor of the Maat of Re
Birth: *rʿ ms sw imn ḥr ḫpš.f* (*ra mes su, imen her khepesh.ef*), Re is the one who bore him, Amun is upon his strong arm

Epithet added to the Throne name:

mry imn (*mery imen*), Beloved of Amun

Epithet added to the Birth name:

nṯr ḥḳ3 iwnw (*netjer, heqa iunu*), The divine one and ruler of Heliopolis

---

185. Gauthier 1914, 191–94; von Beckerath 1999, 168–69.
186. Gauthier 1914, 194–202; von Beckerath 1999, 170–71.
187. The last phrase is an occasional addition.
188. This is sometimes expanded by the phrases *ity nb ḥbw-sd mk kmt*, "The sovereign, possessor of Sed festivals and protector of Egypt"; see Kitchen 1987, 138 n. 4, for the references.

6. Ramses VII[189]

Original titulary

Horus: *kꜣ nḫt ꜥn m nsw* (*ka nakht an em nesu*), Victorious bull, beautiful as king

Two Ladies: *mk kmt wꜥf ḫꜣstyw* (*mek kemet, waf khastiu*), The protector of Egypt who has subdued the foreigners[190]

Golden Horus: *wsr-rnpwt mỉ ỉtmw* (*weser renput mi itemu*), Rich in years like Atum[191]

Throne: *wsr mꜣꜥt rꜥ* (*weser maat ra*), The strong one belonging to the Maat of Re

Birth: *rꜥ ms sw ỉt.ỉ ỉmn* (*ra mes su, it(.i) imen*), Re is the one who bore him, Amun is my father

Additional names

Horus 2: *kꜣ nḫt rꜥ nfr-ḥr* (*ka nakht ra, nefer her*), The victorious bull of Re, beautiful of face[192]

Two Ladies 2: *mk kmt wꜥf pḏwt <9?>* (*mek kemet waf pedjut <9?>*), The protector of Egypt, who has subdued the <Nine?> Bows[193]

Golden Horus 2: *wsr-rnpwt mỉ ỉmn* (*weser renput mi imen*), Rich in years like Amun[194]

Epithet added to the Throne name:

stp n rꜥ mry ỉmn (*setep en ra, mery imen*), Chosen by Re and beloved of Amun

Epithet added to the Birth name:

nṯr ḥḳꜣ ỉwnw (*netjer, heqa iunu*), The divine one and ruler of Heliopolis

7. Ramses VIII[195]

Horus: not known

---

189. Gauthier 1914, 202–04; von Beckerath 1999, 170–73.

190. Compare the original Two Ladies name of Ramses II.

191. This is sometimes expanded by the phrases *ỉty wr-ḥbw-sd mỉ ỉmn-rꜥ nsw nṯrw*, "The sovereign, great of Sed festivals like Amun-Re, King of the gods"; see Kitchen 1987, 138 n. 5, for the references.

192. From a statue found in the Ptah enclosure in Memphis. An epithet was added after the *serekh*: *nb ḥbw-sd mỉ ỉt.f ptḥ-tꜣ-ṯnn*, "Possessor of Sed festivals like his father Ptah-tatjenen"; see KRI VI, 385:3. An additional Horus name from Tell el-Yehudiyeh mentioned by von Beckerath (1999, 170–71 [H3]), *kꜣ nḫt ꜥn m nṯr*, "Victorious bull, beautiful as a god,"is simply the king's original Horus name; see KRIVI, 380:5–6.

193. From the king's tomb in the Valley of the Kings; see KRIVI, 386:8.

194. From a papyrus now in the Louvre (E 8419, for which see Bellion 1987, 221); see KRIVI, 397:3.

195. Gauthier 1914, 205–6; von Beckerath 1999, 172–73.

Two Ladies: not known
Golden Horus: not known
Throne: *wsr mꜣꜥt rꜥ* (*weser maat ra*), The strong one of the Maat of Re
Birth: *rꜥ ms sw stẖ ḥr ḫpš.f* (*ra mes su, seth her khepesh.ef*), Re is the one who bore him, Seth is upon his strong arm

Epithet added to the Throne name:

ꜣḫ n imn (*akh en imen*), Beneficial to Amun

Epithet added to the Birth name:

mry imn (*mery imen*), Beloved of Amun

8. Ramses IX[196]

Horus: *kꜣ nḫt ḫꜥ m wꜣst* (*ka nakht kha em waset*), The victorious bull who has appeared in Thebes
Two Ladies: *wsr-ḫpš sꜥnḫ tꜣwy* (*weser khepesh, sankh tawy*), Powerful of sword, who has sustained the Two Lands
Golden Horus: *wsr-rnpwt mi tꜣ-ṯnn ity wr-nsyt dr pḏwt 9* (*weser renput mi ta-tjenen, ity wer nesyt, der pedjut 9*), Rich in years like Ta-tjenen, the sovereign great of kingship who has repelled the Nine Bows[197]
Throne: *nfr kꜣ rꜥ* (*nefer ka ra*), The perfect one of the ka of Re[198]
Birth: *rꜥ ms sw ḫꜥ m wꜣst* (*ra mes su, kha em waset*), Re is the one who bore him, the one who has appeared in Thebes

Epithets added to the Throne name:

mry mꜣꜥt (*mery maat*), Beloved of Maat[199]
nṯr nfr (*netjer nefer*), Perfect god
stp.n rꜥ (*setep.en ra*), Whom Re chose

Epithets added to the Birth name:

mry imn (*mery imen*), Beloved of Amun
mrr imn (*merrer imen*), Whom Amun continually loves

196. Gauthier 1914, 206–16; von Beckerath 1999, 172–73.

197. A second Golden Horus name from a fragmentary wooden box (von Beckerath 1999, 172–73 [G2]), *wsr-rnpwt mi rꜥ ḏt*, "Rich in years like Re forever," was erroneously suggested by E. A. W. Budge (1896, 350). See KRI VI, 462:15; and Dodson and Reeves (1988, 224 n. 10), who properly restore the king's original Golden Horus name.

198. A slightly different rendering of the name, with the word *kꜣ* pluralized (hence *nfr kꜣw rꜥ*) is found on a stela (Stewart 1976, pl. 45:4), which was perhaps simply a scribal error.

199. So KRI VI, 523 (26), contra von Beckerath's *mry imn*, "Beloved of Amun" (1999, 172–73 [T4]).

9. Ramses X[200]

Original titulary

Horus: *k3 nḫt sḫʿ.n rʿ* (*ka nakht sekha.en ra*), The victorious bull whom Re has caused to appear[201]
Two Ladies: *ʿ3 ////* (*aa-////*), Great of ////[202]
Golden Horus: */// sḫpr t3wy* (*//// sekheper tawy*), ///, who has created[203] the Two Lands[204]
Throne: *ḫpr m3ʿt rʿ* (*kheper maat ra*), The (very) manifestation of the Maat of Re
Birth: *rʿ ms sw ỉmn ḥr ḫpš.f* (*ra mes su, imen her khepesh.ef*), Re is the one who bore him, Amun is upon his strong arm

Additional name

Throne Name 2: *ḫpr m3ʿt n rʿ* (*kheper maat en ra*), The (very) manifestation of the Maat of Re[205]

Epithets added to the Throne name:

mry ỉmn (*mery imen*), Beloved of Amun
stp n rʿ (*setep en ra*), Chosen by Re

Epithet added to the Birth name:

mry ỉmn (*mery imen*), Beloved of Amun

10. Ramses XI[206]

Horus: *k3 nḫt mry rʿ* (*ka nakht mery ra*), Victorious bull, beloved of Re
Two Ladies: *wsr-ḫpš hd ḥfnw* (*weser khepesh, hed hefnu*), The one great of strength who has attacked hundreds of thousands
Golden Horus: *wr-pḥty sʿnḫ t3wy ỉty hr ḥr m3ʿt sḥtp t3wy* (*wer pehty, sankh tawy, ity her her maat, sehetep tawy*), The one great of strength who has sustained the Two Lands, the sovereign who is pleased with Maat and has reconciled the Two Lands

200. Gauthier 1914, 216–19; von Beckerath 1999, 174–75.

201. A reduplicated form of the verb *sḫʿʿ* is found on both outer jambs of the king's tomb (see von Beckerath 1999, 174–75; and KRI VI, 679:13), in which case one would be tempted to render "The victorious bull whom Re is (continually) causing to appear." However, the verb form used is a *sḏm(w).n.f*, which is a past relative tense, so a translation with a past tense is best.

202. KRI VI, 679:13, from the same outer jamb text mentioned in the previous note.

203. Lit. "caused to occur."

204. From a sphinx found at Karnak; see KRI VI, 679:3.

205. The same as the original Throne name, with the added indirect genitive marker.

206. Gauthier 1914, 219–24; von Beckerath 1999, 174–75.

Throne: *mn m3ʿt rʿ* (*men maat ra*), The established one belonging to the Maat of Re
Birth: *rʿ ms sw ḫʿ m w3st* (*ra mes su, kha em waset*), Re is the one who bore him, the one who has appeared in Thebes

Epithets added to the Throne name:

sḫm stp n ptḥ (*sekhem, setep en ptah*), The powerful one who was chosen by Ptah
stp n ptḥ (*setep en ptah*), Chosen by Ptah

Epithets added to the Birth name:

mry ỉmn nṯr ḥḳ3 ỉwnw (*mery imen, netjer, heqa iunu*), Beloved of Amun, the divine one and ruler of Heliopolis
mrr ỉmn nṯr ḥḳ3 ỉwnw (*merrer imen, netjer, heqa iunu*), Whom Amun (continually) loves, the divine one and ruler of Heliopolis

VIII

Third Intermediate Period

Dynasty 21 (1069–945 b.c.e.)[1]

With the death of Ramses XI, a new set of rulers claimed the throne and established themselves at Tanis, north of the previous residence of Per-Ramses. Its first king was Smendes, who may have been married to one of Ramses XI's daughters. The Tanite kings recognized the semi-independent power of the High Priests of Amun in Thebes, and this tenuous relationship was maintained through various marriage ties. Egypt suffered more internal difficulties at this time, including the ongoing robbing of the royal tombs in the Valley of the Kings, which forced the Theban authorities to collect the royal mummies and rebury them in a cliff tomb at Deir el-Bahari (DB 320).

As king, Herihor used a number of epithets that stressed his building activities at Karnak Temple, as befitted his original role of High Priest of Amun,[2] a position perfectly expressed in his unusual Throne name "High Priest of Amun." Smendes was the first to call himself the Dual King *ḥḏ ḫpr rʿ*, "the dazzling one is the manifestation of Re," a phrase that would be subsequently used by a number of Third Intermediate period kings for their Throne names. Following his New Kingdom forebears, he also used a number of aggressive epithets, although he was not specific about which enemy he would strike down. Psusennes I borrowed heavily from earlier kings for his own titulary. He appropriated the phrases *wsr f3w*, "rich in splendor," and *sḫʿ m w3st*, "the one who has been made to appear in Thebes" from Amenhotep II's Two Ladies name; the epithet *w3ḥ-nsyt mi rʿ m pt*, "enduring of kingship like Re in heaven" from Thutmose III's Two Ladies name,[3] the expression *iṯ m sḫm.f m t3w nbw*, "the one who has seized with his strong arm in all lands" from Amenhotep II's Golden Horus name; and the equally aggressive *dr pḏwt 9*, "the one who has repelled the Nine Bows" from Sety II's Two Ladies name. He also modified Thutmose II's Throne name, *ʿ3 ḫpr*

1. The royal texts from Dynasty 21 have been collected in Jansen-Winkeln 2007a; a collection of texts from the period is translated in Ritner 2009, 81–172. For a new study of the Third Intermediate Period, see Dodson 2012.

2. Bonhême 1987, 31.

3. This is from Thutmose III's titulary as sole king.

n rʿ, "the great one is the manifestation of Re," for his own Throne name, *ʿꜣ ḫpr rʿ*, by simply removing the indirect genitive marker *n* from the phrase; the same expression would be used by Osorkon the Elder a few reigns later. And King Amenemope followed the well-established tradition of calling himself the Dual King *wsr mꜣʿt rʿ*, "the strong one belonging to the Maat of Re," after the famous Ramses II.

The order of the names presented here follows that of Peter A. Clayton.[4]

1. Herihor[5]

1. As High Priest

ḥm nṯr tpy n imn-rʿ nsw-nṯrw imy-r mšʿ wr n šmʿw mḥw ḥꜣwty ḥry-ḥr (*hem netjer tepy en imen-ra nesu-netjeru, imy-er mesha wer en shemau mehu, hawty hery hor*), The High Priest of Amun-Re, king of the gods, the great overseer of the army of the south and north and leader, Herihor ("A superior one is Horus")

2. As king

Original titulary

Horus: *kꜣ nḫt sꜣ imn* (*ka nakht sa imen*), Victorious bull and son of Amun
Two Ladies: *sḥtp nṯrw ḳd ḥwt.sn ir hrrt kꜣw.sn* (*sehetep netjeru, qed hut.sen, ir herreret kau.sen*), The one who has satisfied the gods (by) building their temples and who has accomplished what pleases their kas
Golden Horus: *ir ꜣḫwt m ipt-swt n it.f imn ḳmꜣ nfrw.f* (*ir akhut em ipet-sut en it.ef imen, qema neferu.ef*), The one who has accomplished benefits in Karnak for his father Amun, who created his (the king's) perfection
Throne: *ḥm nṯr tpy n imn* (*hem netjer tepy en imen*), High Priest of Amun
Birth: *ḥry ḥr* (*hery hor*), A superior one is Horus

Additional names[6]

Horus 2: *kꜣ nḫt sꜣ imn ir mnw ḥr mnḫt n ms s(w)* (*ka nakht sa imen, ir menu her menkhet en mes s(u)*), Victorious bull and son of Amun, who has made monuments owing to[7] the splendor of the one who bore him
Horus 3: *kꜣ nḫt sꜣ imn wr-ꜣḫwt m ipt-swt* (*ka nakht sa imen, wer akhut em ipet-sut*), Victorious bull and son of Amun, great of benefits in Ipet-sut

4. Clayton 1994, 178.

5. Gauthier 1914, 232–40; von Beckerath 1999, 176–77.

6. All from the temple of Khonsu, in the southern portion of the Karnak Temple complex; see Bonhême 1987, 27–29.

7. Lit. "on account of."

Two Ladies 2: *swꜥb bnbn mḥ sw m mnw sṯḥnt mi ꜣḫt im.s* (*sewab benben, meh su em menu setjehenet mi akhet im.es*), The one who has purified the Benenet[8] and filled it with monuments that gleam like the horizon which is within it

Two Ladies 3: *sḥb wꜣst m mnw wrw* (*seheb waset em menu weru*), The one who has made Thebes festive with great monuments

Two Ladies 4: *wsr-ḫpš ꜥnḫ tꜣwy* (*weser khepesh, ankh tawy*), Powerful of arm, the (very) life of the Two Lands

Golden Horus 2: *ir mꜣꜥt m-ḫt tꜣwy di ḥtp nṯrw nbw m itrt.sn* (*ir maat em-khet tawy, di hetep netjeru nebu em iteret.sen*), The one who has rendered justice[9] throughout the Two Lands and caused all the gods to be satisfied with their shrines

Epithets added to the Birth name:

sꜣ imn (*sa imen*), Son of Amun
mry imn (*mery imen*), Beloved of Amun

2. Nes-ba-neb-djed (Smendes)[10]

Horus: *kꜣ nḫt mry rꜥ swsr imn ḫpš.f r sḳꜣ mꜣꜥt* (*ka nakht mery ra, seweser imen khepesh.ef er seqa maat*), Victorious bull, beloved of Re, whose arm Amun has strengthened in order to offer up[11] Maat

Two Ladies: *sḫm-pḥty ḥwi rḳiw.f bhꜣ.tw.f ḥpt m ////* (*sekhem pehty, hui reqiu.ef beha.tu.ef, hepet em ////*), Powerful of might, who has struck down his opponents who flee from him, who has embraced by means of[12] ///

Golden Horus: /// *ḫsf dndn* (/// *khesef denden*), /// who drove away anger

Throne: *ḥḏ ḫpr rꜥ* (*hedj kheper ra*), The dazzling one is the (very) manifestation of Re

Birth: *n(y)-sw bꜣ-nb-ḏd* (*ni-su ba-neb-djed*), He belongs to the ram, the lord of Mendes

Epithet added to the Throne name:

stp n rꜥ (*setep en ra*), Chosen by Re

Epithet added to the Birth name:

mry imn (*mery imen*), Beloved of Amun

---

8. *bnbn* written for *bnnt*, the temple of Khonsu at Karnak, where this text was found. For the identification, see von Beckerath 1999, 176 n. 2; and PM II², 224.

9. Lit. "accomplished Maat."

10. Gauthier 1914, 287–88; von Beckerath 1999, 178–79.

11. Lit. "make high"; for the interpretation of "offering up," see Grimal 1986, 296 n. 934.

12. Or "in."

3. Amen-em-nisu[13]

Horus: none known
Two Ladies: none known
Golden Horus: none known
Throne: *nfr kꜣ rꜥ* (*nefer ka ra*), The perfect one is the (very) ka of Re
Birth: *ỉmn m nsw* (*imen em nesu*), Amun is king

Epithet added to the Throne name:

ḥkꜣ wꜣst (*heqa waset*), Ruler of Thebes

Epithet added to the Birth name:

mry ỉmn (*mery imen*), Beloved of Amun

4. Pa-seba-kha-en-niut (Psusennes) I[14]

Horus: *kꜣ nḫt m dd ỉmn wsr-fꜣw sḫꜥ m wꜣst* (*ka nakht em ded imen, weser fau, sekha em waset*), Victorious bull through the gift of Amun, rich in splendor, who has been made to appear in Thebes
Two Ladies: *wr-mnw m ỉpt-swt nb pḥty wꜥf tꜣwy wꜣḥ-nsyt mỉ rꜥ m pt* (*wer menu em ipet-sut, neb pehty, waf tawy, wah nesyt mi ra em pet*), Great of monuments in Karnak, the possessor of might who has subdued the Two Lands, the one enduring of kingship like Re in heaven
Golden Horus: *smꜣ tꜣw*[15] *dr pḏwt 9 ỉṯ m sḫm.f m tꜣw nbw* (*sema tau, der pedjut 9, itj em sekhem.ef em tau nebu*), Who has united lands, repelled the Nine Bows, and seized with his strong arm in all lands
Throne: *ꜥꜣ ḫpr rꜥ* (*aa kheper ra*), The great one is a manifestation of Re
Birth: *pꜣ sbꜣ ḫꜥ n nỉwt* (*pa seba kha en niut*), The star who has appeared in Niut (i.e., Thebes)

Additional Birth name:

Birth 2: *rꜥ ms sw <mry> ỉmn pꜣ sbꜣ ḫꜥ n nỉwt* (*ra mes su, <mery> imen, pa seba kha en niut*), Ramses, <beloved of> Amun, the star who has appeared in Thebes[16]

Epithet added to the Birth name:

mry ỉmn (*mery imen*), Beloved of Amun

---

13. Von Beckerath 1999, 178–79.

14. Gauthier 1914, 289–91; von Beckerath 1999, 178–79.

15. The word could also be read as *ḫprw*, "manifestations." The belligerent nature of the epithets, however, would seem to favor "lands," notwithstanding the repetition of the word within a single string of phrases; cf. Bonhême 1987, 66–67, and the references there.

16. From a ring and a fragmentary relief found at Tanis; see Bonhême 1987, 72 nn. 3–4; and Jansen-Winkeln 2007a, 60 (4.98).

Title added to the Birth name:

> *ḥm nṯr tpy n imn* (*hem netjer tepy en imen*), High Priest of Amun

Epithets added to the Throne name:

> *stp n imn* (*setep en imen*), Chosen by Amun
> *mry imn* (*mery imen*), Beloved of Amun
> *stp n mꜣꜥt* (*setep en maat*), Chosen by Maat
> *stp n stẖ* (*setep en setekh*), Chosen by Seth[17]

5. Amenemope[18]

Horus: none known
Two Ladies: none known
Golden Horus: none known
Throne: *wsr mꜣꜥt rꜥ (weser maat ra),* The strong one belonging to the Maat of Re
Birth: *imn m ipt* (*imen em ipet*), Amun is in Ipet (i.e., Luxor)

Epithet added to the Throne name:

> *stp n imn* (*setep en imen*), Chosen by Amun

Epithet added to the Birth name:

> *mry imn* (*mery imen*), Beloved of Amun

Title added to the Birth name:

> *nsw-bity ḥm nṯr tpy n imn-rꜥ nsw nṯrw* (*nesu-bity, hem netjer tepy en imen-ra nesu netjeru*), Dual King and High Priest of Amun-Re, king of the gods

6. Osorkon (the Elder)[19]

Horus: none known
Two Ladies: none known
Golden Horus: none known
Throne: *ꜥꜣ ḫpr rꜥ* (*aa kheper ra*), The great one is a manifestation of Re
Birth: *wsrkn* (*weserken*), Osorkon[20]

Epithet added to the Throne name:

> *stp.n rꜥ* (*setep.en ra*), The one whom Re chose

---

17. An additional epithet tentatively suggested by Bonhême 1987, 70.
18. Gauthier 1914, 292–93; von Beckerath 1999, 180–81.
19. Gauthier 1914, 399–400; von Beckerath 1999, 180–81.
20. On the name, see Bonhême 1987, 149.

7. SIAMUN[21]

Horus: *k3 nḫt mry m3ʿt s3 [mry]*[22] *n imn pr m ḥʿw.f* (*ka nakht mery maat, sa [mery] en imen, per em haw.ef*), Victorious bull, beloved of Maat, the [beloved] son of Amun, who issued from his limbs
Two Ladies: none known
Golden Horus: none known
Throne: *nṯri ḫpr rʿ* (*netjeri kheper ra*), The divine one is a manifestation of Re
Birth: *s3 imn* (*sa imen*), Son of Amun

Epithets added to the Throne name:

stp n imn (*setep en imen*), Chosen by Amun
mry imn (*mery imen*), Beloved of Amun

Epithet added to the Birth name:

mry imn (*mery imen*), Beloved of Amun
mry rʿ (*mery ra*), Beloved of Re

Title added to the Birth name:

nsw (*nesu*), King

8. PA-SEBA-KHA-EN-NIUT (PSUSENNES) II[23]

Horus: none known
Two Ladies: none known
Golden Horus: none known
Throne: *tit ḫprw rʿ* (*tit kheperu ra*), The (very) image of the manifestations of Re
Birth: *p3 sb3 ḫʿ n niwt* (*pa seba kha en niut*), The star who has appeared in Niut[24]

Epithet added to the Birth name:

mry imn (*mery imen*), Beloved of Amun

Epithet added to the Throne name:

stp n rʿ (*setep en ra*), Chosen by Re

Title added to the Birth name:

ḥr (*hor*), The Horus

21. Gauthier 1914, 294–98; von Beckerath 1999, 180–81.
22. Or perhaps *smsw* (*semsu*), "eldest," for which see Bonhême 1987, 88.
23. Gauthier 1914, 301–2; von Beckerath 1999, 180–81.
24. Lit. "the City," a designation of Thebes.

Dynasty 21a

Additional High Priests of Amun who took on royal titularies.

1. Pinodjem I[25]

1. As High Priest

ỉmy-r niwt ṯ3ty ḥm nṯr tpy n ỉmn-rʿ nsw nṯrw ỉmy-r mšʿ wr n t3 r-ḏr.f ḥ3wty p3y nḏm (*imy-er niut, tjaty, hem netjer tepy en imen-ra nesu netjeru, imy-er mesha wer en ta er-djer.ef, hauty, pay nedjem*), The overseer of Niut (i.e., Thebes) and vizier, the High Priest of Amun-Re, king of the gods, the great overseer of the army of the entire land and leader, Pinodjem ("The sweet one")

2. As king

Original titulary

Horus: *k3 nḫt mry ỉmn* (*ka nakht mery imen*), Victorious bull, beloved of Amun
Two Ladies: none known
Golden Horus: none known
Throne: *ḫʿ ḫpr rʿ* (*kha kheper ra*), The (very) appearance of the manifestation of Re[26]
Birth: *p3y nḏm* (*pay nedjem*), The sweet one

Additional names

Horus 2: *k3 nḫt ḫʿ m w3st* (*ka nakht kha em waset*), Victorious bull who has appeared in Thebes[27]
Horus 3: *ḥk3 t3wy wr-nḫtw* (*heqa tawy, wer nakhtu*), Ruler of the Two Lands and great of victories
Horus 4: *ʿ3-pḥty nb šfyt* (*aa pehty, neb shefyt*), Great of might and possessor of majesty[28]

Epithet added to the Throne name:

stp n ỉmn (*setep en imen*), Chosen by Amun

Epithet added to the Birth name:

mry ỉmn (*mery imen*), Beloved of Amun

---

25. Gauthier 1914, 250–52; von Beckerath 1999, 182–83.

26. The name has also been read *ḫpr ḫʿ rʿ* (*kheper kha ra*), "The appearance of Re manifests (itself)," by von Beckerath 1999, 182.

27. From the chapel of Osiris Neb-Ankh at North Karnak; see Jansen-Winkeln 2007a, 6.

28. These two additional Horus names are from the Hypostyle Hall of the temple of Khonsu at Karnak; see Jansen-Winkeln 2007a, 15 (3.18).

2. Menkheperre[29]

1. As High Priest

ḥm nṯr tpy n imn-rꜥ nsw-nṯrw imy-r mšꜥ wr mn ḫpr rꜥ (*hem netjer tepy en imen-ra nesu-netjeru, imy-er mesha wer, men kheper ra*), The High Priest of Amun-Re, king of the gods, and great overseer of the army, "The established one of the manifestation of Re"

2. As king

Horus: none known
Two Ladies: none known
Golden Horus: none known
Throne: *ḥm nṯr tpy n imn* (*hem netjer tepy en imen*), High Priest of Amun
Birth: *mn ḫpr rꜥ* (*men kheper ra*), The established one of the manifestation of Re

3. Pa-seba-kha-en-niut (Psusennes) III[30]

1. As High Priest

ḥm nṯr tpy n imn-rꜥ nsw-nṯrw pꜣ sbꜣ ḫꜥ n niwt (*hem netjer tepy en imen-ra nesu-netjeru, pa seba kha en niut*), The High Priest of Amun-Re, king of the gods, "The star who has appeared in Thebes"

Epithets added to the title:

ir hpw nfrw n kmt ḥꜣwty (*n*) *pr-ꜥꜣ* (*ir hepu neferu en kemet, hauty (en) per-aa*), Who has made perfect laws for Egypt, a leader (for) Pharaoh[31]
mry imn (*mery imen*), Beloved of Amun

2. As king

Horus: none known
Two Ladies: none known
Golden Horus: none known
Throne: *tit ḫprw rꜥ* (*tit kheperu ra*), The (very) image of the manifestations of Re
Birth: *ḥm nṯr tpy n imn pꜣ sbꜣ ḫꜥ n niwt* (*hem netjer tepy en imen, pa seba kha en niut*), The High Priest of Amun, "The star who has appeared in Thebes"

Epithet added to the Throne name:

stp n imn (*setep en imen*), Chosen by Amun

29. Gauthier 1914, 263–74; von Beckerath 1999, 182–83.
30. Von Beckerath 1999, 182–83.
31. Or perhaps "leader and Pharaoh," without the added preposition; see Bonhême 1987, 77.

Epithet added to the Birth name:

mry ỉmn (*mery imen*), Beloved of Amun

Dynasty 22 (945–712 B.C.E.)[32]

The Twenty-Second Dynasty is a line of kings who were descendants of the "Great Chiefs of the Meshwesh," a Libyan tribe. They were military commanders who had been prisoners of war settled into Egypt by Ramses III. Ruling from Tanis, Sheshonq I was powerful enough to intervene in the affairs of the Levant; a great gateway at Karnak Temple shows reliefs commemorating his victory. Osorkon II constructed a portal at Bubastis to honor the Sed festival he celebrated in his twenty-fourth year. An independent line of High Priests of Amun ruled Upper Egypt from Thebes. The latter were often related to the Tanite rulers by blood or marriage ties.

The Twenty-Second Dynasty kings generally did not show a great deal of imagination in choosing their titulary. No fewer than four kings appropriated the expression *ḥḏ ḫpr rʿ*, "the dazzling one is a manifestation of Re," from Smendes, while others simply modified the epithet by calling themselves "the great one" (*ʿ3*), "the true one" (*m3ʿ*), "the ruler" (*ḥḳ3*), "the powerful one" (*sḫm*), and "the (very) image" (*twt*) of "the manifestation of Re." Additionally, Osorkon II, Takelot II, and Sheshonq V claimed to have "appeared in Thebes" (*ḫʿ m w3st*), reflecting Thutmose III's Horus name. However, a number of them did seem to be aware of a mission of sorts, as they maintained they had been made to "appear as kings" (*sḫʿ m nsw*) or had been "put on the throne" (*rdỉ ḥr nst*) in order to "unite" (*sm3*), "establish" (*grg*), or "restore" (*spd*) the Two Lands.[33] One recurring phrase that is unique is the king's declaration of an association with the god Horus as the son of Isis.[34] Sheshonq I and Osorkon I professed to have "struck down" (*ḥwỉ*) or "repelled" (*dr*) the generic Nine Bows, respectively, but only Osorkon II claimed to have specifically "struck down" (*ḥwỉ*) the Mentjyu-bedouin.

As with the previous Intermediate period, the order of kings in a given dynasty is sometimes difficult to establish with any certainty. Unless otherwise noted, the order of kings presented here follows that of Clayton.[35]

32. The royal texts from Dynasties 22–24 have been collected in Jansen-Winkeln 2007b; a collection of texts from the period can be found in Ritner 2009, 173–448.

33. Sheshonq I, Osorkon I, and Osorkon II, respectively.

34. On the motif of the king's affiliation with a divine child in this period, see Bonhême and Forgeau 1988, 315.

35. Clayton 1994, 185.

1. Sheshonq I[36]

Original titulary

Horus: *kȝ nḫt mry rʿ sḫʿ.f m nsw r smȝ tȝwy* (*ka nakht mery ra, sekha.ef em nesu er sema tawy*), Victorious bull, beloved of Re, whom the latter caused to appear as king in order to unite the Two Lands

Two Ladies: *ḫʿ m sḫmty mi ḥr sȝ ȝst sḥtp nṯrw m mȝʿt* (*kha em sekhemty mi hor sa aset sehetep netjeru em maat*), Who has appeared in the Double Crown like Horus, the son of Isis, and pacified the gods with Maat

Golden Horus: *sḫm-pḥty ḥwi pḏwt 9 wr-nḫtw m tȝw nbw* (*sekhem pehty, hui pedjut 9, wer nakhtu em tau nebu*), Powerful of might, who has struck down the Nine Bows, great of victories in all lands

Throne: *ḥḏ ḫpr rʿ* (*hedj kheper ra*), The dazzling one[37] is a manifestation of Re

Birth: *ššnḳ* (*sheshenеq*), Sheshonq

Additional name

Golden Horus 2: /// *sṯtyw* (/// *setjetiu*), [/// who has struck down/repelled?] the Setjetiu-Asiatics[38]

Epithets added to the Throne name:

stp n rʿ (*setep en ra*), Chosen by Re
stp n imn (*setep en imen*), Chosen by Amun
stp n ptḥ (*setep en ptah*), Chosen by Ptah

Epithets added to the Birth name:

mry imn (*mery imen*), Beloved of Amun
sȝ ȝst mry imn (*sa aset, mery imen*), The son of Isis, beloved of Amun

2. Osorkon I[39]

Horus: *kȝ nḫt mry rʿ rdi.n sw itmw ḥr nst.f r grg tȝwy* (*ka nakht mry ra, redi.en su itemu her neset.ef er gereg tawy*), Victorious bull beloved of Re, whom Atum put on his throne in order to establish the Two Lands

Two Ladies: *sʿȝ ḫprw wr-biȝwt* (*saa kheperu, wer biaut*), The one who has magnified (his) manifestations is one great of marvels

Golden Horus: *nḫt-ḫpš dr pḏwt 9 ity iṯ tȝw nbw* (*nakht khepesh, der pedjut 9, ity, itj tau nebu*), The strong-armed one who has repelled the Nine Bows, the sovereign who has seized all lands

36. Gauthier 1914, 307–24; von Beckerath 1999, 184–85.
37. Lit. "bright."
38. From a block found at Herakleopolis; see Meffre 2010.
39. Gauthier 1914, 324–32; von Beckerath 1999, 184–85.

Throne: *sḫm ḫpr rꜥ* (*sekhem kheper ra*), The powerful one is a manifestation of Re
Birth: *wsrkn* (*weserken*), Osorkon

Epithet added to the Throne name:

stp.n rꜥ (*setep.en ra*), The one whom Re chose

Epithet added to the Birth name:

mry ỉmn (*mery imen*), Chosen by Amun

3. Sheshonq IIa[40]

Horus: none known
Two Ladies: none known
Golden Horus: none known
Throne: *ḥḳ3 ḫpr rꜥ* (*heqa kheper ra*), The ruler is the (very) manifestation of Re
Birth: *šš<nḳ>* (*shesh<eneq>*) Shesh<onq>

Epithet added to the Throne name:

stp.n rꜥ (*setep.en ra*), The one whom Re chose

Epithet added to the Birth name:

mry ỉmn (*mery imen*), Beloved of Amun

4. Sheshonq IIb[41]

Horus: none known
Two Ladies: none known
Golden Horus: none known
Throne: *twt ḫpr rꜥ* (*tut kheper ra*), The (very) image of the manifestation of Re
Birth: *ššnḳ* (*sheshenéq*), Sheshonq

Epithet added to the Throne name:

[*stp*] *n* [*rꜥ/ỉmn ?*] ([*setep] en [ra/imen]*), [Chosen] by [Re/Amun]

Epithet added to the Birth name:

mry ỉmn (*mery imen*), Beloved of Amun

---

40. Von Beckerath 1999, 186–87. For the renumbering of the kings named Sheshonq, see Broekman et al. 2008; for his reign, see Broekman 2000.

41. For this newly discovered king, see Lange 2004; Aston 2009, 4, and the references there.

5. Takelot I[42]

Horus: none known
Two Ladies: none known
Golden Horus: none known
Throne: *ḥḏ ḫpr rꜥ* (*hedj kheper ra*), The dazzling one is the (very) manifestation of Re
Birth: *tklt* (*tekelet*), Takelot

Epithet added to the Throne name:

stp n rꜥ (*setep en ra*), Chosen by Re

Epithet added to the Birth name:

mry imn (*mery imen*), Beloved of Amun

6. Osorkon II[43]

Original titulary

Horus: *kꜣ nḫt ḫꜥ m wꜣst* (*ka nakht kha em waset*), The victorious bull who has appeared in Thebes
Two Ladies: *smꜣ psšty mi sꜣ ꜣst dmḏ.f sḫmty m ḥtp* (*sema peseshty mi sa aset demedj.ef sekhemty em hetep*), The one who has united the Two Portions[44] like the son of Isis has assembled[45] the two crowns in peace
Golden Horus: *wr pḥty ḥwi mnṯyw* (*wer pehty, hui mentjyu*), The mighty great one who has struck down the bedouin
Throne: *wsr mꜣꜥt rꜥ* (*weser maat ra*), The strong one belonging to the Maat of Re
Birth: *wsrkn sꜣ bꜣstt* (*weserken, sa bastet*), Osorkon, the son of Bastet

Additional names

From a block found at the Sixth Pylon at Karnak[46]
Horus 2: *kꜣ nḫt mry mꜣꜥt sḫꜥ sw rꜥ r nsw tꜣwy* (*ka nakht mery maat, sekha su ra er nesu tawy*), Victorious bull, beloved of Maat, whom Re caused to appear to be king of the Two Lands
Two Ladies 2: *smꜣ psšty mi sꜣ ꜣst dmḏ.n.f sḫmty m ḥtp dhn ///* (*sema peseshty mi sa aset demedj.en.ef sekhemty em hetep, dehen ///*), The one who has united

42. Von Beckerath 1999, 186–87.
43. Gauthier 1914, 335–47; von Beckerath 1999, 186–89.
44. That is, of the country.
45. Lit. "he has assembled."
46. Jansen-Winkeln 2007b, 118–19 (18.29); for a discussion of these additional names, see Bonhême 1987, 153–60.

the Two Portions like the son of Isis has assembled the two crowns in peace, whom [god X] appointed ///[47]

Golden Horus 2: *wr pḥty ḥwi mnṯyw wsr ///* (*wer pehty, hui mentjyu, weser ///*), The mighty great one who has struck down the bedouin, rich [in splendor?]

Usurped statue of Senwosret III, from Tell el Muqdam (Leontopolis)[48]

Horus 3: */// m nsw r spd t3wy* (*/// em nesu er seped tawy*), /// as king in order to restore the Two Lands

Golden Horus 3: */// dr pḏwt ity sḫm m t3w nbw* (*/// der pedjut, ity, sekhem em tau nebu*), /// who has repelled the (foreign) bowmen, the mighty sovereign in all lands

Granite naos from Bubastis[49]

Two Ladies 3: *sm3 psšty mi s3 3st sḥtp nṯrw m irt m3ʿt* (*sema peseshty mi sa aset, sehetep netjeru em iret maat*), The one who has united the Two Portions like the son of Isis has satisfied the gods by performing Maat

Statue from Tanis[50]

Golden Horus 4: *sḫm pḥty ḥwi ḫftyw.f wsr-f3w* (*sekhem pehty, hui kheftyu.ef, weser fau*), The mighty powerful one who has struck down his enemies is rich in splendor

Queen's statue from Tell Basta[51]

Golden Horus 5: *wr-pḥty ḏr sṯtyw wsr-f3w m t3w nbw* (*wer pehty, der setjetiu, weser fau em tau nebu*), The great of strength one who has repelled the Setjetiu-Asiatics is rich in splendor in all lands

Epithets added to the Throne name:

stp n imn (*setep en imen*), Chosen by Amun
stp n rʿ (*setep en ra*), Chosen by Re

Epithet added to the Birth name:

mry imn (*mery imen*), Beloved of Amun

---

47. Also seen on a statuette from the Karnak Cachette; Jansen-Winkeln 2007b, 133–34 (18.73).

48. Jansen-Winkeln 2007b, 116–17 (18.21).

49. Ibid., 115 (18.16).

50. Ibid., 108–9 (18.3); this object also contains the previous Two Ladies name.

51. See Meffre 2010, 228 n. 42, and the references there.

7. Takelot II[52]

Horus: *k3 nḫt ḫ^c m w3st* (*ka nakht kha em waset*), The victorious bull who has appeared in Thebes
Two Ladies: none known
Golden Horus: none known
Throne: *ḥḏ ḫpr rʿ* (*hedj kheper ra*), The dazzling one is a manifestation of Re
Birth: *tklt* (*tekelet*), Takelot

Epithets added to the Throne name:

stp n rʿ (*setep en ra*), Chosen by Re
nṯr ḥḳ3 w3st (*netjer, heqa waset*), The divine one and ruler of Thebes

Epithets added to the Birth name:

mry ỉmn (*mery imen*), Beloved of Amun
s3 3st mry ỉmn (*sa aset, mery imen*), The son of Isis, beloved of Amun

8. Sheshonq IIc[53]

Horus: none known
Two Ladies: none known
Golden Horus: none known
Throne: *m3ʿ ḫpr rʿ* (*maa kheper ra*), The true one is a manifestation of Re
Birth: *ššnḳ* (*sheshenеq*), Sheshonq

Epithet added to the Throne name:

stp n rʿ (*setep en ra*), Chosen by Re

Epithet added to the Birth name:

mry ỉmn (*mery imen*), Beloved of Amun

9. Sheshonq III[54]

Original titulary

Horus: *k3 nḫt mswt rʿ* (*ka nakht mesut ra*), Victorious bull, the offspring of Re
Two Ladies: none known
Golden Horus: none known
Throne: *wsr m3ʿt rʿ* (*weser maat ra*), The strong one belonging to the Maat of Re
Birth: *ššnḳ* (*sheshenеq*), Sheshonq

52. Gauthier 1914, 351–60; von Beckerath 1999, 192–93. For the difficulty with Takelot II's reign, see Broekman 2005.

53. For the numbering of the king's name, see Broekman et al. 2008; for his reign, see Jansen-Winkeln 1995; and Broekman 2000.

54. Gauthier 1914, 361–68; von Beckerath 1999, 188–89.

Additional names

Horus 2: *k3 nḫt mry rʿ* (*ka nakht mery ra*), Victorious bull, beloved of Re[55]

Epithet added to the latter name:

sḫʿ /// (*sekha ///*), whom [Re?] caused to appear [as king? ///][56]

Horus 3: *k3 nḫt mry m3ʿt* (*ka nakht mery maat*), Victorious bull, beloved of Maat[57]

Epithets added to the Throne name:

stp n rʿ (*setep en ra*), Chosen by Re
stp n imn (*setep en imen*), Chosen by Amun

Epithets added to the Birth name:

mry imn (*mery imen*), Beloved of Amun
s3 b3stt (*sa bastet*), Son of Bastet,
nṯr ḥk3 iwnw (*netjer, heqa iunu*), The god and ruler of Heliopolis
ḏt (*djet*), The eternal one (?)[58]

10. Sheshonq IV[59]

Horus: none known
Two Ladies: none known
Golden Horus: none known
Throne: *ḥḏ ḫpr rʿ* (*hedj kheper ra*), The dazzling one is a manifestation of Re
Birth: *ššnḳ* (*sheshene q*), Sheshonq

Epithet added to the Throne name:

stp n rʿ (*setep en ra*), Chosen by Re

Epithets added to the Birth name:

mry imn (*mery imen*), Beloved of Amun
s3 b3stt (*sa bastet*), Son of Bastet,
nṯr ḥk3 iwnw (*netjer, heqa iunu*), The god and ruler of Heliopolis

55. From a block found at Mendes; see Bonhême 1987, 115–16; and Jansen-Winkeln 2007b, 181 (22.8).

56. From a relief found at Kom el-Hisn; see Bonhême 1987, 115–16; and Jansen-Winkeln 2007b, 182 (22.10).

57. From a Donation Stela found at Mendes, for which see Bonhême 1987, 116; and Jansen-Winkeln 2007b, 199–200 (22.27).

58. The word is written inside the cartouche; see von Beckerath 1999, 189 (E 13).

59. For the numbering of this new king's name, see Broekman et al. 2008.

11. Pamiu[60]

Horus: none known
Two Ladies: none known
Golden Horus: none known
Throne: *wsr mꜣꜥt rꜥ* (*weser maat ra*), The strong one belonging to the Maat of Re
Birth: *pꜣ miw* (*pa miu*), The tomcat

Epithets added to the Throne name:

> *stp n imn* (*setep en imen*), Chosen by Amun
> *stp n rꜥ* (*setep en ra*), Chosen by Re

Epithet added to the Birth name:

> *mry imn* (*mery imen*), Beloved of Amun

12. Sheshonq V[61]

Original titulary

Horus: *wsr-pḥty* (*weser pehty*), Strong of might
Two Ladies: *wsr-pḥty* (*weser pehty*), Strong of might
Golden Horus: *wsr-pḥty* (*weser pehty*), Strong of might
Throne: *ꜥꜣ ḫpr rꜥ* (*aa kheper ra*), The great one is a manifestation of Re
Birth: *šsnḳ* (*sheshenеq*), Sheshonq

Additional names[62]

Horus 2: *kꜣ nḫt ḫꜥ m wꜣst* (*ka nakht kha em waset*), The victorious bull who has appeared in Thebes
Golden Horus 2: *wr-biꜣwt* (*wer biaut*), Great of marvels

Epithet added to the Throne name:

> *stp n rꜥ* (*setep en ra*), Chosen by Re

Epithets added to the Birth name:

> *sꜣ bꜣstt mry imn nṯr ḥḳꜣ wꜣst* (*sa bastet, mery imen, netjer heqa waset*), The son of Bastet, beloved of Amun, the god and ruler of Thebes
> *mry imn nṯr ḥḳꜣ iwnw* (*mery imen, netjer heqa iunu*), Beloved of Amun, the god and ruler of Heliopolis

60. Gauthier 1914, 370–73; von Beckerath 1999, 190–91.
61. Gauthier 1914, 373–75; von Beckerath 1999, 190–91.
62. From a Sed festival chapel from Tanis, for which see Yoyotte 1987; and Jansen-Winkeln 2007b, 268–69 (28.1).

13. Osorkon IV[63]

Horus: none known
Two Ladies: none known
Golden Horus: none known
Throne: *ꜥ3 ḫpr rꜥ* (*aa kheper ra*), The great one is a manifestation of Re[64]
Birth: *wsrkn* (*weserken*), Osorkon[65]

Epithet added to the Throne name:

stp n imn (*setep en imen*), Chosen by Amun

Epithet added to the Birth name:

mry imn (*mery imen*), Beloved of Amun

Dynasty 22a[66]

A ruler at Thebes, contemporaneous with Dynasty 22

1. Harsiese[67]

Horus: *k3 nḫt ḫꜥ m w3st* (*ka nakht kha em waset*), The victorious bull who has appeared in Thebes
Two Ladies: none known
Golden Horus: none known
Throne: *ḥḏ ḫpr rꜥ* (*hedj kheper ra*), The dazzling one is a manifestation of Re
Birth: *ḥr s3 3st* (*hor sa aset*), Horus (is) the son of Isis

Epithet added to the Throne name:

stp n imn (*setep en imen*), Chosen by Amun

Epithet added to the Birth name:

mry imn (*mery imen*), Beloved of Amun

---

63. Gauthier 1914, 399; von Beckerath 1999, 200–201. This Dynasty 22 Osorkon is labeled the Fourth since, chronologically speaking, he came after the Osorkon III mentioned below (Dynasty 23:4). For the two objects that show both the Throne and Birth names of this king, see H. D. Schneider 1985, 264–67.

64. The epithet *n(y)-sw-bity*, "The Dual King," can sometimes appear before the name within the cartouche.

65. As with the Throne name, the epithet *n(y)-sw-bity* can sometimes appear before the name within the cartouche.

66. This numbering of the dynasty is purely for reasons of convenience and is not meant to introduce a new dynasty.

67. Gauthier 1914, 348–50; von Beckerath 1999, 196–97.

Dynasty 23 (818–712 b.c.e.)

The Twenty-Third Dynasty is partly contemporary with both the Twenty-Second and the Twenty-Fourth Dynasties. Its first ruler, Pedubastis, whose authority was recognized by the Thebans, may have been related to the royal family of the Twenty-Second Dynasty. From the reign of Osorkon III on, the priestly function of the Divine Adoratrice of Amun took on ever more importance.

As with the previous dynasty, the choice of epithets in the titularies is rather limited. Of the nine kings in this list, six chose Ramses II's Throne name for their own, while Sheshonq VIa was another king who claimed to be the Dual King *ḥḏ ḫpr rʿ*. It is noteworthy, however, that Osorkon III not only followed Thutmose III's example of being the Horus *kꜣ nḫt ḫʿ m wꜣst,* "Victorious bull who has appeared in Thebes," but also the Two Ladies *st-ib tꜣwy*, "The favorite one of the Two Lands," a phrase that went back to the Fifth Dynasty king Niuserre. Similarly, Peftjauabastet called himself the Dual king Neferkare, patterning himself after Pepy II of the Sixth Dynasty. As has been pointed out,[68] this return to Old Kingdom models occurred just before the period when Egyptian kings emulated their much older predecessors in a consciously archaizing movement.

1. Padibastet (Pedubastis) I[69]

Horus: none known
Two Ladies: none known
Golden Horus: none known
Throne: *wsr mꜣʿt rʿ* (*weser maat ra*), The strong one belonging to the Maat of Re
Birth: *pꜣ di bꜣstt* (*pa di bastet*), The one whom Bastet granted

Epithet added to the Throne name:

stp n imn (*setep en imen*), Chosen by Amun

Epithets added to the Birth name:

sꜣ ꜣst (*sa aset*), The son of Isis
mry imn (*mery imen*), Beloved of Amun

2. Iuput I[70]

Horus: none known
Two Ladies: none known
Golden Horus: none known
Throne: none known

68. Bonhême 1987, 240–42.
69. Gauthier 1914, 378–80; von Beckerath 1999, 192–93.
70. Gauthier 1914, 381–82; von Beckerath 1999, 192–93.

Birth: *iwpwt* (*iuput*), Iuput[71]

Epithet added to the Birth name:

mry imn (*mery imen*), Beloved of Amun

3. Sheshonq VI[72]

Horus: none known
Two Ladies: none known
Golden Horus: none known
Throne: *wsr m3ʿt rʿ* (*weser maat ra*), The strong one belonging to the Maat of Re
Birth: *ššnḳ* (*shesheneq*), Sheshonq[73]

Epithet added to the Throne name:

mry imn (*mery imen*), Beloved of Amun

Epithet added to the Birth name:

mry imn (*mery imen*), Beloved of Amun

4. Osorkon III[74]

Horus: *k3 nḫt ḫʿ m w3st* (*ka nakht kha em waset*), The victorious bull who has appeared in Thebes
Two Ladies: *st-ib t3wy* (*set ib tawy*), The favorite one (lit. "the place of the heart") of the Two Lands
Golden Horus: *ms nṯrw* (*mes netjeru*), Born of the gods
Throne: *wsr m3ʿt rʿ* (*weser maat ra*), The strong one belonging to the Maat of Re
Birth: *wsrkn* (*weserken*), Osorkon[75]

Epithet added to the Throne name:

stp n imn (*setep en imen*), Chosen by Amun

Epithets added to the Birth name:

s3 3st mry imn (*sa aset, mery imen*), The son of Isis, beloved of Amun
nṯr ḥḳ3 w3st (*netjer, heqa waset*), The god and ruler of Thebes

---

71. For this Libyan name, see Bonhême 1987, 212.

72. Von Beckerath 1999, 192–93. This king was previously referred to as Sheshonq IV, for which see Broekman et al. 2008; and Ritner 2009, xi.

73. The epithet *pr-ʿ3*, "Pharaoh," was sometimes written before the name inside the cartouche.

74. Gauthier 1914, 382–89; von Beckerath 1999, 194–95. For the numbering of this king, see the remarks under Osorkon IV (22:13).

75. As with the previous ruler, the epithet *pr-ʿ3*, "Pharaoh," was sometimes written before the name inside the cartouche.

5. Takelot III[76]

Horus: *w3ḏ t3wy* (*wadj tawy*), The sturdy one of the Two Lands
Two Ladies: *w3ḏ t3wy* (*wadj tawy*), The sturdy one of the Two Lands
Golden Horus: *w3ḏ t3wy* (*wadj tawy*), The sturdy one of the Two Lands
Throne: *wsr m3ʿt rʿ* (*weser maat ra*), The strong one belonging to the Maat of Re
Birth: *tklt* (*tekelet*), Takelot

Epithet added to the Throne name:

stp n ỉmn (*setep en imen*), Chosen by Amun

Epithet added to the Birth name:

s3 3st mry ỉmn nṯr ḥḳ3 w3st (*sa aset mery imen netjer heqa waset*), The son of Isis, beloved of Amun, the god, ruler of Thebes

6. Rudamun[77]

Horus: *nb m3ʿ ḫrw* (*neb maa kheru*), The possessor of righteousness[78]
Two Ladies: *ḥkn n m3ʿt* (*heken en maat*), Who has rejoiced at Maat
Golden Horus: none known
Throne: *wsr m3ʿt rʿ* (*weser maat ra*), The strong one belonging to the Maat of Re
Birth: *rwd ỉmn* (*rud imen*), Amun is vigorous

Epithet added to the Throne name:

stp n ỉmn (*setep en imen*), Chosen by Amun

7. Sheshonq VIa[79]

Horus: none known
Two Ladies: none known
Golden Horus: none known
Throne: *ḥḏ ḫpr rʿ* (*hedj kheper ra*), The dazzling one is a manifestation of Re
Birth: *ššnḳ* (*sheshenеq*), Sheshonq

Epithet added to the Birth name:

s3 3st (*sa aset*), The son of Isis

76. Gauthier 1914, 389–91; von Beckerath 1999, 194–95.
77. Gauthier 1914, 392–94; von Beckerath 1999, 196–97. On this king, see Perdu 2002.
78. Lit. "the possessor of (the quality of being) true-of-voice."
79. For the numbering of this king, see Broekman et al. 2008.

8. Iuput II[80]

Horus: none known
Two Ladies: none known
Golden Horus: none known
Throne: *wsr m3ʿt re* (*weser maat ra*), The strong one belonging to the Maat of Re
Birth: *iwpwt* (*iuput*), Iuput

Epithet added to the Throne name:

stp n imn (*setep en imen*), Chosen by Amun

Epithets added to the Birth name:

s3 b3stt mry imn (*sa bastet, mery imen*), The son of Bastet, beloved of Amun

9. Sheshonq VII[81]

Horus: none known
Two Ladies: none known
Throne: *w3s nṯr rʿ* (*was netjer ra*), The (very) divine scepter of Re (?)
Birth: *ššnḳ* (*shesheneq*), Sheshonq

Epithet added to the Throne name:

stp n rʿ (*setep en ra*), Chosen by Re

Epithet added to the Birth name:

mry imn (*mery imen*), Beloved of Amun
nṯr ḥḳ3 w3st (*netjer heqa waset*), The god and ruler of Thebes

Dynasty 23a[82]

Other rulers contemporaneous with Dynasty 23

1. Padibastet (Pedubastis) II[83]

Horus: none known
Two Ladies: none known
Golden Horus: none known

80. Von Beckerath 1999, 204–5.

81. Gauthier 1914, 403. This king was formerly known as Sheshonq VI, for which see Ritner 2009, xii; the name can be seen on a bronze pendant, for which see Petrie 1917, pl. 51D. It is possible that this individual did not actually reign as pharaoh; see Kitchen 1986, 87; Jansen-Winkeln 2007b, 384 (43.1); and Aston 2009, 3.

82. As with the previous "Dynasty 22a," this numbering of the dynasty is purely for reasons of convenience and is not meant to introduce a new dynasty.

83. Von Beckerath 1999, 200–201.

Throne: *wsr mꜣꜥt rꜥ* (*weser maat ra*), The strong one belonging to the Maat of Re
Birth: *pꜣ di bꜣstt* (*pa di bastet*), The one whom Bastet has granted

Epithet added to the Throne name:

stp n imn (*setep en imen*), Chosen by Amun

Epithets added to the Birth name:

sꜣ ꜣst (*sa aset*), The son of Isis
sꜣ bꜣstt (*sa bastet*), The son of Bastet
mry imn (*mery imen*), Beloved of Amun
stp n imn-rꜥ mꜣꜥt (*setep en imen-ra maat*), Chosen by Amun-Re and Maat

A ruler from Herakleopolis, contemporary with Dynasty 23

2. PEFTJAUABASTET[84]

Horus: none known
Two Ladies: none known
Golden Horus: none known
Throne: *nfr kꜣ rꜥ* (*nefer ka ra*), The perfect one is the ka of Re
Birth: *pꜣy.f ṯꜣw* (*m*) *ꜥwy bꜣstt* (*pay.ef tjaw (em) awy bastet*), His breath (comes from) the arms of Bastet

Rulers from Hermopolis, contemporary with Dynasty 23

3. NIMLOT[85]

Horus: none known
Two Ladies: none known
Golden Horus: none known
Throne: none known
Birth: *nmrṯ* (*nemretj*), Nimlot

4. THUTEMHAT[86]

Horus: *ḫꜥ m wn*(*t*) (*kha em wen(et)*), The one who has appeared in the Hermopolitan nome[87]
Two Ladies: none known

84. Gauthier 1914, 400–401; von Beckerath 1999, 204–5.
85. Gauthier 1914, 402; von Beckerath 1999, 204–5.
86. Gauthier 1914, 401–2; von Beckerath 1999, 204–5.
87. A proposed Horus name, *itmw nb m mꜣꜥt*, "Atum is verily a lord (lit. "a lord in truth")" has been shown to be incorrect; see Spencer and Spencer 1986, 199 n. 2.

Golden Horus: none known
Throne: *nfr ḫpr rʿ ḫʿ-ḫʿw* (*nefer kheper ra, kha khau*), The perfect one is the (very) manifestation of Re, radiant of crowns
Birth: *ḏḥwty m-ḥ3t* (*djehuty em-hat*), Thoth is at the forefront

A ruler from Asyut (Lykopolis), contemporary with Dynasty 23

5. Padinemty[88]

Horus: none known
Two Ladies: none known
Golden Horus: none known
Throne: none known
Birth: *p3 di nmty* (*pa di nemty*), The one whom Nemty has granted

Dynasty 24 (727–715 b.c.e.)

Like the previous group, the Twenty-Fourth Dynasty is partly contemporary with both the Twenty-Second and the Twenty-Third Dynasties. Ruling from Sais in the western Delta, its first king, Tefnakht, originally had some success expanding his authority into northern Upper Egypt, but was eventually repulsed by the invading Kushite kings of the Twenty-Fifth Dynasty.

Given the earlier comments about the subsequent archaizing movement, it may be noteworthy that both kings of this dynasty used Throne names that harked back to ancient ancestors. Tefnakht called himself "The noble one belonging to Re" (*špss rʿ*), recalling Shepseskare of the Fifth Dynasty, who was the Dual King "The noble one belonging to the ka of Re" (*špss k3 rʿ*). Similarly, Bakenrenef (Bocchoris) was the "Enduring one belonging to the ka of Re," (*w3ḥ k3 rʿ*), using the same Throne name as the Ninth Dynasty's Wahkare Khety (V).

1. Tefnakht[89]

Horus: *si3 ḫt* (*sia khet*), The one who understands inner (feelings)
Two Ladies: *si3 ḫt* (*sia khet*), The one who understands inner (feelings)[90]
Golden Horus: *ḥr nbw ?* (*hor nebu*), Golden Horus[91]
Throne: *špss rʿ* (*shepses ra*), The noble one belonging to Re

---

88. The name, enclosed in a cartouche, is known only from a fragmentary funerary papyrus; see Bonhême 1987, 226; and von Beckerath 1999, 204–5.

89. Gauthier 1914, 407–9; von Beckerath 1999, 202–3.

90. Lit. "who understands the belly." The name has also been read as *m3ʿ-ḫrw* (*maa kheru*), "true of voice," for which see Bonhême 1987, 230.

91. It is also possible that the actual Golden Horus name was left out and that what is written is simply the title.

Birth: *t3y.f nḫt* (*tay.ef nakht*), His strength[92]

2. Bakenrenef (Bocchoris)[93]

Horus: none known
Two Ladies: none known
Golden Horus: none known
Throne: *w3ḥ k3 rʿ* (*wah ka ra*), The enduring one belonging to the ka of Re
Birth: *b3k n rn.f* (*bak en ren.ef*), The servant of his name[94]

Dynasty 25 (747–656 b.c.e.)[95]

Toward the end of the period of the Twenty-Second to the Twenty-Fourth Dynasties, an energetic family from Napata, downstream from the Fourth Cataract in Upper Nubia, extended its hegemony northward, eventually defeating the various divided Egyptian kingdoms piecemeal. They established themselves as rulers of Egypt, a group we refer to as the Twenty-Fifth Dynasty. The lunette of Piye's Triumphal Stela[96] shows several of the rulers mentioned in the previous sections on Dynasties 22, 23, and 23a kowtowing before the victorious king. Those whose names are written inside cartouches are Osorkon IV, Iuput II, Peftjauabastet, and Nimlot; the latter is shown standing and leading a horse, but his subordinate position is indicated by the fact that his wife precedes him in the scene.

The Twenty-Fifth Dynasty set about asserting its authority and stabilizing the country, all the while enhancing parts of Karnak Temple. Their rule over Egypt did not last long, however, as the Neo-Assyrians invaded Egypt in the mid-seventh century b.c.e. and drove the Kushite kings back to their homeland, where they would set up a dynasty that managed to last until the mid-fourth century c.e.

For his titulary,[97] King Piye mostly borrowed from Thutmose III, whose titulary would have been readily available to him in Upper Nubia, given the preponderance of monuments the earlier king had left behind there, especially at the site

92. This may be an abbreviated form of a fuller theophoric name, "<God X is> his strength."

93. Gauthier 1914, 410–12; von Beckerath 1999, 202–3.

94. Perhaps meaning "a servant to his name"?

95. The royal texts from Dynasty 25 have been collected in Jansen-Winkeln 2007b, 336–65 (Kings Kashta and Piye) and Jansen-Winkeln 2009. Translations of texts from the period can be found in Eide et al. 1994; and Ritner 2009, 449–574. The royal titulary of the complete set of Kushite kings, including the Napatan and Meroitic rulers, is discussed in Török 1997, 198–215.

96. See Grimal 1981. The full text is conveniently translated in Lichtheim 1980, 66–84; Ritner 2003, 367–85; and Ritner 2009, 465–92.

97. The titularies of the Twenty-Fifth Dynasty have been examined by Aufrère 1982, 57; Török 1997, 189–201; and Eide et al. 2000, 1281–86.

of the temple of Amun at Gebel Barkal. Piye's original Horus name, "Victorious bull who has appeared in Napata" (*k3 nḫt ḫꜥ m npt*) was simply a modified version of Thutmose III's own Horus name; his Two Ladies name was the same as the earlier king's; and his Golden Horus name was an expanded version of Thutmose III's Golden Horus name during the latter's sole rule. For his Throne name, Piye used the now time-honored epithet of Ramses II, *wsr m3ꜥt rꜥ*, "the strong one belonging to the Maat of Re." A secondary set of names is found on a stela now in the Louvre, where we see Mentuhotep II's Horus name, *sm3 t3wy*, "The one who has united the Two Lands," used for Piye's Horus name, presumably as a recognition of his role in reuniting the different factions operating in Egypt at the time. On the stela, he also chose Thutmose III's famous epithet, *mn ḫpr rꜥ*, "the established one of the manifestation of Re," for a secondary Throne name. Other monarchs of the Twenty-Fifth Dynasty went back even further in time to formulate their titulary. Shabaka borrowed Pepy II's Throne name, *nfr k3 rꜥ*, "the perfect one of the ka of Re," for his own, while Shabataka appropriated Djedkare's Horus name and slightly modified the latter's Throne name for his own titulary.[98]

1. Alara[99]

Horus: none known
Two Ladies: none known
Golden Horus: none known
Throne: none known
Birth: *ỉlr* (*iler*), Alara

2. Kashta[100]

Horus: none known
Two Ladies: none known
Golden Horus: none known
Throne: *n*(*y*) *m3ꜥt rꜥ* (*ni maat ra*), The one who belongs to the Maat of Re[101]
Birth: *k3št3* (*kashta*), "The Kushite"

3. Piye/Piankhy[102]

Original titulary

Horus: *k3 nḫt ḫꜥ m npt* (*ka nakht kha em nepet*), The victorious bull who has appeared in Napata

98. See Aufrère 1982, 57.
99. Von Beckerath 1999, 206–7.
100. Gauthier 1916, 5–12; von Beckerath 1999, 206–7.
101. For the reading of the name, see Eide et al. 1994, 43.
102. Gauthier 1916, 2–4, 24–28; von Beckerath 1999, 206–7. For the king's names, and their order, see Eide et al. 1994, 51–52; and Török 1997, 153–54.

Two Ladies: *wꜣḥ-nsyt mi rꜥ m pt* (*wah nesyt mi ra em pet*), Enduring of kingship like Re in heaven

Golden Horus: *ḏsr-ḫꜥw sḫm-pḥty ꜥnḫ ḥr-nb n mꜣ.f mi ꜣḫty* (*djeser khau, sekhem pehty, ankh her-neb en ma.ef mi akhty*), Sacred of appearances, powerful of strength, at the sight of whom every one lives like (at the sight of)[103] He-of-the-Horizon

Throne: *wsr mꜣꜥt rꜥ* (*weser maat ra*), The strong one belonging to the Maat of Re

Birth: *pꜣ ꜥnḫy* (*pa ankhy*), "O living one!" (?)[104]

Additional names[105]

Stela Louvre C100[106]

Horus 2: *smꜣ tꜣwy* (*sema tawy*), The one who has united the Two Lands

Two Ladies 2: *ms ḥmwt* (*mes hemut*), The fashioner of crafts

Golden Horus 2: *sꜥšꜣ ḳnw* (*sasha qenu*), The one who has multiplied brave men

Throne 2: *mn ḫpr rꜥ* (*men kheper ra*), The established one of the manifestation of Re[107]

Granite altar from Gebel Barkal[108]

Horus 3: *sḥtp tꜣwy.fy* (*sehetep tawy.fy*), The one who has satisfied his Two Lands

Fragmentary obelisk from the Letti Basin, Sudan[109]

Horus 4: *kꜣ nḫt ḫꜥ m wꜣst* (*ka nakht kha em waset*), The victorious bull who has appeared in Thebes

Horus 5: *kꜣ tꜣwy.fy* (*ka tawy.fy*), The bull of his Two Lands

Two Ladies 3: *ḥḳꜣ kmt* (*heqa kemet*), The ruler of Egypt

Altar (?) from Meroe[110] and mummy bandages[111]

Throne 3: *snfr rꜥ* (*senefer ra*), The one whom Re made perfect[112]

---

103. Cf. Ritner 2009, 464.

104. For the transliteration of this particular version of the name, see Jansen-Winkeln 2007b, 496. It is difficult to know whether the *ankh* sign inside the cartouche is part of the name, thus reading King "Piankhy," or a prospective form of the verb "to live," with the meaning of "Long live Piye."

105. For these, see Eide et al. 1994, 48–52.

106. Gauthier 1916, 404–5; von Beckerath 1999, 196–97; Jansen-Winkeln 2007b, 382–83 (42.2), where, with some hesitation, the stela is attributed to King Iny. The stela is generally accepted to belong to Piye; see Eide et al. 1994, 47, and the references there.

107. Eide et al. 1994, 49.

108. Jansen-Winkeln 2007b, 352 (35.5).

109. Ibid., 365 (35.11).

110. Ibid., 354 (35.12).

111. BM 6640: Jansen-Winkeln 2007b, 363 (35.33).

112. More likely than "The one who has made Re happy."

Epithet added to the Throne name:

mry ỉmn (*mery imen*), Beloved of Amun

Epithets added to the Birth name:

mry ỉmn (*mery imen*), Beloved of Amun
nb ḫʿw (*neb khau*), Lord of appearances
sꜣ bꜣstt (*sa bastet*), Son of Bastet
sꜣ ꜣst (*sa aset*), Son of Isis

4. SHABAKA[113]

Horus: *sb(ꜣ)ḳ tꜣwy* (*sebaq tawy*), The one who has blessed the Two Lands
Two Ladies: *sb(ꜣ)ḳ tꜣwy* (*sebaq tawy*), The one who has blessed the Two Lands
Golden Horus: *sb(ꜣ)ḳ tꜣwy* (*sebaq tawy*), The one who has blessed the Two Lands
Throne: *nfr kꜣ rʿ* (*nefer ka ra*), The perfect one of the ka of Re
Birth: *šꜣbꜣkꜣ* (*shabaka*), Shabaka[114]

Epithet added to the Throne name:

mry ỉmn (*mery imen*), Beloved of Amun

Epithet added to the Birth name:

mry ỉmn (*mery imen*), Beloved of Amun

5. SHABATAKA/SHEBITKO[115]

Original titulary

Horus: *ḏd-ḫʿw* (*djed khau*), Stable of appearances
Two Ladies: *ʿꜣ-šfyt m tꜣw nbw* (*aa shefyt em tau nebu*), Great of majesty in all lands
Golden Horus: *ʿꜣ-ḫpš ḥwỉ pḏwt 9* (*aa khepesh, hui pedjut 9*), The one great of strength who has struck down the Nine Bows
Throne: *ḏd kꜣw rʿ* (*djed kau ra*), The stable one of the kas of Re
Birth: *šꜣbꜣtꜣkꜣ* (*shabataka*), Shabataka

Additional names

From a Karnak chapel now in Berlin:[116]

113. Gauthier 1916, 12–24; von Beckerath 1999, 206–7.
114. For this Kushite name, see Leclant 1965, 336.
115. Gauthier 1916, 28–30; von Beckerath 1999, 208–9.
116. This new set of names is found along with the king's traditional titulary in the chapel; see Jansen-Winkeln 2009, 47–48 (47.7).

Two Ladies 2: *sḫꜥ mꜣꜥt mry tꜣwy* (*sekha maat, mery tawy*), The one who has made Maat appear, the beloved one of the Two Lands
Golden Horus 2: *hr ḥr nḫt* (*her her nakht*), The one who is satisfied with victory

On a Nile level record from Karnak:[117]
Horus 2: *kꜣ nḫt ḫꜥ m wꜣst* (*ka nakht kha em waset*), The victorious bull who has appeared in Thebes
Two Ladies 3: *ḏd-ḫꜥw* (*djed khau*), Stable of appearances

Epithets added to the Birth name:

mry ỉmn (*mery imen*), Beloved of Amun
mry ptḥ (*mery ptah*), Beloved of Ptah

6. Taharqa[118]

Horus: *ḳꜣ-ḫꜥw* (*qa khau*), Exalted of appearances
Two Ladies: *ḳꜣ-ḫꜥw* (*qa khau*), Exalted of appearances
Golden Horus: *ḫw tꜣwy* (*khu tawy*), Protector of the Two Lands
Throne: *ḫw nfr-tm rꜥ* (*khu nefertem ra*), The one whom Nefertum and Re protect
Birth: *tꜣhꜣrḳꜣ* (*taharqa*), Taharqa

Epithet added to the Birth name:

mry ỉmn (*mery imen*), Beloved of Amun

7. Tanutamun[119]

Horus: *wꜣḥ-mrwt* (*wah merut*), Enduring of love
Two Ladies: none known
Golden Horus: none known[120]
Throne: *bꜣ kꜣ rꜥ* (*ba ka ra*), The (very) ba of the ka of Re[121]
Birth: *t(ꜣ) nt ỉmn* (*ta net imen*), The one belonging to Amun

117. Jansen-Winkeln 2009, 40 (47.5).
118. Gauthier 1916, 31–42; von Beckerath 1999, 208–9.
119. Gauthier 1916, 42–45; von Beckerath 1999, 210–11.
120. A Two Ladies name, *sꜥnḫ tꜣwy*, "Who has sustained the Two Lands," and a Golden Horus name, *ḫw tꜣwy ḥkn ///*, "Protector of the Two Lands, who has rejoiced in ///," suggested by Kitchen 1986, 394 n. 886, have been rejected by Eide et al. 1994, 191.
121. The name may also be Kushite; see Leclant 1965, 351.

IX

Late Period

Dynasty 26 (664–525 b.c.e.)

When the Assyrians drove the Kushites back to Napata, they installed a family from Sais as their representatives in Egypt. The new king, Psamtek I, soon took advantage of his masters' absence to declare himself independent, beginning what we designate as the Twenty-Sixth Dynasty. He also secured Upper Egypt and its Theban governor Mentuemhat by having his daughter Nitocris adopted by Shepenwepet II, the Kushite God's Wife of Amun.[1]

In western Asia, the Twenty-Sixth Dynasty backed its Assyrian allies against the growing power of Babylon. Pharaoh's foreign adventures came to a halt in 605 b.c.e. at the hands of King Nebuchadnezzar at the Battle of Carchemish. During this period, the Egyptian army also consisted of a number of Greek mercenaries, some of whom were settled in the newly founded town of Naucratis. This period of independence and high level of creativity was interrupted during the reign of King Psamtek VII by the Persian advance into Egypt in the late sixth century b.c.e.

The Twenty-Fifth Dynasty, and especially the Twenty-Sixth, are characterized by archaizing tendencies in art and language in the so-called Saite Renaissance. Artistic representations from earlier periods were either adapted or copied outright.[2]

Contrary to their late New Kingdom and Third Intermediate period predecessors, the kings of the Saite period did not necessarily wish to be portrayed as bellicose warriors in their titulary.[3] Rather, they went back to much older models, with short phrases that expressed their relationship with the gods. They did not so much borrow old epithets faithfully as refashion them. Thus, Intef II's Horus name and Amenemhat III's Golden Horus name, *wꜣḥ-ꜥnḫ*, "Enduring of life," became Psamtek I's Throne name, *wꜣḥ ib rꜥ*, "The enduring one is the (very)

1. For the so-called Adoption Stela, see Caminos 1964; Der Manuelian 1994, 298–306. On the God's Wife of Amun, see now Ayad 2009.

2. The art of the period has been discussed in W. S. Smith 1998, 232–51, while the language has been studied extensively in Der Manuelian 1994.

3. Spalinger 1978; Pressl 1993.

mind of Re"; Senwosret IV's *snfr ib rꜥ*, "The one whom Re's mind has made perfect," became Psamtek II's Throne name, *nfr ib rꜥ*, "The perfect one of the mind of Re"; and Mentuhotep III's Throne name *sꜥnḫ kꜣ rꜥ*, "The one whom the ka of Re has sustained," became Psamtek III's own Throne name, *ꜥnḫ kꜣ n rꜥ*, "The living one is the (very) ka of Re." Also noteworthy is the way that every king of the dynasty save for the last used a nominal form of a verb followed by the phrase *ib rꜥ*, "the mind of Re." Thus was each king an "enduring one of" (*wꜣḥ*), a "perfect one of" (*nfr*), or else "renewed" (*wḥm*), "continually rejoiced over" (*ḥꜥꜥi*), or were "associated with" (*ẖnm*) the mind of Re.

1. Psamtek (Psammetichus) I[4]

Horus: *ꜥꜣ-ib* (*aa ib*), Strong-minded
Two Ladies: *nb ꜥ* (*neb a*), Possessor of a (strong) arm
Golden Horus: *ḳnw* (*qenu*), The brave one
Throne: *wꜣḥ ib rꜥ* (*wah ib ra*), The enduring one is the (very) mind of Re
Birth: *psmtk* (*psemtek*), Psamtek[5]

2. Nekau (Necho) II[6]

Horus: *siꜣ-ib* (*sia ib*), Perceptive-minded
Two Ladies: *mꜣꜥ-ḫrw* (*maa kheru*), True of voice
Golden Horus: *mry nṯrw* (*mery netjeru*), Beloved of the gods
Throne: *wḥm ib rꜥ* (*wehem ib ra*), Who has renewed the will of Re
Birth: *n(y) kꜣw* (*ni kau*), Who belongs to the kas[7]

3. Psamtek (Psammetichus) II[8]

Horus: *mnḫ-ib* (*menekh ib*), The efficacious one (lit. "Splendid of mind")[9]
Two Ladies: *wsr-ꜥ* (*weser a*), Strong-armed
Golden Horus: *snfr tꜣwy* (*senefer tawy*), Who has made the Two Lands perfect

4. Gauthier 1916, 66–68; von Beckerath 1999, 214–15.

5. A possible etymology of the name is *pꜣ s n mtk* (*pa se en metek*), "The man belonging to the (Libyan divinity) Metek"; see von Beckerath 1999, 214 n. 1.

6. Gauthier 1916, 86–92; von Beckerath 1999, 214–15. This king is labeled as Necho (II) because Necho (I) was simply a vassal of the Assyrians, whose son, Psamtek I, was installed in Egypt by the Assyrians.

7. Although the word *kꜣ*- lifeforce is sometimes written with the bull hieroglyph, the name is less likely to mean "The one who belongs to the bulls."

8. Gauthier 1916, 92–104; von Beckerath 1999, 216–17.

9. A fragmentary granite relief found in the central Delta shows the Horus name to which was added the king's Throne name within the *serekh*, thus giving the fuller phrase *mnḫ-ib nfr ib rꜥ* (Kamal 1906, 238).

Throne: *nfr ib rꜥ* (*nefer ib ra*), The perfect one is the (very) mind of Re[10]
Birth: *psmtk* (*psemtek*), Psamtek

Epithet added to the Birth name:

nb pḥty (*neb pehty*), Possessor of might

4. Wahibre (Apries)[11]

Original titulary

Horus: *wꜣḥ-ib* (*wah ib*), Enduring of mind
Two Ladies: *nb ḫpš* (*neb khepesh*), Possessor of strength
Golden Horus: *swꜣḏ tꜣwy* (*sewadj tawy*), Who has made the Two Lands flourish
Throne: *ḥꜥꜥ ib rꜥ* (*haa ib ra*), Who (continually) rejoices over the mind of Re
Birth: *wꜣḥ ib rꜥ* (*wah ib ra*), The enduring one is the (very) mind of Re

Additional name

Golden Horus 2: *sꜣ ptḥ mry.f* (*sa ptah, mery.ef*), The son of Ptah, his beloved[12]

5. Ahmose (Amasis) III[13]

Horus: *smn mꜣꜥt* (*semen maat*), The one who has established Maat
Two Ladies: *sꜣ nt spd tꜣwy* (*sa neith, seped tawy*), The son of Neith, who has restored the Two Lands (to order)
Golden Horus: *stp nṯrw* (*setep netjeru*), Divinely chosen
Throne: *ẖnm ib rꜥ* (*khnum ib ra*), The one who is associated with the mind of Re
Birth: *iꜥḥ ms(w)* (*iah mesu*), The (moon god) Iah is born

Epithets added to the Birth name:

sꜣ nt (*sa neith*), The son of Neith
sꜣ wsir (*sa wesir*), The son of Osiris

---

10. As with the occurrence of the relief from the central Delta mentioned in the previous note, a graffito in the Wadi Hammamat shows a cartouche that gives the king's Throne name to which was added his Golden Horus name, thus: *snfr tꜣwy nfr ib rꜥ* (Couyat and Montet 1913, no. 100, p. 71).

11. Gauthier 1916, 104–12; von Beckerath 1999, 216–17.

12. A stela from the temple of Ptah at Memphis, for which see von Beckerath 1999, 216–17 (G4). Note the reference to the Memphite god Ptah in the only change to the king's titulary.

13. Gauthier 1916, 113–31; von Beckerath 1999, 216–17.

6. Psamtek (Psammetichus) III[14]

Horus: none known
Two Ladies: none known
Golden Horus: none known
Throne: *ꜥnḫ kꜣ n rꜥ* (*ankh ka en ra*), The living one is the (very) ka of Re
Birth: *psmtk* (*psemtek*), Psamtek

Dynasty 27 (525–404 B.C.E.)[15]

The Persian king Cambyses defeated Egypt at Pelusium in 525 B.C.E., ushering in the Twenty-Seventh Dynasty, wherein Egypt was incorporated into the vast Achaemenid empire as one of its satrapies. This so-called First Persian Domination lasted well over a century but was marked by numerous rebellions on the part of the Egyptians, which the Persians are said to have put down cruelly. The Persian kings ruled as proper pharaohs, being represented in Egyptian garb and taking on a full titulary. In Khargah Oasis in the Western Desert, a large temple dedicated to Amun was built, which shows the cartouches of King Darius. During this time, a Jewish colony flourished at Elephantine in southern Upper Egypt. They left behind many important texts written in Aramaic, which richly illuminate their daily lives.[16] It is also during this period that Herodotus visited Egypt, in the mid-fifth century B.C.E.

The invader Cambyses surely felt like the inaugurator of a new era in the ancient land of Egypt. Thus he became the Horus *smꜣ tꜣwy,* "The one who has united the Two Lands." His Throne name—which the Egyptian courtier Udjahorresnet specifically stated he composed[17]—was then *mswt rꜥ,* "The offspring of Re," presumably in order to show that the new ruler belonged to the long line of kings, each of whom had been "the son of Re." The next king, Darius I, may have borrowed his Horus name, *mnḫ-ib,* "The efficacious one," from Psamtek II. He then continued his predecessor's theme of being the heir of the sun god by calling himself the Dual King *stwt rꜥ,* "The progeny of Re."

1. Cambyses[18]

Horus: *smꜣ tꜣwy* (*sema tawy*), The one who has united the Two Lands
Two Ladies: none known
Golden Horus: none known

14. Gauthier 1916, 131–32; von Beckerath 1999, 218–19.
15. For a list of sources from this period, see Kuhrt 2007.
16. On these, see especially Porten et al. 1996.
17. For a convenient translation of the text, see Lichtheim 1980, 36–41; the passage in question is found on p. 38.
18. Gauthier 1916, 136–39; von Beckerath 1999, 220–21.

Throne: *mswt rʿ* (*mesut ra*), The offspring of Re
Birth: *kmbwd* (*kembud*), Cambyses

2. Darius I[19]

Original titulary

Horus: *mnḫ-ib* (*menekh ib*), The efficacious one[20]
Two Ladies: none known
Golden Horus: none known
Throne: *stwt rʿ* (*setut ra*), Progeny of Re
Birth: *driwš* (*deriush*), Darius

Additional names

Horus 2: *wr nb mry šmʿw* (*wer neb, mery shemau*), Chieftain and lord, beloved of Upper Egypt[21]

Temple of Hibis:[22]
Throne 2: *mry imn-rʿ* (*mery imen-ra*), Beloved of Amun-Re
Throne 3: *mry imn-rʿ nb hbt nṯr ʿ3 nḫt-ḫpš* (*mery imen-ra, neb hebet, netjer aa, nakht khepesh*), Beloved of Amun-Re, lord of Hibis (temple), the great god, the one strong of arm

3. Xerxes I[23]

Horus: none known
Two Ladies: none known
Golden Horus: none known
Throne: none known
Birth: *ḫšyrš* (*kheshyresh*), Xerxes

4. Artaxerxes I[24]

Horus: none known
Two Ladies: none known
Golden Horus: none known
Throne: none known
Birth: *3rtḫšsš* (*artekhshesesh*), Artaxerxes

---

19. Gauthier 1916, 140–50; von Beckerath 1999, 220–21.
20. Lit. "splendid of mind."
21. From a fragmentary piece of jewelry found in the Karnak Cachette; see Legrain 1907.
22. Von Beckerath 1999, 220–21.
23. Gauthier 1916, 150–52; von Beckerath 1999, 220–21.
24. Gauthier 1916, 152–54; von Beckerath 1999, 220–21.

5. Xerxes II

6. Darius II

7. Artaxerxes II

Kings Xerxes II, Darius II, and Artaxerxes II are not known from Egyptian hieroglyphic texts

Dynasty 28 (404–399 B.C.E.)

A revolt by the Saites against the rule of the Persians constitutes the short-lived Twenty-Eighth Dynasty. Attested in Manetho,[25] it may have had suzerainty only over the Delta and consists of a single king, who is known only from a cartouche around his Birth name.

1. Amenirdis (Amyrtaios)[26]

Horus: none known
Two Ladies: none known
Golden Horus: none known
Throne: none known
Birth: *ỉmn ỉr di.s*(*w*) (*imen ir di s*(*u*)), Amun is the one who created him

Dynasty 29 (399–380 B.C.E.)

King Nepherites I was a ruler from Mendes who replaced the Twenty-Eighth Dynasty in the Delta. Although short-lived, this dynasty is attested in Manetho.[27] It was beset by internal struggles and was eventually displaced by the Thirtieth Dynasty's Nectanebo I.

Nepherites I borrowed his Horus name from Psamtek I and appropriated Merenptah's Throne name for his own. His successor Psammuthis went even further back in time for his own Throne name, as he adapted Niuserre's *n*(*y*) *wsr rꜥ*, "who belongs to the power of Re," into the shorter phrase *wsr rꜥ*, "The powerful one of Re." Of course, we cannot tell whether a king removed twenty centuries from a given predecessor had access to the latter's full titulary. Perhaps Psammuthis's court simply expanded on Nepherites I's theme of a king's *bꜣ*-spirit, altering his predecessor's *bꜣ n rꜥ*, "the spirit of Re," into "the powerful one of Re." This is certainly true of the last ruler of the dynasty, Achoris, who built

25. Waddell 1940, 178–79.
26. Gauthier 1916, 159–60; von Beckerath 1999, 222–23.
27. Waddell 1940, 178–81.

on Nepherites I's titulary. Both Achoris's Horus and Golden Horus names relied heavily on the former king's epithets to compose his own. Additionally, Achoris's Throne name, *ḫnm mꜣʿt rʿ*, "the one associated with the Maat of Re," could have been patterned after Amasis's Throne name, *ḫnm ib rʿ*, "the one associated with the mind of Re."

1. Nefaarudu (Nepherites) I[28]

Horus: *ʿꜣ-ib* (*aa ib*), Strong-minded
Two Ladies: none known
Golden Horus: *stp nṯrw* (*setep netjeru*), Divinely chosen
Throne: *bꜣ n rʿ* (*ba en ra*), The (very) spirit of Re
Birth: *nꜣy.f ʿꜣw rwḏw* (*nay.ef aau rudju*), His ancestors are flourishing[29]

Epithet added to the Throne name:

mry nṯrw (*mery netjeru*), Beloved of the gods

2. Pasherimut (Psammuthis)[30]

Horus: *ʿꜣ-pḥty mʿr-spw* (*aa pehty, mar sepu*), Great of strength and successful of occasions
Two Ladies: none known
Golden Horus: none known
Throne: *wsr rʿ* (*weser ra*), The powerful one of Re
Birth: *pꜣ šri mwt* (*pa sheri mut*), The child of (the goddess) Mut

Epithet added to the Throne name:

stp n ptḥ (*setep en ptah*), Chosen by Ptah

3. Hakor (Achoris)[31]

Horus: *ʿꜣ-ib mry tꜣwy* (*aa ib, mery tawy*), Strong-minded and beloved of the Two Lands
Two Ladies: *ḳnw* (*qenu*), The brave one
Golden Horus: *sḥtp nṯrw* (*sehetep netjeru*), Who has satisfied the gods
Throne: *ḫnm mꜣʿt rʿ* (*khnum maat ra*), The one who is associated with the Maat of Re
Birth: *hgr/hkr/hḳr* (*heger/heker/heqer*), Achoris

28. Gauthier 1916, 161–63; von Beckerath 1999, 224–25.
29. So T. Schneider (1996, 275); one might also render "His greatness is flourishing," using the plural nominative subject as a collective.
30. Gauthier 1916, 168–69; von Beckerath 1999, 224–25.
31. Gauthier 1916, 164–68; von Beckerath 1999, 224–25.

Epithets added to the Throne name:

stp n ḫnmw (*setep en khnum*), Chosen by Khnum
stp n in-ḥrt (*setep en in-heret*), Chosen by Onuris

4. Nefaarudu (Nephérites) II

King Nepherites II is not known from hieroglyphic sources

Dynasty 30 (380–343 B.C.E.)

The first king of the Thirtieth Dynasty[32] was Nectanebo I, a military commander from the city of Samannud, Greek Sebennytos. The last gasp of Egyptian independence, the dynasty had a certain measure of success. It undertook military campaigns in western Asia and managed to repulse an attempted Persian invasion. The Decree of Naucratis,[33] by which the king granted revenues to the temple of Neith at Sais, was promulgated during the reign of Nectanebo I. The latter also undertook considerable building activities, notably the temple of Behbeit el-Hagar in the Delta[34] and at Karnak Temple, the current temenos wall of which dates to this period. A final Persian invasion in 342 B.C.E. ended the last native Egyptian dynasty.

Although there are a few borrowings in the formation of the titulary of the Thirtieth Dynasty kings, notably Nectanebo I's use of Senwosret I's Throne name,[35] what really distinguishes their titulary is the recognition of their role as native defenders of Egypt. The kings claimed to have "made potent" (*smnḫ*) or "guided" (*sšm*) the Two Lands, and to have "protected" (*ḫw*) the country by "subduing foreign lands" (*wꜥf ḫ3swt*). All of this was obviously done according to divine will, as they had "accomplished what the gods desired" (*ir mrt nṯrw*) by making "the gods' temples glorious" (*s3ḫ prw nṯrw*), which "pleased the gods' minds" (*shr ib nṯrw*) and "contented Re" (*snḏm ib rꜥ*).

1. Nakhtnebef (Nectanebo) I[36]

Horus: *ṯm3-ꜥ* (*tjema a*), The sturdy-armed one
Two Ladies: *smnḫ t3wy* (*semenekh tawy*), Who has made the Two Lands potent
Golden Horus: *ir mrt nṯrw* (*ir meret netjeru*), Who has accomplished what the gods desired
Throne: *ḫpr k3 rꜥ* (*kheper ka ra*), The (very) manifestation of the ka of Re

---

32. Waddell 1940, 182–85.
33. Conveniently translated in Lichtheim 1980, 86–89.
34. For an easily accessible summary of the site, see Favard-Meeks 1999.
35. See Koemoth 2002, 55.
36. Gauthier 1916, 183–92; von Beckerath 1999, 226–27.

Birth: *nḫt nb.f* (*nakht neb.ef*), The strong one for (lit. "of") his lord[37]

2. Djedhor (Tachos/Teos)[38]

Horus: *ḫ῾ m m3῾t sšm t3wy* (*kha em maat, seshem tawy*), The one who has appeared through Maat[39] and guided the Two Lands
Two Ladies: *mry m3῾t s3ḫ prw nṯrw* (*mery maat, sakh peru netjeru*), Beloved of Maat, who has made the gods' temples glorious
Golden Horus: *ḫw b3ḳt w῾f ḫ3swt* (*khu baqet, waf khasut*), The one who has protected Baqet[40] and subdued the foreign lands
Throne: *ỉr m3῾t n r῾* (*ir maat en ra*), The one who has accomplished Maat for Re
Birth: *ḏd ḥr* (*djed hor*), Horus says[41]

Epithet added to the Birth name:

stp n ỉn-ḥr (*setep en inher(et)*), Chosen by Onuris

3. Nakhthorhebyt (Nectanebo II)[42]

Original titulary

Horus: *mry t3wy* (*mery tawy*), Beloved of the Two Lands
Two Ladies: *shr ỉb nṯrw* (*seher ib netjeru*), The one who has pleased the gods' minds
Golden Horus: *smn hpw* (*semen hepu*), The establisher of laws
Throne: *snḏm ỉb r῾* (*senedjem ib ra*), The one who has contented[43] Re
Birth: *nḫt ḥr* (*n*) *ḥbyt* (*nakht hor (en) hebyt*), The strong one of Horus of Hebit[44]

Additional names

Offering table from Abu Roash (CG 23115):[45]
Horus 2: *mry t3wy mk kmt* (*mery tawy, mek kemet*), The beloved of the Two Lands and guardian of Egypt

37. Or perhaps "His lord is strong."
38. Gauthier 1916, 182–83; von Beckerath 1999, 226–27.
39. Or "in righteousness."
40. A designation of Egypt in the Late Period (*Wb* I, 425:18).
41. The construction is either a short version of the name "Horus says 'He will live,'" or may be an ancient misreading of the original hieratic Nes-Hor, "The one who belongs to Horus," for which see Ranke 1935, 1:409 n. 1.
42. Gauthier 1916, 171–81; von Beckerath 1999, 228–29.
43. Lit. "made pleasant the mind."
44. Behbeit el–Hagar, a city in the Delta near ancient Sebennytos, the home town of the kings of Dynasty Thirty. It was the site of an important temple of Isis, for which see Baines and Málek 1980, 171; and Favard-Meeks 1991, 1999, and 2002.
45. Kamal 1909, 94–95.

Two Ladies 2: *shr ỉb nṯrw tkn ḫ3swt* (*seher ib netjeru, teken khasut*), The one who has pleased the gods' minds by attacking the foreign lands
Golden Horus 2: *smn hpw ḥwi pḏwt 9* (*semen hepu, hui pedjut 9*), The establisher of laws, who has struck down the Nine Bows

Epithets added to the Throne name:

stp n ỉn-ḥr (*setep en inher(et)*), Chosen by Onuris
stp n ḥt-ḥr (*setep en hut-hor)*), Chosen by Hathor

Epithets added to the Birth name:

mry ỉn-ḥr (*mery inher(et)*), Beloved of Onuris
mry ỉn-ḥr s3 ḥt-ḥr (*mery inher(et), sa hut-hor*), Beloved of Onuris, the son of Hathor
s3 mry ḥt-ḥr (*sa mery hut-hor*), The beloved son of Hathor
mry ḥt-ḥr (*mery hut-hor*), Beloved of Hathor
mry ỉn-ḥr s3 b3stt (*mery inher(et), sa bastet*), Beloved of Onuris, the son of Bastet

Dynasty 31 (343–332 B.C.E.)

The so-called Second Persian Domination[46] comprised three Persian kings and one minor Egyptian ruler with the very non-Egyptian name of Khababash. Egypt was once again simply part of the Achaemenid empire.

1 Artaxerxes III

2. Arses

Kings Artaxerxes III and Arses are not known from hieroglyphic sources

3. Darius III[47]

Horus: none known
Two Ladies: none known
Golden Horus: none known
Throne: none known
Birth: *drỉwš* (*deriush*), Darius

An additional minor king, the last native Egyptian ruler, is known from this period.

---

46. The number thirty-one was given to the dynasty by Manetho, for which see Waddell 1940, 184–87.
47. Von Beckerath 1999, 230–31.

4. Khababash[48]

Horus: none known
Two Ladies: none known
Golden Horus: none known
Throne: *snn stp.n ptḥ* (*senen setep.en ptah*), The likeness that Ptah chose
Birth: *ḫbbš* (*khabebesh*), Khababash[49]

---

48. Gauthier 1916, 195–96; von Beckerath 1999, 230–31.
49. The name may be Libyan; see T. Schneider 1996, 144.

X

The Macedonian and Ptolemaic Dynasties

Macedonian Dynasty (332–305 B.C.E.)

Alexander the Great defeated the Persians and invaded Egypt in 332 B.C.E. He immediately endeared himself to the Egyptians by adopting their ways and paying homage to their gods. For the latter, he went as far as the Oasis of Siwa in the Western Desert, where he was purported to have been confirmed as pharaoh by the oracle of the temple of Amun there. He founded the city of Alexandria, his new capital on the Mediterranean in the northwestern Delta. Unfortunately, Alexander's success was short-lived. He died in Babylon in 323 B.C.E., and his hard-won empire was soon divided among his generals.

Fully realizing his role as the liberator of Egypt, Alexander diplomatically patterned himself after the last native Egyptian pharaoh. Borrowing one of Nectanebo II's secondary Horus names, he called himself the Horus *mk kmt*, "the protector of Egypt,"[1] using a phrase first seen in New Kingdom royal titularies.[2] His successor, Philip Arrhidaeus, used a similar phrase by claiming to be the Horus *ḫw t3wy*, "the protector of the Two Lands." Interestingly, he also called himself the Two Ladies *ḥḳ3 ḫ3swt*, "the ruler of foreign countries," recalling the term "Hyksos." The last Macedonian ruler, Alexander II, began a trend followed by the succeeding Ptolemies when he legitimized his rule by claiming to be "one to whom his father's office had been given" (*rdỉ n.f ỉ3wt it.f*) in part of his Two Ladies name.

1. Alexander the Great[3]

Original titulary

Horus: *mk kmt* (*mek kemet*), The guardian of Egypt
Two Ladies: none known
Golden Horus: none known

---

1. See also Hölbl 2001, 79.
2. Sety I first used the phrase for a Two Ladies name on an obelisk at Heliopolis and was then followed by his son Ramses II for part of the latter's original Two Ladies name. The phrase was subsequently used by Sety II, Ramses III, IV, VI, and VII.
3. Gauthier 1916, 199–203; von Beckerath 1999, 232–33.

Throne: *stp n rʿ mry ỉmn* (*setep en ra, mery imen*), Chosen by Re and beloved of Amun

Birth: *ꜣlksndrs/ꜣlksỉndrs* (*aleksendres/aleksindres*), Alexander

Additional names

Horus 2: *ḥḳꜣ ḳnỉ* (*heqa qeni*), The brave ruler[4]

Horus 3: *ḥḳꜣ ḳnỉ tkn ḫꜣswt* (*heqa qeni, teken khasut*), The brave ruler who has attacked foreign lands[5]

2. Philip Arrhidaeus[6]

Original titulary

Horus: *ḫ[w] tꜣwy* (*khu tawy*), The protector of the Two Lands

Two Ladies: *ḥḳꜣ ḫꜣswt* (*heqa khasut*), The ruler of foreign countries

Golden Horus: *mrỉyw* (*meriu*), The beloved one

Throne: *stp n rʿ mry ỉmn* (*setep en ra, mery imen*), Chosen by Re and beloved of Amun

Birth: *p(h)lpws* (*p(h)elepus*), P(h)ilippos

Additional names

Horus 2: *kꜣ nḫt mry mꜣʿt* (*ka nakht, mery maat*), The victorious bull, beloved of Maat[7]

Throne 2: *stp n kꜣ rʿ mry ỉmn* (*setep en ka ra, mery imen*), Chosen by the ka of Re and beloved of Amun[8]

3. Alexander II/IV[9]

Horus: *ḥwnw wsr-pḥty* (*hunu, weser pehty*), The youthful one, powerful of strength

Two Ladies: *mry nṯrw rdỉ n.f ỉꜣwt n ỉt.f* (*mery netjeru, redi en.ef iaut en it.ef*), Beloved of the gods, to whom the office of his father was given

Golden Horus: *ḥḳꜣ nḫt m tꜣ (r)-ḏr.f* (*heqa nakht em ta (er)-djer-ef*), Victorious ruler in the entire land

Throne: *ḥʿʿ ỉb rʿ stp n ỉmn* (*haa ib ra, setep en imen*), Who (continually) rejoices over the mind of Re, chosen by Amun

Birth: *ꜣlksndrs/ꜣlksỉndrs* (*aleksendres/aleksindres*), Alexander

---

4. From Karnak Temple; see LD IV, 3a.
5. From a structure of Thutmose III at Karnak Temple; see LD IV, 4a.
6. Gauthier 1916, 204–7; von Beckerath 1999, 232–33.
7. From the sanctuary of Thutmose III at Karnak; see Gauthier 1916, 205, V.
8. From a temple at Hermopolis (Ashmunein); see Gauthier 1916, 206, XI.
9. Gauthier 1916, 207–11; von Beckerath 1999, 232–33.

Ptolemaic Dynasty (305–30 B.C.E.)

When General Ptolemy, son of Lagos, was given Egypt in 305 B.C.E. as his share of Alexander the Great's empire, he ushered in a glorious new era for the country. He was the first ruler of the so-called Ptolemaic Dynasty, which would rule Egypt for close to three centuries, not an inconsiderable amount of time. The dynasty first brought stability and prosperity to the country, as it pursued its commercial and military interests in the eastern Mediterranean. By the middle of the dynasty, however, bloody internal strife developed, which weakened the rulers' ability to survive the growing power of Rome. The society was divided between its Greek-speaking monarchs and the native Egyptian population, which once again felt displaced by foreign rulers.[10]

The Ptolemies' legacy lay in their cultural achievements, as they erected the Lighthouse at Alexandria, one of the classical Seven Wonders of the World, as well as the famous library, built under Ptolemy II in the same city. The best-preserved temples in Egypt today—at Dendera, Edfu, Kom Ombo, and Philae—were either constructed or received their final treatment during this period. A decree in honor of the young king Ptolemy V (205–180 B.C.E.) was drawn up in two languages (Greek and Egyptian) and three scripts (Greek, a cursive writing used in the Late period called Demotic, and hieroglyphs) and probably deposited at Naucratis. It was found in 1799 by a member of Napoleon's forces at the site of Rosetta in the western Delta, from where it gets its modern name. The Egyptian priest Manetho, who came from the city of Sebennytos, was tasked by a Ptolemaic ruler, possibly Ptolemy II, to write a history of Egypt in Greek; for better or for worse, his division of Egypt's long history into dynasties is still followed today.

The last of the Ptolemies was the famous queen Cleopatra VII (51–30 B.C.E.), who first allied herself with Julius Caesar then with General Mark Antony. When the latter was defeated at the Battle of Actium by Octavian in 30 B.C.E., the queen committed suicide, effectively ending ancient Egyptian history. Egypt would at that point become part of the Roman empire for over four centuries.

The Ptolemaic kings' titularies are characterized by a series of themes used throughout the period.[11] The most obvious is the issue of legitimizing their rule by claiming to be the proper "heir" (*iwꜥ*) of their predecessor,[12] and further confirming this by asserting that they had been specifically enthroned by their father[13] or

10. For a contrasting approach to the period, see Manning 2010.

11. Ptolemaic titularies have been discussed by, among others, Koenen (1993, 57–66), Samuel (1993, 168–69 and n. 2), Chauveau (1997, 49, 61–63), Hölbl (2001, 79–81), and Stanwick (2002, 43–46). See also Huß 2001 and Manning 2010.

12. Used by Ptolemy III, IV, VI, VIII, IX, X, XII, and XIV as part of their Throne names, save for Ptolemy IX, who also used the word in one of his Two Ladies names. See also Chauveau 1997, 61; and Stanwick 2002, 46.

13. Ptolemy II, III, IV, V, and VIII.

their mother.[14] As the first of his line, Ptolemy I not surprisingly claimed to have "seized (the throne) by (his own) power" (*iṯ m sḫm*). In contrast, toward the end of the period Ptolemy XII was content with having simply "assumed the crown of kingship for himself" (*šsp n.f ḫꜥ m nsw*), demonstrating the king's tenuous hold on the throne at this point.

A second motif was that of taking care of their subjects. Thus did Ptolemy III claim to be a "potent wall for the Beloved Land" (*inb mnḫ n tꜣ mry*), and Ptolemy IV assured his subjects that he would "safeguard" (*swḏꜣ*) them and be their "savior" (*nḏty*). One of the ways kings would do this was by "establishing laws" (*smn hpw*), which Ptolemy IV, IX, and XII wished to do. This was not necessarily a new concept in royal titularies,[15] but its frequency in Ptolemaic phraseology is noteworthy.

Another important theme was a comparison of the king to a divinity. Rather than the traditional motifs of being sustained, endowed, protected, or chosen by a god, the kings were now actually compared to various gods through the use of the preposition *mi*, "like," in the epithets.[16] Thus, Ptolemy III, IV, V, VI, VIII, and XII were each said to be "a sovereign like Re," while Ptolemy VI was stated to be the "twin brother" (*ḥtr*) of the Apis bull.

1. Ptolemy I Soter ("Savior") [17]

Horus: *wr-pḥty nsw ḳni* (*wer pehty, nesu qeni*), Great of strength and brave king
Two Ladies: *iṯ m sḫm ḥḳꜣ ṯl* (*itj em sekhem, heqa tjel*), Who has seized with (his own) power, the ruler of Sile[18]
Golden Horus: none known
Throne: *stp n rꜥ mry imn* (*setep en ra, mery imen*), Chosen by Re and beloved of Amun
Birth: *ptwlmys* (*ptolemys*), Ptolemy

2. Ptolemy II Philadelphus ("Brother-loving")[19]

Horus: *ḥwnw ḳni* (*hunu qeni*), Brave youth

---

14. Ptolemy IX and X.

15. The notion of "establishing laws" went back to Amenhotep III's original Two Ladies name, a phrase subsequently used by Merenptah in a secondary Two Ladies name and Nectanebo II in his original Golden Horus name. Tutankhamun claimed to be "perfect of laws" (*nfr-hpw*) in his Two Ladies name and Psusennes III would also maintain that he had "made perfect laws" (*ir hpw nfw*).

16. For a discussion of this phraseology, see particularly Derchain-Urtel 1975.

17. Gauthier 1916, 214–21; von Beckerath 1999, 234–35.

18. Also referred to as Tjaru or Tharu, a site at the very northeastern part of Egypt long considered the starting point for the Sinai; see Montet 1957, 190–91. For texts pertaining to the site, see al-Ayedi 2006, 28–79.

19. Gauthier 1916, 222–45; von Beckerath 1999, 234–35.

Two Ladies: *wr-pḥty* (*wer pehty*), Great of strength
Golden Horus: *sḫꜥ.n sw it.f* (*sekha.en su it.ef*), Whose father enthroned him[20]
Throne: *wsr kꜣ rꜥ* (*weser ka ra*), The strong one of the ka of Re
Birth: *ptwlmys* (*ptolemys*), Ptolemy

Epithet added to the Throne name:

mry imn (*mery imen*), Beloved of Amun

2A. Arsinoe II[21]

Throne: *ẖnm(t) ib n mꜣꜥt mr(t) nṯrw* (*khneme(t) ib en maat, mer(et) netjeru*), Whose mind is united with Maat, beloved of the gods
Birth: *ir-si-nꜣt* (*ir-si-nat*), Arsinoe

3. Ptolemy III Euergetes ("Benefactor")[22]

Original titulary

Horus: *ḥkn nṯrw rmṯ ḥr.f* (*heken netjeru remetj her.ef*), The one over whom gods and people have rejoiced
Two Ladies: *ḳn nḏti nṯrw inb mnḫ n tꜣ mry* (*qen, nedjti netjeru, ineb menekh en ta mery*), The brave one who has protected the gods, a potent wall for Ta-mery[23]
Golden Horus: *wr-pḥty ir ꜣḫwt nb ḥbw-sd mi ptḥ tꜣ-ṯnn ity mi rꜥ* (*wer-pehty, ir akhut, neb hebu-sed mi ptah ta-tjenen, ity mi ra*), The one great of strength who has done beneficial things, the possessor of Sed festivals like Ptah Tatjenen and a sovereign like Re
Throne: *iwꜥ n snwy nṯrwy stp (n) rꜥ sḫm ꜥnḫ n imn* (*iwa en senwy netjerwy, setep (en) ra, sekhem ankh en imen*), The heir of the two divine brothers, chosen by Re, the living image of Amun
Birth: *ptwlmys* (*ptolemys*), Ptolemy

Additional names

Horus 2: *ḥkn nṯrw rmṯ ḥr.f m šsp.f nsyt m-ꜥ it.f* (*heken netjeru remetj her.ef em shesep.ef nesyt em a it.ef*), The one over whom gods and people rejoiced when he has received the kingship from his father's hand[24]
Horus 3: *wr-pḥty ir ꜥḏt m bdšw.f* (*wer pehty, ir adjet em bedshu.ef*), The one great of strength, who has brought about slaughter among those who rebelled against him[25]

20. Lit. "caused him to appear."
21. Gauthier 1916, 239–44; von Beckerath 1999, 234–35.
22. Gauthier 1916, 245–63; von Beckerath 1999, 234–37.
23. "The Beloved Land," a designation of Egypt.
24. From the temple of Philae; see Gauthier 1916, 254, XXXVIII.
25. Lit. "has accomplished slaughter among his rebels." From a temple wall relief; see von Beckerath 1999, 234–35 (H3).

Epithet added to the Birth name:

ʿnḫ ḏt mry ptḥ (*ankh djet, mery ptah*), Who lives eternally, beloved of Ptah

3a. Berenike II[26]

Horus: *s3t ḥḳ3 irt.n ḥḳ3* (*sat heqa, iret.en heqa*), Daughter of the ruler, whom the ruler begat
Birth: *br-ny-kt* (*ber-ny-ket*), Berenike

Epithet added to the Birth name:

nṯrt mnḫ(t) mr(t) nṯrwt (*netjeret menkhe(t) mer(et) netjerut*), Potent goddess, beloved of the goddesses

4. Ptolemy IV Philopator ("Father-loving")[27]

Horus: *ḥwnw ḳni sḫʿ.n sw it.f* (*hunu qeni, sekha.en su it.ef*), The brave youth whose father enthroned him
Two Ladies: *wr-pḥty mnḫ-ib ḫr nṯrw nb(w) nḏty n ḥnmmt* (*wer pehty, menekh ib kher netjeru neb(u), nedjty en henmemet*), Great of strength, efficacious before all the gods, and the savior of mankind
Golden Horus: *swḏ3 b3ḳt sḥḏ gsw-prw smn hpw mi ḏḥwty ʿ3 ʿ3 nb ḥbw sd mi ptḥ t3-ṯnn ity mi rʿ* (*sewedja baqet, sehedj gesu-peru, semen hepu mi djehuty aa aa, neb hebu-sed mi ptah ta-tjenen, ity mi ra*), Who has kept Baqet[28] safe (by) illuminating the temples and establishing laws like the twice-great Thoth,[29] a possessor of Sed festivals like Ptah Ta-tjenen and a sovereign like Re
Throne: *iwʿ n nṯrwy mnḫwy stp(.n) ptḥ wsr k3 rʿ sḫm ʿnḫ imn* (*iwa en netjerwy menekhwy, setep(.en) ptah, weser ka ra, sekhem ankh imen*), The heir of the two potent gods,[30] chosen by Ptah, the strong one of the ka of Re, the living image of Amun
Birth: *ptwlmys* (*ptolemys*), Ptolemy

Epithet added to the Birth name:

ʿnḫ ḏt mry 3st (*ankh djet, mery aset*), Living forever, beloved of Isis

---

26. Gauthier 1916, 259–62; von Beckerath 1999, 236–37.
27. Gauthier 1916, 263–74; von Beckerath 1999, 236–37.
28. That is, Egypt.
29. A common epithet of the god; see *Wb* I, 163:5; and Leitz 2002, 16.
30. Horus and Seth.

5. Ptolemy V Epiphanes ("Who manifests himself")[31]

Horus: *ḥwnw ḫꜥ m nsw ḥr st it.f* (*hunu kha em nesu her set it.ef*), The youth who has appeared[32] as king on his father's throne

Two Ladies: *wr-pḥty smn tꜣwy snfr tꜣ-mry mnḫ-ib ḫr nṯrw* (*wer pehty, semen tawy, senefer ta-mery, menekh ib kher netjeru*), The one great of strength, who has established the Two Lands and made Ta-mery perfect (by) being efficacious before the gods

Golden Horus: *wꜣḏ ꜥnḫ n ḥnmmt nb ḥbw-sd mi ptḥ tꜣ-ṯnn ity mi rꜥ* (*wadj ankh en henmemet, neb hebu-sed mi ptah ta-tjenen, ity mi ra*), The one who has made the life of mankind flourish, a possessor of Sed festivals like Ptah Ta-tjenen and a sovereign like Re

Throne: *iwꜥ n nṯrwy mrwy it, stp(n) ptḥ wsr kꜣ rꜥ sḫm ꜥnḫ imn* (*iwa en netjerwy merwy it, setep(en) ptah, weser ka ra, sekhem ankh imen*), The heir of the two gods who love (their?) father, chosen by Ptah, the strong one of the ka of Re, the living image of Amun

Birth: *ptwlmys* (*ptolemys*), Ptolemy

Epithet added to the Birth name:

ꜥnḫ ḏt mry ptḥ (*ankh djet, mery ptah*), Living forever, beloved of Ptah

5a. Cleopatra I[33]

Horus: *ḥwn(t) sꜣt ḥkꜣ ir(t).n ḥkꜣ mr(t) nṯrw bꜣḳt ḫkr(t).n ḫnmw ṯꜣtt sꜣt ḏḥwty wr(t)-pḥty shr(t) tꜣwy rdi n.s nbty rḫyt n nfrw ḳni sy nt nb(t) sꜣw ṯni sy ḥt-ḥr m mrwt.s* (*hun(et), sat heqa, ir(et).en heqa, mer(et) netjeru baqet, kheqer(et). en khnemu, tjatet, sat djehuty, wer(et)-pehty, seher(et) tawy, redi en.es nebty rekhyet en neferu, qeni sy net neb(et) saw, tjeni sy hut-hor em merut.es*), The youthful one and the daughter of a ruler, whom a ruler begat, beloved of the gods of Baqet, whom Khnum ornamented, vizier,[34] daughter of Thoth, great of strength, who has pleased the Two Lands, to whom the Two Ladies have given the common folk because of (her) perfection, whom Neith, mistress of Sais, has made brave, and whom Hathor has elevated through love of her

Birth: *ḳlw-pꜣ-trꜣ/ḳlꜣw-pꜣ-drꜣ* (*qlu-pa-tra/qliu-pa-dra*), Cleopatra

31. Gauthier 1916, 275–88; von Beckerath 1999, 236–39.
32. Note the Egyptian word that recalls the Greek *epiphanēs*.
33. Gauthier 1916, 286–87; von Beckerath 1999, 238–39.
34. Written with a feminine ending.

6. Ptolemy VI Philometor ("Mother-loving")[35]

Horus: *ṯnỉ m ḫt ḥtr ḥpw ꜥnḫ ḥr msḫn(t).sn* (*tjeni em khet, heter hapu ankh her meskhen(et).sen*), Distinguished in the sanctuary,[36] the twin brother[37] of the living Apis bull upon their birth-stool[38]

Two Ladies: *m mꜣꜥt sḫꜥ.n sw ỉt.f* (*em maat, sekha.en su it.ef*), Truly, whose father enthroned him

Golden Horus: *wr-pḥty nb ḥbw-sd mỉ ptḥ tꜣ-ṯnn ỉt nṯrw ỉty mỉ rꜥ* (*wer pehty, neb hebu-sed mi ptah ta-tjenen, it netjeru, ity mi ra*), The one great of strength, a possessor of Sed festivals like Ptah Ta-tjenen, the father of the gods, and a sovereign like Re

Throne: *ỉwꜥ n nṯrwy prw stp n ptḥ-ḫprỉ ỉr mꜣꜥt (n) ỉmn-rꜥ* (*iwa en netjerwy peru, setep en ptah-khepri, ir maat (en) imen-ra*), Heir of the two "Epiphanes" gods,[39] chosen by Ptah-Khepri, who has carried out Maat for Amun-Re[40]

Birth: *ptwlmys* (*ptolemys*), Ptolemy

Epithet added to the Birth name:

ꜥnḫ ḏt mry ptḥ (*ankh djet, mery ptah*), Living forever, beloved of Ptah

7. Ptolemy VII Neos Philopator ("The young father-lover")[41]

No royal titulary is attested in hieroglyphs

8. Ptolemy VIII Euergetes II Tryphon ("The magnificent benefactor")[42]

Original titulary

Horus: *ḥwnw ḥkn.tw m ꜥnḫ.f ḥr nst ỉt.f mꜥr-spw ḏsr msḫꜥw.f ḥnꜥ ḥpw ꜥnḫ* (*hunu, heken.tu em ankh.ef her neset it.ef, mar sepu, djeser meskhau.ef hena hapu ankh*), The youthful one, about whose life on his father's throne one is joyful, successful of deeds, and whose appearances with the living Apis bull are sacred

Two Ladies: *shr tꜣwy* (*seher tawy*), Who has pleased the Two Lands

Golden Horus: *wr-pḥty nb ḥbw-sd mỉ ỉt.f ptḥ tꜣ-ṯnn ỉt nṯrw ỉty mỉ rꜥ* (*wer pehty, neb hebu-sed mi it.ef ptah ta-tjenen it netjeru, ity mi ra*), The one great of

35. Gauthier 1916, 288–307; von Beckerath 1999, 238–39.

36. *Wb* III, 358:13.

37. *Wb* III, 199:7.

38. Or perhaps "twin brother of the living Apis, the bull upon his [*sic* for "their"] birth-stool."

39. Lit. "the two gods who have emerged," that is, Ptolemy V and Cleopatra I.

40. One example of this Throne name adds "forever" at the end.

41. Gauthier 1916, 341–45; von Beckerath 1999, 238–39.

42. Gauthier 1916, 307–35; von Beckerath 1999, 240–41.

strength, a possessor of Sed festivals like his father Ptah Ta-tjenen, the father of the gods, and a sovereign like Re

Throne: *iwꜥ n nṯrwy prw stp n ptḥ ir mꜣꜥt-rꜥ sḫm ꜥnḫ (n) imn (iwa en netjerwy peru, setep en ptah, ir maat ra, sekhem ankh (en) imen)*, Heir of the two "Epiphanes" gods, chosen by Ptah, who has accomplished the Maat (of?) Re, the living image of Amun

Birth: *ptwlmys (ptolemys)*, Ptolemy

Additional names

Horus 2: *ḥwnw ḥkn.tw ḥr nst it.f tit ḏsr(t) nt nsw nṯrw stp n itmw ḏs.f (hunu, heken. tu her neset it.ef, tit djeser(et) net nesu netjeru, setep en itmu djes.ef)*, The youthful one, about whose father's throne one is joyful, the sacred image of the king of the gods, chosen by Atum himself

Horus 3: *ḥwnw ḥry-tp pḏt 9 sꜣ wsir ms.n ꜣst šsp n.f nsyt rꜥ m-ꜥ it.f (hunu, hery-tep pedjet 9, sa wesir, mes.en aset, shesep en.ef nesyt ra em-a it.ef)*, The youthful one, leader of the Nine Bows, the son of Osiris, whom Isis has borne, who has received for himself the kingship of Re from his father's hand[43]

Epithet added to the Birth name:

ꜥnḫ ḏt mry ptḥ (ankh djet, mery ptah), Living forever, beloved of Ptah

8A. Cleopatra II[44]

Birth: *ḳlꜣw-pꜣ-drꜣ (qliu-pa-dra)*, Cleopatra

Epithet added to the Birth name:

nṯrt mr(t) mwt (netjeret, mer(et) mut), The goddess, beloved of Mut

9. Ptolemy IX Philometor Soter II ("Mother-loving and a savior")[45]

Original titulary

Horus: *ḏsr-mswt ḥnꜥ ḥpw ꜥnḫ nṯri-ḫpr(w) ḥtr msḫn(t) nt sꜣ ꜣst (djeser mesut hena hapu ankh, netjeri kheper(u), heter meskhen(et) net sa aset)*, Sacred of birth together with the living Apis, divine of manifestations, and twin brother of the birth-stool of the son of Isis

Two Ladies: *sḫꜥ sw mwt.f ḥr nst it.f iṯ tꜣwy m mꜣꜥ-ḫrw (sekha su mut.ef her neset it.ef, itj tawy em maa-kheru)*, The one whom his mother has enthroned on the throne of his father, who seized the Two Lands in justification

43. Both additional Horus names are from the Philae obelisk that is now at Kingston Lacy, Dorset, England; see Gauthier 1916, 323, LVIII, C–D.

44. Gauthier 1916, 330–32; von Beckerath 1999, 240–41.

45. Gauthier 1916, 346–65; von Beckerath 1999, 240–43.

Golden Horus: *nb tꜣ mry ḥkꜣ.f m hꜥꜥw nb ḥbw-sd mi tꜣ-ṯnn it nṯrw nsw(?) ity smn hpw mi ḏḥwty ꜥꜣ ꜥꜣ* (*neb ta mery, heqa.ef em haau, neb hebu-sed mi ta-tjenen it netjeru, nesu(?) ity semen hepu mi djehuty aa aa*), The Lord of the Beloved Land, he rules in jubilation, the possessor of Sed festivals like Ta-tjenen, the father of the gods, king(?) and sovereign who has established laws like twice-great Thoth

Throne: *iwꜥ (n) nṯr mnḫ nṯrt mr(t) mwt.s nḏt stp n ptḥ ir mꜣꜥt rꜥ sḫm ꜥnḫ imn* (*iwa (en) netjer menekh netjeret mer(et) mut.es, nedjet, setep en ptah, ir maat ra, sekhem ankh imen*), Heir of the potent god and of the goddess who loves her mother, the savior, chosen by Ptah, who has accomplished the Maat of Re, and the living image of Amun

Birth: *ptwlmys* (*ptolemys*), Ptolemy

Additional names[46]

Horus 2: *kꜣ nḫt ity psḏ m tꜣ-mry mi ḥpw ꜥnḫ rdi n.f ḥbw-sd ꜥšꜣw wrw mi ptḥ tꜣ-ṯnn it nṯrw* (*ka nakht, ity pesedj em ta-mery mi hapu ankh, redi en.ef hebu-sed ashau weru mi ptah ta-tjenen it netjeru*), The victorious bull and sovereign who shines in Ta-mery like the living Apis bull, to whom has been given a great many Sed festivals like Ptah Ta-tjenen, and father of the gods

Two Ladies 2: *wr-pḥty ḫnty-š nḥḥ smn hpw mi ḏḥwty ꜥꜣ ꜥꜣ* (*wer pehty, khenty-she neheh, semen hepu mi djehuty aa aa*), The one great of strength and the foremost one of the sea forever, who has established laws like the twice-great Thoth

Two Ladies 3: *wr-pḥty sḫm wꜣḏ-wr iṯ iwꜥ tꜣwy m mꜣꜥ-ḫrw mnḫ-ib ḫr nṯrw rmṯw* (*wer pehty, sekhem wadj-wer, itj iwa tawy em maa-kheru, menekh-ib kher netjeru remetju*), The great of strength and the powerful one of the Mediterranean, who has seized the inheritance of the Two Lands in justification and is efficacious before gods and men

Golden Horus 2: *šsp tꜣ mry ḥkꜣ.f m hꜥꜥw nb ḥbw-sd ꜥšꜣw wrw mi it.f ptḥ tꜣ-ṯnn smsw nṯrw šsp.n.f nsyt n rꜥ m ḳnw nḫt ity wḏꜥ mꜣꜥt smn hpw mi ḏḥwty ꜥꜣ ꜥꜣ* (*shesep ta mery, heqa.ef em haau, neb hebu-sed ashau weru mi it.ef ptah ta-tjenen semsu netjeru, shesep.en.ef nesyt en ra em qenu nakht, ity wedja maat, semen hepu mi djehuty aa aa*), The one who has received the Beloved Land, he rules in jubilation, the possessor of a great many Sed festivals like his father Ptah Ta-tjenen, the eldest of the gods, as he has received the kingship of Re in victorious bravery, the sovereign who discerns Maat and establishes laws like twice-great Thoth

Throne 2: *iwꜥ (n) nṯrwy mnḫwy stp n ptḥ ir mꜣꜥt rꜥ sḫm ꜥnḫ n imn* (*iwa (en) netjerwy menekhwy setep en ptah ir maat ra sekhem ankh en imen*), Heir of the two

---

46. All additional names are from the temple of Edfu; see Gauthier 1916, 359, XLV.A; 359, XLV.B; 358, XLII.A; von Beckerath 1999, 242–43 (G2); and Gauthier 1916, 358, XLII.A, respectively.

potent gods, chosen by Ptah, who has accomplished the Maat of Re, the living image of Amun

Epithet added to the Birth name:

ꜥnḫ ḏt mry ptḥ (*ankh djet, mery ptah*), Living forever, beloved of Ptah

10. Ptolemy X Alexander I[47]

Original titulary

Horus: *nṯri m ḫt ẖnm.n sw ḥpw ꜥnḫ ḥr msḫn(t) ḥwnw nfr bnr-mrwt sḫꜥ.n sw mwt.f ḥr nst it.f ṯmꜥ-ꜥ ḥwi ḫ3swt iṯ m sḫm.f mi rꜥ psḏ.f m 3ḫt* (*netjeri em khet, khnum.en su hapu ankh her meskhen(et), hunu nefer, bener merut, sekha.en su mut.ef her neset it.ef, tjema-a hui khasut, itj em sekhem.ef mi ra pesedj.ef em akhet*), The divine one in the sanctuary, whom the living Apis bull has united with the birth-stool, the perfect youth sweet of love, whom his mother enthroned on his father's throne, the sturdy-armed one who has struck down foreign countries and seized with his power like Re when he shines in the horizon

Two Ladies: *shr t3wy k3 nḫt sḫm nḥḥ* (*seher tawy, ka nakht, sekhem neheh*), Who has made the Two Lands content, victorious bull, eternal power

Golden Horus: *ꜥ3-ib mry nṯrw ity b3ḳt ḥḳ3 w3ḏty ꜥḳ.f t3-mry m ḥtp* (*aa ib, mery netjeru, ity baqet, heqa wadjty aq.ef ta-mery em hetep*), The great-hearted one who is beloved of the gods, sovereign of Baqet and ruler of the two crowns when he enters Ta-mery in peace

Throne: *iwꜥ (n) nṯr mnḫ nṯrt mnḫt s3t rꜥ stp n ptḥ ir m3ꜥt rꜥ snn ꜥnḫ n imn* (*iwa (en) netjer menekh netjeret menkhet, sat ra, setep en ptah, ir maat ra, snn ankh en imen*) Heir of the potent god and of the potent goddess, the daughter of Re, chosen by Ptah, who has accomplished the Maat of Re, the living likeness of Amun

Birth: *ptwlmys ḏd(w) n.f ilk-sntrs* (*ptolemys djed(u) en.ef ilek-sentres*), Ptolemy, also called[48] Alexander

Additional name

Throne 2: *mry nṯr mnḫ nṯrt mnḫt s3t rꜥ stp n ptḥ ir m3ꜥt rꜥ snn ꜥnḫ n imn* (*mery netjer menekh netjeret menkhet, sat ra, setep en ptah, ir maat ra, snn ankh en imen*), Beloved of the potent god and of the potent goddess, the daughter of Re, chosen by Ptah, who has accomplished the Maat of Re, the living likeness of Amun[49]

---

47. Gauthier 1916, 366–90; von Beckerath 1999, 242–43.

48. Lit. "to whom is said."

49. From the eastern temenos wall of the temple of Edfu; see Gauthier 1916, 387, LXXXVIII.

Epithet added to the Birth name:

ʿnḫ ḏt mry ptḥ (*ankh djet, mery ptah*), Living forever, beloved of Ptah

11. Ptolemy XI Alexander II

No royal titulary is attested in hieroglyphs

12. Berenike[50]

Horus: none attested
Two Ladies: none attested
Golden Horus: none attested
Throne: none attested
Birth: *iry-pʿtt wr(t)-ḥsw(t) birnikt* (*iry-patet, wer(et)-hesu(t), birniket*), The hereditary princess who is great of praise, Berenike

13. Ptolemy XII Neos Dionysos Auletes ("Flute-player")[51]

Original titulary

Horus: *ḥwnw nfr bnr-mrwt ṯni sw nbty rḫyt ḥnʿ k3.f dw3 n.f ẖnmw šps r šsp n.f ḫʿ m nsw snsn.n sḥnw m ḥʿʿw mi nḏt it.f ṯḥn-msw(t) ḥr nst it.f mi ḥr k3 nḫt ity psḏ m t3-mry mi ḥpw ʿnḫ rdi n.f ḥbw-sd ʿš3w wrw mi ptḥ t3-ṯnn it nṯrw* (*hunu nefer, bener-merut, tjeni su nebty rekhyet hena ka.f, dua en.ef khnum, shepes er shesep en.ef kha em nesu, sensen.en sehnu em haaw mi nedjet it.ef tjehen mesu(t) her neset it.ef mi hor ka nakht, ity pesedj em ta-mery mi hapu ankh, redi en.ef hebu-sed ashau weru mi ptah ta-tjenen it netjeru*), The perfect youth sweet of love, whom the Two Mistresses and the common folk have elevated along with his ka, whom the august Khnum praised in order to assume the crown of kingship for himself, with whom commanders have readily (lit. "in joy") associated like the Protector-of-his-Father,[52] dazzling of birth on the throne of his father like Horus, the victorious bull, the sovereign who shines in Ta-mery like the living Apis bull, to whom has been given a great many Sed festivals like Ptah Ta-tjenen, the father of the gods
Two Ladies: *wr-pḥty ḫnty š nḥḥ smn hpw mi ḏḥwty ʿ3 ʿ3* (*wer pehty, khenty she neheh, semen hepu mi djehuty aa aa*), The one great of strength and foremost one of the sea forever, who has established laws like the twice-great Thoth
Golden Horus: *ʿ3-ib ity nb ḳnw nḫt mi s3 3st* (*aa-ib, ity, neb qenu nakht mi sa aset*), The one great of mind, the sovereign, the possessor of bravery and strength like the son of Isis
Throne: *iwʿ n p3 nṯr nty nḥm stp n ptḥ ir m3ʿt rʿ sḫm ʿnḫ imn* (*iwa en pa netjer nety*

50. Gauthier 1916, 389–91; von Beckerath 1999, 244–45.
51. Gauthier 1916, 392–410; von Beckerath 1999, 244–45.
52. Horus.

nehem, setep en ptah, ir maat ra, sekhem ankh imen), Heir of the god-who-rescues, chosen by Ptah, who has accomplished the Maat of Re, the living image of Amun

Birth: *ptwlmys* (*ptolemys*), Ptolemy

Additional names

Two Ladies 2: *wr-pḥty ḫnty š nḥḥ nfr-ib wṯs nfrw mi ḏḥwty ꜥ3 ꜥ3* (*wer pehty, khenty she neheh, nefer ib, wetjes neferu mi djehuty aa aa*), The one great of strength and foremost one of the sea forever, perfect of mind, who has raised perfection like the twice-great Thoth[53]

Golden Horus 2: *ꜥ3-ib mry nṯrw b3ḳt ity mi rꜥ ḥḳ3 w3ḏty* (*aa ib, mery netjeru baqet, ity mi ra, heqa wadjty*), The one great of mind who is beloved of the gods of Baqet, a sovereign like Re and ruler of the two crowns[54]

Throne 2: *iwꜥ n p3 nṯr nty nḥm stp n ptḥ ir m3ꜥt imn-rꜥ* (*iwa en pa netjer nety nehem, setep en ptah, ir maat imen-ra*), Heir of the god-who-rescues, chosen by Ptah, who has accomplished the Maat of Amun-Re[55]

Throne 3: *p3 nṯr mry it sn wsir ḥwnw* (*pa netjer, mery it sen, wesir hunu*), The god who is beloved of his father and brother, the youthful Osiris ("Neos Dionysos")[56]

Epithet added to the Birth name:

> *ꜥnḫ ḏt mry ptḥ 3st* (*ankh djet, mery ptah aset*), Living forever, beloved of Ptah and Isis

14. Cleopatra VII Philopator ("Father-loving")[57]

Original titulary

Horus: *wr(t) nb(t) nfrw 3ḫ(t)-sḥ* (*wer(et), neb(et) neferu, akh(et) seh*), The great one, possessor of perfection and splendid of shrine

Two Ladies: none attested

Golden Horus: none attested

Throne: none attested

Birth: *ḳliw-p3-dr3* (*qliu-pa-dra*), Cleopatra

53. From the ceiling of the Hypostyle Hall at the temple of Kom Ombo; see Gauthier 1916, 402, XXXIX, A.

54. From a pylon at the temple of Philae; see Gauthier 1916, 401, XXXIV.

55. From an architrave at the temple of Philae; see Gauthier 1916, 401, XXXII.

56. From a reused block found near the temple of Hathor at Philae; see Gauthier 1916, 401, XXXV.

57. Gauthier 1916, 410–22; von Beckerath 1999, 244–45. Chauveau (1997, 62) points out that, like her ancestor Cleopatra I, Cleopatra VII was not given a full titulary, possibly out of reluctance to accept the fact of having a queen on the throne.

Additional names

Horus 2: *wrt twt n ỉt.s* (*weret, tut en it.es*), The great one and the (very) image of her father[58]

Epithet added to the Birth name:

nṯrt mr(t) ỉt.s (*netjeret, mer(et) it.es*), The goddess, beloved of her father

15. Ptolemy XIII

No royal titulary is attested in hieroglyphs

16. Ptolemy XIV

No royal titulary is attested in hieroglyphs

17. Ptolemy XV Caesarion[59]

Original titulary

Horus: *ḥwnw nfr bnr-mrwt* (*hunu nefer, bener merut*), The perfect youth who is sweet of love
Two Ladies: none attested
Golden Horus: none attested
Throne: *ỉwꜥ (n) pꜣ nṯr nty nḥm stp n ptḥ ỉr mꜣꜥt rꜥ sḫm n ỉmn* (*iwa (en) pa netjer nety nehem, setep en ptah, ir maat ra, sekhem en imen*), Heir (of) the god-who-rescues, chosen by Ptah, who has accomplished the Maat of Re, the image of Amun
Birth: *ptwlmys* (*ptolemys*), Ptolemy

Additional names

Horus 2: *kꜣ nḫt ỉꜣḫw stwt rꜥ ỉꜥḥ* (*ka nakht, iakhu setut ra iah*), Victorious bull, the light of the sun and the moon's rays
Birth 2: *kỉsrs* (*kiseres*), Caesar[60]
Birth 3: *ptwlmys ḏd.tw n.f kisrs* (*ptolemys djed.tu enef kiseres*), Ptolemy, also called Caesar[61]

Epithet added to the Birth name:

ꜥnḫ ḏt mry ptḥ ꜣst (*ankh djet, mery ptah aset*), Living forever, beloved of Ptah and Isis

---

58. Part of a scene from the temple of Armant, showing scenes of the divine birth of her son Caesarion; see Gauthier 1916, 417–17, XVIII,H.

59. Gauthier 1916, 419–21; von Beckerath 1999, 246–47.

60. The additional Horus name and second Birth name are from the previously mentioned scenes of the divine birth of Caesarion at Armant; see LD IV, 60b; and LD IV, 63a.

61. From a similar scene on a reused block found at Coptos; see Gauthier 1916, 419, XXVII.A.e.

Appendix A

Index of Royal Names

Included here are all the royal names listed alphabetically, as they would be found in a scholarly Egyptian to English dictionary. Note that the small epithets added to the Throne and Birth names, such as "Beloved of Amun" and "Chosen by Re," have not been added here.

Abbreviations used
B = Birth name
C = Later Cartouche name
G = Golden Horus name
H = Horus name
N = Nebty/Two Ladies name
T = Throne name

ꜣw-ib rꜥ (*au ib ra*), The (very) joy of Re, Hor (I) T, Awibre T
ꜣlksndrs / *ꜣlksindrs* (*aleksendres/aleksindres*), Alexander B
ꜣḫ n itw.f skꜣ pr.sn (*akh en itu.ef, seqa per.sen*), The one beneficial to his fathers, who has exalted their temples, Sety I G2
ꜣḫ n itn (akh en aten), Beneficial to the Aten, Akhenaten B2
ꜣḫ n rꜥ stp.n rꜥ (*akh en ra, setep.en ra*), Beneficial to Re, whom Re chose, Siptah T2

i nb /// (*i neb ///*), O the lord /// (?), I-neb /// B
ii m ḥtp (*ii em hetep*), The one who has come in peace, Imhotep T
iy (*iy*), "Hey!", Iy B
iy ṯnw (*iy tjenu*), The one who has come (already) distinguished, Iytjenu B
iꜥrt nbw (*iaret nebu*), The golden uraeus, Den G
iꜥḥ ms(w) (iah mes(u)), Iah (= the moon god) is born, Ahmose I to III B
iwꜥ n pꜣ nṯr nty nḥm stp n ptḥ ir mꜣꜥt imn-rꜥ (*iwa en pa netjer nety nehem, setep en ptah, ir maat imen-ra*), Heir of the god-who-rescues, chosen by Ptah, who has accomplished the Maat of Amun-Re, Ptolemy XII T2
iwꜥ n pꜣ nṯr nty nḥm stp n ptḥ ir mꜣꜥt rꜥ sḫm ꜥnḫ imn (*iwa en pa netjer nety nehem, setep en ptah, ir maat ra, sekhem ankh imen*), Heir of the god-who-rescues,

chosen by Ptah, who has accomplished the Maat of Re, the living image of Amun, Ptolemy XII T1

iwꜥ (n) pꜣ nṯr nty nḥm stp n ptḥ ir mꜣꜥt rꜥ sḫm n imn (*iwa (en) pa netjer nety nehem, setep en ptah, ir maat ra, sekhem en imen*), Heir (of) the god-who-rescues, chosen by Ptah, who has accomplished the Maat of Re, the image of Amun, Ptolemy XV T

iwꜥ (n) nṯr mnḫ nṯrt mnḫt sꜣt rꜥ stp n ptḥ ir mꜣꜥt rꜥ snn ꜥnḫ n imn (*iwa (en) netjer menekh netjeret menkhet, sat ra, setep en ptah, ir maat ra, snn ankh en imen*) Heir of the potent god and of the potent goddess, the daughter of Re, chosen by Ptah, who has accomplished the Maat of Re, the living likeness of Amun, Ptolemy X T1

iwꜥ (n) nṯr mnḫ nṯrt mr(t) mwt.s nḏt stp n ptḥ ir mꜣꜥt rꜥ sḫm ꜥnḫ imn (*iwa (en) netjer menekh netjeret mer(et) mut.es, nedjet, setep en ptah, ir maat ra, sekhem ankh imen*), Heir of the potent god and of the goddess who loves her mother, the savior, chosen by Ptah, who has accomplished the Maat of Re, and the living image of Amun, Ptolemy IX T1

iwꜥ n nṯrwy prw stp n ptḥ ir mꜣꜥt-rꜥ sḫm ꜥnḫ (n) imn (*iwa en netjerwy peru, setep en ptah, ir maat ra, sekhem ankh (en) imen*), Heir of the two "Epiphanes" gods, chosen by Ptah, who has accomplished the Maat (of?) Re, the living image of Amun, Ptolemy VIII T

iwꜥ n nṯrwy prw stp n ptḥ-ḫpri ir mꜣꜥt (n) imn-rꜥ (*iwa en netjerwy peru, setep en ptah-khepri, ir maat (en) imen-ra*), Heir of the two "Epiphanes" gods, chosen by Ptah-Khepri, who has carried out Maat for Amun-Re, Ptolemy VI T

iwꜥ (n) nṯrwy mnḫwy stp n ptḥ ir mꜣꜥt rꜥ sḫm ꜥnḫ n imn (*iwa (en) netjerwy menekhwy, setep en ptah, ir maat ra sekhem, ankh en imen*), Heir of the two potent gods, chosen by Ptah, who has accomplished the Maat of Re, the living image of Amun, Ptolemy IX T2

iwꜥ n nṯrwy mnḫwy stp (n) ptḥ wsr kꜣ rꜥ sḫm ꜥnḫ imn (*iwa en netjerwy menekhwy, setep (en) ptah, weser ka ra, sekhem ankh imen*), The heir of the two potent gods, chosen by Ptah, the strong one of the ka of Re, the living image of Amun, Ptolemy IV T

iwꜥ n nṯrwy mrwy it, stp (n) ptḥ wsr kꜣ rꜥ sḫm ꜥnḫ imn (*iwa en netjerwy merwy it, setep (en) ptah, weser ka ra, sekhem ankh imen*), The heir of the two gods who love (their?) father, chosen by Ptah, the strong one of the ka of Re, the living image of Amun, Ptolemy V T

iwꜥ n snwy nṯrwy stp (n) rꜥ sḫm ꜥnḫ n imn (*iwa en senwy netjerwy, setep (en) ra, sekhem ankh en imen*), The heir of the two divine brothers, chosen by Re, the living image of Amun, Ptolemy III T

iwpwt (*iuput*), Iuput B

iw.f n.i (*iu.ef en.i*), He belongs to me, Iufni B

ib iꜥ(w) (*ib iau*), The quiet one (lit. "whose heart/mind is washed"), Ib-iau B

ip /// (*ip ///*), Ip /// B

ibi (*ibi*), The kid (lit. "the young goat"), Qakare Ibi I B, Ibi II B

imy-r mšʿ (*imy-er mesha*), The General, Imy-ra Mesha B
imn ir di.s(*w*) (*imen ir di s(u)*), Amun is the one who created him, Amenirdis B
imn m ipt (*imen em ipet*), Amun is in Ipet, Amenemope B
imn m nsw (*imen em nesu*), Amun is king, Amen-em-nisu B
imn m ḥ3t (*imen em hat*), Amun is at the forefront, Amenemhat I to VII
imn-m-ḥ3t <*s3*> *sbk ḥtp*(*w*) (*imen em hat* <*sa*> *sobek hetep(u)*), Amenemhat's son, Sobekhotep ("Sobek is satisfied"), Sobekhotep I B
imn-m-ḥ3t <*s3*> *snb.f* (*imen em hat* <*sa*> *seneb.ef*), Amenemhat's son, Senbef, Senbef B
imn ms sw mry rʿ ḥḳ3 w3st (*imen mes su, mery ra, heqa waset*), Amun is the one who bore him, the beloved of Re and Ruler of Thebes, Amenmesse B
imn ḥtp(*w*) *(imen hetpu),* Amun is satisfied, Amenhotep I to IV B
imny (*s3*) *ḳm3w* (*imeny (sa) qemau*), Ameny's son, Qemau ("the begotten one"), Qemau B
in.i (*in.i*), The one whom I have brought forth, Ini I B
ini (*ini*), The delayed one, Ini II B
ini (*ini*), Ini (as a nickname), Niuserre B
in it.f (*in it.ef*), The one whom his father has brought forth, Intef I to VII B
in it.f ʿ3 (*in it.ef aa*), Intef the Great, Intef II B, Intef V B and VII B 2
in it.f nḫt(*w*) (*in it.ef nakht(u)*), Intef the Victorious, Intef VI B 2
in ḥtp (*in hetep*), The one who has brought peace, Dedumose I G
in-k (*in-ek*), Inek B
inḳ t3w (*ineq tau*), Who has embraced the lands, Khyan H
inḳ t3wy (*ineq tawy*), Who has embraced the Two Lands, Sobekemsaf II G
ind (*ined*), The sad one, Ined B
ilr (*iler*), Alara b
ir 3ḫwt m ipt-swt n it.f imn ḳm3 nfrw.f (*ir akhut em ipet-sut en it.ef imen, qema neferu.ef*), The one who has accomplished benefits in Karnak for his father Amun, who created his (the king's) perfection, Herihor G1
ir b3w r t3 n tmḥw (*ir bau er ta en temehu*), Who has exercised power against the land of the Temehu, Merenptah N1
ir m ʿwy.f(*y*) (*ir em awy.fy*), Who has acted with his arms, Merenptah N3
ir m3ʿt (*ir maat*), The one who has accomplished Maat, Userkaf H N
ir m3ʿt m-ḫt t3wy di ḥtp nṯrw nbw m itrt.sn (*ir maat em-khet tawy, di hetep netjeru nebu em iteret.sen*), The one who has rendered justice throughout the Two Lands and caused all the gods to be satisfied with their shrines, Herihor G2
ir m3ʿt n psḏt sḥb r3.w-pr rʿ nb (*ir maat en pesdjet, seheb rau-per ra neb*), Who has accomplished Maat for the Ennead and made (their) temples festive daily, Ramses III N3
ir m3ʿt n rʿ (*ir maat en ra*), The one who has accomplished Maat for Re, Tachos T
ir mrt nṯrw (*ir meret netjeru*), Who has accomplished what the gods desire, Nectanebo I G
ir t3š.f (*ir tash.ef*), The one who has made his (own) border, Seker-her G

iry-nbty (*iry-nebty*), He who is connected to the Two Ladies, Semerkhet N
iry-ḥr (*iry-hor*), The companion of Horus, Iry-Hor H
izi (*izi*), Izi, Nefer(ef)re B
izzi (*izezi*), Izezi, Djedkare B
isw (*isu*), The ancient one (?), Isu B
ik3w (*ikau*), Ikau, Menkauhor B2
ik3w ḥr (*ikau hor*), Ikauhor, Menkauhor B1
it nṯr iy (it netjer iy), The god's father Ay, Ay B
it-nṯrw mnṯw-ḥtp(.w) ꜥ3 mry stt nbt 3bw (*it netjeru mentu hotep aa, mery Satet nebet Abu*), The Gods' Father Mentuhotep ("Montu is satisfied") the Great, beloved of Satet, mistress of Elephantine, Mentuhotep I B
it3 (*ita*), The sovereign (?), Djet C
ity (*ity*), The sovereign, Aha C, Djer C, Djet C, Iti T
ity wsr-ḫꜥw wr-bi3wt (*ity, weser khau, wer biaut*), The sovereign who is rich in appearances and great of marvels, Merenptah N4
iṯ iwꜥt t3wy (*itj iwat tawy*), The one who has seized the inheritance of the Two Lands, Amenemhat III N
iṯ m nḫtw (*itj em nakhtu*), Who has seized through victories, Djehuty H
iṯ m sḫm ḥk3 ṯl (*itj em sekhem, heqa tjel*), Who has seized with (his own) power, the ruler of Sile, Ptolemy I N
iṯ m sḫm.f m t3w nbw (itj em sekhem.ef em tau nebu), Who has seized by means of his strong arm in all lands, Amenhotep II G1
iṯ sḫm.f (*itj sekhem.ef*), The one who has seized his power, Senbef N
iṯ t3w nbw (itj tau nebu), Who has seized all lands, Thutmose I N2
i /// rꜥ (*i /// ra*), I /// Re, I /// re B

yꜥ-mw (*ya-mu*), "Where is the uncle?," Iamu B
y3-k-b-mw (*yakeb mu*), "(the goddess) Aya is a rock," Yakob-mu B
yꜥ-kb-hr (*ya-keb-her*), "(the god) Haddad protects," Yakub-her B

ꜥ (*a*), The (raised?) arm, Horus "A" H
ꜥ3-ib (*aa ib*), Strong-minded, Psamtek I H, Nepherites I H
ꜥ3-ib ity nb ḳnw nḫt mi s3 3st (*aa-ib, ity, neb qenu nakht mi sa aset*), The one great of mind, the sovereign, the possessor of bravery and strength like the son of Isis, Ptolemy XII G1
ꜥ3-ib mry nṯrw ity b3ḳt ḥk3 w3ḏty ꜥḳ.f t3-mry m ḥtp (*aa ib, mery netjeru, ity baqet, heqa wadjty aq.ef ta-mery em hetep*), The great-hearted one who is beloved of the gods, sovereign of Baqet and ruler of the Two Crowns when he enters Ta-mery in peace, Ptolemy X G
ꜥ3-ib mry nṯrw b3ḳt ity mi rꜥ ḥk3 w3ḏty (*aa ib, mery netjeru baqet, ity mi ra, heqa wadjty*), The one great of mind who is beloved of the gods of Baqet, a sovereign like Re and ruler of the Two Crowns, Ptolemy XII G2

ˁ3-ib mry t3wy (aa ib, mery tawy), Strong-minded and beloved of the Two Lands, Achoris H
ˁ3 wsr rˁ (aa weser ra), The great one whom Re has made strong, Apophis T2
ˁ3-b3w (aa bau), Great of might, Amenemhat III H
ˁ3-pḥty (aa pehty), Great of strength, Amenemhat VII G, Neferhotep III Iykher-nofret N
ˁ3-pḥty wr-nḫtw (aa pehty, wer nakhtu), Great of might and important of victories, Merenptah N5
ˁ3-pḥty wsr-ḫpš w3ḏ-rnpwt m ḥwt-ˁ3t m3ˁt (aa pehty weser khepesh wadj renput em hut-aat maat), Great of strength and strong-armed, enduring of years in the temple of Maat, Thutmose I G3
ˁ3-pḥty mˁr spw (aa pehty, mar sepu), Great of strength and successful of occasions, Psammuthis H
ˁ3-pḥty nb šfyt (aa pehty, neb shefyt), Great of might and possessor of majesty, Pinodjem I H4
ˁ3-mw (aa mu), "The Asiatic," Aamu B
ˁ3-n3-ti (aa-na-ti), Anati B
ˁ3-nrw (aa neru), Great of dread, Amenhotep I N
ˁ3-nrw m t3w nbw (aa neru em tau nebu), Great of dread in all lands, Sety II G1
ˁ3-nrw ḥr ḫ3st nbt (aa neru her khaset nebet), Great of dread in every foreign land, Amenhotep III N4
ˁ3-nḫtw m t3w nbw (aa nakhtu em tau nebu), Great of victories in all lands, Sety II G2
ˁ3 ḥtp rˁ (aa hetep ra), The great one is the (very) peace of Re, Aamu T
ˁ3 ḫpr n rˁ (aa kheper en ra), The great one is the manifestation of Re, Thutmose II T
ˁ3 ḫpr rˁ (aa kheper ra), The great one is a manifestation of Re, Psusennes I T, Osorkon the Elder T, Sheshonq V T, Osorkon IV T
ˁ3 ḫpr k3 rˁ (aa kheper ka ra), The great one is the manifestation of the ka of Re, Thutmose I T
ˁ3-ḫprw (aa kheperu), Great of manifestations, Ahmose (II) H1
ˁ3 ḫprw rˁ (aa kheperu ra), The great one of the manifestations of Re, Amenhotep II T
ˁ3-ḫpš mry t3wy (aa khepesh, mery tawy), Great of effectiveness, beloved of the Two Lands, Ramses II G3
ˁ3-ḫpš ḥwi pḏwt 9 (aa khepesh, hui pedjut 9), The one great of strength who has struck down the Nine Bows, Thutmose III (b) G3, Shabataka G1
ˁ3-ḫpš ḥwi sṯtyw (aa khepesh, hui setjetiu), The great-of-strength one who has struck down the Asiatics, Amenhotep III G1
ˁ3-ḫpš sˁ3 w3st n ms sw (aa khepesh, saa waset en mes su), The one great of might, who has magnified Thebes for the one who bore him, Amenmesse G1
ˁ3 sḥ rˁ (aa seh ra), The great one of the shrine of Re, Nehsy T

ꜥ3-šfyt m t3w nbw (*aa shefyt em tau nebu*), Great of majesty in all lands, Thutmose III (b) N3, Shabataka N1
ꜥ3 ḳn.n rꜥ (*aa qen.en ra*), The great one, whom Re has made brave, Apophis T1
ꜥ3 k3 rꜥ (*aa ka ra*), The great one of the ka of Re, Aakare T
ꜥ3 /// (*aa-///*), Great of ///, Ramses X N
ꜥn n nsw mi itmw mr.tw.f 3b.tw.f mi ḥm n rꜥ (*an en nesu mi itemu, mer.tu.ef ab.tu. ef mi hem en ra*), Beautiful as king like Atum, he is loved and wished for like the majesty of Re, Ramses III H16
ꜥn ḥr srḫ mi s3 3st (*an her serekh mi sa aset*), Beautiful on the throne like the son of Isis, Ramses III H9
ꜥn tnr / ṯl m msw nṯrw nṯrywt ḳ3b ꜥ3bt.sn (*an tener / tjel em mesu netjeru ntjeriut qab aabet.sen*), Beautiful and mighty, as the (very) progeny of gods and goddesses, who has doubled their offerings, Ramses III G4
ꜥnw (*anu*), The beautiful one, Neferkamin Anu C2
ꜥnḫ ib t3wy (*ankh ib tawy*), The (very) life of the heart of the Two Lands, Sobekhotep IV H
ꜥnḫ mswt (*ankh mesut*), The one who has lived the (re)birth, Senwosret I H G N
ꜥnḫ nṯrw (*ankh netjeru*), The (very) life of the gods, Sobekhotep I G
ꜥnḫ rnpwt (*ankh renput*), (Fully) Alive of years, Sekhemre Khutawy G
ꜥnḫ ḫꜥw (*ankh khau*), (Whose) appearances are (very much) alive, Merenre H
ꜥnḫ ḫꜥw nbty (*ankh khau nebty*), (The one for whom) The appearances of the Two Ladies are alive, Merenre N
ꜥnḫ ḫprw rꜥ (ankh kheperu ra), The (very) life of the manifestations of Re, Neferneferu-aten T
ꜥnḫ k3 n rꜥ (*ankh ka en ra*), The living one is the (very) ka of Re, Psamtek III T
ꜥḥ3 (*aha*), The fighter, Aha H
ꜥḥ3 n ḥḥw m3i sḫm-ib (*aha en hehu, mai sekhem-ib*), Who has fought for millions, a stout-hearted lion, Ramses II N2
ꜥḥ3 ḥr ḫpš.f mk mšꜥw.f (*aha her khepesh.ef, mek meshau.ef*), Who has fought with his sword/strong arm, the protector of his armies, Ramses II N3
ꜥš3-mnw (*asha menu*), With many monuments, Ramses III H7
ꜥš(3)-ḫprw (*ash(a) kheperu*), Numerous of manifestations, Sobekemsaf II N
ꜥḏ-ib (*adj ib*), Hale-hearted, Adjib H

w3ḥ-ib (*wah ib*), Enduring of mind, Apries H
w3ḥ ib rꜥ (*wah ib ra*), The enduring one is the (very) mind of Re, Ib-iau T, Psamtek I T, Apries B
w3ḥ-ꜥnḫ (*wah ankh*), Enduring of life, Intef II H, Amenemhat III G, Rahotep H
w3ḥ-mrwt (*wah merut*), Enduring of love, Tanutamun H
w3ḥ-mswt (*wah mesut*), Enduring of birth, Khendjer N
w3ḥ-nsyt (wah nesyt), Enduring of kingship, Thutmose III (a) N1
w3ḥ-nsyt mi rꜥ m pt (wah nesyt, mi ra em pet), Enduring of kingship like Re in heaven, Thutmose III (b) N1, Piye N1

wꜣḥ-rnpwt (wah renput), Enduring of years, Amenhotep I G
wꜣḥ-rnpwt ꜥšꜣ-ḥbw (wah renput, asha hebu), Enduring of years and numerous of festivals, Amenhotep III H3
wꜣḥ kꜣ rꜥ (*wah ka ra*), The enduring one of the ka of Re, Khety (V) T, Bakenrenef T
wꜣs nṯr rꜥ (*was netjer ra*), The (very) divine scepter of Re (?), Sheshonq VII T
wꜣḏ ꜥnḫ n ḥnmmt nb ḥbw-sd mi ptḥ tꜣ-ṯnn ity mi rꜥ (*wadj ankh en henmemet, neb hebu-sed mi ptah ta-tjenen, ity mi ra*), The one who has made the life of mankind flourish, a possessor of Sed festivals like Ptah Ta-tjenen and a sovereign like Re, Ptolemy V G
wꜣḏ m nbty (*wadj em nebty*), The one who is sturdy by means of the Two Ladies, Unas N
wꜣḏ-ns (*wadj-nes*), Sturdy (lit. "hale") of tongue, Weneg C
wꜣḏ-ḫꜥw (*wadj khau*), Flourishing of appearances, Sobekhotep IV N, Neferhotep III Iykhernofret H, Dedumose I H
wꜣḏ ḫpr rꜥ (*wadj kheper ra*), The flourishing one is the manifestation of Re, Kamose T
wꜣḏ kꜣ rꜥ (*wadj ka ra*), The flourishing one of the ka of Re, Wadjkare T
wꜣḏ-kꜣw nfr-rnpwt nb ḥbw-sd (wadj kau, nefer renput, neb hebu sed), Sturdy of sustenance, perfect of years, and lord of Sed festivals, Amenhotep III G8
wꜣḏ tꜣwy (*wadj tawy*), The sturdy one of the Two Lands, Unas H, Takelot III H N G
wꜣḏ /// (*wadj///*), Flourishing of ////, Rahotep G
wꜣḏt (*wadjet*), The cobra, Djet/Wadjet H
wꜣḏt-rnpwt (wadjet renput), Flourishing of years, Hatshepsut N
wꜣḏd ,Wadjed B
wꜥf bštw (*waf beshtu*), Who has subdued the rebellious ones, Ramses II G4
wꜥf pḏwt (*waf pedjut*), The one who has subdued the Nine Bows, Seker-her N
wꜥf ḫꜣswt dr bštw (*waf khasut, der beshtu*), Who has subdued foreign countries and repelled the rebellious ones, Ramses II G5
wꜥf ḫꜣswt dr mntyw (*waf khasut, der mentiu*), Who has subdued the foreign lands and repelled the bedouin, Sety I N4
wbn rꜥ (*weben ra*), The (very) rising of Re, Webenre I T
wp-wꜣwt m sꜣ.f (*wepwawet em sa.ef*), Wepwawet is his protection, Wepwawetem-saf B
wp mꜣꜥt (*wep maat*), Who has inaugurated Maat, Neferhotep I N, Intef V H
wnis (*wenis*), Unas, Unas B
wng (*weneg*), The *weneg*-plant, Weneg N
wr ꜥḥ imn (*wer ah imen*), The great one of the palace of Amun, Tutankhamun N3
wr-biꜣwt (*wer biaut*), Great of marvels, Sheshonq V G2
wr-biꜣwt m ipt swt (wer biaut em ipet sut), Great of marvels in Ipet-sut, Horemheb N , Amenmesse N1
wr-pḥty (*wer pehty*), Great of strength, Ptolemy II N

wr-pḥty ir ꜣḫwt nb ḥbw-sd mi ptḥ tꜣ-ṯnn ity mi rꜥ (*wer-pehty, ir akhut, neb hebu-sed mi ptah ta-tjenen, ity mi ra*), The one great of strength who has done beneficial things, the possessor of Sed festivals like Ptah Tatjenen and a sovereign like Re, Ptolemy III G

wr-pḥty ir ꜥḏt m bdšw.f (*wer pehty, ir adjet em bedshu.ef*), The one great of strength, who has brought about slaughter among those who rebelled against him, Ptolemy III H3

wr-pḥty mi imn (*wer pehty mi imen*), Great of strength like Amun, Amenmesse H2

wr-pḥty mi sꜣ nwt (*wer pehty mi sa nut*), Great of might like the son of Nut, Ramses II N4

wr-pḥty mnḫ-ib ḫr nṯrw nb(*w*) *nḏty n ḥnmmt* (*wer pehty, menekh-ib kher netjeru neb(u), nedjty en henmemet*), Great of strength, efficacious before all the gods, and the savior of mankind, Ptolemy IV N

wr-pḥty nb ḥbw-sd mi it.f ptḥ tꜣ-ṯnn it nṯrw ity mi rꜥ (*wer pehty, neb hebu-sed mi it.ef ptah ta-tjenen it netjeru, ity mi ra*), The one great of strength, a possessor of Sed festivals like his father Ptah Ta-tjenen, the father of the gods, and a sovereign like Re, Ptolemy VIII G

wr-pḥty nb ḥbw-sd mi ptḥ tꜣ-ṯnn it nṯrw ity mi rꜥ (*wer pehty, neb hebu-sed mi ptah ta-tjenen, it netjeru, ity mi ra*), The one great of strength, a possessor of Sed festivals like Ptah Ta-tjenen, the father of the gods, and a sovereign like Re, Ptolemy VI G

wr-pḥty nsw ḳni (*wer pehty, nesu qeni*), Great of strength and brave king, Ptolemy I H

wr pḥty ḥwi mnṯyw (*wer pehty, hui mentjyu*), The mighty great one who has struck down the bedouin, Osorkon II G1

wr pḥty ḥwi mnṯyw wsr /// (*wer pehty, hui mentjyu, weser ///*), The mighty great one who has struck down the bedouin, rich [in splendor?], Osorkon II G2

wr-pḥty ḫnty š nḥḥ nfr-ib wṯs nfrw mi ḏḥwty ꜥꜣ ꜥꜣ (*wer pehty, khenty she neheh, nefer ib, wetjes neferu mi djehuty aa aa*), The one great of strength and foremost one of the sea forever, perfect of mind, who has raised perfection like the twice-great Thoth, Ptolemy XII N2

wr-pḥty ḫnty š nḥḥ smn hpw mi ḏḥwty ꜥꜣ ꜥꜣ (*wer pehty, khenty she neheh, semen hepu mi djehuty aa aa*), The one great of strength and foremost one of the sea forever, who has established laws like the twice-great Thoth, Ptolemy IX N2, Ptolemy XII N1

wr-pḥty sꜥnḫ tꜣwy ity hr ḥr mꜣꜥt sḥtp tꜣwy (*wer pehty, sankh tawy, ity her her maat, sehetep tawy*), The one great of strength who has sustained the Two Lands, the sovereign who is pleased with Maat and has reconciled the Two Lands, Ramses XI G

wr-pḥty smn tꜣwy snfr tꜣ-mry mnḫ-ib ḫr nṯrw (*wer pehty, semen tawy, senefer ta-mery, menekh-ib kher netjeru*), The one great of strength, who has established the Two Lands and made Ta-mery perfect (by) being efficacious before the gods, Ptolemy V N

wr-pḥty sḫm w3ḏ-wr iṯ iwꜥ t3wy m m3ꜥ-ḫrw mnḫ-ib ḫr nṯrw rmṯw (*wer pehty, sekhem wadj-wer, itj iwa tawy em maa-kheru, menekh-ib kher netjeru remetju*), The great of strength and the powerful one of the Mediterranean, who has seized the inheritance of the Two Lands in justification and is efficacious before gods and men, Ptolemy IX N3

wr-pḥty ḏr sṯtyw wsr-f3w m t3w nbw (*wer pehty, der setjetiu, weser fau em tau nebu*), The great of strength one who has repelled the Setjetiu-Asiatics is rich in splendor in all lands, Osorkon II, G5

wr-f3wt sḫm-pḥty (*wer fawet, sekhem pehty*), Great of splendor and powerful of strength, Ramses II G6

wr-mnw m ipt-swt nb pḥty wꜥf t3wy w3ḥ-nsyt mi rꜥ m pt (*wer menu em ipet-sut, neb pehty, waf tawy, wah nesyt mi ra em pet*), Great of monuments in Karnak, the possessor of might who has subdued the Two Lands, the one enduring of kingship like Re in heaven, Psusennes I N

wr-mnw m pr ẖnmw (*wer menu em per khnemu*), Great of monuments in the temple of Khnum, Ramses II N5

wr-mnw r ḏ3t pḥty.f (wer menu er djat pehty.ef), Great of monuments so as to extend his strength, Amenhotep III N3

wr nb mry šmꜥw (*wer neb, mery shemau*), Chieftain and lord, beloved of Upper Egypt, Darius I H2

wr-nḫtw ḥr ḫ3st nbt (*wer nakhtu her khaset nebet*), Great of victories in every foreign country, Ramses II G7

wr-nsyt m 3ḫt-itn (wer nesyt em akhet iten), Great of kingship in Akhetaten, Akhenaten N

wr-nsyt m ipt swt (wer nesyt em ipet sut), Great of kingship in Ipet-sut, Amenhotep IV N

wr-ḥbw-sd mi t3-ṯnn (*wer hebu sed mi ta-tjenen*), Great of Sed festivals like Ta-tjenen, Ramses II H2 and N6, Ramses III N1

wr ḥbw-sd mi t3-ṯnn ptpt tḥnw m iwnw ḥr st.sn (*wer hebu-sed mi ta-tjenen, petpet tjehenu em iunu her set.sen*), Great of Sed festivals like Ta-tjenen, who has trampled the Tehenu-Libyans into piles (of corpses) right there and then, Ramses III N4

wr-šfyt mk kmt (*wer shefyt, mek kemet*), Great of majesty, the protector of Egypt, Ramses II N6

wr(t) nb(t) nfrw 3ḫ(t) sḥ (*wer(et), neb(et) neferu, akh(et) seh*), The great one, possessor of perfection and splendid of shrine, Cleopatra VII H1

wrt twt n it.s (*weret, tut en it.es*), The great one and the (very) image of her father, Cleopatra VII H2

wḥm ib rꜥ (*wehem ib ra*), Who has renewed the will of Re, Nekau II T

wḥm ꜥnḫ (*wehem ankh*), The one who has repeated life, Senwosret IV H *wḥm mnw* (*wehem menu*), Who has renewed (lit. "repeated") monuments, Kamose N

wḥm mswt (*wehem mesut*), The one who has repeated births, Amenemhat I (b) H N G

wḥm mswt sḫm-ḫpš dr pḏwt 9 (*wehem mesut, sekhem khepesh, der pedjut 9*), Renewing births, the strong-armed one who has repelled the Nine Bows, Sety I N1

wḥm ḫʿw wsr-pḏwt m t3w nbw (*wehem khau, weser pedjut em tau nebu*), Who has repeated appearances, strong of troops in all lands, Sety I G1

wḥm ḏd (*wehem djed*), The one who has repeated stability, Sekhemre Khutawy N

wḫ3 mi imy w3st (*wekha, mi imy waset*), A (veritable) pillar, like the one who is in Thebes, Ramses II G8

wsr-ib (*weser ib*), Strong-minded, Khafre H

wsr-ʿ (*weser a*), Strong-armed, Psamtek II N

wsr-b3w (*weser bau*), Rich in might, Sobekhotep IV G

wsr-pḥty (*weser pehty*), Strong of might Sheshonq V H1 N G1

wsr-pḥty mi it.f mnṯw sksk pḏwt 9 dr m t3.sn (*weser pehty mi it.ef mentju, seksek pedjut 9, der em ta.sen*), Powerful of strength like his father Montu, who has annihilated the Nine Bows and repelled (them) in their (own) countries, Ramses III N2

wsr-f3w sḫʿ m w3st (weser fau, sekha em waset), Rich in splendor, who has been made to appear in Thebes, Amenhotep II N1

wsr m nbty (*weser em nebty*), Who is strong by means of the Two Ladies, Khafre N

wsr m3ʿt rʿ (*weser maat ra*), The strong one belonging to the Maat of Re, Ramses II T, Ramses III T, Ramses IV T1, Ramses V T, Ramses VII T1, Ramses VIII T, Amenemope T, Osorkon II T, Sheshonq III T, Pamiu T, Pedubastis I T, Sheshonq VI T, Osorkon III T, Takelot III T, Rudamun T, Iuput II T, Pedubastis II T, Piye T1

wsr m3ʿt rʿ 3ḫ n imn (*weser maat ra, akh en imen*), The strong one of the Maat of Re , Beneficial to Amun, Ramses VIII T

wsr m3ʿt rʿ mry imn (*weser maat ra, mery imen*), The strong one of the Maat of Re, beloved of Amun, Ramses III T1

wsr rʿ (*weser ra*), The powerful one of Re, Psammuthis T

wsr-rnpwt (*weser renput*), Rich in years, Rahotep N

wsr-rnpwt ʿ3-nḫtw (*weser renput, aa nakhtu*), Rich in years and great of victories, Ramses II G1

wr-rnpwt ʿ3-nsyt mi itmw ity ms nṯrw sḫpr t3wy (*weser renput, aa nesyt mi itemu, ity, mes netjeru, sekheper tawy*), Rich in years and great of kingship like Atum, the sovereign whom the gods fashioned, the one who has fostered the Two Lands, Ramses II G9

wsr-rnpwt wr-nḫtw ity ms nṯrw sḫpr t3wy (*weser renput, wer nakhtu, ity, mes netjeru, sekheper tawy*), Rich of years and great of victories, the sovereign whom the gods bore, who has created the Two Lands, Ramses IV G *wsr-rnpwt mi imn* (*weser renput mi imen*), Rich in years like Amun, Ramses VII G2

wsr-rnpwt mi itmw (*weser renput mi itemu*), Rich in years like Atum, Ramses III G1, Ramses V G, Ramses VII G1

wsr-rnpwt mi itmw ity mk kmt wꜥf ḫꜣswt (*weser renput mi itemu, ity mek kemet, waf khasut*), Rich in years like Atum, the sovereign and protector of Egypt, who has subdued the foreign countries, Ramses III G2

wsr-rnpwt mi tꜣ-ṯnn (*weser renput mi ta-tjenen*), Rich in years like Ta-tjenen, Ramses VI G

wsr-rnpwt mi tꜣ-ṯnn ity wr-nsyt dr pḏwt 9 (*weser renput mi ta-tjenen, ity wer nesyt, der pedjut 9*), Rich in years like Ta-tjenen, the sovereign great of kingship who has repelled the Nine Bows, Ramses IX G

wsr-ḫꜥw (*weser khau*), Strong of appearances, Neferirkare H, Userkhau N, Djehuty G

wsr-ḫꜥw nbty (*weser khau nebty*), Strong of appearances <by means of> the Two Ladies, Neferirkare N2

wsr ḫꜥw rꜥ (*weser khau ra*), The strong one of the appearances of Re, Sethnakht T

wsr ḫprw rꜥ (*weser kheperu ra*), The strong one of the manifestations of Ra, Sety II T

wsr-ḫpš (*weser khepesh*), Strong of might, Ramses II G10

wsr-ḫpš ꜥnḫ tꜣwy (*weser khepesh, ankh tawy*), Powerful of arm, the (very) life of the Two Lands, Herihor N4

wsr-ḫpš mry tꜣwy (*weser khepesh, mery tawy*), Strong of might, beloved of the Two Lands, Ramses II G11

wsr-ḫpš hd ḥfnw (*weser khepesh, hed hefnu*), The one great of strength who has attacked hundreds of thousands, Ramses VI N, Ramses XI N

wsr-ḫpš sꜥnḫ tꜣwy (*weser khepesh, sankh tawy*), Powerful of sword, who has sustained the Two Lands, Ramses IX N

wsr-ḫpš dr pḏwt 9 (weser khepesh, der pedjut 9), The one great of strength who has repelled the Nine Bows, Thutmose IV G1, Ramses II G12

wsr kꜣ rꜥ (*weser ka ra*), The strong one belonging to the ka of Re, Userkare T/B, [User]kare T, Khendjer T, Ptolemy II T

wsr kꜣ.f (*weser ka.ef*), His ka is strong, Userkaf B

wsrt-kꜣw (weseret kau), Powerful of kas, Hatshepsut H

wsr /// rꜥ (*weser /// ra*), The powerful one /// of Re, User /// re I and II T

wsrkn (*weserken*), Osorkon I to IV B

wgꜣ.f (*wega.ef*), May he chew (?), Wegaf B

wṯs rn n itn (wetjes ren en iten), Who has elevated the name of the Aten, Akhenaten G

wṯs ḥḏt mry iwnw (wetjes hedjet, mery iunu), Who has raised the White Crown, the beloved one of Heliopolis, Amenhotep III H4

wṯs ḫꜥw it.f rꜥ (wetjes khau it.ef ra), Who has elevated the appearances of his father Re, Tutankhamun G2

wṯs-ḫꜥw m iwnw šmꜥw (wetjes khau em iunu shemau), Elevated of appearances in southern Heliopolis, Amenhotep IV G

wṯs-ḫꜥw sḥtp nṯrw (wetjes khau, sehetep netjeru), Elevated of appearances, who has satisfied the gods, Tutankhamun G1

bꜣ n nṯr (*ba en netjer*), The spirit of the god, Ninetjer C

bꜣ n rꜥ (*ba en ra*), The (very) spirit of Re, Merenptah T, Nepherites I T

bꜣ n rꜥ ḏt itmw (*ba en ra, djet itemu*), The spirit of Re and (the very) body of Atum, Merenptah H3

bꜣ kꜣ rꜥ (*ba ka ra*), The (very) *ba* of the ka of Re, Tanutamun T

bꜣw.f rꜥ (*bau.ef ra*), His *bas* are those of Re, Baufre C

bꜣk n rn.f (*bak en ren.ef*), The servant of his name, Bakenrenef B

bik ꜥꜣ /// (*bik aa ///*), Great falcon ///, [Weser]kare G

bik nbw (*bik nebu*), The golden falcon, Khaba G, Snefru G

bik nbw wꜣḏ (*bik nebu wadj*), The sturdy golden falcon, Unas G

bik nbw nfr (*bik nebu nefer*), The perfect golden falcon, Userkaf G, Nefer(ef)re G

bik nbw nṯri (*bik nebu netjeri*), The divine golden falcon, Niuserre G

bik nbw ḥḏ (*bik nebu hedj*), The radiant golden falcon, Menkauhor G

bik nbw sḫm (*bik nebu sekhem*), The powerful golden falcon, Pepy II G

bik nbw ḏd (*bik nebu djed*), The enduring golden falcon, Djedkare G

bikw nbw (*biku nebu*), The triple falcons are golden, Pepy I G

bikw (*nṯrw*) *nbw* (*biku (netjeru) nebu*), The (divine) falcons are golden, Radjedef G

bikwy nbw (*bikwy nebu*), The golden double falcon, Khufu G, Sahure G, Merenre G

bity wr-mnw wr-biꜣwt mḥ ipt-swt ḥr rn.f (*bity, wer menu, wer biaut, meh ipet-sut her ren.ef*), The king of Lower Egypt, great of monuments and great of wonders, who has filled Ipet-sut with his renown, Ramses III H10

b-b-n-m (*bebnem*), Bebnem B

bby / bbty (*beby / bebty*), Beby/Bebty, Khasekhem/Kasekhemwy C

bbi ꜥnḫ(*w*) (*bebi ankh(u)*), Bebi is alive, Bebiankh B

bḏꜣw (*bedjau*), Bedjau, Hetepsekhemwy C

p (*?*) (*pe*?), The (very) throne of Horus, Horus "Pe" H

pꜣ ꜥnḫy (*pa ankhy*), "O living one!" (?), Piye B

pꜣ miw (*pa miu*), The tomcat, Pamiu B

p(*ꜣ*) *n ṯni* (*pa en tjeny*), Pantjeny ("The man of Thinis") B

pꜣ nṯr mry it sn wsir ḥwnw (*pa netjer, mery it sen, wesir hunu*), The god who is beloved of his father and brother, the youthful Osiris, Ptolemy XII T3

pꜣ šri mwt (*pa sheri mut*), The child of (the goddess) Mut, Psammuthis B

pꜣ di bꜣstt (*pa di bastet*), The one whom Bastet granted, Pedubastis I and II B

pꜣ di nmty (*pa di nemty*), The one whom Nemty has granted, Padinemty B

p3y.f ṯ3w (m) ʿwy b3stt (*pay.ef tjaw (em) awy bastet*), His breath (comes from) the arms of Bastet, Peftjauabastet B
p3y nḏm (*pay nedjem*), The sweet one, Pinodjem I B
ppy (*pepy*), Pepy, Pepy I B, Pepy II B
ppy snb(.w) (*pepy senbu*), Pepy is healthy, Neferkare Pepysenbu C2
pr ib.sn (*per ib.sen*), (For whom) Their will has come forth, Peribsen N T
p(h)lpws (*p(h)elepus*), P(h)ilippos, Philip Arrhidaeus B
psmtk (*psemtek*), Psamtek B
ptpt iwntyw iṯ t3.sn (petpet iuntiu, itj ta.sen), Who has trampled Asiatics and seized their land, Amenhotep III G7

m m3ʿt sḫʿ.n sw it.f (*em maat, sekha.en su it.ef*), Truly, whose father enthroned him, Ptolemy VI N
m3ʿ ib rʿ (*maa ib ra*), The righteous one is the heart of Re, Sheshi T
m3ʿ ḫpr rʿ (*maa kheper ra*), The true one is a manifestation of Re, Sheshonq IIc T
m3ʿ-ḫrw (*maa kheru*), Righteous of voice, Amenemhat II G1, Nekau II N
m3ʿ ḫrw m nb [*t3wy?*] (*maa kheru em neb [tawy]*), Righteous of voice as the Lord of [the Two Lands?], Amenemhat II G2
m3ʿ ḫrw rʿ (*maa kheru ra*), The righteous one of Re, Amenemhat IV T
m3ʿt k3 rʿ (maat ka ra), The true one of the ka of Re, Hatshepsut T
mn w3ḏ rʿ (*men wadj ra*), The established and flourishing one of Re, Sahathor T
mn pḥty rʿ (*men pehty ra*), The established one of the might of Re, Ramses I T
mn m3ʿt rʿ (*men maat ra*), The established one belonging to the Maat of Re, Sety I T, Ramses XI T
mn mi rʿ stp n rʿ mry imn (*men mi ra, setep en ra, mery imen*), Established like Re, chosen by Re and beloved of Amun, Amenmesse T
mn-mnw m ḥwt-ʿ3t m3ʿt (*men menu em hut-aat maat*), Enduring of monuments in the Great Mansion of Maat, Sety I N2
mn-mnw ḏt nḥḥ (*men menu djet neheh*), Enduring of monuments forever and ever, Sety I N3
mn-mrwt (*men merut*), Enduring of love, Neferhotep I G
mn-ḫʿw (*men khau*), Established of appearances, Menkauhor H
mn ḫʿw rʿ (*men khau ra*), The established one is (like) the appearances of Re, Senaaib T
mn ḫpr rʿ (men kheper ra), The established one of the manifestation of Re, Thutmose III (a) T1, III (b), Menkheperre B, Piye T2
mn ḫpr k3 rʿ (men kheper ka ra), The established one of the manifestation of the ka of Re, Thutmose III (a) T2
mn ḫprw rʿ (men kheperu ra), The established one of the manifestations of Re, Thutmose IV T
mn k3 rʿ (*men ka ra*), The established one of the ka of Re, Menkare C
mn k3w rʿ (*men kau ra*), The established one of the kas of Re, Menkaure T
mn k3w ḥr (*men kau hor*), The established one of the kas of Horus, Menkauhor T

mn /// (*men ///*), Established of ///, Neferhotep III Iykhernofret G
mn /// rꜥ (*men /// ra*), The established one of /// of Re, Men /// re T
mnḫ-ib (*menekh ib*), The efficacious one, Psamtek II H, Darius I H1
mnḫ- /// (*menekh ///*), Potent of ///, Sobekhotep I H
mntw m s3.f (*mentu em sa.ef*), Montu is his protection, Montuemsaf B
mnṯw n t3 mk kmt (*mentju en ta mek kemet*), Montu of the land, the protector of Egypt, Sety I N5
mnṯw ḥtp(.w) (*mentu hetpu*), Montu is satisfied, Mentuhotep I to VII
[*mr?*] *ib rꜥ* (*[mer?] ib ra*), The one whom the mind of Re has loved, Seth T
mr wsr rꜥ (*mer weser ra*), The beloved one of the strength of Re, Yakub-her T
mr.n rꜥ (*mer.en ra*), The one whom Re has loved, Merenre T
mr.n rꜥ [*nmty?*] *m z3.f* (*mer.en ra [nemty?] em za.ef*), The one whom Re has loved, [Nemty] is his protection, Merenre II T
mr.n rꜥ sꜥ3 k3.f (*mer.en ra, saa ka.ef*), Whom Re has loved, who has magnified his ka, Sety I G4
mr nfr rꜥ (*mer nefer ra*), Whom the perfection of Re has loved, Iy T
mr ḥtp rꜥ (*mer hetep ra*), The one whom the peace of Re has appreciated, Sobekhotep V T, Ini I T
mr /// rꜥ (*mer /// ra*), The beloved one of /// of Re, Mer[///]re T
mr ḏf3 rꜥ (*mer djefa ra*), The one whom Re's bounty has loved, Merdjefare T
mry (*?*) (*mery* ?), The beloved one, Khety (VIII) G
mry 3ḫ n it.f (*mery akh en it.ef*), The beloved one, who is beneficial to his father, Ramses II N7
mry ib t3wy (*mery ib tawy*), Beloved of the mind of the Two Lands, Khety (VIII) H N
mry ib rꜥ (*mery ib ra*), The beloved one of the mind of Re, Khety (VIII) T
mry imn-rꜥ (*mery imen-ra*), Beloved of Amun-Re, Darius I T2
mry imn-rꜥ nb hbt nṯr ꜥ3 nḫt ḫpš (*mery imen-ra, neb hebet, netjer aa, nakht khepesh*), Beloved of Amun-Re, lord of Hibis (temple), the great god, and powerful of arm, Darius I T3
mry itn (mery iten), Beloved of Aten, Akhenaten H
mr(y) ꜥnḫ rꜥ (*mer(y) ankh ra*), The beloved one of the life of Re, Mentuhotep VII T
mr(y) bi3 p (*mer(y) bia pe*), The eternally beloved of the throne, Adjib C
mr p bi3i (*mer pe biai*), The one who wished the eternal throne, Adjib T
mry m3ꜥt (*mery maat*), Beloved of Maat, Ahmose (I) H
mry m3ꜥt s3ḫ prw nṯrw (*mery maat, sakh peru netjeru*), Beloved of Maat, who has made the gods' temples glorious, Tachos N
mry n ptḥ ḥtp-ḥr m3ꜥt (*mery en ptah, hetep her maat*), Beloved of Ptah, satisfied with Maat, Merenptah B
mr(y) n ḥr (*mer(y) en hor*), Beloved of Horus, Merenhor C
mry nṯr mnḫ nṯrt mnḫt s3t rꜥ stp n ptḥ ir m3ꜥt rꜥ snn ꜥnḫ n imn (*mery netjer menekh netjeret menkhet, sat ra, setep en ptah, ir maat ra, snn ankh en imen*),

Beloved of the potent god and of the potent goddess, the daughter of Re, chosen by Ptah, who has accomplished the Maat of Re, the living likeness of Amun, Ptolemy X T2

mry nṯrw (*mery netjeru*), Beloved of the gods, Nekau II G

mry nṯrw rdi n.f iꜣwt n it.f (*mery netjeru, redi en.ef iaut en it.ef*), Beloved of the gods, to whom the office of his father was given, Alexander II / IV N

mry rꜥ (*mery ra*), Beloved of Re, Pepy I T2, Thutmose III (b) H5

mry rꜥ ḫꜥ m ḥḏt (mery ra, kha em hedjet), The one beloved of Re, who has appeared in the White Crown, Thutmose I H3

mry rꜥ ḳꜣ-ḥḏt (mery ra, qa-hedjet), Beloved of Re, (whose) White Crown is high, Thutmose III (b) H2

mr(y) ḫpr rꜥ (*mer(y) kheper ra*), The beloved one of the manifestation of Re, Merkheperre T

mry ḫt nbty (*mery khet nebty*), Beloved of the Two Ladies' bodies, Pepy I N

mry sḫm rꜥ (*mery sekhem ra*), The beloved one of the power of Re, Ined T, Neferhotep II T

mry šps rꜥ (*mery shepes ra*), Beloved of the grandeur of Re, Ini II T

mry kꜣ rꜥ (*mery ka ra*), The beloved one of the ka of Re, Merykare T, Merka[re] T

mry kꜣw rꜥ (*mery kau ra*), Beloved of the kas of Re, Sobekhotep VII T

mr(y) grg pn (*mer gereg pen*), The beloved of this establishment, Adjib C

mry tꜣwy (*mery tawy*), Beloved of the Two Lands, Pepy I H, Merytawy H , Wegaf G, Nectanebo II H1

mry tꜣwy mk kmt (*mery tawy, mek kemet*), The beloved of the Two Lands and guardian of Egypt, Nectanebo II H2

mriyw (*meriu*), The beloved one, Philip Arrhidaeus G

mry /// (*mery ///*), Beloved of [divine name], Mery /// B

mry /// ḫty (*mery /// [khety]*), Beloved of [Khety], Khety (IV) T and B

mryt rꜥ (*meryt ra*), The one beloved of Re, Sobeknefru H

mḥ ib tꜣwy (*meh ib tawy*), The confidante (lit. "who fills the heart") of the Two Lands, Senbef H

ms ḥmwt (*mes hemut*), The fashioner of crafts, Piye N2

msy (*mesy*), The one who was born, Amenmesse (short form)

ms nṯrw (*mes netjeru*), Born of the gods, Osorkon III G

mswt rꜥ (*mesut ra*), The offspring of Re, Cambyses T

mk kmt (*mek kemet*), The guardian of Egypt, Alexander the Great H1

mk kmt wꜥf pḏwt 9 (*mek kemet waf pedjut 9*), The protector of Egypt who has subdued the Nine Bows, Ramses IV N, Ramses VII N2

mk kmt wꜥf ḫꜣswt (*mek kemet, waf khasut*), The protector of Egypt who has subdued foreign countries, Ramses II N1, Sety II N3

mk kmt wꜥf ḫꜣswt rꜥ ms nṯrw grg tꜣwy (*mek kemet, waf khasut, ra mes netjeru, gereg tawy*), Protector of Egypt, who has subdued foreign lands, a Re whom the gods have borne, the founder of the Two Lands, Ramses II N10

mk kmt wꜥf ḫꜣstyw (*mek kemet, waf khastiu*), The protector of Egypt who has subdued the foreigners, Ramses VII N1
mḏd r nbty (*medjed er nebty*), Who has adhered to the Two Ladies, Khufu N
mḏdw (*medjedu*), Who has been adhered to/followed, Khufu H

nꜣy.f ꜥꜣw rwḏw (*nay.ef aau rudju*), His ancestors are flourishing, Nepherites I B
n(y) wsr rꜥ (*ni weser ra*), Who belongs to the power of Re, Niuserre T
n(y) mꜣꜥt rꜥ (*ni maat ra*), The one who belongs to the Maat of Re, Amenemhat III T, Kashta T
n(y)-nbw (*ni-nebu*), He who belongs to the Golden One, Djer G
n(y)-nt (*ni-net*), The one who belongs to (the goddess) Neith, Ny-Neith H
n(y)-nṯr (*ni-netjer*), The one who belongs to the divinity of the Two Ladies, Ninetjer N
n(y)-nṯr (*ni-netjer*), The one who belongs to the god, Ninetjer H
n(y)-<ḥr> (*ny-<her>*), The one who belongs to <Horus>, Ny-<Hor> H
n(y)-sw bꜣ-nb-ḏd (*ni-su ba-neb-djed*), He belongs to the ram, the lord of Mendes, Smendes B
n(y)-kꜣ rꜥ (*ny-ka ra*), Who belongs to the ka of Re, Nikare C
n(y) kꜣw (*ni kau*), Who belongs to the kas, Nekau II B
nu-ya, Nuya B
nꜥr mr, (*nar mer*), The menacing catfish, Narmer H
nb iry r ꜣw (*nb iry er au*), The possessor of all, Nebiryerau I B1
nb iry <r> ꜣw rꜥ (*nb iry <er> au ra*), The possessor of all (the things of) Re, Nebiryerau I B2, and Nebiryerau II
nb ꜥ (*neb a*), Possessor of a (strong) arm, Psamtek I N
nb ꜥḥꜥw mi it.f rꜥ (*neb ahau mi it.ef ra*), Lord of a lifetime like his father Re, Ramses III H11
nb pḥty rꜥ (neb pehty ra), The possessor of the might of Re, Ahmose (II) T
nb fꜣw rꜥ (*neb fau ra*), The possessor of the splendor of Re, Nebfaure T
nb mꜣꜥ ḫrw (*neb maa kheru*), The possessor of righteousness, Rudamun H
nb mꜣꜥt (*neb maat*), Possessor of Maat, Snefru H1 N
nb mꜣꜥt rꜥ (*neb maat ra*), The possessor of the truth of Re, Nebmaatre T, Amenhotep III T, Ramses VI T
nb mꜣꜥt snfr w(i) (*neb maat senefer wi*), The lord of Maat has made me perfect, Snefru H2
nb nnw (*neb nenu*), (My) lord is Nun, Nebnun B
nb rꜥ (*neb ra*), My lord is the sun god, Nebre H
nb ḥbw ḫꜥw (*neb hebu khau*), Possessor of Appearance Festivals, Merenptah H8
nb ḥbw-sd mi tꜣ-ṯnn (*neb hebu sed mi ta-tjenen*), Possessor of Sed festivals like Ta-tjenen, Ramses II H3, Amenmesse H3, Ramses III H14
nb ḥpt rꜥ (*neb hepet ra*), The possessor of the steering oar of Re, Mentuhotep II (b-c) T
nb ḫꜥw (*neb khau*), Possessor of appearances, Sahure H N

nb ḫprw rʿ (neb kheperu ra), The possessor of the manifestations of Re, Tutankhamun T

nb ḫpš (*neb khepesh*), Possessor of strength, Apries N

nb.sn rʿ (*neb.sen ra*), Their lord is Re, Nebsenre B

nb snḏ ʿꜣ-šfyt (*neb senedj, aa shefyt*), Lord of fear and great of majesty, Merenptah G1

nb kꜣ (*neb ka*), Lord of the ka, Sanakht T

nb kꜣ rʿ (*neb ka ra*), The possessor of the ka of Re, Nebkare C

nb kꜣw rʿ (*neb kau ra*), The possessor of the kas of Re, Khety (VII) T

nb tꜣ mry ḥḳꜣ.f m ḥʿʿw nb ḥbw-sd mi tꜣ-ṯnn it nṯrw nsw(?) ity smn hpw mi ḏḥwty ʿꜣ ʿꜣ (*neb ta mery, heqa.ef em haau, neb hebu-sed mi ta-tjenen it netjeru, nesu(?) ity semen hepu mi djehuty aa aa*), The Lord of the Beloved Land, he rules in jubilation, the possessor of Sed festivals like Ta-tjenen, the father of the gods, king(?) and sovereign who has established laws like twice-great Thoth, Ptolemy IX G1

nb tꜣwy (*neb tawy*), The lord of the Two Lands, Mentuhotep IV H N, Ramses II N8

nb tꜣwy rʿ (*neb tawy ra*), The possessor (or “lord”) of the Two Lands of Re, Mentuhotep IV

nb ḏfꜣ rʿ (*neb djefa ra*), The possessor of Re’s bounty, Nebdjefare T

nbw wsr rʿ (*nebu weser ra*), The golden one is the strength of Re, Iamu T

nbw nfr (*nebu nefer*), The perfect golden one, Nebre T

nbw nṯrw (*nebu netjeru*), The golden one of the gods, Mentuhotep IV G

nbw ḫpr rʿ (*nebu kheper ra*), The golden one is the (very) manifestation of Re, Intef VI T

nbw kꜣw rʿ (*nebu kau ra*), The golden one of the kas of Re, Amenemhat II T

nby (*neby*), Who belongs to <his> lord, Neferkare Nebi B

nfr ib rʿ (*nefer ib ra*), The perfect one is the (very) mind of Re, Neferibre T, Psamtek II T

nfr ir kꜣ rʿ (*nefer ir ka ra*), The perfect one is the one whom the ka of Re has engendered, Neferirkare (I) T, Neferirkare (II) C

nfr m nbty (*nefer em nebty*), Who is perfect by means of the Two Ladies, Nefer(ef)re N

nfr rʿ (*nefer ra*), The (very) perfection of Re, Nefer(ef)re T1

nfr.f rʿ (*nefer.ef ra*), He is perfect (in the manner of) Re, Nefer(ef)re T2

nfr nfrw itn (nefer neferu iten), Perfect is the perfection of Aten, Nefer-neferu-aten B

nfr nṯrw (*nefer netjeru*), The perfect one of the gods, Hor (I) G

nfr-rnpwt sʿnḫ ibw (nefer renput, sankh ibu), The one perfect of years, who has sustained minds, Thutmose I G1

nfr-rnpwt sʿnḫ tꜣwy (*nefer renput, sankh tawy*), Perfect of years, who has sustained the Two Lands, Sety I, Abydos 7. Ceiling G *nfr-hpw sgrḥ t3wy (nefer hepu, segereh tawy),* Perfect of laws, who has quieted down the Two Lands, Tutankhamun N1

nfr-hpw sgrḥ t3wy sḥtp nṯrw nbw (nefer hepu, segereh tawy, sehetep netjeru nebu), Perfect of laws, who has quieted down the Two Lands and pacified all the gods, Tutankhamun N2

nfr ḥtp (*nefer hetep*), The beautiful/perfect one is satisfied, Neferhotep I to III

nfr ḥtp ii ẖr nfrt (*nefer hetep, ii kher nefret*), The beautiful/perfect one is satisfied, the one who has come bearing happiness, Neferhotep III Iykhernofret B

nfr ḫʿw (*nefer khau*), Perfect of appearances, Nefer(ef)re H, Hor (I) N, Nebiry-erau I G, Senwosret IV G

nfr ḫpr rʿ ḫʿ ḫʿw (*nefer kheper ra, kha khau*), The perfect one is the (very) manifestation of Re, radiant of crowns, Thutemhat T

nfr-ḫprw (*nefer kheperu*), Perfect of manifestations, Intef VI H1

nfr ḫprw rʿ wʿ n rʿ (nefer kheperu ra, wa en ra), The perfect one of the manifestations of Re, the unique one of Re, Amenhotep IV and Akhenaten T

nfr ḫ3b t3wy (*nefer, khab tawy*), The perfect one is the sickle of the Two Lands, Kamose H2

nfr z3 ḥr (*nefer za hor*), Perfect is the protection of Horus, Pepy I T1

nfr k3 mnw (*nefer ka menu*), The perfect one of the ka of (the god) Min, Neferka-min C, Neferkamin Anu C1

nfr k3 rʿ (*nefer ka ra*), The perfect one of the ka of Re, Seneferka C, Neferkare (I) C, Pepy II T, Neferkare (II) C, Neferkare Nebi T, Neferkare Khendu C1, Neferkare Tereru T, Neferkare Pepysenbu C 1, Neferkare (III) T, Ramses IX T, Peftjauabastet T, Shabaka T

nfr k3 rʿ ḥḳ3 w3st (*nefer ka ra, heqa waset*), The perfect one is the (very) ka of Re, Ruler of Thebes, Amen-em-nisu T

nfr k3 ḥr (*nefer ka hor*), The perfect one of the ka of Horus, Neferkahor C

nfr k3w rʿ (*nefer kau ra*), The perfect one of the kas of Re, Neferkaure T

nfr k3w ḥr (*nefer kau hor*), The perfect one of the kas of Horus, Neferkauhor Khuwihapi T

nfr k3 skr (*nefer ka seker*), The perfect one of the ka of Sokar, Neferkasokar C

nfrtm /// rʿ (*nefertum /// ra*), Re is the /// of Nefertum (?), Nefertum /// re T

nmrṯ (*nemretj*), Nimlot B

nmty m z3.f (*nemty em za.ef*), (The god) Nemty is his protection, Merenre (I) B, Merenre II B

nr k3 rʿ (*ner ka ra*), The feared one is the (very) ka of Re, Nerkare T

nḥsy (*nehsy*), The Nubian, Nehsy B

nḫt nb tp-nfr (*nakht neb tep-nefer*), The possessor of a perfect beginning is victorious, Intef III H

nḫt nb.f (*nakht neb.ef*), The strong one for (lit. "of") his lord, Nectanebo I and II B

nḫt ḥr (*n*) *ḥbyt* (*nakht hor (en) hebyt*), The strong one of Horus of Hebit, Nectanebo II B

nḫt-ḫpš dr pḏwt 9 (*nakht khepesh, der pedjut 9*), The strong-armed one who has repelled the Nine Bows, Sety II N1
nḫt ḫpš dr pḏwt 9 ỉty ỉṯ t3w nbw (*nakht khepesh, der pedjut 9, ity, itj tau nebu*), The strong-armed one who has repelled the Nine Bows, the sovereign who has seized all lands, Osorkon I G
nsw ḥwỉ (*nesu hui*), The smiting king, Huni T
nt ỉḳrt (*net iqeret*), (The goddess) Neith is excellent, Nitocris C
nṯr(ỉ) wsr (*netjer weser*), The divine and strong one, Shepseskare B
nṯrỉ-b3w (*netjeri-bau*), Divine of might, Hetepsekhemwy C, Neferkauhor Khuwihapi H, Amenemhat VII N
nṯrỉ bỉk nbw (*netjeri bik nebu*), The golden falcon is divine, Menkaure G
nṯrỉ m pr.f m ḫt swḥt ỉḳrt sbḳt n ḥr-3ḫty (*netjeri em per.ef em khet suhet iqeret sebqet en hor-akhty*), Divine as soon as he emerged from the womb, the excellent and precious egg of Harakhty, Ramses III G3
nṯrỉ m ḫt ḫnm.n sw ḥpw ꜥnḫ ḥr msḫn(t) ḥwnw nfr bnr-mrwt sḫꜥ.n sw mwt.f ḥr nst ỉt.f ṯmꜥ-ꜥ ḥwỉ ḫ3swt ỉṯ m sḫm.f mỉ rꜥ psḏ.f m 3ḫt (*netjeri em khet, khnum.en su hapu ankh her meskhen(et), hunu nefer, bener merut, sekha.en su mut.ef her neset it.ef, tjema-a hui khasut, itj em sekhem.ef mi ra pesedj.ef em akhet*), The divine one in the sanctuary, whom the living Apis bull has united with the birth-stool, the perfect youth sweet of love, whom his mother enthroned on his father's throne, the sturdy-armed one who has struck down foreign countries and seized with his power like Re when he shines in the horizon, Ptolemy X H
nṯrỉ-mswt (*netjeri mesut*), Divine of births, Senwosret III N
nṯrỉ-nsyt (netjeri nesyt), Divine of kingship, Thutmose II N
nṯrỉ ḥḏt (*netjeri hedjet*), Whose White Crown is divine, Mentuhotep II (b) H N
nṯrỉ ḫꜥw (*netjeri khau*), Divine of appearances, Pepy II H
nṯrỉ ḫꜥw nbty (*netjeri khau nebty*), The divine one of the appearances of the Two Ladies, Pepy II N
nṯrỉ ḫpr rꜥ (*netjeri kheper ra*), The divine one is a manifestation of Re, Siamun T
nṯrỉ ḫprw (*netjeri kheperu*), Divine of manifestations, Senwosret III H, Nebiryerau I N
nṯrỉ-ḫt (*netjeri-khet*), The one (whose) body is divine, Djoser H N
nṯrỉ k3 rꜥ (*netjeri ka ra*), The divine one of the ka of Re, Netjerikare C
nṯrt-ḫꜥw (netjeret khau), Divine of appearances, Hatshepsut G
nḏ ḥr ỉt.f mỉty m3ꜥt (*nedj her it.ef, mity maat*), Protector of his father, the likeness of Maat, Merenptah H5
nḏm ỉb rꜥ (*nedjem ib ra*), The pleasant one of the mind of Re, Nedjemibre T

rꜥ ms sw (*ra mes su*), Re is the one who bore him, Ramses I to XI
rꜥ ms sw ỉmn ḥr ḫpš.f (*ra mes su, imen her khepesh.ef*), Re is the one who bore him, Amun is upon his strong arm, Ramses V B, Ramses VI B, Ramses X B

rʿ ms sw ỉt.ỉ ỉmn nṯr ḥḳꜣ ỉwnw (*ra mes su, it(.i) imen, netjer, heqa iunu*), Re is the one who bore him, Amun is my father, the divine one and ruler of Heliopolis, Ramses VII B

rʿ ms sw <mry> ỉmn pꜣ sbꜣ ḫʿ n nỉwt (*ra mes su, <mery> imen, pa seba kha en niut*), Ramses, <beloved of> Amun, the star who has appeared in Niut, Psusennes I B2

rʿ ms sw ḫʿ m wꜣst (*ra mes su, kha em waset*), Re is the one who bore him, the one who has appeared in Thebes, Ramses IX B, Ramses XI B

rʿ ms sw stẖ ḥr ḫpš.f (*ra mes su, seth her khepesh.ef*), Re is the one who bore him, Seth is upon his strong arm, Ramses VIII B

rʿ ḥtp (*ra hetep(u)*), Re is satisfied, Rahotep B

rʿ ḏd.f (*ra djed.ef*), Re is his stability, Radjedef T

rwd ỉmn (*rud imen*), Amun is vigorous, Rudamun B

rn nbw (*ren nebu*), The golden named one, Ninetjer G

rn.ỉ snb(*w*) (*ren.i seneb(u)*), My name is healthy, Reniseneb B

hr ỉb rʿ (*her ib ra*), Who has pleased Re's mind, Heribre T

hr nṯrw (?) (*her netjeru*), The one who has pleased the gods, Mentuhotep VI H

hr ḥr mꜣʿt sḫpr tꜣwy (heru her maat, sekheper tawy), Pleased with Maat, who (re-) created the Two Lands, Horemheb G

hr ḥr nḫt (*her her nakht*), Satisfied with victory, Shabataka G2

hr ḥr nḫtw (her her nakhtu), Pleased with (his) victories, Thutmose III (b) G2

hr ḥr nḫtw ḥwỉ ḥḳꜣw ḫꜣswt pḥw sw (her her nakhtu, hui heqau khasut pehu su), Pleased with (his) victories, the one who has struck down the rulers of the foreign lands who approached him, Thutmose III (b) G4

hr ḥr nst.f (*her her neset.ef*) Pleased with his throne, Intef VI N

hgr / hkr / hḳr (*heger / heker / heqer*), Achoris B

ḥꜣty-<ḥr> (*haty-<hor>*), The foremost one of <Horus>, Haty-Hor H

ḥʿ ḥr mꜣʿt mỉ ꜣḫty (*ha her maat mi akhty*), Who has rejoiced in Maat like The One of the Two Horizons, Ramses II N10

ḥʿʿ ỉb rʿ (*haa ib ra*), Who (continually) rejoices over the mind of Re, Apries T

ḥʿʿ ỉb rʿ stp n ỉmn (*haa ib ra, setep en imen*), Who (continually) rejoices over the mind of Re, chosen by Amun, Alexander II/IV T

ḥwỉ pḏwt-9 (*hui pedjut-9*), Who has struck down the Nine Bows, Thutmose I G2

ḥwỉ pḏwt 9 ʿn m nsyt (<*hui*> *pedjut 9, an em nesyt*), <Who has struck> the Nine Bows, beautiful in kingship, Sethnakht G2

ḥwỉ mntyw dr ṯḥnw (hui mentiu, der tjehenu), Who has struck down the bedouin and repelled the Tjehenu-Libyans, Amenhotep III G2

ḥwnỉ (*huni*), The smiter, Huni C

ḥwnw wsr-pḥty (*hunu, weser pehty*), The youthful one, powerful of strength, Alexander II/IV H *ḥwnw nfr bnr-mrwt* (*hunu nefer, bener merut*), The perfect youth who is sweet of love, Ptolemy XV H1

ḥwnw nfr bnr-mrwt ṯnỉ sw nbty rḫyt ḥnʿ kꜣ.f dwꜣ n.f ḫnmw šps r šsp n.f ḫʿ m nsw snsn.n sḥnw m ḥʿʿw mỉ nḏt ỉt.f ṯḥn msw(t) ḥr nst ỉt.f mỉ ḥr kꜣ nḫt ỉty psḏ m tꜣ-mry mỉ ḥpw ʿnḫ rdỉ n.f ḥbw-sd ʿšꜣw wrw mỉ ptḥ tꜣ-ṯnn ỉt nṯrw (*hunu nefer, bener-merut, tjeni su nebty rekhyet hena ka.f, dua en.ef khnum, shepes er shesep en.ef kha em nesu, sensen.en sehnu em haaw mi nedjet it.ef tjehen mesu(t) her neset it.ef mi hor ka nakht, ity pesedj em ta-mery mi hapu ankh, redi en.ef hebu-sed ashau weru mi ptah ta-tjenen it netjeru*), The perfect youth sweet of love, whom the Two Mistresses and the common folk have elevated along with his ka, whom the august Khnum praised in order to assume the crown of kingship for himself, with whom commanders have readily (lit. "in joy") associated like the Protector-of-his-Father, gleaming of birth on the throne of his father like Horus, the victorious bull, the sovereign who shines in Ta-mery like the living Apis bull, to whom has been given a great many Sed festivals like Ptah Ta-tjenen, the father of the gods, Ptolemy XII H

ḥwnw ḥry-tp pḏt 9 sꜣ wsỉr ms.n ꜣst šsp n.f nsyt rʿ m-ʿ ỉt.f (*hunu, hery-tep pedjet 9, sa wesir, mes.en aset, shesep en.ef nesyt ra em-a it.ef*), The youthful one, leader of the Nine Bows, the son of Osiris, whom Isis has borne, who has received for himself the kingship of Re from his father's hand, Ptolemy VIII H3

ḥwnw ḥkn.tw m ʿnḫ.f ḥr nst ỉt.f mʿr spw ḏsr msḫʿw.f ḥnʿ ḥpw ʿnḫ (*hunu, heken. tu em ankh.ef her neset it.ef, mar sepu, djeser meskhau.ef hena hapu ankh*), The youthful one, about whose life on his father's throne one is joyful, successful of deeds, and whose appearances with the living Apis bull are sacred, Ptolemy VIII H1

ḥwnw ḥkn.tw ḥr nst ỉt.f tỉt ḏsr(t) nt nsw nṯrw stp n ỉtmw ḏs.f (*hunu, heken.tu her neset it.ef, tit djeser(et) net nesu netjeru, setep en itmu djes.ef*), The youthful one, about whose father's throne one is joyful, the sacred image of the king of the gods, chosen by Atum himself, Ptolemy VIII H2

ḥwnw ḫʿ m nsw ḥr st ỉt.f (*hunu kha em nesu her set it.ef*), The youth who has appeared as king on his father's throne, Ptolemy V H

ḥwnw ḳnỉ (*hunu qeni*), Brave youth, Ptolemy II H

ḥwnw ḳnỉ sḫʿ.n sw ỉt.f (*hunu qeni, sekha.en su it.ef*), The brave youth whose father enthroned him, Ptolemy IV H

ḥwn(t) sꜣt ḥḳꜣ ỉr(t).n ḥḳꜣ mr(t) nṯrw bꜣḳt ḫkr(t).n ḫnmw ṯꜣtt sꜣt ḏḥwty wr(t)-pḥty sḥr(t) tꜣwy rdỉ n.s nbty rḫyt n nfrw ḳnỉ sy nt nb(t) sꜣw ṯnỉ sy ḥt-ḥr m mrwt.s (*hun(et), sat heqa, ir(et).en heqa, mer(et) netjeru baqet, kheqer(et).en khnemu, tjatet, sat djehuty, wer(et)-pehty, seher(et) tawy, redi en.es nebty rekhyet en neferu, qeni sy net neb(et) saw, tjeni sy hut-hor em merut.es*), The youthful one and the daughter of a ruler, whom a ruler begat, beloved of the gods of Baqet, whom Khnum ornamented, vizier, daughter of Thoth, great of strength, who has pleased the Two Lands, to whom the Two Ladies have given the common folk because of (her) perfection, whom Neith, mistress of Sais, has made brave, and whom Hathor has elevated through love of her, Cleopatra I H

ḥ(w) ḏfꜣ (*hu djefa*), Hudjefa (I) and (II) C

ḥ /// (*h[u?]///*), The smiter (?) ///, Hu /// B

ḥpw (*hepu*), The runner, Hepu B

ḥfnw-ḥbw mity rꜥ (hefenu hebu, mity ra), Immeasurable of festivals, the (very) likeness of Re, Amenhotep III G4

ḥm nṯr tpy n imn (*hem netjer tepy en imen*), High Priest of Amun, Menkheperre T

ḥnk sw n rꜥ m ḫrt-hrw (*henek su en ra em kheret-heru*), Who offers it (i.e., Maat) to Re in the course of every day, Merenptah H2

ḥr (*hor*), Horus, Hor I and II B

ḥr m ḥb (hor em heb), Horus is festive (lit. "in holiday"), Horemheb B

ḥr nbw (*hor nebu*), Golden Horus, Tefnakht G

ḥr sꜣ ꜣst (*hor sa aset*), Horus (is) the son of Isis, Harsiese B

ḥri (*hori*), Hori ("Who belongs to Horus"), Hori B

ḥry ḥr (*hery hor*), A superior one is Horus, Herihor B

ḥry-tp tꜣwy (*hery tep tawy*), The chieftain of the Two Lands, Amenemhat VII H

ḥrwy (*herwy*), The double falcon, Horwy H

ḥḥy ꜣḫwt n ms sw (*hehy akhut en mes su*), Who seeks benefits for the one who bore him, Ramses II G13

ḥḳꜣ mꜣꜥt (*heqa maat*), The ruler of Maat, Amenemhat VI G

ḥḳꜣ mꜣꜥt rꜥ (*heqa maat ra*), The ruler of the truth of Re, Ramses IV T2

ḥḳꜣ mꜣꜥt sḫpr tꜣwy (heqa maat, sekheper tawy), The ruler of Maat, who has created the Two Lands, Ay G

ḥḳꜣ n ḥwt-wꜥrt (*heqa en hut-waret*), The ruler of Avaris, Apophis B

ḥḳꜣ nḫt m tꜣ (*r*)*-ḏr.f* (*heqa nakht em ta (er)-djer-ef*), Victorious ruler in the entire land, Alexander II/IV G

ḥḳꜣ ḫꜣswt (*heqa khasut*), The Ruler of Foreign Lands, Semqen T, Aper-anati T, Seker-her T, Philip Arrhidaeus N

ḥḳꜣ ḫpr rꜥ (*heqa kheper ra*), The ruler is the (very) manifestation of Re, Sheshonq IIa T

ḥḳꜣ kmt (*heqa kemet*), The ruler of Egypt, Piye N3

ḥḳꜣ ḳni (*heqa qeni*), The brave ruler, Alexander the Great H2

ḥḳꜣ ḳni tkn ḫꜣswt (*heqa qeni, teken khasut*), The brave ruler who has attacked foreign lands, Alexander the Great H3

ḥḳꜣ tꜣwy wr-nḫtw (*heqa tawy, wer nakhtu*), Ruler of the Two Lands and great of victories, Pinodjem I H3

ḥkn m mꜣꜥt (*heken em maat*), The one who has been acclaimed by Maat, Amenemhat II H N

ḥkn n mꜣꜥt (*heken en maat*), Who has rejoiced at Maat, Rudamun N

ḥkn nṯrw rmṯ ḥr.f (heken netjeru remetj her.ef), The one over whom gods and people have rejoiced, Ptolemy III H1
ḥkn nṯrw rmṯ ḥr.f m šsp.f nsyt m-ˁ it.f (heken netjeru remetj her.ef em shesep.ef nesyt em a it.ef), The one over whom gods and people rejoiced when he has received the kingship from his father's hand, Ptolemy III H2
ḥtp (hetep), The one who is at peace, Hotep B
ḥtp (hetep), The Two Ladies are satisfied, Hetepsekhemwy N
ḥtp ib rˁ (hetep ib ra), The satisfied one of the mind of Re, Khamudi T
ḥtp ib t3wy (hetep ib tawy), The mind of the Two Lands is satisfied, Hor (I) H
ḥtp nṯrw (hetep netjeru), (With whom) the gods are satisfied, Senwosret II G, Sobekemsaf II H
ḥtp ḥr m3ˁt (hetep her maat), Contented with Maat, Sobekhotep III G
ḥtp ḥr m3ˁt mi t3-ṯnn (hetep her maat mi ta-tjenen), Satisfied with Maat, like Tatjenen, Merenptah H4
ḥtp sḫmy (hetep sekhemwy), The two powers are satisfied, Hetepsekhemwy H
ḥtp(w) (hetep), The one who is satisfied, Mentuhotep III G1
ḥḏ ḫpr rˁ (hedj kheper ra), The dazzling one is the (very) manifestation of Re, Smendes T, Sheshonq I T, Takelot I T, Takelot II T, Sheshonq IV T, Harsiese T, Sheshonq VIa T
ḥḏw-ḥr (hedju-her), The maces (of?) Horus, Hedju-Hor H

ḫ(3)mwdi (khamudi), Khamudi B
ḫ3sty (khasety), The highlander, Den T
ḫy3n (khyan), Khyan B
ḫˁ ˁnḫ rˁ (kha ankh ra), The living appearance of Re, Sobekhotep II T
ḫˁ wsr rˁ (kha weser ra), The (very) appearance of the strength of Re, Qareh T
ḫˁ b3 (kha ba,) The (very) appearance of a *ba*, Khaba H
ḫˁ b3w, (kha bau), The (very) appearance of power/might, Neferkaure H, Sekhemre Khutawy H, Wegaf N
ḫˁ.f rˁ (kha.ef ra), He appears (as) Re, Khafre T
ḫˁ m w3st (kha em waset), The one who has appeared in Thebes, Seqenenre Tao H
ḫˁ m wn(t) (kha em wen(et)), The one who has appeared in the Hermopolitan nome, Thutemhat H
ḫˁ m m3ˁt sšm t3wy (kha em maat, seshem tawy), The one who has appeared through Maat and guided the Two Lands, Tachos H
ḫˁ m nbty (kha em nebty), Who has appeared by means of the Two Ladies, Neferirkare N1
ḫˁ m nsw mi itmw (kha em nesu mi itemu), Who has appeared as king like Atum, Ramses I N
ḫˁ m nsrt ˁ3 -pḥty (kha em nesret, aa pehty), The one who has appeared by means of the serpent goddess, the one great of might, Thutmose I N1
ḫˁ m sḫm.f (kha em sekhem.ef), Who has appeared through his power, Sobekhotep III N

ḫʿ m sḫmty mỉ ḥr s3 3st sḥtp nṯrw m m3ʿt (*kha em sekhemty mi hor sa aset sehetep netjeru em maat*), Who has appeared in the Double Crown like Horus, the son of Isis, and pacified the gods with Maat, Sheshonq I N

ḫʿ mỉ ptḥ m ḫnw ḥfnw r smn hpw nfrw m-ḫt ỉdbwy (*kha mi ptah em khenu hefnu er semen hepu neferu em-khet idebwy*), Who has appeared like Ptah amidst hundreds of thousands in order to establish the perfect laws throughout the Two Banks, Merenptah N2

ḫʿ-mw-rʿ, Khamure B

ḫʿ nfr rʿ (*kha nefer ra*), The (very) appearance of the perfection of Re, Sobekhotep IV T

ḫʿ ḥr nst.f (*kha her neset.ef*), The one who has appeared on his throne, Kamose H1

ḫʿ ḥtp rʿ (*kha hetep ra*), The (very) appearance of the peace of Re, Sobekhotep VI T

ḫʿ-ḫʿw m ỉpt-swt (kha khau em ipet-sut), Radiant of crowns in Ipet-sut, Amenhotep II N2

ḫʿ ḫpr rʿ (*kha kheper ra*), The (very) appearance of the manifestation of Re, Senwosret II T, Pinodjem I T

ḫʿ ḫrw rʿ (*kha kheru ra*), The (very) appearance of the voice of Re, Khakherure T

ḫʿ sḫm (*kha sekhem*), The powerful one has appeared, Khasekhem/Kasekhemwy H1

ḫʿ sḫm rʿ (*kha sekhem ra*), The (very) appearance of the power of Re, Neferhotep I T

ḫʿ sḫmy nbw ḫt.sn (*kha sekhemwy nebu khet.sen*), The two powerful ones have appeared, the golden one of their bodies, Khasekhem/Kasekhemwy N2

ḫʿ sḫmy nbwy ḥtp(.w) ỉm.f (*kha sekhemwy nebwy hetep(u) im.ef*), The two powerful ones have appeared, the two lords being satisfied with him, Khasekhem/Kasekhemwy H2 and Seth name N1

ḫʿ k3 rʿ (*kha ka ra*), The (very) appearance of the ka of Re, Khakare T

ḫʿ k3w rʿ (*kha kau ra*), The (very) appearance of the kas of Re, Senwosret III T

ḫw wỉ (*khu wi*), The one who protects me, Khui B

ḫw wỉ ḥʿpy (*khu wi hapy*), (The Nile god) Hapy protects me, Neferkauhor Khuwihapi B

ḫw b3ḳt wʿf ḫ3swt (*khu baqet, waf khasut*), The one who has protected Baqet and subdued the foreign lands, Tachos G

ḫw.f wỉ (*khu.ef wi*), He protects me, Khufu T1

ḫw nfr-tm rʿ (*khu nefertem ra*), The one whom Nefertum and Re protect, Taharqa T

ḫw t3wy (*khu tawy*), The protector of the Two Lands, Sobekhotep III H, Taharqa G, Philip Arrhidaeus H1

ḫw t3wy rʿ (*khu tawy ra*), The protector of the Two Lands of (?) Re, Wegaf T

ḫnḏr (*khendjer*), The wild boar, Khendjer B

ḫpr (*kheper*), The one who has manifested (himself), Radjedef H, Senwosret III G
ḫpr m nbty (*kheper em nebty*), Who has manifested (himself) by means of the Two Ladies, Radjedef N
ḫpr m3ʿt n rʿ (*kheper maat en ra*), The (very) manifestation of the truth of Re, Ramses X T2
ḫpr m3ʿt rʿ (*kheper maat ra*), The (very) manifestation of the truth of Re, Ramses X T1
ḫpr ḫprw (*kheper kheperu*), The (very) manifestation of manifestations, Amenemhat IV H, Intef VI H2
ḫpr ḫprw rʿ ir m3ʿt (kheper kheperu ra, ir maat), The (very) manifestation of the manifestations of Re, who has accomplished Maat, Ay T
ḫpr k3 rʿ (*kheper ka ra*), The (very) manifestation of the ka of Re, Senwosret I T, Nectanebo I T
ḫndw (*khendu*),The wanderer, Neferkare Khendu C2

ẖnm ib rʿ (*khnum ib ra*), The one who is associated with the mind of Re, Amasis T
ẖnm m3ʿt rʿ (*khnum maat ra*), The one who is associated with the truth of Re, Achoris T
ẖnmw ḫw.f wi (*khnum khu.ef wi*), Khnum, he protects me, Khufu T2
ẖnm(t) ib n m3ʿt mr(t) nṯrw (*khneme(t) ib en maat, mer(et) netjeru*), Whose mind is united with Maat, beloved of the gods, Arsinoe II T
ẖnmt imn ḥ3t špswt (khnemet imen, hat shepsut), United with Amun, foremost of noble women, Hatshepsut B
ẖty (*khety*), The one belonging to the divine corporation, Khety II to VIII B

zmty (*zemty*), The desert man, Den C

s n wsrt (*s en wosret*), The man belonging to (the goddess) Wosret, Senwosret I to IV
s-sw (*se-su*), short form of name Ramses (II)
s3 imn (*sa imen*), Son of Amun, Ramses III H12, Siamun B
s3 ptḥ (*sa ptah*), The son of Ptah, Siptah B
s3 ptḥ mry.f (*sa ptah, mery.ef*), The son of Ptah, his beloved, Apries G2
s3 nt spd t3wy (*sa neith, seped tawy*), The son of Neith, who has restored the Two Lands, Amasis N
s3 nḫt (*sa nakht*), The powerful protector, Sanakht H
s3 ḥt-ḥr (*sa hut-hor*), Son of Hathor, Sahathor B
s<3?>b (*s<a>b*), The jackal (?), Seb/Sab B
s3ḥ w(i) rʿ (*sah w(i) ra*), Re has endowed me, Sahure B
s3t rʿ (*sat ra*), Daughter of Re, Tawosret T
s3t ḥḳ3 irt.n ḥḳ3 (*sat heqa, iret.en heqa*), Daughter of the ruler, whom the ruler begat, Berenike II H

sꜣt sḫm nbt tꜣwy (*sat sekhem nebet tawy*), The daughter of the powerful one is (now) Mistress of the Two Lands, Sobeknefru N

siꜣ-ib (*sia ib*), Perceptive-minded, Nekau II H

siꜣ ẖt (*sia khet*), The one who understands inner (feelings), Tefnakht H N

sꜥꜣ iwnw ḳꜣb ꜥꜣbt di mꜣꜥt n rꜥ m ẖrt-hrw (*saa iunu, qab aabet, di maat en ra em kheret heru*), Who has magnified Heliopolis, doubled the offerings, and presented Maat to Re every day, Siptah N

sꜥꜣ ḥwt.f nt ḏt (saa hut.ef net djet), Who has magnified his temple of eternity, Amenhotep III G5

sꜥꜣ ḫꜥw mi ꜣḫty wbn.f ꜥnḫ rḫyt (*saa khau mi akhty weben.ef, ankh rekhyet*), Who has magnified (his) appearances like the One of the Two Horizons when he rises, the (very) life of the *rekhyet*-people, Ramses III H13

sꜥꜣ ḫprw wr-biꜣwt (*saa kheperu, wer biaut*), The one who has magnified (his) manifestations is one great of marvels, Osorkon I N

sꜥnḫ ib rꜥ (*sankh ib ra*), The one whom the mind of Re has sustained, Amenemhat VI T, Sankhibre T

sꜥnḫ ib tꜣwy (*sankh ib tawy*), Who has sustained the mind of the Two Lands, Mentuhotep II (a) H

sꜥnḫ ptḥ (*sankh ptah*), The one whom Ptah sustains, Sankhptah B

sꜥnḫ.n rꜥ (*sankh.en ra*), The one whom Re made live, Sewadjtu T, Mentuhotep VI T

sꜥnḫ kꜣ rꜥ (*sankh ka ra*), The one whom the ka of Re has sustained, Mentuhotep III T1

sꜥnḫ tꜣwy (*sankh tawy*), The one who has sustained the Two Lands, Senwosret IV N

sꜥnḫ tꜣwy.f(y) (*sankh tawy.f(y)*), The one who has sustained his Two Lands, Mentuhotep III H N

sꜥr mꜣꜥt sḥtp rꜥ (sar maat, sehetep ra), Who has elevated Maat and satisfied Re, Thutmose III (b) G5

sꜥšꜣ ḳnw (*sasha qenu*), The one who has multiplied brave men, Piye G2

swꜣḥ.n rꜥ (*sewah.en ra*), The one whom Re has made enduring, Senebmiu T

swꜣḏ.n rꜥ (*sewadj.en ra*), The one whom Re has made flourish, Nebiryerau I T

swꜣḏ kꜣ rꜥ (*sewadj ka ra*), The one whom the ka of Re has made flourish, Sewadjkare (I) T, Hori T, Sewadjkare (II) T

swꜣḏ tꜣwy (*sewadj tawy*), The one who has made the Two Lands flourish, Nebiryerau I H, Senaaib H, Apries G1

swꜣḏ.tw (*sewadj.tu*),<He> was made to flourish, Sewadjtu B

swꜥb bnbn mḥ sw m mnw sṯḥnt mi ꜣḫt im.s (*sewab benben, meh su em menu setjehenet mi akhet im.es*), The one who has purified the Benenet and filled it with monuments that gleam like the horizon which is within it, Herihor N2

swsr.n rꜥ (*seweser.en ra*), The one whom Re has made strong, Khyan T, Bebiankh T

swsḫ tꜣwy (*sewesekh tawy*), Who has widened the Two Lands, Sehetepibre H

swḏꜣ bꜣḳt sḥḏ gsw-prw smn hpw mi͗ ḏḥwty ꜥꜣ ꜥꜣ nb ḥbw-sd mi͗ ptḥ tꜣ-ṯnn i͗ty mi͗ rꜥ (*sewedja baqet, sehedj gesu-peru, semen hepu mi djehuty aa aa, neb hebu-sed mi ptah ta-tjenen, ity mi ra*), Who has kept Baqet safe (by) illuminating the temples and establishing laws like the twice-great Thoth, a possessor of Sed festivals like Ptah Ta-tjenen and a sovereign like Re, Ptolemy IV G

swḏꜥ rꜥ (*sewedja ra*), Whom Re has made a judge, Mentuhotep V T

sbk m sꜣ.f (*sobek em sa.ef*), Sobek is his protection, Sobekemsaf I and II B

sbk nfrw (*sobek nefru*), Sobek is perfect, Sobeknefru B

sbk ḥtp(w) (*sobek hetep(u)*), Sobek is satisfied, Sobekhotep I to VIII

sb(ꜣ)ḳ tꜣwy (*sebaq tawy*), The one who has blessed the Two Lands, Shabaka H N G

spꜣty (*sepaty*), He of the two districts, Den C

smꜣ (*sema*), The uniter, Teti G, Amenemhat I (a) G

smꜣ psšty mi͗ sꜣ ꜣst sḥtp nṯrw m i͗rt mꜣꜥt (*sema peseshty mi sa aset sehetep netjeru em iret maat*), The one who has united the Two Portions like the son of Isis has satisfied the gods by performing Maat, Osorkon II N3

smꜣ psšty mi͗ sꜣ ꜣst dmḏ.f sḫmty m ḥtp (*sema peseshty mi sa aset demedj.ef sekhemty em hetep*), The one who has united the Two Portions like the son of Isis has assembled the Two Crowns in peace, Osorkon II N1

smꜣ psšty mi͗ sꜣ ꜣst dmḏ.n.f sḫmty m ḥtp dhn /// (*sema peseshty mi sa aset demedj.en.ef sekhemty em hetep, dehen ///*), The one who has united the Two Portions like the son of Isis has assembled the Two Crowns in peace, whom [god X] appointed ///, Osorkon II N2

smꜣ tꜣw dr pḏwt 9 i͗ṯ m sḫm.f m tꜣw nbw (*sema tau, der pedjut 9, itj em sekhem.ef em tau nebu*), Who has united lands, repelled the Nine Bows, and seized with his strong arm in all lands, Psusennes I G

smꜣ tꜣwy (*sema tawy*), The uniter of the Two Lands, Mentuhotep II (c) H N, Sobekhotep II H, Piye H2, Cambyses H

smn mꜣꜥt (*semen maat*), The one who has established Maat, Amasis H

smn mꜣꜥt ḫt tꜣwy (*semen maat khet tawy*), Who has established Maat throughout the Two Lands, Ramses I G

smn.n rꜥ (*semen.en ra*), The one whom Re has established, Hepu T, Semenenre T

smn hpw (*semen hepu*), The establisher of laws, Nectanebo II G1

smn hpw mi͗ nb wꜣst (semen hepu mi neb waset), Who has established laws like the lord of Thebes, Amenhotep III N5

smn hpw ḥwi͗ pḏwt 9 (*semen hepu, hui pedjut 9*), The establisher of laws, who has struck down the Nine Bows, Nectanebo II G2

smn hpw sgrḥ tꜣwy (semen hepu, segereh tawy), Who has established laws and pacified the Two Lands, Amenhotep III N1

smn hpw ṯs tꜣwy (semen hepu, tjes tawy), Who has established laws and raised up the Two Lands, Amenhotep III N2

smn kꜣ rꜥ (*semen ka ra*), The one whom the ka of Re has established, Nebnun T

smnḫ mnw m i͗pt-rsy(t) n i͗t.f i͗mn di͗ sw ḥr nst.f (*semenekh menu em ipet-resy(t) en it.ef imen di su her neset.ef*), Who has made monuments splendid in Ipet-Resyt for his father Amun, who put him on his throne, Ramses II N11

smnḫ k3 rʿ (*semenekh ka ra*), The one whom the ka of Re has made potent, Imy-ra Mesha T

smnḫ k3 rʿ ḏsr-ḫprw (semenekh ka ra, djeser kheperu), Whom the ka of Re has made potent, sacred of manifestations, Smenkhkare T B

smnḫ t3wy (*semenekh tawy*), Who has made the Two Lands potent, Nectanebo I N

smr ẖt (*semer khet*), Friend of the (divine) body, Semerkhet H

smsw (*semsu*), The eldest, Semerkhet C

sn (*sen*), The one whom the Two Ladies have kissed, Qaa N2

snʿʿ ỉb (*senaa ib*), The soother (lit. "who has made the heart smooth"), Senaaib B

snb mỉ ỉw (*seneb mi iu*), Healthy like one who has arrived, Senebmiu B

snfr ỉb rʿ (*senefer ib ra*), The one whom Re's mind has made perfect, Senwosret IV T

snfr w(ỉ) (*senefer wi*), <God N> has made me perfect, Snefru T

snfr rʿ (*senefer ra*), The one whom Re made perfect, Piye T3

snfr k3 (*senefer ka*), The one whom a ka has made perfect, Seneferka H

snfr k3 rʿ (*senefer ka ra*), The one whom the ka of Re has made perfect, Mentuhotep III T2

snfr /// rʿ (*senefer /// ra*), Whom the /// of Re has made perfect, Senefer /// re T

snfr t3wy (*senefer tawy*), Who has made the Two Lands perfect, Psamtek II G

snn stp.n ptḥ (*senen setep en ptah*), The likeness that Ptah chose, Khababash T

snn/// (*senen///*), The (very) likeness [of ? ///], Senen /// C

snḫt.n rʿ (*senakht.en ra*), The one whom Re has made victorious, Senakhtenre Ahmose (I) T

snḫt kmt dr pḏwt 9 r dỉt ḥtp nṯrw m mr.sn (*senakht kemet, der pedjut 9 er dit hetep netjeru em mer.sen*), Who has strengthened Egypt and repelled the Nine Bows in order to satisfy the gods with what they love/wish for, Merenptah G2

snd (*sened*), The frightful one, Sened B and C (both later names)

snḏm ỉb rʿ (*senedjem ib ra*), The one who has contented Re, Nectanebo II T

srḳ (*sereq*), The scorpion, Scorpion H

shr ỉb nṯrw (*seher ib netjeru*), The one who has pleased the gods' minds, Nectanebo II N1

shr ỉb nṯrw tkn ḫ3swt (*seher ib netjeru, teken khasut*), The one who has pleased the gods' minds by attacking the foreign lands, Nectanebo II N2

shr t3wy (*seher tawy*), Who has made the Two Lands content, Intef I H, Amenemhat VI H, Kamose G, Ptolemy VIII N

shr t3wy k3 nḫt sḫm nḥḥ (*seher tawy, ka nakht, sekhem neheh*), Who has made the Two Lands content, victorious bull, eternal power, Ptolemy X N

sḥb w3st m mnw wrw (*seheb waset em menu weru*), The one who has made Thebes festive with great monuments, Herihor N3

sḥb rʿ (*seheb ra*), The one who has made Re festive, Sehebre T

sḥb t3wy (*seheb tawy*), The one who has made the Two Lands festive, Amenemhat IV N
sḥḳ3.n rˁ (*seheqa.en ra*), Whom Re has made a ruler, Sankhptah T
sḥtp ib rˁ (*sehetep ib ra*), The one who has propitiated the mind of Re, Amenemhat I (a-b) T, Sa-Hornedjheritef T, Sehetepibre T
sḥtp ib t3wy (*sehetep ib tawy*), The one who has propitiated the mind of the Two Lands, Amenemhat I (a) H N
sḥtp nbty (*sehetep nebty*), The one who has satisfied the Two Ladies, Qaa N3, Teti N
sḥtp nṯrw (*sehetep netjeru*), Who has satisfied the gods, Achoris G
sḥtp nṯrw ḳd ḥwt.sn ir hrrt k3w.sn (*sehetep netjeru, qed hut.sen, ir herreret kau.sen*), The one who has satisfied the gods (by) building their temples and who has accomplished what pleases their kas, Herihor N1
sḥtp rˁ m mrrt.f (*sehetep ra em merret.ef*), Who pleases Re with whatever he (i.e., Re) wishes, Sety I G3
sḥtp k3 rˁ (*sehetep ka ra*), The one who has propitiated the ka of Re, Intef IV T
sḥtp t3wy (*sehetep tawy*), The one who has satisfied the Two Lands, Teti H, Apophis H
sḥtp t3wy.fy (*sehetep tawy.fy*), The one who has satisfied his Two Lands, Piye H3
sḫˁ m3ˁt (*sekha maat*), The one who has caused Maat to appear, Senwosret II N
sḫˁ m3ˁt mry t3wy (*sekha maat, mery tawy*), Who has made Maat appear, the beloved one of the Two Lands, Thutmose III (b) N2, Shabataka N2
sḫˁ.n ptḥ (*sekha.en ptah*), The one whom Ptah has caused to appear/crowned, Sekhaenptah T
sḫˁ.n rˁ (*sekha.en ra*), The one whom Re has caused to appear, Sekhaenre T, Yakob-mu T, Siptah T1
sḫˁ.n sw it.f (*sekha.en su it.ef*), Whose father enthroned him, Ptolemy II G
sḫˁ sw mwt.f ḥr nst it.f iṯ t3wy m m3ˁ-ḫrw (*sekha su mut.ef her neset it.ef, itj tawy em maa-kheru*), The one whom his mother has enthroned on the throne of his father, who seized the Two Lands in justification, Ptolemy IX N1
sḫpr.n rˁ (*sekheper.en ra*), The one whom Re has brought into being, Sekheperenre T
sḫm (*sekhem*), The one who is powerful, Mentuhotep III G2
sḫm-ib (*sekhem-ib*), The resolute one, Sekhemib H1
sḫm-ib pr.n m3ˁt (*sekhem-ib per.en maat*), The resolute one, (for whom) Maat has come forth, Sekhemib H2 N
sḫm bik nbw (*sekhem bik nebu*), The golden falcon is powerful, Khafre G
sḫm-pḥty hd ḥfnw dḫ n3 pḥw sw dmḏ (*ḫr*) *ṯbwy.f* (*y*) (*sekhem pehty, hed hefnu, dekh na pehu su demedj (kher) tjebwy.fy*), Powerful of strength, who has attacked hundreds of thousands, overthrown those who have attacked him, and gathered (them) (under) his sandals, Ramses III H8
sḫm-pḥty ḥwi pḏwt 9 wr nḫtw m t3w nbw (*sekhem pehty, hui pedjut 9, wer nakhtu*

em tau nebu), Powerful of might, who has struck down the Nine Bows, great of victories in all lands, Sheshonq I G1

sḫm-pḥty ḥwi rḳiw.f bh3.tw.f ḥpt m //// (*sekhem pehty, hui reqiu.ef beha.tu.ef, hepet em ////*), Powerful of might, who has struck down his opponents who flee from him, who has embraced by means of ///, Smendes N

sḫm-pḥty ḥwi ḫftyw.f wsr-f3w (*sekhem pehty, hui kheftyu.ef, weser fau*), The mighty powerful one who has struck down his enemies is rich in splendor, Osorkon II G4

sḫm-pḥty dr sttyw (sekhem pehty, der setetiu), Powerful of might, who has repelled the Asiatics, Ay N

sḫm nṯri ir.n ḫpri (*sekhem netjeri, ir.en khepri*), Divine power, whom Khepri has begotten, Sety I G5

sḫm nṯrw (*sekhem netjeru*), The powerful one of the gods, Amenemhat IV G, Wegaf H

sḫm rʿ w3ḥ ḫʿw (*sekhem ra, wah khau*), The powerful one of Re is enduring of appearances, Rahotep T

sḫm rʿ w3ḏ-ḫʿw (*sekhem ra, wadj khau*), The powerful one of Re is flourishing of appearances, Sobekemsaf II T

sḫm rʿ wp m3ʿt (*sekhem ra wep maat*), The powerful one of Re is the one who has discerned Maat, Intef V T

sḫm rʿ nfr-ḫʿw (*sekhem ra, nefer khau*), The powerful one of Re is perfect of appearances, Wepwawetemsaf T

sḫm rʿ hr ḥr m3ʿt (*sekhem ra her her maat*), The powerful one of Re, who is pleased with Maat, Intef VII T

sḫm rʿ ḫw t3wy (*sekhem ra khu tawy*), The powerful one of Re is the protection of the Two Lands, Sobekhotep I T, Sekhemre Khutawy T, Pantjeny T

sḫm rʿ sʿnḫ t3wy (*sekhem ra, sankh tawy*), The powerful one of Re, who has sustained the Two Lands, Neferhotep III Iykhernofret T

sḫm rʿ sw3ḏ t3wy (*sekhem ra, sewadj tawy*), The (very) power of Re, who has made the Two Lands flourish, Sobekhotep III T

sḫm rʿ swsr t3wy (*sekhem ra, seweser tawy*), The powerful one of Re, who has strengthened the Two Lands, Sobekhotep VIII T

sḫm rʿ smn t3wy (*sekhem ra, semen tawy*), The powerful one of Re, who has made the Two Lands firm, Djehuty T

sḫm rʿ šd w3st (*sekhem ra shed waset*), The powerful one of Re, who has rescued Thebes, Sekhemreshedwaset T

sḫm rʿ šd t3wy (*sekhem ra shed tawy*), The powerful one of Re is the one who has rescued the Two Lands, Sobekemsaf I T

sḫm ḫʿw (*sekhem khau*), Powerful of appearances, Shepseskare H, Amenemhat VI N

sḫm-ḫʿw m t3w nbw (sekhem khau em tau nebu), Powerful of appearances in all lands, Thutmose IV N2 *sḫm ḫpr rʿ (sekhem kheper ra)*, The powerful one is a manifestation of Re, Osorkon I T

sḫm-ḫprw (sekhem kheperu), Powerful of manifestations, Thutmose II G

sḫm-ḫpš dr pḏwt 9 (sekehm khepesh, der pedjut 9), The powerful of arm/sword, who has repelled the Nine Bows, Ramses II G14, Sety II N2

sḫm-ḫpš dr rḳyw.f (sekhem khepesh, der reqyu.ef), Powerful of effectiveness, who has subdued his enemies, Sethnakht G1

sḫm-ḫt (sekhem-khet), The one (whose) body is powerful, Sekhemkhet H

sḫm k3 rʿ (sekhem ka ra), The powerful one of the ka of Re, Sekhemkare T, Senbef T, Amenemhat V T

sḫm /// rʿ (sekhem /// ra), The powerful one of the /// of Re, Sekhem /// re T

sḫmw nbw (sekhemu nebu), The triple power, Neferirkare G

sḫr pḥw sw in pḥwy t3 (sekher pehu su in pehwy ta), Who has felled those who attacked him and who has captured the ends of the earth, Ramses II N12

sšm t3wy (seshem tawy), The one who has guided the Two Lands, Senwosret II H

sḳn.n rʿ (seqen.en ra), The one whom Re has made brave, Seqenenre Tao T

st-ib nbty (set-ib nebty), The favorite of the Two Ladies, Niuserre N

st-ib t3wy (set-ib tawy), The favorite of the Two Lands, Niuserre H, Osorkon III N

stwt rʿ (setut ra), Progeny of Re, Darius I T1

stp nṯrw (setep netjeru), Divinely chosen, Amasis G, Nepherites I G

stp n rʿ mry imn (setep en ra, mery imen), Chosen by Re and beloved of Amun, Alexander the Great T, Philip Arrhidaeus T1, Ptolemy I T

stp n k3 rʿ mry imn (setep en ka ra, mery imen), Chosen by the ka of Re and beloved of Amun, Philip Arrhidaeus T2

stḫ (seth), Seth, Seth B

stḫ pr(w) ib.sn (per(u) ib.sen), Seth, (for whom ?) their will has come forth, Peribsen Seth name

stḫ nḫt(.w) (seth nakht(u)), Seth is strong, Sethnakht B

stḫy (sethy), The one who belongs to (the god) Seth, Sety I and II B

sḏf3 k3 rʿ (sedjefa ka ra), The one whom the ka of Re has endowed, Amenemhat VII T

sḏf3 t3wy (sedjefa tawy), The one who has provisioned the Two Lands, Kamose H3

sḏs (sedjes), Broken, Sedjes C

s[///] rʿ (se[///].en ra), Whom Re has ///, Se [///] re T

s/// rʿ ḫty (se/// ra khety), Who /// Re, Khety (VI) T B

s/// k3 rʿ (se/// ka ra), Who makes the ka of Re ///, Se /// kare T

š3b3k3 (shabaka), Shabaka B

š3b3t3k3 (shabataka), Shabataka B

šps <m> nbty (shepes <em> nebty), The noble one <by means of> the Two Ladies, Shepseskaf N

šps ḫt (shepes khet), The noble one of the (divine) Corporation, Shepseskaf H

špss rʿ (*shepses ra*), The noble one belonging to Re, Tefnakht T
špss kꜣ rʿ (*shepses ka ra*), The noble one of the ka of Re, Shepseskare T
špss kꜣ.f (*shepses ka.ef*), His ka is noble, Shepseskaf T
šmꜣy (*shemay*), The foreigner, Djedkare Shemay C2
šny (*sheny*), The crocodile, Crocodile H
š-n-ḥ, Sheneh B
š-n-š-k (*shenshek*), "the rescuer" (?), Shenshek B
šndt (*shendet*), The crocodile, Crocodile H
šsp ʿnḫ n itmw ḫpr m ḫpri ḥtp bꜣw iwnw ḥr mꜣʿt.f (shesep ankh en itemu, kheper em khepri, hetep bau iunu her maat.ef), Living image of Atum who has appeared as Khepri, with whose offerings the Souls of Heliopolis are satisfied, Thutmose III (b) N4
šsp nṯri n ḫpri (*shesep netjeri en khepri*), The divine image of Khepri, Ramses II N13
šsp tꜣ mry ḥḳꜣ.f m ḥʿʿw nb ḥbw-sd ʿšꜣw wrw mi it.f ptḥ tꜣ-ṯnn smsw nṯrw šsp.n.f nsyt n rʿ m ḳnw nḫt ity wḏʿ mꜣʿt smn hpw mi ḏḥwty ʿꜣ ʿꜣ (*shesep ta mery, heqa.ef em haau, neb hebu-sed ashau weru mi it.ef ptah ta-tjenen semsu netjeru, shesep.en.ef nesyt en ra em qenu nakht, ity wedja maat, semen hepu mi djehuty aa aa*), The one who has received the Beloved Land, he rules in jubilation, the possessor of a great many Sed festivals like his father Ptah Ta-tjenen, the eldest of the gods, as he has received the kingship of Re in victorious bravery, the sovereign who discerns Maat and establishes laws like twice-great Thoth, Ptolemy IX G2
š-š-i (*sheshi*), Sheshi, Sheshi B
ššnḳ (*shesheneq*), Sheshonq I to VII B
šd /// (*shed///*), The savior ///, Shed /// B
šd tꜣwy (*shed tawy*), The one who has rescued the Two Lands, Dedumose I N

ḳꜣ-ʿ (*qa-a*), (Whose) arm is raised, Qaa H N1
ḳꜣ-r-ḥ (*qareh*), The bald one, Qareh B
ḳꜣ-ḥḏt (*qa-hedjet*), (Whose) White Crown is high, Huni H
ḳꜣ-ḥḏt mry rʿ (qa-hedjet, mery ra), (Whose) White Crown is high, beloved of Re, Thutmose III (b) H6
ḳꜣ-ḫʿw (*qa khau*), Exalted of appearances, Taharqa H N
ḳꜣ-šwty (*qa shuty*), High of plumes, Mentuhotep II (c) G
ḳꜣ kꜣ rʿ (*qa ka ra*), The exalted (lit. "high") one of the ka of Re, Qakare Ibi I T
ḳbḥ (*qebeh*), The cool one, Qaa C
ḳmꜣw sꜣ-ḥr-nḏ-ḥr-it.f (*qemau sa-hor-nedj-her-it.ef*), Qemau's son "Son-of-Horus is the protector of his father," Sa-Hornedjheritef B
ḳn nb ḫpš ir tꜣš r mr.f m-sꜣ ḫftyw.f (*qen neb khepesh ir tash er mer.ef em-sa kheftiu.ef*), The brave one, possessor of a strong arm, who has made (his) border as he wished, on the back of his enemies, Ramses III G5
ḳn nḏti nṯrw inb mnḫ n tꜣ mry (*qen, nedjti netjeru, ineb menekh en ta mery*), The

brave one who has protected the gods, a potent wall for Ta-mery, Ptolemy III N
ḳnw (*qenu*), The brave one, Psamtek I G, Achoris N

k3 (*ka*), The ka-life force, Ka H
k3 wʿf t3w (ka waf tau), Bull who has subdued the lands, Amenhotep I H
k3 pḥty sḫm-ḫpš nḫt-ʿ nb nrw m t3w ḫ3swt fnḫw tmḥw (*ka pehty, sekhem khepesh, nakht-a, neb neru, em tau khasut fenkhu temehu*), Powerful bull, potent of sword, strong-armed, lord of dread in the lowlands and the highlands of the Fenkhu-Asiatics and the Temehu-Libyans, Ramses III H2
k3 m w3st (ka em waset), Bull in Thebes, Ahmose (II) H2
k3 <*m*> *nbty* (*ka* <*em*> *nebty*), The bull <by means of> the Two Ladies, Menkaure N
k3 ms(*w*) (*ka mes(u)*), Kamose ("The bull is born"), Kamose B1
k3 ms(*w*) *nḫt*(*w*) (*ka mes(u) nakht(u)*), Kamose the victorious, Kamose B2
k3 n nsww dr pḏwt 9 (ka en nesu, der pedjut 9), The bull of kings who has repelled the Nine Bows, Amenhotep III G6
k3 n rʿ sḫm (*ka en ra, sekhem*), The bull of Re, the powerful one, Ramses II H4
k3 nḫt 3ḫ n itmw (*ka nakht akh en itemu*), Victorious bull, beneficial to Atum, Merenptah H11
k3 nḫt i3ḫw stwt rʿ iʿḥ (*ka nakht, iakhu setut ra iah*), Victorious bull, the light of the sun and the moon's rays, Ptolemy XV H2
k3 nḫt ir.n rʿ (*ka nakht ir.en ra*), Victorious bull, begotten of Re, Sety I, Abydos 3. He
k3 nḫt ity psḏ m t3-mry mi ḥpw ʿnḫ rdi n.f ḥbw-sd ʿš3w wrw mi ptḥ t3-ṯnn it nṯrw (*ka nakht, ity pesedj em ta-mery mi hapu ankh, redi en.ef hebu-sed ashau weru mi ptah ta-tjenen it netjeru*), The victorious bull and sovereign who shines in Ta-mery like the living Apis bull, to whom has been given a great many Sed festivals like Ptah Ta-tjenen, and father of the gods, Ptolemy IX H2
k3 nḫt-ʿ dm ḥnwty mn-ib wr-pḥty ḥr b3wy n ḳnw (*ka nakht-a, dem henuty, men ib, wer pehty her bawy en qenu*), The strong-armed bull who has sharpened (his) two horns, decisive and great of strength on the battlefield of bravery, Ramses III H6
k3 nḫt ʿ3-pḥty (ka nakht aa pehty), Victorious bull, great of might, Amenhotep II H2
k3 nḫt ʿ3-nḫtw sʿnḫ t3wy (*ka nakht aa nakhtu, sankh tawy*), The victorious bull great of victories, who has sustained the Two Lands, Ramses VI H
k3 nḫt ʿ3-nsyt (*ka nakht aa nesyt*), Victorious bull, great of kingship, Ramses II H5, Ramses III H1
k3 nḫt ʿ3-ḫpš (*ka nakht aa khepesh*), Victorious bull, great of strong arm, Sety I H13
k3 nḫt ʿ3-šfyt (*ka nakht aa shefyt*), Victorious bull, great of majesty, Ramses II H5

k3 nḫt ꜥ3-šfyt mry rꜥ (ka nakht aa shefyt, mery ra), The victorious bull, great of majesty and beloved of Re, Sety I H9

k3 nḫt ꜥn m nsw (ka nakht an em nesu), Victorious bull, beautiful as king, Ramses VII H1

k3 nḫt ꜥnḫ m m3ꜥt nb ḥbw-sd mi it.f ptḥ-t3-ṯnn (ka nakht ankh em maat neb hebu-sed mi it.ef ptah-ta-tjenen), The victorious bull who lives on Maat, and lord of Sed festivals like his father Ptah-Ta-tjenen, Ramses IV H

k3 nḫt ꜥḥ3 ḥr ḫpš.f (ka nakht aha her khepesh.ef), Victorious bull, who has fought with his strong arm/sword, Ramses II H6

k3 nḫt w3ḥ-nsyt (ka nakht wah nesyt), The victorious bull, enduring of kingship, Sety I, Abydos 2. He

k3 nḫt w3ḏ-nsyt (ka nakht wadj nesyt), Victorious bull, flourishing of kingship, Ramses I H

k3 nḫt wꜥf ḫ3swt (ka nakht waf khasut), Victorious bull, who has subdued the foreign lands, Ramses II H7

k3 nḫt wr-pḥty (ka nakht wer pehty), Victorious bull, great of might, Amenhotep II H1, Ramses II H8, Sety II H1, Siptah H2, Sethnakht H

k3 nḫt wr-nḫtw ꜥḥ3 ḥr ḫpš.f (ka nakht wer nakhtu, aha her khepesh.ef), Victorious bull, great of victories, who fought with his strong arm/sword, Ramses II H9

k3 nḫt wr-nsyt (ka nakht wer nesyt), The victorious bull, who is great of kingship, Sety I, Abydos 7. He

k3 nḫt wr-ḥbw-sd (ka nakht wer hebu sed), Victorious bull, great of Sed festivals, Ramses II H10

k3 nḫt wr-ḥbw-sd mry t3wy (ka nakht wer hebu sed, mery tawy), Victorious bull, great of Sed festivals and beloved of the Two Lands, Ramses II H11

k3 nḫt wḥm mswt (ka nakht wehem mesut), The victorious bull who has renewed births, Sety I, Abydos 1. Hb, Abydos 5. Hb, Abydos 6. Hb, Abydos 7. Hb

k3 nḫt wḥm mswt sḫm-ḫpš (ka nakht wehem mesut sekhem khepesh), The victorious bull who has renewed births, the powerful of arm/sword, Sety I, Abydos 2. Hb

k3 nḫt wḥm ḫꜥw (ka nakht wehem khau), The victorious bull who has repeated appearances, Sety I, Abydos 1. Hd, Abydos 5. Hc, Abydos 6. Hc, Abydos 7. Hc

k3 nḫt wḥm-ḫꜥw <dr> pḏwt 9 (ka nakht wehem khau, <der> pedjut 9), The victorious bull who has repeated appearances and <repelled> the Nine Bows, Sety I, Abydos 2. Hc

k3 nḫt wsr-pḥty (ka nakht weser pehty), Victorious bull, strong of might, Thutmose II H, Ramses II H12

k3 nḫt wsr-pḏwt (ka nakht weser pedjut), The victorious bull, strong of troops, Sety I, Abydos 2. Hd

k3 nḫt wsr-m3ꜥt (ka nakht weser maat), Victorious bull, strong of Maat/Truth, Ramses II H13 *k3 nḫt wsr-rnpwt* (*ka nakht weser renput*), Victorious bull, rich in years, Ramses II H14

k3 nḫt wsr-ḫpš (*ka nakht weser khepesh*), Victorious bull, strong of effectiveness/sword, Ramses II H15

k3 nḫt wsr-k3w (*ka nakht weser kau*), The victorious bull, who is strong of kas, Sety I, Abydos 7. Hd

k3 nḫt wṯs m3ʿt (*ka nakht wetjes maat*), Victorious bull, who has upheld Maat, Ramses II H16

k3 nḫt pr m rʿ (*ka nakht per em ra*), Victorious bull, who has emerged from Re, Merenptah H6

k3 nḫt m dd imn wsr-f3w sḫʿ m w3st (*ka nakht em ded imen, weser fau, sekha em waset*), Victorious bull through the gift of Amun, rich in splendor, who has been made to appear in Thebes, Psusennes I H

k3 nḫt m3i pḥty nḫt-ʿ nb ḫpš ḥ3ḳ sttiw (*ka nakht mai pehty, nakht a, neb khepesh, haq setetiu*), Victorious bull and powerful lion, strong of arm, the lord of strength who has captured the Asiatics, Ramses III H3

k3 nḫt m3i ḥbn.n.f (*ka nakht mai heben.en.ef*), Victorious bull, a lion who has triumphed, Merenptah H13

k3 nḫt mitt mnṯw (*ka nakht mitet mentju*), The victorious bull and the (very) likeness of Montu, Sety I H6

k3 nḫt mn-ib sḫm-pḥty (*ka nakht men ib, sekhem pehty*), Victorious bull, decisive and powerful of might, Ramses II H17

k3 nḫt mn-m3ʿt (*ka nakht men maat*), Victorious bull, enduring of Maat, Ramses V H

k3 nḫt mnḫ-mnw sḥtp nb-r-ḏr m n3y.f 3ḫwt (*ka nakht menekh menu, sehetep neb-er-djer em nay.ef akhut*), Victorious bull, splendid of monuments, who has satisfied the Lord of All with his benefactions, Ramses III H4

k3 nḫt mr.n imn (*ka nakht mer.en imen*), Victorious bull, whom Amun has loved, Sety I, Abydos 4. He

k3 nḫt mry imn (*ka nakht, mery imen*), Victorious bull, beloved of Amun, Pinodjem I H1

k3 nḫt mry w3st (ka nakht mery waset), Victorious bull, beloved of Thebes, Thutmose IV H2

k3 nḫt mry ptḥ (*ka nakht mery ptah*), Victorious bull, beloved of Ptah, Ramses II H18

k3 nḫt mry m3ʿt (ka nakht mery maat), Victorious bull, beloved of Maat, Thutmose I H1, Ramses II H1, Sheshonq III H3, Philip Arrhidaeus H2

k3 nḫt mry m3ʿt nb ḥb(w)-sd mi it.f ptḥ-t3-ṯnn (*ka nakht mery maat, neb hebu sed mi it.ef ptah-ta- tjenen*), Victorious bull, beloved of Maat, possessor of Sed festivals like his father Ptah-Ta-tjenen, Ramses II H19

k3 nḫt mry m3ʿt s3 [*mry*] *n imn pr m ḥʿw.f* (*ka nakht, mery maat, sa [mery] en imen, per em haw.ef*), Victorious bull, beloved of Maat, the [beloved] son of Amun, who issued from his limbs, Siamun H *k3 nḫt mry m3ʿt smn t3wy* (*ka nakht mery maat, semen tawy*), Victorious bull, beloved of Maat, who has perpetuated the Two Lands, Amenmesse H1

k3 nḫt mry m3ʿt sḫʿ sw rʿ r nsw t3wy (*ka nakht, mery maat, sekha su ra er nesu tawy*), Victorious bull, beloved of Maat, whom Re caused to appear to be king of the Two Lands, Osorkon II H2

k3 nḫt mry mwt.f ḥwt-ḥr (*ka nakht mery mut.ef hut-hor*), Victorious bull, beloved of his mother Hathor, Ramses II H20

k3 nḫt mry mntw (*ka nakht mery montu*), Victorious bull, beloved of Montu, Ramses II H21

k3 nḫt mry rʿ (ka nakht mery ra), Victorious bull, beloved of Re, Thutmose III (b) H3, Sety I H2, Abydos 3. Hb, Ramses II H22, Sety II H2, Ramses XI H, Sheshonq III H2

k3 nḫt mry rʿ ptpt ḫ3swt nb(w)t ḫr ṯbwt.f (*ka nakht mery ra, petpet khasut neb(u)t kher tjebut.ef*), Victorious bull, beloved of Re, who has trampled all the foreign countries under his sandals, Ramses II H23

k3 nḫt mry rʿ m3ʿt (*ka nakht mery ra maat*), Victorious bull, beloved of Re and Maat, Sety I H4

k3 nḫt mry rʿ swsr imn ḫpš.f r sḳ3 m3ʿt (*ka nakht, mery ra, seweser imen khepesh.ef er seqa maat*), Victorious bull, beloved of Re, whose arm Amun has strengthened in order to offer up Maat, Smendes H

k3 nḫt mry rʿ sḫʿ.f m nsw r sm3 t3wy (*ka nakht, mery ra, sekha.ef em nesu er sema tawy*), Victorious bull, beloved of Re, whom the latter caused to appear as king in order to unite the Two Lands, Sheshonq I H

k3 nḫt mry rʿ rdi.n sw itmw ḥr nst.f r grg t3wy (*ka nakht, mry ra, redi.en su itemu her neset.ef er gereg tawy*), Victorious bull beloved of Re, whom Atum put on his throne in order to establish the Two Lands, Osorkon I H

k3 nḫt mry ḥʿpy sʿnḫ t3 nb m k3.f rʿ-nb (*ka nakht mery hapy, sankh ta neb em ka.ef ra neb*), Victorious bull, beloved of Hapy, who has sustained every land by means of his ka daily, Siptah H1

k3 nḫt mry stḫ (*ka nakht mery setekh*), Victorious bull, beloved of Seth, Ramses II H24

k3 nḫt mry(t) m3ʿt nb(t) ʿn m nsw mi itmw (*ka nakht mery(t) maat, neb(et) an em nesu mi itmu*), Victorious bull, beloved of Maat and possessor of beauty as king like Atum, Tawosret H

k3 nḫt mswt rʿ (*ka nakht, mesut ra*), Victorious bull, the offspring of Re, Sheshonq III H1

k3 nḫt mk kmt (*ka nakht mek kemet*), The victorious bull and protector of Egypt, Sety II H3

k3 nḫt n rʿ (ka nakht en ra), The victorious bull of Re, Thutmose I H2

k3 nḫt n rʿ sḏ sṯtyw (*ka nakht en ra, sedj setjetyu*), Victorious bull of Re, who has shattered the Asiatics, Ramses II H25

k3 nḫt nb t3wy (*ka nakht neb tawy*), Victorious bull and lord of the Two Lands, Ramses II H26

kȝ nḫt nsw tȝwy (*ka nakht nesu tawy*), Victorious bull and king of the Two Lands, Merenptah H9
kȝ nḫt nḏty rʿ (*ka nakht nedjty ra*), The victorious bull and protector of Re, Sety I, Abydos 6. He
kȝ nḫt rʿ nfr-ḥr (*ka nakht ra, nefer her*), The victorious bull of Re, beautiful of face, Ramses VII H2
kȝ nḫt ḥʿ m mȝʿt (ka nakht ha em maat), Victorious bull, who has rejoiced in Maat, Thutmose III (b) H4, Merenptah H1
kȝ nḫt ḥʿ ḥr mȝʿt (*ka nakht ha her maat*), Victorious bull, who has rejoiced over Maat, Ramses II H27
kȝ nḫt ḥwi tȝ nb (*ka nakht hui ta neb*), Victorious bull who has struck every land, Ramses II H28
kȝ nḫt ḥkȝ ḥkȝw (ka nakht heqa heqau), The victorious bull and ruler of rulers, Amenhotep III H5
kȝ nḫt ḥtp ḥr mȝʿt (*ka nakht hetep her maat*), The victorious bull who is satisfied with Maat, Sety I H5
kȝ nḫt ḫʿ m wȝst (ka nakht kha em waset), The victorious bull who has appeared in Thebes, Thutmose III (a-b) H1, Ramses IX H, Pinodjem I H2, Osorkon II H1, Takelot II H, Sheshonq V H2, Harsiese H, Osorkon III H, Piye H4, Shabataka H2
kȝ nḫt ḫʿ m wȝst sʿnḫ tȝwy (*ka nakht kha em waset, sankh tawy*), The victorious bull who has appeared in Thebes and sustained the Two Lands, Sety I H1 (also Abydos 1. Ha; Abydos 2. Ha; Abydos 3. Ha; Abydos 4. Ha; Abydos 5. Ha; Abydos 6. Ha; Abydos 7. Ha), Ramses II H29
kȝ nḫt ḫʿ m mȝʿt (ka nakht kha em maat), The victorious bull who has appeared in Truth, Thutmose III (b) H7, Amenhotep III H1
kȝ nḫt ḫʿ m npt (*ka nakht, kha em nepet*), The victorious bull who has appeared in Napata, Piye H1
kȝ nḫt ḫʿ m ḥḏt (*ka nakht kha em hedjet*), The victorious bull who has appeared in the White Crown, Sety I, Abydos 7. Ceiling H
kȝ nḫt ḫʿ m ḥḏt mry rʿ (*ka nakht kha em hedjet, mery ra*), The victorious bull who has appeared in the White Crown, the beloved of Re, Sety I H8
kȝ nḫt ḫʿ-ḫʿw (*ka nakht kha khau*), Victorious bull, the (very) appearance of appearances, Sety I H14
kȝ nḫt sȝ imn (*ka nakht sa imen*), The victorious bull and son of Amun, Sety I, Abydos 4. Hb, Ramses II H30, Merenptah H12, Herihor H1
kȝ nḫt sȝ imn ir mnw ḥr mnḫt n ms s(*w*) (*ka nakht, sa imen, ir menu her menkhet en mes s(u)*), Victorious bull and son of Amun, who has made monuments owing to the splendor of the one who bore him, Herihor H2
kȝ nḫt sȝ imn wr-ȝḫwt m ipt-swt (*ka nakht, sa imen, wer akhut em ipet-sut*), Victorious bull and son of Amun, great of benefits in Ipet-sut, Herihor H3
kȝ nḫt sȝ itmw (*ka nakht sa itemu*), The victorious bull and the son of Atum, Sety I H7, Ramses II H31

k3 nḫt s3 wsir (*ka nakht sa wesir*), The victorious bull and son of Osiris, Sety I, Abydos 5. Hd, Abydos 6. Hd

k3 nḫt s3 ptḥ (*ka nakht sa ptah*), Victorious bull, son of Ptah, Ramses II H32

k3 nḫt s3 rꜥ (*ka nakht sa ra*), Victorious bull, the son of Re, Merenptah H10

k3 nḫt s3 ḫpri (*ka nakht sa khepri*), Victorious bull, the son of Khepri, Sety I, Abydos 3. Hc, Ramses II H33

k3 nḫt s3 t3-ṯnn (*ka nakht sa ta-tjenen*), Victorious bull, son of Ta-tjenen, Ramses II H34

k3 nḫt swsḫ kmt wsr-ḫpš nḫt-ꜥ sm3 ṯḥnw (*ka nakht sewesekh kemet, weser khepesh, nakht a, sema tjehenu*), The victorious bull who has widened (the boundaries of) Egypt, the one powerful of sword and strong of arm who has slaughtered the Tjehenu-Libyans, Ramses III H5

k3 nḫt spd-ꜥbwy (ka nakht seped abwy), Victorious bull, sharp of horns, Amenhotep II H3, Ramses II H35

k3 nḫt spd-sḫrw (ka nakht seped sekheru), The victorious bull, who is clever of plans, Horemheb H

k3 nḫt sḫꜥ.n rꜥ (*ka nakht sekha.en ra*), The victorious bull whom Re has caused to appear, Ramses X H

k3 nḫt sḫpr t3wy (*ka nakht sekheper tawy*), The victorious bull who has created the Two Lands, Sety I H11

k3 nḫt sḫm-pḥty (ka nakht sekhem pehty), Victorious bull, powerful of might, Amenhotep II H4, Sety I H12, Ramses II H36

k3 nḫt sḫm-f3w (ka nakht sekhem fau), The victorious bull powerful of splendor, Amenhotep III H2

k3 nḫt sḫm-ḫpš (*ka nakht sekhem khepesh*), The victorious bull powerful of arm/sword, Sety I, Abydos 1. Hc

k3 nḫt sḳ3 w3st (*ka nakht seqa waset*), Victorious bull, who has exalted Thebes, Ramses II H37

k3 nḫt stp.n imn (*ka nakht setep.en imen*), Victorious bull, whom Amun has chosen, Sety I, Abydos 4. Hd

k3 nḫt sḏ sṯtyw (*ka nakht sedj setjetyu*), Victorious bull who has shattered the Asiatics, Ramses II H38

k3 nḫt ḳ3-ḥḏt (*ka nakht qa hedjet*), Victorious bull, (whose) White Crown is high, Ramses II H39

k3 nḫt ḳ3-ḥḏt mry m3ꜥt (*ka nakht qa hedjet, mery maat*), Victorious bull, (whose) White Crown is high, the beloved of Maat, Sety I H10

k3 nḫt ḳ3-šwty (ka nakht qa shuty), Victorious bull, high of plumes , Amenhotep IV H

k3 nḫt k3 n ḥḳ3w (*ka nakht ka en heqau*), Victorious bull, bull of the rulers, Ramses II H40

k3 nḫt tit imn (*ka nakht tit imen*), The victorious bull and the (very) image of Amun, Sety I, Abydos 4. Hc *kꜣ nḫt tỉt rꜥ ỉtmw* (*ka nakht tit ra itmu*), Victorious bull, the (very) image of Re-Atum, Sety I, Abydos 3. Hd

kꜣ nḫt twt mswt (ka nakht tut mesut), Victorious bull, the (very) image of (re-) birth, Tutankhamun H

kꜣ nḫt twt-ḫꜥw (ka nakht tut khau), Victorious bull, the (very) image of appearances, Thutmose IV H1, Ramses II H41

kꜣ nḫt ṯḥn-ḫꜥw (ka nakht tjehen khau), Victorious bull, dazzling of appearances, Ay H1

kꜣ nḫt ṯḥn-ḫprw (ka nakht tjehen kheperu), Victorious bull, dazzling of manifestations, Ay H2

skꜣ nḫt ṯs tꜣwy (*ka nakht tjes tawy*), Victorious bull who has governed the Two Lands, Ramses II H42

kꜣ nḫt dr pḏwt 9 (*ka nakht der pedjut 9*), Victorious bull who has repelled the Nine Bows, Merenptah H7

kꜣ nḫt dr ḫꜣswt m nḫtw.f (*ka nakht der khasut em nakhtu.ef*), The victorious bull who has repelled foreign lands with his victories, Sety I H3

kꜣ nḫt /// (*ka nakht ///*), The victorious bull and ///, Sety I, Abydos 5. He

kꜣ ḫt (*ka khet*), The bull of the (divine) Corporation, Menkaure H

kꜣ sbk rꜥ (*ka sobek ra*), The (very) ka of (the god) Sobek-Re, Sobeknefru T

kꜣ kꜣ.ỉ (*ka ka.i*), My ka is a (true) ka (?), Neferirkare B

kꜣ kꜣw (*ka kau*), Bull of bulls, Nebre C

kꜣ km{t} rꜥ (*ka kem{et} ra*), The black bull of Re, Kakemre T

kꜣ tꜣwy.fy (*ka tawy.fy*), The bull of his Two Lands, Piye H5

kꜣy (*kay*), Who belongs to the ka, Kay B

kꜣy <*sꜣ*> *ỉmn-m-ḥꜣt* (*kay* <*sa*> *imen em hat*), Kay's <son>, Amenemhat ("Amun is in front"), Amenemhat VII B

kꜣw nṯrw (*kau netjeru*), (Possessor of?) The kas of the gods, Sobekhotep II G

kꜣštꜣ (*kashta*), "The Kushite," Kashta B

grg tꜣwy (*gereg tawy*), The founder of the Two Lands, Neferhotep I H

grg(t) kmt wꜥf(t) ḫꜣswt (*gereg(et) kemet, waf(et) khasut*), Who has founded Egypt and subdued foreign countries, Tawosret N

tꜣ wsrt (*ta wosret*), The one (fem.) who belongs to (the goddess) Wosret, Tawosret B

t(ꜣ) nt ỉmn (*ta net imen*), The one belonging to Amun, Tanutamun B

tꜣy.f nḫt (*tay.ef nakht*), His strength, Tefnakht B

tꜣhꜣrḳꜣ (*taharqa*), Taharqa B

tỉt rꜥ ḫnty tꜣwy (tit ra, khenty tawy), The (very) image of Re, who is at the head of the Two Lands, Amenhotep III H6

tỉt ḫprw rꜥ (*tit kheperu ra*), The (very) image of the manifestations of Re, Psusennes II T, Psusennes III T

twt ʿnḫ imn ḥḳ3 iwnw šmʿw (tut ankh imen, heqa iunu shemau), The living image of Amun, ruler of Southern Heliopolis, Tutankhamun B2
twt ʿnḫ itn (tut ankh aten), The living image of Aten, Tutankhamun B1
twt mswt (tut mesut), The (very) image of (re-)birth, Ahmose (II) N
twt-ḫʿw mi t3-ṯnn (*tut-khau mi ta-tjenen*) The (very) image of appearances like Ta-tjenen, Sethnakht N
twt ḫpr rʿ (*tut kheper ra*), The (very) image of the manifestation of Re, Sheshonq IIb T
tp ʿ (*tepy a*), "The ancestor", Mentuhotep I H
trrw (*tereru*), The respected one (?), Neferkare Tereru B
tklt (*tekelet*), Takelot I to III B
tti (*teti*), Teti, Aha C, Sekhemkhet C , Teti B

ṯm3-ʿ (*tjema a*), The sturdy-armed one, Nectanebo I H
ṯni m ḫt ḥtr ḥpw ʿnḫ ḥr msḫn(t).sn (*tjeni em khet, heter hapu ankh her meskhen(et).sen*), Distinguished in the sanctuary, the twin brother of the living Apis bull upon their birth-stool, Ptolemy VI H
ṯḥn-ḫʿw (*tjehen-khau*), Dazzling of appearances, Ramses III H15
ṯḥn-ḫʿw wr-šfyt (tjehen khau, wer shefyt), Dazzling of appearances and great of majesty, Amenhotep III N6
ṯḥn-ḫprw wr-bi3wt (tjehen kheperu, wer biaut), Dazzling of manifestations and great of wonders, Amenhotep III G3
ṯs t3wy (tjez tawy), The one who has bound the Two Lands, Ahmose (II) G

di kmt m ršwt m šnyt.f imyw m ḥʿʿ m mrwt.f (*di kemet em reshwet em shenyt.ef, imyu em haa em merut.ef*), Who caused Egypt to delight in his company; those who are in it continually rejoice because of love of him, Ramses II G2
dw3 itmw ḫʿ-ḫʿw (dua itemu, kha khau), Who worships Atum, radiant of appearances, Thutmose I N3
dmḏ ib t3wy (*demedj ib tawy*), Who has united (lit. "assembled") the will (lit. "mind") of the Two Lands, Wadjkare H
dn (*den*), The severer (of heads), Den H
ddw msw (*dedu mesu*), The one (whose) birth has been granted, Dedumose I and II B

ḏ3ḏ3y (*djadjay*), The head-man, Khasekhem/Kasekhemwy C
ḏr (*djer*), The one who repulses (enemies), Djer H
ḏḥwty (*djehuty*), (the god) Thoth, Djehuty B
ḏḥwty ʿ3(w) ḳn (*djehuty aa qen*), Tao ("Thoth is great") the Brave, Seqenenre Tao B
ḏḥwty m-ḥ3t (*djehuty em-hat*), Thoth is at the forefront, Thutemhat B
ḏḥwty ms(w) (djehuty mes(u)), Thoth is born, Thutmose I to IV
ḏsr (*djeser*), The sacred one, Djoser C

ḏsr-mswt ḥnꜥ ḥpw ꜥnḫ nṯri ḫpr(w) ḥtr msḫn(t) nt sꜣ ꜣst (*djeser mesut hena hapu ankh, netjeri kheper(u), heter meskhen(et) net sa aset*), Sacred of birth together with the living Apis, divine of manifestations, and twin brother of the birth-stool of the son of Isis, Ptolemy IX H1

ḏsr nbty ꜥnḫ.t(i) (*djeser nebty ankh.t(i)*), The sacred one of the Two Ladies, (long) may you live, Sekhemkhet N

ḏsr-ḫꜥw (djeser khau), Sacred of appearances, Thutmose III (a) G1

ḏsr-ḫꜥw sḫm-pḥty (djeser khau, sekhem pehty), Sacred of appearances and powerful of might, Thutmose III (b) G1

ḏsr-ḫꜥw sḫm-pḥty ꜥnḫ ḥr-nb n mꜣ.f mi ꜣḫty (*djeser-khau, sekhem-pehty, ankh her-neb en ma.ef mi akhty*), Sacred of appearances, powerful of strength, at the sight of whom every one lives like (at the sight of) He-of-the-Horizon, Piye G1

ḏsr ḫprw rꜥ (djeser kheperu ra), The sacred one of the manifestations of Re, Horemheb T

ḏsr kꜣ rꜥ (djeser ka ra), The sacred one of the ka of Re, Amenhotep I T

ḏsr tti (*djeser teti*), Teti is sacred, Sekhemkhet C

ḏt (*djet*), The cobra, Djet/Wadjet H

ḏd ꜥnḫ rꜥ (*djed ankh ra*), The stable one belonging to the life of Re, Montuemsaf T

ḏd msw(t) (*djed mesu(t)*), Stable of births, [User]kare N

ḏd nfr rꜥ (*djed nefer ra*), The stable one of the perfection of Re, Dedumose II T

ḏd-nsyt mi itmw (djed nesyt mi itemu), Stable of kingship like Atum, Thutmose IV N1, Ramses II N14

ḏd ḥr (*djed hor*), Horus says, Tachos B

ḏd ḥtp rꜥ (*djed hetep ra*), The stable one of the peace of Re, Dedumose I T

ḏd-ḫꜥw (*djed khau*), Stable of appearances, Djedkare H, Sobekhotep II N, Shabataka H1 N3

ḏd-ḫꜥw nbty (*djed khau nebty*), Stable of appearances <by means of?> the Two Ladies, Djedkare G

ḏd-ḫprw (*djed kheperu*), Stable of manifestations, [User]kare H

ḏd ḫrw rꜥ (*djed kheru ra*), The stable one of the voice of Re, Djedkherure T

ḏd kꜣ rꜥ (*djed ka ra*), The stable one of the ka of Re, Djedkare T1, Djedkare Shemay C1, Anati T

ḏd kꜣ ḥr (*djed ka hor*), The stable one of the ka of Horus, Djedkare T2

ḏd kꜣw rꜥ (*djed kau ra*), The stable one of the kas of Re, Shabataka T

ḏd- ///////// mi [*ḥr*]*-ꜣḫty (djed ///////// mi [her]-akhty),* Stable /// like [Hor]-akhty, Thutmose IV G2

ḏd /// rꜥ (*djed /// ra*), The stable one of the /// of Re, Djed /// re T

ḏdt-ḫꜥw (*djedet khau*), Stable (fem.) of appearances, Sobeknefru G

[///]*i <sꜣ> ḥr* (*[///]-i <sa> her*), ///-i (son of) Hor, [Weser]kare B

[///] *ꜥnḫ*, ([///] *ankh*), /// alive ///, Khendjer H

/// wbn rꜥ (*/// weben ra*), /// Re's rising/shining ///, /// Hor II T, Webenre II and III T

/// m nsw r spd tꜣwy (*/// em nesu er seped tawy*), /// as king in order to restore the Two Lands, Osorkon II H3

[///] *mꜣꜥt rꜥ* (*/// maat ra*), The truth of Re is ///, Ibi II T

/// mỉ ỉt.f rꜥ ỉty sꜥnḫ ỉbw n rḫyt dỉ kmt m <r>š<wt?> (*//// mi it.ef ra, ity, sankh ibu en rekhyet, di kemet em reshwet(?)*), /// like his father Re, the sovereign who has sustained the common folks' hearts, and brought joy to Egypt, Siptah G

[///] *ms rꜥ* (*/// mes ra*), The one whom Re bore (?), [///]-mesra T

/// nṯrw (*/// netjeru*), /// of the gods ///, Intef VI G

/// rꜥ (*/// ra*), /// of Re ///, Hotep T, [///]re T

/// ḥb rꜥ (*/// heb ra*), [Who makes the /// of?] Re festive, /// hebre I (and II?) T

/// ḫsf dndn (*/// khesef denden*), /// who drove away anger, Smendes G

/// sḫpr tꜣwy (*/// sekheper tawy*), ///, who has created the Two Lands, Ramses X G

/// sṯtyw (*/// setjetiu*), [/// who has struck down?] the Setjetiu-Asiatics, Sheshonq I G2

/// kꜣ rꜥ (*/// ka ra*), The /// of the ka of Re, Bebnem T

/// dr pḏwt ỉty sḫm m tꜣw nbw (*/// der pedjut, ity, sekhem em tau nebu*), /// who has repelled the (foreign) bowmen, the mighty sovereign in all lands, Osorkon II G3

/// ḏfꜣ rꜥ (*/// djefa ra*), The one whom Re's bounty ///, /// djefare T

/// ḏḥwty (*/// djehuty*), /// Thoth, Djehuty N

Appendix B

Alphabetical List of Kings

The first number refers to the dynasty while the second refers to the placement of the king within that dynasty.

“A” (Horus), 0:11
Aakare*, 14:31
Aamu, 14:4
Adjib, 1:5
Aha, 1:1
Ahmose I (Senakhtenre), 17:26
Ahmose II (Nebpehtyre), 18:1
Ahmose (Amasis) III (Khnumibre), 26:5
Akhenaten, see Amenhotep IV
Alara, 25:1
Alexander the Great, Macedonian:1
Alexander II / IV, Macedonian:3
Amen-em-nisu (Neferkare), 21:3
Amenemhat I (Sehetepibre), 12:1
Amenemhat II (Nebukaure), 12:3
Amenemhat III (Nimaatre), 12:6
Amenemhat IV (Maakherure), 12:7
Amenemhat V (Sekhemkare), 13:4
Amenemhat VI (Sankhibre), 13:8
Amenemhat VII (Sedjefakare), 13:20
Amenemope (Usermaatre Setepenamun), 21:5
Amenhotep I (Djeserkare), 18:2
Amenhotep II (Aakheperure), 18:7
Amenhotep III (Nebmaatre), 18:9
Amenhotep IV / Akhenaten (Neferkheperure waenre), 18:10
Amenirdis (Amyrtaios), 28:1
Amenmesse (Menmire), 19:6
Anati*, 14:33
Anu*, 8:13
Apepi (Apophis), 15:5

Aper-anati, 15:2
Arses, 31:2
Arsinoe II, Ptolemaic:2a
Artaxerxes I, 27:4
Artaxerxes II, 27:7
Artaxerxes III, 31:1
Awibre*, 14:17
Ay (Kheperkheperure), 18:14
Bakenrenef (Bocchoris), 24:2
Baufre*, 4:5
Bebiankh, 16:9
Bebnem*, 14:34
Berenike II, Ptolemaic:3a
Berenike, Ptolemaic:12
Cambyses, 27:1
Cleopatra I, Ptolemaic:5a
Cleopatra II, Ptolemaic:8a
Cleopatra VII Philopator, Ptolemaic:14
Crocodile, 0:5
Darius I, 27:2
Darius II, 27:6
Darius III, 31:3
Dedumose I (Djedhetepre), 16a:1
Dedumose II (Djedneferre), 16a:2
Den, 1:4
Djed /// re*, 14:45
Djedhor (Tachos / Teos), 30:2
Djedkare, 5:8
Djedkare Shemay*, 8:5
Djedkherure*, 14:23
/// djefare*, 14:15
Djehuty, 16:2
Djer, 1:2
Djet / Wadjet, 1:3
Djoser*, 3:1
Hakor (Achoris), 29:3
Harsiese, 22a:1
Hatshepsut, 18:6
Haty-Hor, 0:8
/// heb (?)-re*, 17:15
/// hebre*, 17:11
Hedju-Hor, 0:6
Hepu*, 14:32

Heribre*, 14:18
Herihor, 21:1
Hetepsekhemwy, 2:1
Hor I (Auibre), 13:15
Hor II* (/// webenre), 13:53
Horemheb (Djeserkheperure), 18:15
Hori*, 13:37
Horwy, 0:9
Hotep, 8a:5
Hu ////*, 9-10a:9
Hudjefa (I)*, 2a:2
Hudjefa (II)*, 3a:2
Hui, 3:5
Huni*, 3:5
I /// re*, 14:29
I-neb ///, 14:50
Iamu, 14:2
Ib-iau, 13:32
Ibi I, 8:14
Ibi II* (/// maatre ///), 13:52
Imhotep, 8a:4
Imy-ra Mesha, 13:23
Ined*, 13:36
Inek*, 14:49
Ini I (Merhetepre), 13:34
Ini II (Meryshepesre), 13a:1
Intef I (Sehertawy), 11a:2
Intef II (Wahankh), 11a:3
Intef III (Nakhtnebtepnefer), 11a:4
Intef IV (Sehetepkare), 13:24
Intef V (Sekhemrewepmaat), 17:22
Intef VI (Nebukheperre), 17:23
Intef VII (Sekhemreherhermaat), 17:24
Ip-///*, 14:51
Iry-Hor, 0:1
Isu, 8a:6
Iti, 8a:3
Iufni*, 13:7
Iuput I, 23:2
Iuput II (Usermaatre), 23:8
Iy, 13:33
Iykhernofret, 16:4
Iytjenu, 8a:8

Ka, 0:2
Kakemre*, 14:27
Kamose (Wadjkheperre), 17:28
Kashta, 25:2
Kay, 13:19
Khaba, 3:3
Khababash, 31:4
Khafre (Chephren), 4:4
Khakare*, 14:30
Khakherure*, 14:7
Khamudi, 15:6
Khamure, 14a:5
Khasekhem / Khasekhemwy, 2:8
Khendjer, 13:22
Khendu*, 8:6
[Khety I]*, 9-10a:1
Khety II*, 9-10a:4
[Khety III]*, 9-10a:6
[Khety IV]*, 9-10a:7
Khety V (Wahkare), 9-10b:1
Khety VI, 9-10b:3
Khety VII, (Nebkaure), 9-10b:4
Khety VIII, (Meryibre), 9-10b:5
Khufu (Cheops), 4:2
Khui, 8a:6
Khuwihapi, 8:16
Khyan, 15:4
Men /// re*, 14:44
Menkare*, 8:2
Menkauhor, 5:7
Menkaure (Mycerinus), 4:6
Menkheperre, 21a:2
Mentuhotep I, 11a:1
Mentuhotep II (Nebhepetre), 11b:5
Mentuhotep III (Sankhkare), 11b:6
Mentuhotep IV (Nebtawyre), 11b:7
Mentuhotep V (Sewedjkare), 13:50
Mentuhotep VI (Sankhenre), 16:5
Mentuhotep VII (Meryankhre), 16a:4
Merdjefare*, 14:10
Merenhor*, 8:7
Merenptah / Merneptah (Baenre), 19:4
Merenre I, 6:4

Merenre II, 6:6
Merkare*, 13:48
Merkheperre, 13:47
Mery ///, 9-10b:2
Meryibre Khety (VIII), 9-10b:5
Merykare, 9-10b:6
Merytawy, 13a:5
Mer[///]re*, 13:46
Montuemsaf, 16a:3
Nakhtnebef (Nectanebo I) (Kheperkare), 30:1
Nakhthorhebyt (Nectanebo II) (Senedjemibre), 30:3
Narmer, 0:3
Nebdjefare*, 14:12
Nebfaure*, 14:8
Nebi, 8:4
Nebiryerau I (Sewadjenre), 16:6
Nebiryerau II*, 16:7
Nebkare*, 3a:4
Nebkaure Khety (VII), 9-10b:4
Nebmaatre, 17a:1
Nebnun, 13:9
Nebre, 2:2
Nebsenre, 14:19
Nedjemibre*, 13:12
Nefaarudu (Nepherites) I (Baenre), 29:1
Nefaarudu (Nepherites) II, 29:4
Nefer(ef)re, 5:5
Nefer-neferu-aten, 18:11
Neferhotep I (Khasekhemre), 13:27
Neferhotep II (Merysekhemre), 13a:2
Neferhotep III Iykhernofret (Sekhemresankhtawy), 16:4
Neferibre*, 14:28
Neferirkare (I), 5:3
Neferirkare II*, 8:17
Neferkahor*, 8:11
Neferkamin*, 8:8
Neferkamin Anu*, 8:13
Neferkare (I)*, 3a:3
Neferkare (II)*, 8:3
Neferkare (III), 9-10a:3
Neferkare Khendu*, 8:6
Neferkare Nebi, 8:4
Neferkare Pepysenbu*, 8:12

Neferkare Tereru, 8:10
Neferkasokar*, 2a:1
Neferkauhor Khuwihapi, 8:16
Neferkaure, 8:15
Nefertum /// re*, 14:25
Nehsy, 14:6
Neith-iqeret (Nitocris*) (Queen), 6:7
Nekau (Necho) II, 26:2
Nerkare, 13:3
Nes-ba-neb-djed (Smendes) (Hedjkheperre Setepenre), 21:2
Netjerikare*, 8:1
Netjerikhet, 3:1
Nikare*, 8:9
Nimlot, 23a:3
Ninetjer, 2:3
Niuserre, 5:6
Nuya, 14a:1
Ny-<Hor>, 0:7
Ny-Neith, 0:10
Osorkon the Elder (Aakhepere setepenre), 21:6
Osorkon I (Sekhemkheperre), 22:2
Osorkon II (Usermaatre), 22:6
Osorkon III (Usermaatre), 23:4
Osorkon IV (Aakheperre), 22:13
Padibastet (Pedubastis) I (Usermaatre Setepenamun), 23:1
Padibastet (Pedubastis) II (Usermaatre Setepenamun), 23a:1
Padinemty, 23a:5
Pamiu, 22:11
Pantjeny, 17:18
Pa-seba-kha-en-niut (Psusennes) I (Aakheperre), 21:4
Pa-seba-kha-en-niut (Psusennes) II (Titkheperure Setepenre), 21:8
Pa-seba-kha-en-niut (Psusennes) III (Titkheperure Setepenamun), 21a:3
Pasherimut (Psammuthis), 29:2
"Pe" (Horus), 0:12
Peftjauabastet, 23a:2
Pepy I (Meryre), 6:3
Pepy II (Neferkare), 6:5
Pepysenbu*, 8:12
Peribsen, 2:7
Philip Arrhidaeus, Macedonian:2
Piankhy, 25:3
Pinodjem I, 21a:1
Piye, 25:3

Psamtek (Psammetichus) I (Wahibre), 26:1
Psamtek (Psammetichus) II (Neferibre), 26:3
Psamtek (Psammetichus) III (Ankhkaenre), 26:6
Ptolemy I Soter, Ptolemaic:1
Ptolemy II Philadelphus, Ptolemaic:2
Ptolemy III Euergetes, Ptolemaic:3
Ptolemy IV Philopator, Ptolemaic:4
Ptolemy V Epiphanes, Ptolemaic:5
Ptolemy VI Philometor, Ptolemaic:6
Ptolemy VII Neos Philopator, Ptolemaic:7
Ptolemy VIII Euergetes II Tryphon, Ptolemaic:8
Ptolemy IX Philometor Soter II, Ptolemaic:9
Ptolemy X Alexander I, Ptolemaic:10
Ptolemy XI Alexander II, Ptolemaic:11
Ptolemy XII Neos Dionysos Auletes, Ptolemaic:13
Ptolemy XIII, Ptolemaic:15
Ptolemy XIV, Ptolemaic:16
Ptolemy XV Caesarion, Ptolemaic:17
Qaa, 1:7
Qahedjet, 3:5
Qakare Ibi I, 8:14
Qareh, 14:3
Qemau, 13:5
Radjedef, 4:3
Rahotep, 17:20
Ramses I (Menpehtyre), 19:1
Ramses II (Usermaatre), 19:3
Ramses III (Usermaatre Meryamun), 20:2
Ramses IV (Heqamaatre Setepenamun), 20:3
Ramses V (Usermaatre Sekheperenre), 20:4
Ramses VI (Nebmaatre Meryamun), 20:5
Ramses VII (Usermaatre Setepenre Meryamun), 20:6
Ramses VIII (Usermaatre Akhenamun), 20:7
Ramses IX (Neferkare Setepenre), 20:8
Ramses X (Khepermaatre Setepenre), 20:9
Ramses XI (Menmaatre Setepenptah), 20:10
Reniseneb, 13:14
Rudamun (Usermaatre), 23:6
Sa-Hornedjheritef, 13:6
Sahathor, 13:28
Sahure, 5:2
Sanakht, 3:4
Sankhibre*, 14:24

Sankhptah, 13:55
Scorpion, 0:4
Se /// kare*, 13:54
Se [///] re*, 13:57
Seb / Sab (?), 13:18
Sedjes*, 3a:1
Sehebre*, 14:9
Sehetepibre, 13:10
Seker-her, 15:3
Sekhaenptah, 13a:7
Sekhaenre, 13a:4
Sekhem /// re*, 14:26
Sekhemib, 2:6
Sekhemkare, 8a:1
Sekhemkhet, 3:2
Sekhemre Khutawy, 13:16
Sekhemreshedwaset*, 16:10
Sekheperenre, 14:22
Semenenre, 16:8
Semerkhet, 1:6
Semqen, 15:1
Senaaib, 17:19
Senbef, 13:2
Senebmiu, 13a:3
Sened*, 2:5
Senefer /// re*, 14:43
Seneferka, 2:9
Senen ////*, 9-10a:5
Senwosret I (Kheperkare), 12:2
Senwosret II (Khakheperre), 12:4
Senwosret III (Khakaure), 12:5
Senwosret IV (Seneferibre), 16a:5
Seqenenre Tao, 17:27
Seth, 13:25
Sethnakht (Userkhaure), 20:1
Sety I (Menmaatre), 19:2
Sety II (Userkheperure), 19:5
Sewadjkare (I)*, 13:11
Sewadjkare (II)*, 14:11
Sewadjtu, 13:35
Shabaka, 25:4
Shabataka / Shebitko, 25:5
Shed ////*, 9-10a:8

Shemay*, 8:5
Sheneh, 14a:2
Shenshek, 14a:3
Shepseskaf, 4:7
Shepseskare, 5:4
Sheshi, 14:5
Sheshonq I (Hedjkheperre), 22:1
Sheshonq IIa (Heqakheperre), 22:3
Sheshonq IIb (Tutkheperre), 22:4
Sheshonq IIc (Maakheperre), 22:8
Sheshonq III (Usermaatre), 22:9
Sheshonq IV (Hedjkheperre), 22:10
Sheshonq V (Aakheperre), 22:12
Sheshonq VI (Usermaatre), 23:3
Sheshonq VIa (Hedjkheperre), 23:7
Sheshonq VII (Wasnetjerre), 23:9
Siamun (Netjerikhepere), 21:7
Siptah (Sekhaenre), 19:7
Smenkhkare, 18:12
Snefru, 4:1
Sobekemsaf I (Sekhemreshedtawy), 17:21
Sobekemsaf II (Sekhemrewadjkhau), 17:25
Sobekhotep I (Sekhemrekhutawy), 13:1
Sobekhotep II (Khaankhre), 13:13
Sobekhotep III (Sekhemresewadjtawy), 13:26
Sobekhotep IV (Khaneferre), 13:29
Sobekhotep V (Merhetepre), 13:30
Sobekhotep VI (Khahetepre), 13:31
Sobekhotep VII (Merykaure), 13:38
Sobekhotep VIII (Sekhemresewesertawy), 16:3
Sobeknefru (Queen), 12:8
Taharqa, 25:6
Takelot I (Hedjkheperre), 22:5
Takelot II (Hedjkheperre), 22:7
Takelot III (Usermaatre), 23:5
Tanutamun, 25:7
Tao (Seqenenre), 17:27
Tawosret (Satre), 19:8
Tefnakht, 24:1
Teos, see Tachos
Tereru, 8:10
Teti: 6:1
Thutemhat, 23a:4

Thutmose I (Aakheperkare), 18:3
Thutmose II (Aakheperenre), 18:4
Thutmose III (Menkheperre), 18:5a-b
Thutmose IV (Menkheperure), 18:8
Tutankhamun (Nebkheperure), 18:13
Unas, 5:9
Userkaf, 5:1
Userkare (I), 6:2
[User]kare (II), 13:17
Userkhau, 13a:6
User /// re (I)*, 17:1
User /// re (II)*, 17:2
Wadjed, 14a:4
Wadjet / Djet, 1:3
Wadjkare, 8a:2
Wahibre (Apries), 26:4
Wahkare Khety (V), 9-10b:1
Webenre I*, 14:13
/// webenre II*, 14:16
/// webenre III*, 17:16
Wegaf (Khutawyre), 13:21
Weneg, 2:4
Wepwawetemsaf, 17:17
Xerxes I, 27:3
Xerxes II, 27:5
Yakob-mu, 14:1
Yakub-her, 14a:6
[///]-mesra*, 13:51
[///] re*, 13:56

Appendix C

Greek–Egyptian Equivalents of Royal Names

Note that this list gives only the names that will be commonly found in scholarly studies, not a complete list of suggested equivalents between Egyptian sources and Manetho's names.

Achoris = Hakor
Achthoes/Akhtoy = Khety
Amenophis = Amenhotep
Ammenemes = Amenemhat
Amasis/Amosis = Ahmose
Amyrtaios = Amenirdis
Apophis = Apepi
Apries = Wahibre
Bocchoris = Bakenrenef
Cheops = Khufu
Chephren = Khafre
Menes = Meni
Mycerinus = Menkaure
Necho = Nekau
Nectanebo = Nakhtnebef/Nakhthorhebyt
Nepherites = Nefaarudu
Nitocris = Neith-iqeret
Pedubastis/Petubastis = Pa-di-bastet
Phiops = Pepy
Psammetichus = Psamtek
Psammuthis = Pasherimut
Psusennes = Pa-seba-kha-en-niut
Sesostris = Senwosret
Sethos = Sety
Smendes = Nes-ba-neb-djed
Tachos/Teos = Djedhor
Thutmose/Thutmosis = Djehutymes

Bibliography

Allen, James P. 1976. "The Funerary Texts of King Wahkare Akhtoy on a Middle Kingdom Coffin." Pages 1–29 in *Studies in Honor of George R. Hughes: January 12, 1977*. Edited by J. H. Johnson and E. F. Wente. SAOC 39. Chicago: Oriental Institute of the University of Chicago.

———, trans. 2005. *The Ancient Egyptian Pyramid Texts*. SBLWAW 23. Atlanta: Society of Biblical Literature.

———. 2010. "The Second Intermediate Period in the Turin King-List." Pages 1–10 in *The Second Intermediate Period (Thirteenth–Seventeenth Dynasties): Current Research, Future Prospects*. Edited by Marcel Marée. OLA 192. Leuven: Peeters.

Anthes, Rudolf. 1928. *Die Felseninschriften von Hatnub nach den Aufnahmen Georg Möllers*. Untersuchungen zur Geschichte und Altertumskunde Ägyptens 9. Leipzig: J. C. Hinrichs.

Arnold, Dieter. 1969. "Zur frühen Namensform des Königs *mnṯw-ḥtp nb-ḥpt-rꜥ*." *MDAIK* 24:38–42.

Arnold, Dorothea. 1991. "Amenemhat I and the Early Twelfth Dynasty at Thebes." *MMJ* 26:5–48.

Aston, David A. 2009. "Takeloth II, a King of the Herakleopolitan/Theban Twenty-Third Dynasty Revisited: The Chronology of Dynasties 22 and 23." Pages 1–28 in *The Libyan Period in Egypt: Historical and Cultural Studies into the 21st–24th Dynasties. Proceedings of a Conference at Leiden University, 25–27 October 2007*. Edited by G. P. F. Broekman, R. J. Demarée, and O. E. Kaper. Egyptologische uitgaven 23. Leuven: Peeters.

Aufrère, Sydney H. 1982. "Contribution à l'étude de la morphologie du protocole 'classique.'" *BIFAO* 82:19–73.

———. 2001. "Le roi Aouibrê Hor: Essai d'interprétation du matériel découvert par Jacques de Morgan à Dahchour (1894)." *BIFAO* 101:1–41.

Ayad, Mariam. 2009. *God's Wife, God's Servant: The God's Wife of Amun (c. 740–525 BC)*. New York: Routledge.

Ayedi, Abdul Rahman al-. 2006. *The Inscriptions of the Ways of Horus*. Ismailia: Obelisk Publications.

Baines, John. 1986. "*mswt* 'Manifestations'?" Pages 43–50 in *Hommages à François Daumas*. Publication de la Recherche, Université de Montpellier. Montpellier: Institut d'Égyptologie, Université Paul Valéry.

———. 1995. "Kingship, Definition of Culture, and Legitimation." Pages 3–47 in *Ancient Egyptian Kingship.* Edited by David O'Connor and David P. Silverman. Probleme der Ägyptologie 9. Leiden: E. J. Brill.

Baines, John, and Jaromir Málek. 1980. *Atlas of Ancient Egypt.* New York: Facts on File.

Bard, Kathryn A. 2000. "The Emergence of the Egyptian State (c. 3200–2686 BC)." Pages 61–88 in *The Oxford History of Ancient Egypt.* Edited by Ian Shaw. Oxford: Oxford University Press.

Barguet, Paul. 1951. "Un groupe d'enseignes en rapport avec les noms du roi." *RdE* 8:9–19.

———. 1953. *La stèle de la famine, à Séhel.* BdÉ 24. Cairo: IFAO.

Barta, Winfried.1969. "'Falke des Palastes' als ältester Königstitel." *MDAIK* 24:51–57.

———. 1982. "Zur Namensform und zeitlichen Einordung des Königs 'Ro.'" *GM* 53:11–13.

Baud, Michel. 1998. "Une épithète de Rêdjedef et la prétendue tyrannie de Chéops: Études sur la statuaire de Rêdjedef, II." *BIFAO* 98:15–30.

———. 1999. *Famille royale et pouvoir sous l'Ancien Empire égyptien.* 2 vols. BdÉ 126. Cairo: IFAO.

———. 2007. *Djéser et la IIIe dynastie.* Paris: Pygmalion.

Baud, Michel, and Vassil Dobrev. 1995. "De nouvelles annales de l'ancien empire égyptien: Une "Pierre de Palerme" pour la VIe dynastie." *BIFAO* 95:23–92.

Baumgartel, Elise J. 1975. "Some Remarks on the Origins of the Titles of the Archaic Egyptian Kings." *JEA* 61:28–32.

Beckerath, Jürgen von. 1962. "The Date of the End of the Old Kingdom of Egypt." *JNES* 21:140–47.

———. 1966. "Die Dynastie der Herakleopoliten (9./10. Dynastie)." *ZÄS* 93:13–20.

———. 1980. "Merikare." Column 94 in *Lexikon der Ägyptologie IV.* Edited by Wolfgang Helck and Eberhard Otto. Wiesbaden: Harrassowitz.

———. 1984. *Handbuch der ägyptischen Königsnamen.* MÄS 20. Munich and Berlin: Deutscher Kunstverlag.

———. 1999. *Handbuch der ägyptischen Königsnamen.* 2nd ed. MÄS 49. Mainz am Rhein: von Zabern.

Bell, Lanny. 1985. "Luxor Temple and the Cult of the Royal Ka." *JNES* 44:251–94.

Bellion, Madeleine. 1987. *Égypte Ancienne: Catalogue des manuscrits hiéroglyphiques et hiératiques et des dessins sur papyrus, cuir ou tissu, publiés ou signalés.* Paris: M. Bellion.

Bennett, John. 1965. "The Meaning of the Royal Nomen and Prenomen." *JEA* 51:206–7.

Ben-Tor, D., Susan J. Allen, and James P. Allen. 1999. "Seals and Kings." *BASOR* 315:47–74.

Berman, Lawrence M. 1985. "Amenemhet I." Ph.D. dissertation, Yale University Ann Arbor: University Microfilms International.

Bietak, Manfred. 1999. "Tell ed-Deba'a, Second Intermediate Period." Pages 778–82 in *Encyclopedia of the Archaeology of Ancient Egypt.* Edited by Kathryn A. Bard. London and New York: Routledge.

Birkstam, Bengt. 1984. "Reflections on the Association between the Sun-God and Divine Kingship in the 18th Dynasty." Pages 33–42 in *Sundries in Honor of Torgny Säve-Söderbergh.* Edited by R. Holthoer and T. Linders. Acta Universitatis Upsaliensis. Boreas 13. Uppsala: Almqvist and Wiksell.

Biston-Moulin, Sébastien. 2012. "Le roi Sénakht-en-Rê Ahmès de la XVIIe dynastie." *ENIM* 5:61–72.

Blyth, Elizabeth. 2006. *Karnak: Evolution of a Temple.* London and New York: Routledge.

Bonhême, Marie-Ange. 1978. "Les désignations de la 'titulature' royale au Nouvel Empire." *BIFAO* 78:347–87.

———. 1987. *Les noms royaux dans l'Égypte de la troisième période intermédiaire.* BdÉ 98. Cairo: IFAO.

Bonhême, Marie-Ange, and Annie Forgeau. 1988. *Pharaon. Les secrets du pouvoir.* Paris: Armand Colin.

Borghouts, Joris F. 1982. "Divine Intervention in Ancient Egypt and Its Manifestation (*bꜣw*)." Pages 1–70 in *Gleanings from Deir el-Medina.* Edited by Robert J. Demarée and Jac J. Janssen. Egyptologische uitgaven 1. Leiden: Nederlands Instituut voor het Nabije Oosten.

Borrego Gallardo, Francisco L. 2010. *El "título áureo" del rey durante el Reino Antiguo egipcio: Estudio textual, semiológico e histórico.* Madrid: Facultad de Filosofía y Letras, Universidad Autónoma de Madrid.

Brand, Peter J. 2000. *The Monuments of Seti I: Epigraphic, Historical & Art Historical Analysis.* Probleme der Ägyptologie 16. Leiden: E. J. Brill.

Broekman, Gerard P. F. 2000. "Shoshenq Maäkheperre and Shoshenq Heqakheperre." *GM* 176:39–46.

———. 2005. "The Reign of Takeloth II, a Controversial Matter." *GM* 205:21–33.

Broekman, Gerard P.F., et al. 2008. "The Numbering of Kings called Shoshenq." *GM* 216:9–10.

Bryan, Betsy M. 1991. *The Reign of Thutmose IV.* Baltimore: Johns Hopkins University Press.

Budge, E.A. Wallis. 1896. *Some Account of the Collection of Egyptian Antiquities in the Possession of Lady Meux of Theobald's Parks, Waltham Cross.* Second Edition. London: Harrison & Sons.

Cabrol, Agnès. 2000. *Amenhotep III: le magnifique.* Champollion. Paris: Éditions du Rocher.

Callender, Vivienne G. 2002. "The Innovations of Hatshepsut's Reign." *BACE* 13:29–46.

Caminos, Ricardo. 1964. "The Nitocris Adoption Stela." *JEA* 50:71–101.

Černý, Jaroslav. 1958. "Name of the King of the Unfinished Pyramid at Zawiyet el-Aryān." *MDAIK* 16:25–29.

Chauveau, Michel. 1997. *L'Egypte au temps de Cléopâtre, 180–30 av. J.-C.* Vie quotidienne: Antiquité. Paris: Hachette Littératures.

Clayton, Peter A. 1994. *Chronicle of the Pharaohs: The Reign-by-Reign Record of the Rulers and Dynasties of Ancient Egypt.* London: Thames & Hudson.

Clère, Jacques J., and Jacques Vandier. 1948. *Textes de la première période intermédiaire et de la XIème dynastie.* Bibliotheca Aegyptiaca 10. Brussels: Fondation Égyptologique Reine Élisabeth.

Cline, Eric H., and David O'Connor, eds. 2006. *Thutmose III: A New Biography.* Ann Arbor: University of Michigan Press.

Coche-Zivie, Christiane. 1972. "Nitocris, Rhodopis et la troisième pyramide de Giza." *BIFAO* 72:115–38.

Couyat, Jules, and Pierre Montet. 1913. *Les inscriptions hiéroglyphiques et hiératiques du Ouâdi Hammâmât.* MIFAO 34. Cairo: IFAO.

Daressy, Georges. 1916. "Le Pierre de Palerme et la chronologie de l'Ancien Empire." *BIFAO* 12:161–214.

———. 1920. "L'obélisque de Qaha." *ASAE* 19:131–35.

Darnell, John Coleman, ed. 2002. *Theban Desert Road Survey in the Egyptian Western Desert.* Vol. 1, *Gebel Tjauti Rock Inscriptions 1–45 and Wadi el-Ḥôl Rock Inscriptions 1–45.* OIP 119. Chicago: Oriental Institute of the University of Chicago.

Dautzenberg, Norbert. 1997a. "Einige Bemerkungen zu einigen Thronnamen des Neuen Reiches und ihren politischen Aussagen sowie zur Person des Sethnacht." *GM* 156:37–46.

———. 1997b. "Die Wahl des Königsnamens in der Hyksoszeit: Das Entstehen einer eigenen Tradition, Bezüge zu den thebanischen Herrschern und Schlussfolgerungen für die Chronologie." *GM* 159:43–51.

Davies, Vivian W. 1998. "A Statue of the 'King's Son, Sahathor', from Thebes." Pages 177–79 in *Stationen: Beiträge zur Kulturgeschichte Ägyptens. Rainer Stadelmann gewidmet.* Edited by Heike Guksch and Daniel Polz. Mainz am Rhein: von Zabern.

———. 2003. "Sobeknakht's Hidden Treasure." *British Museum Magazine* (Summer): 18–19.

Delia, Robert D. 1980. "A Study of the Reign of Senwosret III." Ph.D. dissertation, Columbia University. Ann Arbor: University Microfilms International.

Derchain-Urtel, Maria-Theresa. 1975. "Gott oder Mensch?" *SAK* 3:25–41.

Der Manuelian, Peter. 1987. *Studies in the Reign of Amenophis II.* HÄB 26. Hildesheim: Gerstenberg.

———. 1994. *Living in the Past: Studies in Archaism of the Egyptian Twenty-Sixth Dynasty.* New York: Kegan Paul.

Dessoudeix, Michel. 2008. *Chronique de l'Égypte ancienne: Les pharaons, leur règne, leurs contemporains.* Arles: Actes Sud.

Dobrev, Vassil. 1993. "Considérations sur les titulatures des rois de la IVe dynastie égyptienne." *BIFAO* 93:179–204.

Dodson, Aidan. 1981. "King 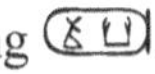." *ZÄS* 108:171.

———. 1995. *Monarchs of the Nile.* Cairo: American University in Cairo Press.

———. 2000. Review of Ryholt 1997a, *BiOr* 57:48–52.

———. 2012. *Afterglow of Empire: Egypt from the Fall of the New Kingdom to the Saite Renaissance.* Cairo: American University in Cairo Press.

Dodson, Aidan, and Nicholas Reeves. 1988. "A Casket Fragment of Ramesses IX in the Museum of Archaeology and Anthropology, Cambridge." *JEA* 74:223–26.

Doxey, Denise M. 1998. *Egyptian Non-Royal Epithets in the Middle Kingdom: A Social and Historical Analysis.* Probleme der Ägyptologie 12. Leiden: E. J. Brill.

Dreyer, Günter. 1992a. "Recent Discoveries at Abydos Cemetery U." Pages 293–99 in *The Nile Delta in Transition, 4th.–3rd. Millennium B.C.: Proceedings of the Seminar Held in Cairo, 21.–24. October 1990, at the Netherlands Institute of Archaeology and Arabic Studies.* Edited by Edwin C. M. van den Brink. Tel Aviv: The Israel Exploration Society.

———. 1992b. "Horus Krokodil, ein Gegenkönig der Dynastie 0." Pages 259–64 in *The Followers of Horus: Studies Dedicated to Michael Allen Hoffman 1944–1990.* Edited by Renée Friedman and Barbara Adams. Egyptian Studies Association Publication 2. Oxbow Monograph 20. Oxford: Oxbow Books.

———. 1998. *Umm el-Qaab.* Vol. 1, *Das prädynastische Königsgrab U-j und seine frühen Schriftzeugnisse.* Archäologische Veröffentlichungen 86. Mainz am Rhein: von Zabern.

Dreyer, Günter, et al. 1996. "Umm el-Qaab: Nachuntersuchungen im frühzeitlichen Königsfriedhof, 7./8. Vorbericht." *MDAIK* 52:11–81.

Drioton, Étienne. 1954. "Une liste de rois de la IVe dynastie dans l'Ouâdi Hammamât." *BSFE* 16:41–49.

Edel, Elmar. 1955/1964. *Altägyptische Grammatik,* vols. I and II. Analecta Orientalia 34, 39. Rome: Pontificium Institutum Biblicum.

———. 1960. "Altägyptische Personennamen." *ZÄS* 85:79–83.

———. 1972. " *nj-rmṯw-nswt,* 'ein Besitzer von Menschen ist der König.'" *GM* 2:15–17.

Eide, Tormod, Tomas Hägg, Richard Holton Pierce, and László Török. 1994. *Fontes Historiae Nubiorum: Textual Sources for the History of the Middle Nile Region between the Eighth Century BC and the Sixth Century AD.* Vol. 1, *From the Eighth to the Mid-fifth Century BC.* Bergen: University of Bergen.

———. 1996. *Fontes Historiae Nubiorum: Textual Sources for the History of the Middle Nile Region between the Eighth Century BC and the Sixth Century AD.* Vol. 2, *From the Mid-Fifth to the First Century BC.* Bergen: University of Bergen.

———. 1998. *Fontes Historiae Nubiorum: Textual Sources for the History of the Middle Nile Region between the Eighth Century BC and the Sixth Century AD.* Vol. 3, *From the First to the Sixth Century AD.* Bergen: University of Bergen.

———. 2000. *Fontes Historiae Nubiorum: Textual Sources for the History of the Middle Nile Region between the Eighth Century BC and the Sixth Century AD.* Vol. 4, *Corrigenda and Indices.* Bergen: University of Bergen.

Evans, Linda. 2011. "The *Shedshed* of Wepwawet: An Artistic and Behavioural Interpretation." *JEA* 97:103–15.

Fakhry, Ahmed. 1961. *The Pyramids.* Chicago: University of Chicago Press.

Faulkner, Raymond O. 1969. *The Ancient Egyptian Pyramid Texts.* Warminster: Aris & Phillips.

Favard-Meeks, Christine. 1991. *Le temple de Behbeit el-Hagara: Essai de reconstitution et d'interprétation.* Studien zur altägyptischen Kultur 6. Hamburg: Helmut Buske.

———. 1999. "Behbeit el-Hagara." Pages 165–67 in *Encyclopedia of the Archaeology of Ancient Egypt.* Edited by Kathryn A. Bard. London and New York: Routledge.

———. 2002. "The Present State of the Site of Behbeit el-Hagar," *British Museum Studies in Ancient Egypt and Sudan* 3:31–41.

Fischer, Henry G. 1963. "A Stela of the Heracleopolitan Period at Saqqara: The Osiris *Iti.*" *ZÄS* 90:35–41.

———. 1973. "An Eleventh Dynasty Couple Holding the Sign of Life." *ZÄS* 100:16–28.

———. 1989a. "On Some Reinterpretations of Royal Names." *GM* 108:21–29.

———. 1989b. "The Transcription of the Royal Name Pepy." *JEA* 75:214–15.

Forman, Werner, and Stephen Quirke. 1996. *Hieroglyphs and the Afterlife in Ancient Egypt.* London: British Museum Press.

Franke, Detlef. 1988. "Zur Chronologie des Mittleren Reiches (12.–18. Dynastie). Teil II, Die sogenannte 'Zweite Zwischenzeit' Altägyptens." *Or* 57:245–74.

———. 2001. "First Intermediate Period." Pages 526–32 in *The Oxford Encyclopedia of Ancient Egypt.* Vol. 1. Edited by Donald B. Redford. New York: Oxford University Press.

Frankfort, Henry. 1926. "Egypt and Syria in the First Intermediate Period." *JEA* 12:80–99.

Gabolde, Luc. 1990. "Nerkarê a-t-il existé?" *BIFAO* 90:213–22.

Gabolde, Marc. 1998. *D'Akhenaton à Toutânkhamon.* Collection de l'Institut d'archéologie et d'histoire de l'antiquité 3. Lyon: Université Lumière-Lyon 2, Institut d'archéologie et d'histoire de l'antiquité.

Galán, José M. 1995. *Victory and Border: Terminology Related to Egyptian Imperialism in the XVIIIth Dynasty.* HÄB 40. Hildesheim: Gerstenberg.

Gardiner, Alan H. 1936. "The Egyptian Origin of Some English Personal Names." *JAOS* 56:189–97.

———. 1943. “The god Semseru.” *JEA* 29:75–76.

———. 1953. “The Coronation of King Haremhab.” *JEA* 39:13–31.

———. 1956. “The First King Menthotpe of the Eleventh Dynasty.” *MDAIK* 14:42–51.

———. 1957a. *Egyptian Grammar: Being an Introduction to the Study of Hieroglyphs.* 3rd ed. Oxford: Griffith Institute.

———. 1957b. *The Royal Canon of Turin.* Oxford: Griffith Institute.

———. 1961. *Egypt of the Pharaohs: An Introduction.* Oxford: Oxford University Press.

Gardiner, Alan H., and T. Eric Peet. 1955. *The Inscriptions of Sinai.* 2 vols. Egypt Exploration Society Memoir 36. London: Egypt Exploration Society.

Garstang, John. 1903. *Maḥâsna and Bêt Khallâf.* London: Bernard Quaritch. Egyptian Research Account, 1901.

Gauthier, Henri. 1907. *Le livre des rois d’Égypte: Recueil de titres et protocoles royaux.* Vol. 1, *Des origines à la XIIe dynastie.* MIFAO 17. Cairo: IFAO.

———. 1912. *Le livre des rois d’Égypte: Recueil de titres et protocoles royaux.* Vol. 2, *De la XIIIe dynastie à la fin de la XVIIIe dynastie.* MIFAO 18. Cairo: IFAO.

———. 1914. *Le livre des rois d’Égypte: Recueil de titres et protocoles royaux.* Vol. 3, *De la XIXe à la XXIVe dynastie.* MIFAO 19. Cairo: IFAO.

———. 1916. *Le livre des rois d’Égypte: Recueil de titres et protocoles royaux.* Vol. 4, *De la XXVe dynastie à la fin des Ptolémées.* MIFAO 20. Cairo: IFAO.

Gilroy, Thomas D. 2001. “‘Forgotten’ *Serekhs* in the Royal Ontario Museum.” *GM* 180:67–76.

Gilula, Mordechai. 1982. “An Egyptian Etymology of the Name of Horus?” *JEA* 68:259–65.

Godron, Gérard. 1949. “À propos du nom royal [*mry nʿrỉ*].” *ASAE* 49: 217–20.

———. 1990. *Études sur l’Horus Den et quelques problèmes de l’Égypte archaïque.* Cahiers d’Orientalisme 19. Geneva: Patrick Cramer.

Goebs, Katja. 1998. “Some Cosmic Aspects of the Royal Crowns.” Pages 447–60 in *Proceedings of the Seventh International Congress of Egyptologists, Cambridge, 3–9 September 1995*. Edited by C. J. Eyre. OLA 82. Leuven: Peeters.

Goedicke, Hans. 1956. “King *ḥwḏfꜣ* (?).” *JEA* 42:50–53.

———. 1960. *Die Stellung des Königs im Alten Reich.* Ägyptologische Abhandlungen 2. Wiesbaden: Otto Harrassowitz.

———. 1995. “Narmer.” *WZKM* 85:81–84.

Gomaà, Farouk. 1980. *Ägypten während der Ersten Zwischenzeit.* Beihefte zum Tübingen Atlas des Vorderen Orients: Reihe B, Geisteswissenschaften 27. Wiesbaden: Reichert.

Graefe, Erhart. 1995. “Zur Struktur der Thronnamen der ägyptischen Könige und der Lesung des Thronnamen der Königin Hatschepsut.” Pages 119–27, in *Divitiae Aegypti: Koptologische und verwandte Studien zu Ehren von Martin Krause.* Edited by Cäcilia Fluck et al. Wiesbaden: Reichert.

Grajetzki, Wolfram. 2005. *Ancient Egyptian Queens: A Hieroglyphic Dictionary.* London: Golden House.

———. 2006. *The Middle Kingdom of Ancient Egypt: History, Archaeology and Society.* London: Duckworth.

Grandet, Pierre. 1993. *Ramsès III. Histoire d'un règne.* Bibliothèque de l'Egypte ancienne. Paris: Pygmalion/Gérard Watelet.

Grdseloff, Bernhard. 1944. "Notes d'épigraphie archaique." *ASAE* 44:279–306.

Green, Michael. 1980. "A Means of Discouraging Perjury." *GM* 39:33–39.

Grimal, Nicolas Christophe. 1981. *Études sur la propagande royale égyptienne.* Vol. 1, *La stèle triomphale de Pi(ankh)y au Musée du Caire. JE 48862 et 47086–47089.* MIFAO 105. Cairo: IFAO.

———. 1986. *Les termes de la propagande royale égyptienne de la XIXe dynastie à la conquête d'Alexandre.* Mémoires de l'Académie des inscriptions et belles-lettres n.s. 6. Paris: Imprimerie nationale.

Gundlach, Rolf. 1979. "Der Obelisk Tuthmosis I: Textthematik und Funktion." Pages 192–226 in *Festschrift Elmar Edel. 12. März 1979.* Edited by Manfred Görg and Edgar Pusch. Studien zu Geschichte, Kultur und Religion Ägyptens und des Alten Testaments 1. Bamberg: M. Görg.

———. 2003. "Sethos I. und Ramses II: Tradition und Entwicklungsbruch in der frühramessidischen Königsideologie." Pages 17–53 in *Das Königtum der Ramessidenzeit: Voraussetzungen, Verwirklichung, Vermächtnis. Akten des 3. Symposions zur ägyptischen Königsideologie in Bonn 7.–9.6. 2001.* Edited by Rolf Gundlach and Ursula Rössler-Köhler. Ägypten und Altes Testament 36. Beiträge zur altägyptischen Königsideologie 3. Wiesbaden: Harrassowitz.

Habachi, Labib. 1963. "King Nebhepetre Mentuhotp: His Monuments, Place in History, Deification and Unusual Representations in the Form of Gods." *MDAIK* 19:16–52.

———. 1974. "Sethos I's Devotion to Seth and Avaris." *ZÄS* 100:95–102.

Hannig, Rainer. 2003. *Ägyptisches Wörterbuch.* Vol. 1, *Altes Reich und Erste Zwischenzeit.* Mainz am Rhein: von Zabern.

———. 2006a. *Ägyptisches Wörterbuch.* Vol. 2, *Mittleres Reich und Zweite Zwischenzeit.* Teil 1. Mainz am Rhein: von Zabern.

———. 2006b. *Ägyptisches Wörterbuch.* Vol. 2, *Mittleres Reich und Zweite Zwischenzeit.* Teil 2. Mainz am Rhein: von Zabern.

Hardwick, Tom. 2006. "The Golden Horus Name of Amenmesse?" *JEA* 92:255–60.

Hari, Robert. 1964. *Horemheb et la reine Moutnedjemet: ou, la fin d'une dynastie.* Geneva: Imprimerie la Sirène.

Hart, George. 1986. *A Dictionary of Egyptian Gods and Goddesses.* London: Routledge & Kegan Paul.

Harvey, Stephen P. 2007. "King Heqatawy: Notes on a Forgotten Eighteenth Dynasty Royal Name." Pages 343–56 in *The Archaeology and Art of Ancient*

Egypt: Essays in Honor of David B. O'Connor. Edited by Zahi A. Hawass and Janet E. Richards. Annales du Service des Antiquités de l'Égypte 36. Cairo: Conseil Suprême des Antiquités de l'Égypte.

Hayes, William C. 1946. "Royal Decrees from the Temple of Min at Coptus." *JEA* 32:3–23.

———. 1948. "Minor Art and Family History in the Reign of Amun-Hotpe III." *BMMA* 6:272–79.

———. 1953. *The Scepter of Egypt: A Background for the Study of the Egyptian Antiquities in The Metropolitan Museum of Art.* Vol. 1. *From the Earliest Times to the End of the Middle Kingdom.* New York: The Metropolitan Museum of Art.

Hendrickx, Stan. 1999. "Elkab." Pages 289–93 in *Encyclopedia of the Archaeology of Ancient Egypt.* Edited by Kathryn A. Bard. London and New York: Routledge.

Hölbl, Günther. 2001. *A History of the Ptolemaic Empire.* London and New York: Routledge.

Hölscher, Uvo. 1941. *The Mortuary Temple of Ramses III.* Part 1, *The Excavation of Medinet Habu,* vol. 3. Chicago: University of Chicago Press.

Hornung, Erik. 1999. *Akhenaten and the Religion of Light.* Ithaca, N.Y.: Cornell University Press.

Huß, Werner. 2001. *Ägypten in hellenistischer Zeit, 332–30 v. Chr.* Munich: C. H. Beck.

Ikram, Salima. 2001. "The Home of the Giant Catfish." *Nekhen News* 13:10.

———. 2004. "An Early Dynastic *serekh* from the Kharga Oasis." *JEA* 90:211–15.

Ikram, Salima, and Aidan Dodson. 1998. *The Mummy in Ancient Egypt: Equipping the Dead for Eternity.* London: Thames & Hudson.

Iskander, Sameh. 2002. "The Reign of Merenptah." Ph.D. dissertation. New York University.

Iverson, Erik. 1988. "Reflections on Some Egyptian Royal Names." Pages 78–88 in *Pyramid Studies and Other Essays Presented to I.E.S. Edwards.* Edited by John Baines et al. Occasional Publications 7. London: Egypt Exploration Society.

Jansen-Winkeln, Karl. 1995. "Historische Probleme der 3. Zwischenzeit." *JEA* 81:129–49.

———. 2007a. *Inschriften der Spätzeit:* Teil I, *Die 21. Dynastie.* Wiesbaden: Harrassowitz.

———. 2007b. *Inschriften der Spätzeit:* Teil II, *Die 22.–24. Dynastie.* Wiesbaden: Harrassowitz.

———. 2009. *Inschriften der Spätzeit:* Teil III, *Die 25. Dynastie.* Wiesbaden: Harrassowitz.

Jéquier, Gustave. 1933. *Les Pyramides des reines Neit et Apouit.* Cairo: IFAO.

———. 1935. *La Pyramide d'Aba.* Cairo: IFAO.

Jiménez-Serrano, Alejandro. 2001. "Horus Ka and the Cemetery of Helwan." *GM* 180:81–87.

Jones, Dilwyn. 2000. *An Index of Ancient Egyptian Titles, Epithets and Phrases of the Old Kingdom.* 2 vols. BAR International Series 866. Oxford: Archaeopress.

Kahl, Jochem. 1994. *Das System der ägyptischen Hieroglyphenschrift in der 0.-3. Dynastie.* Göttinger Orientforschungen. Reihe 4. Ägypten 29. Wiesbaden: Harrassowitz.

Kahl, Jochem, et al. 1995. *Die Inschriften der 3. Dynastie: Eine Bestandsaufnahme.* Ägyptologische Abhandlungen 56. Wiesbaden: Harrassowitz.

———. 2002. *Frühägyptisches Wörterbuch: Erste Lieferung ꜣ – f.* Wiesbaden: Harrassowitz.

Kaiser, Werner. 1957. "Zur Inneren Chronologie der Naqadakultur." *Archaeologia Geographica* 6:69–77.

Kaiser, Werner, and Günther Dreyer. 1982. "Umm el-Qaab: Nachuntersuchungen im frühzeitlichen Königsfriedhof. 2. Vorbericht." *MDAIK* 38:211–69.

Kamal, Ahmed Bey. 1906. "Rapport sur quelques localités de la Basse Époque." *ASAE* 7:232–40.

———. 1909. *Tables d'offrande.* vol. 1. Cairo Catalogue Général. Cairo: IFAO.

———. 1910. "Un monument nouveau du pharaon Khatouî." *ASAE* 10:185–86.

———. 1912. "Fouilles à Dara et à Qoçéîr el-Amarna." *ASAE* 12:128–42.

Kanawati, Naguib. 2003. *Conspiracies in the Egyptian Palace: Unis to Pepy I.* London and New York: Routledge.

Kaplony, Peter. 1958. "Sechs Königsnamen der 1. Dynastie in neuer Deutung." *Orientalia Suecana* 7:54–69.

———. 1972. "Adjib." Columns 62–64 in *Lexikon der Ägyptologie I.* Edited by Wolfgang Helck and Eberhard Otto. Wiesbaden: Harrassowitz.

Kemp, Barry J. 2000. "The Colossi from the Early Shrine at Coptos in Egypt." *CAJ* 10:211–42.

———. 2006. *Ancient Egypt: Anatomy of a Civilization.* 2nd ed. London and New York: Routledge.

Kitchen, Kenneth A. 1982. *Pharaoh Triumphant: The Life and Times of Ramesses II, King of Egypt.* Warminster: Aris & Phillips.

———. 1986. *The Third Intermediate Period in Egypt (1100–650 B.C.).* 2nd ed. with suppl. Warminster: Aris & Phillips.

———. 1987. "The Titularies of the Ramesside Kings as Expression of Their Ideal Kingship." *ASAE* 71:131–41.

———. 1993. *Ramesside Inscriptions: Translated and Annotated. Translations.* Vol. 1, *Ramesses I, Sethos I and Contemporaries.* Oxford: Blackwell.

Klug, Andrea. 2002. *Königliche Stelen in der Zeit von Ahmose bis Amenophis III.* Fondation Égyptologique Reine Élisabeth. Monumenta Aegyptiaca 8. Turnhout: Brepols.

Koemoth, Pierre P. 2002. "Le couronnement du faucon-roi à Pi-Sopdou, d'après le naos de Saft el-Henna (*CG* 70021)." *DE* 52:13–55.

Koenen, Ludwig. 1993. "The Ptolemaic King as a Religious Figure." Pages 25–115 in *Images and Ideologies: Self-definition in the Hellenistic World*. Edited by Anthony Bulloch et al. Hellenistic Culture and Society 12. Berkeley: University of California Press.

Köhler, E. Christiana. 1995. "The State of Research on Late Predynastic Egypt: New Evidence for the Development of the Pharaonic State?" *GM* 147:79–92.

———. 2011. "The Rise of the Egyptian State." Pages 123–25 in *Before the Pyramids: The Origins of Egyptian Civilization*. Edited by Emily Teeter. Oriental Institute Museum Publications 33. Chicago: Oriental Institute of the University of Chicago.

Köhler, E. Christiana, and Edwin C. M. van den Brink. 2002. "Four Jars with Incised *Serekh*-Signs from Helwan Recently Retrieved from the Cairo Museum." *GM* 187:59–81.

Kozloff, Arielle P. 2012. *Amenhotep III: Egypt's Radiant Pharaoh*. Cambridge: Cambridge University Press.

Krauss, Rolf. 1978. *Das Ende der Amarnazeit: Beiträge zur Geschichte und Chronologie des Neuen Reiches*. HÄB 7. Hildesheim: Gerstenberg.

Kuhrt, Amélie. 2007. *The Persian Empire. A Corpus of Sources from the Achaemenid Period*. London: Routledge.

Lacau, Pierre. 1967. "Le tableau central de la stèle-porte égyptienne." *RdE* 19:39–50.

Lacau, Pierre, and Henri Chevrier. 1956, 1965. *Une Chapelle de Sésostris Ier à Karnak*. Cairo: IFAO.

Lange, Eva R. 2004. "Ein neue König Schoschenk in Bubastis." *GM* 203:65–72.

Leclant, Jean. 1965. *Recherches sur les monuments thébains de la XXVe dynastie dite éthiopienne*. BdÉ 36. Cairo: IFAO.

Legrain, Georges. 1903. "Notes d'inspection." *ASAE* 4:193–226.

———. 1907. "Notes d'inspection: XXXI, Le nom d'Horus de Darius." *ASAE* 8:51.

Leitz, Christian. 2002. *Lexikon der ägyptischen Götter und Götterbezeichnungen*. Vol. 2. Leuven: Peeters.

Leprohon, Ronald J. 1980. "The Reign of Amenemhat III." Ph.D. dissertation. University of Toronto.

———. 1996. "The Programmatic Use of the Royal Titulary in the Twelfth Dynasty." *JARCE* 33:165–71.

———. 2009. "The Cairo Stela of Sehetepibre (CG 20538): Borrowings and Innovation." Pages 277–92 in *Archaism and Innovation: Recent Perspectives on Middle Kingdom Egypt*. Edited by David P. Silverman, William Kelly Simpson, and Josef Wegner. Philadelphia: University of Pennsylvania Museum of Archaeology and Anthropology.

———. 2010a. “The Royal Titulary in the 18th Dynasty: Change and Continuity.” *JEGH* 3:7–45.

———. 2010b. “Patterns of Royal Name-giving,” in *UCLA Encyclopedia of Egyptology.* Edited by Elizabeth Frood and Willeke Wendrich. Online at http://digital2.library.ucla.edu/viewItem.do?ark=21198/zz001nx697, 1–10.

Lichtheim, Miriam. 1973. *Ancient Egyptian Literature: A Book of Readings.* Vol. 1, *The Old and Middle Kingdoms.* Berkeley: University of California Press.

———. 1980. *Ancient Egyptian Literature: A Book of Readings.* Vol. 3, *The Late Period.* Berkeley: University of California Press.

———. 1988. *Ancient Egyptian Autobiographies Chiefly of the Middle Kingdom: A Study and an Anthology.* OBO 84. Freiburg, Schweiz: Universitätsverlag.

Málek, Jaromir. 1982. “The Original Version of the Royal Canon of Turin.” *JEA* 68:93–106.

Malek, Jaromir, and Werner Forman. 1986. *In the Shadow of the Pyramids. Egypt during the Old Kingdom.* London: Orbis.

Manning, Joseph G. 2010. *The Last Pharaohs: Egypt under the Ptolemies, 305–30 BC.* Princeton: Princeton University Press.

Maruéjol, Florence. 2007. *Thoutmosis III et la corégence avec Hatchepsout.* Grands pharaons. Paris: Pygmalion.

Maspero, Gaston. 1891. “Notes au jour le jour: §10.” *PSBA* 13:429–31.

McCormack, Dawn. 2010. “Establishing the Legitimacy of Kings in Dynasty Thirteen.” Pages 375–85 in *Millions of Jubilees: Studies in Honor of David P. Silverman.* Edited by Zahi Hawass and Jennifer Houser Wegner. Cairo: American University in Cairo Press.

Meffre, Raphaële. 2010. “Un nouveau nom d’Horus d’or de Sheshonq Ier sur le bloc Cairo JE 39410.” *BIFAO* 110:221–33.

Meltzer, Edmund S. 1971. “A Reconsideration of  .” *JEA* 57:202–3.

———. 1972. “Horus *dn,* ‘cutter’, ‘severer (of heads)’?” *JNES* 31:338–39.

Midant-Reynes, Béatrix. 2000. *The Prehistory of Egypt: From the First Egyptians to the First Pharaohs.* Oxford: Blackwell.

Möller, Georg. 1911. *Hieratische Papyrus aus den königlichen Museen zu Berlin.* Vol. 3. Leipzig: J. C. Hinrichs.

Monnet Saleh, Janine. 1986. “Interprétation globale des documents concernant l’unification de l’Egypte.” *BIFAO* 86: 227–38.

Montet, Pierre. 1957. *Géographie de l’Égypte ancienne.* Première partie, *To-mehou, La Basse Égypte.* Paris: Imprimerie Nationale.

Moran, William L. 1992. *The Amarna Letters.* Baltimore: Johns Hopkins University Press.

Morgan, Jacques de. 1894. *Catalogue des monuments et inscriptions de l’Égypte antique.* Vol. 1. *De la frontière de Nubie à Kom Ombos.* Vienna: Holzhausen.

Murnane, William J. 1977. *Ancient Egyptian Coregencies.* SAOC 40. Chicago: Oriental Institute of the University of Chicago.

———. 1990. *The Road to Kadesh: A Historical Interpretation of the Battle Reliefs of King Sety I at Karnak.* SAOC 42. Chicago: Oriental Institute of the University of Chicago.

———. 2001. "The End of the Amarna Periode Once Again." *OLZ* 96:9–22.

Newberry, Percy E. 1943. "Queen Nitocris of the Sixth Dynasty." *JEA* 29:51–54.

Nims, Charles F. 1969. "Thutmosis III's Benefactions to Amon." Pages 69–74 in *Studies in Honor of John A. Wilson: September 12, 1969.* Edited by E. B. Hauser. SAOC 35. Chicago: Oriental Institute of the University of Chicago.

Obsomer, Claude. 1995. *Sésostris Ier: Étude chronologique et historique du règne.* Etude 5. Brussels: Connaissance de l'Égypte ancienne.

O'Connor, David, and Eric H. Cline, eds. 1998. *Amenhotep III: Perspectives on his Reign.* Ann Arbor: University of Michigan Press.

O'Connor, David, and David P. Silverman. 1995."Introduction." Pages xvii–xxvii in *Ancient Egyptian Kingship.* Edited by David O'Connor and David P. Silverman. Probleme der Ägyptologie 9. Leiden: E. J. Brill.

O'Mara, Patrick F. 1986. "Is the Cairo Stone a Fake? An Example of Proof by Default." *DE* 4:33–40.

———. 1999a. "The Cairo Stone: Questions of Workmanship and Provenance." *GM* 168:73–82.

———. 1999b. "The Cairo Stone II. The Question of Authenticity." *GM* 170:69–82.

Parent, Firmin. 1992. "Seth dans l'Horus d'Or des titres royaux." Pages 347–54 in *Amosiadès: Mélanges offerts au Professeur Claude Vandersleyen par ses anciens étudiants.* Edited by Claude Obsomer and Ann-Laure Oosthoek. Louvain-la-Neuve; Université Catholique de Louvain.

Parkinson, Richard B. 1991. *The Tale of the Eloquent Peasant.* Oxford: Griffith Institute, Ashmolean Museum.

Parlebas, Jacques. 1975. "Sur l'origine de la valeur *ḏḥwty* de θ et le groupe  dans les noms de personnes." *GM* 15:39–43.

Peden, A. J. 1994. *The Reign of Ramesses IV.* Warminster: Aris & Phillips.

Perdu, Olivier. 2002. "Le roi Roudamon en personne!" *RdE* 53:157–78.

Petrie, W. M. Flinders. 1891. *Illahun, Kahun and Gurob, 1889–90.* London: David Nutt.

———. 1902. *Abydos I.* London: Kegan Paul, Trench, Trübner.

———. 1906. *Hyksos and Israelite Cities.* British School of Archaeology in Egypt and Egyptian Research Account Twelfth Year, 1906. London: Bernard Quaritch.

———. 1917. *Scarabs and Cylinders with Names.* British School of Archaeology in Egypt and Egyptian Research Account Twenty-first Year, 1915. London: Bernard Quaritch.

Pignattari, Stefania. 2008. *Due donne per il trono d'Egitto: Neferuptah e Sobekneferu.* Imola: Editrice La Mandragora.

Porten, Bezalel, et al., eds. 1996. *The Elephantine Papyri in English. Three Millennia of Cross-Cultural Continuity and Change.* Documenta et monumenta Orientis antiqui 22. Leiden: E. J. Brill. .

Postel, Lilian. 2003. "'Rame' ou 'course'? Enquête lexicographique sur le terme .'' *BIFAO* 103:377–420.

———. 2004. *Protocole des souverains égyptiens et dogme monarchique au début du Moyen Empire.* Monographies reine Elisabeth 10. Turnhout: Brepols.

Pressl, Diana A. 1993. "Zur Königsideologie der 26. Dynastie." *SAK* 20:223–54.

Pusch, Edgar B., and Anja Herold. 1999. "Qantir/Pi-Ramses." Pages 647–49 in *Encyclopedia of the Archaeology of Ancient Egypt.* Edited by Kathryn A. Bard. London and New York: Routledge.

Quibell, James E., and W. M. Flinders Petrie. 1900. *Hierakonpolis 1.* London: Bernard Quaritch.

Quirke, Stephen. 1986. "The Regular Titles of the Late Middle Kingdom." *RdE* 37:107–30.

———. 1990. *Who Were the Pharaohs? A History of their Names with a List of Cartouches.* London: British Museum Publications.

———. 2011. *The Cult of Ra: Sun-Worship in Ancient Egypt.* London: Thames & Hudson.

Raffaele, Francesco. 2003. "Dynasty 0." Pages 99–141 in *Basel Egyptology Prize 1: Junior Research in Egyptian History, Archaeology, and Philology.* Edited by Susanne Bickel and Antonio Loprieno. Aeyptiaca Helvetica 17. Basel: Schwabe.

Ranke, Hermann. 1935. *Die ägyptischen Personennamen.* Vol. 1. Glückstadt: J. J. Augustin.

Ray, John D. 2003. "The Name of King Narmer." *Lingua Aegyptia* 11:131–38.

———. 2004. "The Name of King Narmer. Postscript." *GM* 201:111.

Redford, Donald B. 1970. "The Hyksos in History and Tradition." *Or* 39:1–52.

———. 1986. *Pharaonic King-Lists, Annals and Day-Books.* Mississauga: Benben Books.

———. 1995. "The Concept of Kingship during the Eighteenth Dynasty." Pages 157–84 in *Ancient Egyptian Kingship.* Edited by David O'Connor and David P. Silverman. Probleme der Ägyptologie 9. Leiden: E. J. Brill.

———. 1997. "Textual Sources for the Hyksos Period." Pages 1–44 in *The Hyksos: New Historical and Archaeological Perspectives.* Edited by Eliezer Oren. University Museum Monograph 96. Philadelphia: University Museum, University of Pennsylvania.

Regulski, Ilona. 2008. "Online Database of Early Dynastic Inscriptions." *GM* 219:79–85.

Richards, Janet. 2002. "Text and Context in Late Old Kingdom Egypt: The Archaeology and Historiography of Weni the Elder." *JARCE* 39:75–102.

———. 2010. "Spatial and Verbal Rhetorics of Power: Constructing Late Old Kingdom History." *JEGH* 3:339–66.

———. Forthcoming. *Writing Ancient Lives: Weni the Elder and Ancient Egyptian Responses to Political Crisis.* Cambridge: Cambridge University Press.

Ritner, Robert K. 2003. "The Victory Stela of Piye," and "The Famine Stela." Pages 367–91 in *The Literature of Ancient Egypt: An Anthology of Stories, Instructions, Stelae, Autobiographies, and Poetry.* Edited by William K. Simpson. 3rd ed. New Haven and London: Yale University Press.

———. 2009. *The Libyan Anarchy: Inscriptions from Egypt's Third Intermediate Period.* Writings from the Ancient World 21. Atlanta: Society of Biblical Literature.

Robins, Gay. 1999. "The Names of Hatshepsut as King." *JEA* 85:103–12.

———. 2000. *The Art of Ancient Egypt.* Cambridge, Mass.: Harvard University Press.

Roeder, Günther. 1913. *Aegyptische Inschriften aus den königlichen Museen zu Berlin:* I, *Inschriften von der ältesten Zeit bis zum Ende der Hyksoszeit.* Leipzig: Hinrichs.

Ryholt, Kim S. B. 1997a. *The Political Situation in Egypt during the Second Intermediate Period c. 1800–1550 B.C.* CNI Publications 20. Copenhagen: Museum Tusculanum Press.

———. 1997b. "A Bead of King Ranisonb and a Note on King Qemau." *GM* 156:95–100.

———. 2008. "King Seneferka in the King-Lists and His Position in the Early Dynastic Period." *JEGH* 1:159–73.

Samuel, Alan E. 1993. "The Ptolemies and the Ideology of Kingship." Pages 168–210 in *Hellenistic History and Culture.* Edited by Peter Green. Hellenistic Culture and Society 9. Berkeley: University of California Press.

Schade-Busch, Mechthild. 1992. *Zur Königsideologie Amenophis' III: Analyse der Phraseologie historischer Texte der Voramarnazeit.* HÄB 35. Hildesheim: Gerstenberg.

Schaden, Otto J. 1978. "The God's Father Ay." Ph.D. dissertation. University of Minnesota.

Scheele-Schweitzer, Katrin. 2007. "Zu den Königsnamen der 5. und 6. Dynastie." *GM* 215:91–94.

Schmitt, Lionel. 2004. "Un bloc inédit au nom d'Horus Sehertaouy à l'Université Marc Bloch de Strasbourg (IES 346)." *RdE* 55:172–81.

Schmitz, Franz-Jürgen. 1978. *Amenophis I: Versuch einer Darstellung der Regierungszeit eines ägyptischen Herrschers der frühen 18. Dynastie.* HÄB 6. Hildesheim: Gerstenberg.

Schneider, Hans D. 1985. "A Royal Epigone of the 22nd Dynasty." Pages 261–67 in *Mélanges Gamal eddin Mokhtar II.* Edited by P. Posener-Kriéger. BdÉ 97/2. Cairo: IFAO.

Schneider, Thomas. 1996. *Lexikon der Pharaonen.* Munich: Deutscher Taschenbuch Verlag.

———. 1998. *Ausländer in Ägypten während des Mittleren Reiches und der Hyksoszeit:* Teil 1, *Die ausländischen Könige.* Wiesbaden: Harrassowitz.

Schott, Siegfried. 1969. "Zur Unvergänglichkeit des Namens." *MDAIK* 25:131–35.

Shaw, Ian, and Paul Nicholson. 1995. *The Dictionary of Ancient Egypt.* New York: Harry N. Abrams.

Simpson, William K. 1974. *The Terrace of the Great God at Abydos: The Offering Chapels of Dynasties 12 and 13.* Publications of the Pennsylvania–Yale Expedition to Egypt 5. New Haven and Philadelphia: The Peabody Museum of Natural History of Yale University and The University Museum of the University of Pennsylvania.

Smith, Harry S. 1992. "The Making of Egypt: A Review of the Influence of Susa and Sumer on Upper Egypt and Lower Nubia in the 4th Millennium B.C." Pages 235–46 in *The Followers of Horus: Studies Dedicated to Michael Allen Hoffman 1944–1990.* Edited by Renée Friedman and Barbara Adams. Egyptian Studies Association Publication 2. Oxbow Monograph 20. Oxford: Oxbow Books.

Smith, William S. 1971. "The Old Kingdom in Egypt and the Beginning of the First Intermediate Period." Pages 145–207 in *The Cambridge Ancient History.* 3rd ed. Vol. 1, Part 2. Edited by I. E. S. Edwards, C. J. Gadd, and N. G. L. Hammond. Cambridge: Cambridge University Press.

———. 1998. *The Art and Architecture of Ancient Egypt.* Rev. ed., with additions by William K. Simpson. New Haven: Yale University Press.

Sourouzian, Hourig. 1989. *Les Monuments du roi Merneptah.* Mainz am Rhein: von Zabern.

Spalinger, Anthony. 1978. "The Concept of the Monarchy during the Saite Epoch: An Essay of Synthesis." *Or* 47:12–36.

Spencer, Patricia A., and A. Jeffrey Spencer. 1986. "Notes on Libyan Egypt." *JEA* 72:198–201.

Stanwick, Paul E. 2002. *Portraits of the Ptolemies: Greek Kings as Egyptian Pharaohs.* Austin: University of Texas Press.

Stewart, Harry M. 1976. *Egyptian Stelae, Reliefs and Paintings from the Petrie Collection: The New Kingdom.* Warminster: Aris & Phillips.

Strudwick, Nigel. 2005. *Texts from the Pyramid Age.* Writings from the Ancient World 16. Atlanta: Society of Biblical Literature.

Takács, Gábor. 1997. "Note on the Name of King Narmer of the Egyptian Predynastic Period." *Folia Orientala* 33:139–42.

Tiradritti, Francesco. 1999. *Egyptian Treasures from the Egyptian Museum in Cairo.* New York: Harry N. Abrams.

Tobin, Vincent A. 2003. "The Teaching for King Merykare." Pages 152–65 in *The Literature of Ancient Egypt* Third edition. Edited by William K. Simpson. New Haven and London: Yale University Press.

Török, László. 1997. *The Kingdom of Kush. Handbook of the Napatan-Meroitic Civilization.* Handbuch der Orientalistik 1, Nahe und der Mittlere Osten 31. Leiden: E. J. Brill.

Uphill, Eric. 1965–66. "The Nine Bows." *JEOL* 19:393–420.

Valbelle, Dominique. 1990. *Les neufs arcs: L'Égyptien et les étrangers de la préhistoire à la conquête d'Alexandre.* Paris: Armand Colin.

Vandersleyen, Claude. 1995. *L'Égypte et la vallée du Nil:* Tome 2, *De la fin de l'ancien empire à la fin du nouvel empire.* Paris: Presses universitaires de France.

Vandier, Jacques. 1950. *Mo'alla. La tombe d'Ankhtifi et la tombe de Sébekhotep.* BdÉ 18. Cairo: IFAO.

———. 1968. "Une stèle égyptienne portant un nouveau nom royal de la troisième dynastie." *Comptes rendus de l'Académie des Inscriptions et Belles-Lettres* 112:16–22.

Vercoutter, Jean. 1992. *L'Egypte et la vallée du Nil.* Tome 1. *Des origines à la fin de l'ancien empire, 12000–2000 av. J.- C.* Paris: Presses universitaires de France.

Vergote, Jozef. 1961. "Le nom du roi 'Serpent'." *Or* 30:355–65.

Verner, Miroslav. 1985. "Un roi de la Ve dynastie: Rêneferef ou Rênefer?" *BIFAO* 85:281–84.

Vernus, Pascal. 1976. "Inscriptions de la Troisième Période Intermédiaire (III)." *BIFAO* 76:1–15.

———. 1980. "Name." Columns 320–26 in *Lexikon der Ägyptologie IV.* Edited by Wolfgang Helck and Eberhard Otto. Wiesbaden: Harrassowitz.

———. 1986. *Le surnom au moyen empire: Répertoire, procédés d'expression et structures de la double identité du début de la XIIe dynastie à la fin de la XVIIe dynastie.* Studia Pohl. Dissertationes scientificae de rebus orientis antiqui 13. Rome: Biblical Institute Press.

———. 1993. *Affaires et scandales sous les Ramsès: La crise des valeurs dans l'Égypte du Nouvel Empire.* Paris: J'ai lu.

Waddell, William G. 1940. *Manetho.* Loeb Classical Library. Cambridge, Mass.: Harvard University Press.

Ward, William A. 1982. *Index of Egyptian Administrative and Religious Titles of the Middle Kingdom.* Beirut: American University in Beirut.

Way, Thomas von der. 1999. "Buto (Tell el Fara'in)." Pages 180–84 in *Encyclopedia of the Archaeology of Ancient Egypt.* Edited by Kathryn A. Bard. London and New York: Routledge.

Weigall, Arthur E. P. 1908. "Upper Egyptian Notes." *ASAE* 9:105–12.

Whitehouse, Helen. 2009. *Ancient Egypt and Nubia in the Ashmolean Museum.* Oxford: Ashmolean Museum.

Wildung, Dietrich. 2003. "Looking Back into the Future. The Middle Kingdom as a Bridge to the Past." Pages 61–78 in *'Never Had the Like Occurred': Egypt's View of Its Past.* Edited by John Tait. London: University College London, Institute of Archaeology, Cavendish Publishing.

Wilkinson, Richard H. 1985. "The Horus Name and the Form and Significance of the Serekh in the Royal Egyptian Titulary." *JSSEA* 15:98–104.

———. 2003. *The Complete Gods and Goddesses of Ancient Egypt.* London: Thames & Hudson.

———. 2011. *The Temple of Tausret: The University of Arizona Egyptian Expedition Tausret Temple Project, 2004–2011.* Tucson: University of Arizona Egyptian Expedition.

———, ed. 2012. *Tausret: Forgotten Queen and Pharaoh of Egypt.* New York: Oxford University Press.

Wilkinson, Toby A. H. 1993. "The Identification of Tomb B1 at Abydos: Refuting the Existence of a King *Ro/*Iry-Hor," *JEA* 79:241–43.

———. 1995. "A New King in the Western Desert." *JEA* 81:205–10.

———. 2000. "What a King Is This: Narmer and the Concept of the Ruler." *JEA* 86:23–32.

———. 2001. *Early Dynastic Egypt.* London: Routledge.

Yoyotte, Jean. 1987. "À propos de la titulature de Chéchanq V." *Cahiers de Tanis* 1: 145–49.

Žabkar, Louis. 1968. *A Study of the Ba Concept in Ancient Egyptian Texts.* SAOC 34. Chicago: Oriental Institute of the University of Chicago.

Zayed, Abdel Hamid. 1985. "Une représentation inédite des campagnes d'Aménophis II." Pages 5–17, pls. 1–2, in *Mélanges Gamal eddin Mokhtar I.* Edited by Paule Posener-Kriéger. BdÉ 97/1. Cairo: IFAO.

Indexes

Names of Kings

The references are to page and footnote numbers, and will only occur when a king is mentioned within the text.

Achoris, 170
Adjib, 8, 17
Aha, 15
Ahmose (I), 87, 95n12
Ahmose (II), 13n104, 87, 93, 94, 108, 126
Akhenaten, 13n104, 93, 94, 105n52, 106n60
Alexander the Great, 175, 177
Alexander II, 175
Amasis, 170
Amenemhat I, 56, 58n32, 94, 108
Amenemhat III, 8, 16n119, 60, 60n48, 164
Amenemhat VI, 60, 61
Amenemhat VII, 61n53
Amenemope, 137
Amenhotep I, 94
Amenhotep II, 5, 7n51, 13, 93, 95, 136
Amenhotep III, 93, 95, 95n11, 178n15
Amenhotep IV, see Akhenaten
Apophis, 81
Apries, 4, 5
Ay, 13n104

Bakenrenef, 158
Baufre, 34, 36n38

Cambyses, 167
Cleopatra I, 182n39, 187n57
Cleopatra VII, 177, 187n52

Darius I, 167
Den, 8, 15, 17, 22n13
Dewen, 26n39
Djedkare, 38, 160
Djehuty, 83n16
Djet, 14 fig 3, 16
Djoser, 31, 33n13, 37

Elephant, 23n16

Hatshepsut, 2, 8, 9, 93, 98n26
Herihor, 136
Horemheb, 13n104, 95, 106n57, 107
Huni, 31, 33n17, 34, 34n25

Imy-ra Mesha, 61n53
Intef I, 60, 87
Intef II, 3, 87, 164
Intef V, 87
Intef VII, 87
Iny, 161n106
Iuput II, 159

Kamose, 87
Khaba, 15
Khafre, 5, 16, 34, 35, 36n38, 38
Khasekhem, 27
Khasekhemwy, 27
Khenty-pe, 24n22
Khufu, 5, 34, 35n29, 35n32, 36n38, 38n49, 42n76
Khyan, 81

Menes, 22n12
Menkaure, 34, 35
Mentuhotep II, 53n31, 54, 60, 160
Mentuhotep III, 4, 54, 165
Mentuhotep IV, 54, 56
Merenptah, 108, 109, 109n69, 109n70, 125, 169, 178n15
Meryibre Khety, 49
Merykare, 49, 52n22

Narmer, 14, 22n12, 23, 23n18
Nebkaure Khety, 49
Necho (I), 165n6
Nectanebo I, 169, 171
Nectanebo II, 175, 178n15
Nefer-neferu-aten, 13n104
Nefer(ef)re, 38
Neferhotep I, 87
Neferhotep III, 83n16
Neferirkare, 37, 38
Neferkare, 45n96, 49, 50n6
Nepherites I, 169, 170
Nimlot, 159
Nitocris (Queen), 2
Niuserre, 37, 38, 153, 169

Osorkon I, 144, 144n33
Osorkon II, 144, 144n33
Osorkon III, 152n63, 153
Osorkon IV, 152n63, 159
Osorkon the Elder, 137

Pantjeny, 87
Pedubastis, 153
Peftjauabastet, 153, 159
Pepy I, 41, 42n72, 42n74, 42n75, 43n81, 49
Pepy II, 44, 49, 153, 160
Peribsen, 27
Philip Arrhidaeus, 175
Piye, 159, 160, 161n104, 161n106
Psammuthis, 169
Psamtek I, 164, 165n6, 169
Psamtek II, 165, 167
Psamtek III, 165
Psamtek VII, 164
Psusennes I, 136
Psusennes III, 178n15
Ptolemy I, 178
Ptolemy II, 177, 177n13
Ptolemy III, 177n12, 177n13, 178
Ptolemy IV, 177n12, 177n13, 178
Ptolemy V, 177, 177n13, 178
Ptolemy VI, 177n12, 178
Ptolemy VIII, 177n12, 177n13, 178
Ptolemy IX, 177n12, 178, 178n14
Ptolemy X, 177n12, 178n14
Ptolemy XII, 178
Ptolemy XIV, 177n12

Qahedjet Huni, 31, 33n15

Radjedef, 8n56, 19, 34, 35, 36n35, 36n37, 36n38
Rahotep, 87
Ramses I, 107, 108, 109, 126
Ramses II, 4, 12, 19, 107, 108, 109, 109n69, 110n76, 118n116, 124n138, 126, 132n190, 137, 153, 160, 175n2
Ramses III, 3, 17, 125, 126, 126n146, 144, 175n2
Ramses IV, 126, 126n146, 175n2
Ramses VI, 175n2
Ramses VII, 126, 126n146, 175n2
Ramses VIII, 126
Ramses IX, 126n146
Ramses XI, 125, 136
Ro, 22n9

Sahure, 37, 38, 42n76
Sanakht, 8, 33n13
Sankhptah, 61n53
Scorpion, 14, 21
Sehetepre, 42n72
Sekhemib, 5, 29n75
Sekhemre Khutawy, 87
Sekhemreshedwaset, 83
Semerkhet, 8, 15
Senakhtenre Ahmose (I), 87, 95n12
Senwosret I, 57, 58n31, 94, 171
Senwosret II, 32n4, 57, 58n30
Senwosret III, 8, 57, 148
Senwosret IV, 165
Seqenenre Tao, 87, 91n69
Sethnakht, 125, 126, 126n146
Sety I, 12, 24, 107, 108, 109, 109n69, 109n70, 117, 122, 123n134, 175n2
Sety II, 12, 126, 136, 175n2
Sewadjkare (I), 61n53
Sewadjtu, 61n53
Shabaka, 160
Shabataka, 160
Shepseskaf, 35

Shepseskare, 38, 158
Sheshonq I, 144, 144n33
Sheshonq V, 144
Sheshonq VIa, 153
Siptah, 123n134
Smendes, 5, 136, 144
Snefru, 27n56, 34, 35n32
Sobekemsaf I, 87
Sobekemsaf II, 87
Sobekhotep I, 87
Sobekhotep III, 87
Sobekhotep VIII, 83n16
Sobeknefru (Queen), 2

Takelot II, 144
Tawosret (Queen), 2, 109, 109n69
Tefnakht, 158
Teti, 41, 42n78, 43n81
Thamphthis, 37n41
Thutmose I, 8, 9n71, 10, 11 fig 2, 13n104, 18, 93, 94, 95, 95n11, 99n30, 108
Thutmose II, 13n104, 94, 136
Thutmose III, 5, 7n50, 7n51, 9, 13n104, 17, 18, 19, 93, 95, 95n11, 108, 136, 136n3, 144, 153, 159, 160, 176n5, 176n7
Thutmose IV, 13n104, 94, 95, 95n11
Tutankhamun, 2n5, 13n104, 19n141, 93, 95, 178n15

Udimu, 26n39
Unas, 37, 38, 41
Userkaf, 37, 38
Usertesen, 58n31
Wadjkare, 40n64
Wahkare Khety, 49, 158
Wepwawetemsaf, 87

Deities

Divine names commonly found in theophoric names, such as Amenhotep, Mentuhotep, or Thutmose, will be excluded from this list.

Amun, 5, 18n 137, 113, 136, 144, 153, 160, 164, 167, 175
Amun-Re, 9, 95
Apis, 178, 182, 183, 184, 185, 186, 207, 209, 221, 228, 229
Atum, 18n137, 97, 99, 100, 101, 102, 104, 109, 110, 113, 117, 118, 119, 120, 121, 125, 127, 129, 131, 132, 145, 157n87, 183

Bastet, 147, 150, 151, 153, 156, 157, 162, 173

Ennead, 26, 31, 32n3, 50n5, 129

Hapy, 47, 124
Harakhty, 102, 112, 112n90, 129, 207
Hathor, 12, 13, 16, 16n121, 18n137, 27, 27n60, 29nn80–82, 114, 180n30, 186n52
Horus, 1, 6, 10, 12, 13, 16n21, 18n137, 27n60, 29nn 80–82, 114, 145, 180n30, 186n52
Horus of Hebit, 172

Iah, 188
Isis, 113, 128, 144, 145, 147, 148, 149, 152, 153, 154, 155, 157, 162, 172n44, 180, 183, 186, 187, 188

Khepri, 99, 111, 113, 117, 118, 182
Khnum, 35, 118, 171, 181, 186

Lord of All (sun god), 127

Maat, *passim*
Min, 45, 46
Montu, 7n51, 110, 111, 116, 120, 129
Mut, 103, 125, 129n171, 183

Nefertum, 77, 163
Neith, 23, 43, 166, 171, 181

Nekhbet, 13, 14
Nemty, 43, 158
Nun, 63
Nut, 118

Onuris, 18n137, 171, 172, 173
Osiris, 37, 113, 142, 166, 183, 187

Ptah, 18n137, 72, 73, 91n67, 112, 114, 115, 116, 117, 118, 120, 121, 123, 124, 129, 130, 132n192, 135, 145, 163, 166, 166n12, 170, 174, 180, 181, 182, 183, 184, 185, 186, 187, 188
Ptah-Khepri, 182
Ptah Ta-tjenen, 116, 130, 132n192, 179, 180, 181, 182, 183, 184, 186

Re, 8, 17, 18, 19, 37
Re-Atum, 113
Re-Harakhty, 112

Satet, 53
Sekhmet, 96n18
Seth, 16, 16n121, 17, 27, 27n60, 29, 29n81, 66, 110n74, 117, 123, 133, 140, 180n30
Sobek-Re, 60
Sokar, 60
Souls of Heliopolis, 99

Ta Tjenen, 115, 117, 121, 124, 126, 127, 128, 129, 131, 133, 184
Tefnet, 96n18
Thoth, 83, 91, 91n70, 180, 181, 184, 186, 187

Wadjet, 13, 14
Wepwawet, 15n114

Personal Names

Ankhtyfy (Nomarch), 50n6

Dedi (Supervisor of the regiments of Pharaoh), 93n3
Djehuty (High Priest of Amun), 96n14

Harkhuf (Overseer of Upper Egypt), 41
Hattusilis III (King of Hatti), 108
Heqaib, sanctuary of, 53n29
Herodotus, 167
Hordjedef, 36n38

Imhotep, 31
Iput (Queen), 45n96
Isu-ankhu (King's Son), 48n124

Julius Caesar, 177

Kagemni (Vizier), 41
Khnumhotep II (Nomarch), 58n30

Lagos (father of Ptolemy), 177

Manetho, 24, 37, 41, 44, 49, 82, 169, 173n46, 177, 241
Mark Antony, 177
Mehu (Vizier),41
Mentuemhat (Governor of Thebes), 164

Nebuchadnezzar (King of Babylon), 164
Nefertiti (Queen), 105n53
Nitocris (God's Wife of Amun), 164

Octavian, 177

Ptolemy son of Lagos, 177

Seniseneb (Queen), 10
Shepenwepet II (God's Wife of Amun), 164

Tetisheri (Queen), 96n13
Tjunuroy, 24
Turi, 10
Tushratta (King of Mitanni), 93n2

Udjahorresnet, 167

Weni the Elder, 41

Zat-Iytjenu, 48n125

Place Names

Abu Roash, 172
Abu Simbel, 115, 115n107
Abusir, 37
Abydos, 15, 16, 21, 22, 24, 25, 27, 33n13, 41, 87, 96n13, 111, 115, 116
Alexandria, 175, 177
Amada, 121, 122
Armant, 188n58, 188n60
Asyut, 48n122, 49, 158
Avaris, 81, 82, 110

Baqet (Egypt), 172, 180, 181, 185, 187
Behbeit el-Hagar, 171, 172n44
Beit Khallaf, 8n57, 33n13
Beni Hasan, 58n30
Bubastis, 144, 148
Buhen, 11n90, 124n141
Buto, 14, 15, 23n19

Coptos, 47n111, 188n161

Dahshur, 27n56, 34
Dara, 48n122
Deir el-Bahari, 55n12, 136
Deir el Medina, 116
Dendera, 100n34, 177
Derr, 115n107, 118, 119

Edfu, 111n80, 177, 184n46, 185n49
Elephantine, 10, 41, 47n117, 53, 57, 118, 167
El-Kab, 14

Faras, 106n59
Fayum, 8

Gebel Barkal, 7n51, 160, 161
Gebel Silsileh, 48n124
Gerza, 23n15
Giza, 34, 37

Hatnub, 42n77, 51n15
Hebit, 172
Heliopolis, 37, 99, 100, 101, 103, 104, 106, 110, 114, 117, 120, 121, 124, 130, 131, 132, 135, 150, 151, 175n2
Helwan, 23n20
Herakleopolis, 49, 50n4, 52, 54, 116, 145n38, 157
Hermopolis, 157, 176n8
Hibis Temple, Khargah Oasis, 168
Hierakonpolis, 14, 15, 21, 22n13, 97n22

Illahun, 106n58
Ipet (Luxor), 140
Ipet-Resyt (LuxorTemple), 118
Ipet-sut (Karnak Temple), 95, 101, 104, 107, 123, 128, 137, 139
Itj-tawy, 56, 58n28, 60

Kanais, 111
Karnak, 9, 32n4, 94, 95, 97, 99, 99n30, 101n37, 103, 104, 106n57, 107n65, 123, 129, 134n204, 136, 137, 139, 144, 147, 159, 162, 163, 171, 176n4, 176n5,176n7
Karnak Cachette, 115, 117, 118,119, 148n47, 168n21
Karnak, Festival Hall, 7n50
Karnak, Khonsu Temple, 137n6, 138n8, 142n28
Karnak, Mut Temple, 103
Karnak, Osiris chapel, 142n27
Karnak, Ptah Temple, 91n67
Karnak, White Chapel, 94
Kerma, 81
Khargah Oasis, 167
Kom el-Hisn, 150n56
Kom Ombo, 177, 187n53
Kumma, 98n24

Leontopolis, 148
Letti Basin (Sudan), 161
Lisht, 52n21, 56, 58n28
Luxor, 7n51, 103, 115, 116, 117, 118, 119, 140

Medinet Habu, 115, 126, 127
Meidum, 34
Meir, 48n122, 52n20
Memphis, 24, 44, 58n28, 102n40, 115, 118, 121, 122, 132n192, 166n12
Mendes, 138, 150n55, 150n57, 169

Meroe, 161
Mo`alla, 50n6
Musturud, 115

Nagada, 1n1, 12n98, 15, 16, 21
Napata, 2n3, 159, 160, 164
Naucratis, 164, 171, 177
Neni-Nesu, 49
Niut (Thebes), 139, 141, 142, 143

Pelusium, 167
Per-Ramses, 107, 136
Philae, 177, 179n24, 183n43, 187n54, 187n55, 187n56

Qaha, 121n124
Qantir, 107, 110n74
Qurnah, 117, 122, 123n134

Sais, 158, 164, 171, 181, 210
Samannud, 171
Saqqara, 27, 31, 37, 45n96, 46n109, 48n125
Sebennytos, 171, 172n44, 177
Semna, 57
Shatt er Rigal, 25n36
Sile (Tharu), 178, 192
Sinai, 26n41, 57, 126n149, 178n18
Siwa Oasis, 175
Soleb, 7n51, 95, 102
Southern Heliopolis (Thebes), 104, 106

Tanis, 115, 116, 117, 118, 121, 136, 139n16, 144, 148, 151n62
Tarkhan, 23n15
Tell el-Debaa, 81
Tell el Muqdam, 148
Tell el-Yehudiyeh, 132n192
Tharu (Sile), 178n18
Thebes, 7, 52, 56, 58n28, 83, 85, 87, 91, 94, 96, 98–103, 104, 107–9, 110n77, 112–14, 117, 119–20, 123, 125, 133, 135–36, 138–39, 141n24, 142–44, 147, 149, 151–56, 161, 163, 164
Thinis, 89
This, 24
Tod, 53n31
Tomas, 42n77
Turah, 23n18, 23n19, 101

Valley of the Kings, 107n63, 124n140, 125, 132n93, 136

Wadi Hammamat, 36n38, 42n74, 48n119, 48n120
Wadi Tumilat, 51n18

Xois, 121

Subjects

Actium, Battle of, 177
Adoption Stela, 164n1
Amarna Letter EA 20, 93n2
Assyria, 108, 159, 164, 165n6

Babylon, 164, 175
Battlefield Palette, 12n97
Benben stone, 37

Carchemish, Battle of, 164
Coffin Texts, Spell 148, 12n99

Decree of Naucratis, 171
Divine Adoratrice of Amun, 153

Fenkhu-Asiatics, 126, 127

God's Wife of Amun, 164

High Priest of Amun, 136, 137, 140, 142, 143, 144
Hittites, 107, 108
Hyksos, 81, 83, 86, 87, 93, 94, 96n13, 175

Israel Stela, 108
Iuntiu-Asiatics, 95, 103

Jewish colony, Elephantine, 167

Kadesh, Battle of, 108
King Lists, 3, 44, 49

Libya, 95, 103, 108, 109, 120n122, 126–29, 144, 154n71, 165n5, 174n49
Libyan Palette, 12n96, 12n97

Mediterranean, 14, 93, 175, 177, 184
Megiddo, Siege of, 7n50
Memnon Colossus, Thebes, 103
Memphite Theology col. 55, 5n11
Mentiu/Mentjyu-bedouin, 95, 103, 109, 110, 144, 147, 148
Meshwesh-Libyans, 144
Mitanni, 93, 93n2

Narmer Palette, 14, 15n114, 40
Nine Bows, 12, 82, 95, 97, 100, 101, 103, 108, 109, 110, 112, 119, 121, 122, 126, 129, 130, 132, 133, 136, 139, 144, 145, 162, 173, 183
Nomarchs, 37, 49, 50n6, 52, 57
Nubia, 2, 2n3, 7n51, 10, 37, 41, 42n77, 57, 75, 81, 93, 95, 98n24, 102, 106n59, 108, 115, 118, 119, 121, 124n141, 125, 126, 159

Obelisks, 3, 37, 95, 97, 99, 110, 115–19, 121, 161, 175n2, 183n43

Peace Treaty (Ramses II), 108
Persia, 164, 167, 169, 171, 173, 175
Punt, 37
Pyramid Texts, Spell 267, 31
Pyramid Texts, Spell 523, 34
Pyramid Texts, Spell 627, 12n99

Restoration Stela, Tutankhamun, 19n141
Rome, 177
Rosetta Stone, 17n126, 177
Rulers of the Foreign Lands, 100

Scorpion Macehead, 14, 21
Sea Peoples, 108
Sed festival, 12, 95, 97, 99, 102n42, 103n47, 104, 115, 116, 124, 127–30, 131n188, 132n191, 144, 151n62, 179–84, 186
Serekh, 13, 13n106, 14 fig. 3, 15, 16, 21, 21n7, 23, 23n19, 29n81, 132n192, 165n9
Setetiu/Setjetiu-Asiatics, 95, 102, 106, 109, 117, 126, 127, 145, 148
Sphinx, 103, 134n204
Step Pyramid, Saqqara, 31

Tehenu/Tjehenu -Libyans, 95, 103, 126, 127, 129, 197
Temehu-Libyans, 109, 120, 126, 127

Western Asia, 37, 41, 57, 81, 164, 171

Sources

Abydos King List, 24, 44, 49
Ashmolean Museum AN1896-1908.E3632 (macehead), 21

Bentresh Stela, 117, 118, 119
Berlin 3023 (papyrus), 51n18
Berlin 7702 (statue), 32n4
Berlin 10499 (papyrus), 51n18
Berlin 10523 (papyrus), 47n117
Berlin 13725 (stela), 11n90
British Museum 6640 (mummy bandages), 161n111
Buhen ST9 (stela), 11n90

Cairo Annals, 24
Cairo CG 20538 (stela), 5n19
Cairo CG 23115 (offering table), 172
Cairo CG 28088 (coffin), 51n14
Cairo CG 34002 (Tetisheri Donation Stela), 96n13
Cairo CG 34006 (stela), 11n90
Cairo JE 39410 (block), 145n38
Coptos Decrees, (h), 47n111; (j) to (q), 47n113; (r), 47n118

Donation Stela (Abydos), 96n13

Eloquent Peasant B1 104, R 17.1, 51n18

Famine Stela (Sehel), 32n4

Hammamat 100, 166n10
Hammamat 168–69, 42n74, 48n119
Hammamat 199, 58n30
Hammamat 206, 48n120

Karnak King List, 53n27

Leiden V 4 (stela), 58n36
Louvre C100 (stela), 161
Louvre E 8419 (papyrus), 132n194

New York, MMA 14.2.6 (stela), 53n34

Pap. Westcar (1,14), 32n4
Piye Stela, 159

Saqqara King List, 24
Sinai 271, 126n149

Turin Canon of Kings, 24, 30n92, 44, 49, 56, 74, 82
Turin Museum 1380 (statue), 118n116

Urk. VII, 26:20, 58n30

Concordances

Texts in *Urkunden* IV

2:5, **6n33**
80:11, **9n75**
80–81, **10n89**
92–94, **97n19**
135, **97n22**
160:10–11, **9n70**
160:11, **10n83**
160–61, **18n138**
161:9–12, **18n140**
252:3,6, **10n87**
261:2–4, **9n72**
261:11–13, **9n73**
261:17, **8n64**
261–62, **8n62**
276:11, **9n82**
285:6, **10n83**
358:14, **9n80**
366:15, **5n12**
383:12, **9n77, 80**
600:5–6, **99n32**
608:14, **53n27**
609:15, **56n17**
661:6, **7n50**
740:1, **7n52**
995:11, **94n3**
1250:16, **7n51**
1252:7, **7n51**
1254:9, **7n50**
1268:2, **7n54**
1283:3, **5n20**
1295:7–8, **5n21**
1297:8, **7n48**
1302:3, **7n47**
1355:9, **7n51**
1405:19, **7n55**
1410:4, **6n34**
1421:19, **7n52**
1446:12, **6n41**
1446:18, **6n40**
1493:7, **6n43**
1504:8, **6n40**
1537:2, **6n27**
1554:2, **7n55**
1601:2, **6n28**
1626:15, **6n25**
1641:19, **6n40**
1650:5, **7n53**
1652:12, **7n48**
1655:2, **7n51**
1668:10, **7n51**
1685:14, **5n16**
1693:17, **5n16**
1709:17, **7n51**
1710:7, **5n15, 7n51**
1746, **103n43**
1747, **103n46**
1748–49, **103n47**
1752:11, **5n15, 7n51**
1758:10, **7n55**
1778:3, **5n22**
1785:14, **6n23**
1796:15, **7n55**
1800:19, **6n31**
1805:4, **6n24, 29**
1808:11, **6n40**
1818:10, **6n32**
1822:11, **5n17**
1835:9, **6n26**
1845:20, **6n25**
1846:15, **6n26**
1875:18, **6n23**
1912:6, **6n31**
1913:20, **6n40**
1919:3, **6n40**
1921:1, **5n15**
1934:15, **5n18**
1939:16, **6n42**
1950:12, **6n42**
2026:18–19, **19n141**
2033, **106n57**
2044, **106n59**
2118:11, **9n75**
2123:16, **9n75**
2175:14, **107n65**

Texts in Kitchen, *Ramesside Inscriptions*

I, 66:5, **5n13**
I, 66:11, **7n46**
I, 70–71, **111n80**
I, 71:14, **111n80**
I, 118–20, **110n76**
I, 134:12, **111n81**
I, 147–49, **112n86**
I, 147–62, **112n85**
I, 149–50, **112n87**
I, 151–52, **112n89**
I, 153–54, **113n93**
I, 154–57, **113n94**
I, 157–59, **113n95**
I, 159–62, **114n96**
I, 178, **24n25**
I, 178:11–179:1, **44n90**
I, 185:8, **111n82**
I, 185:10, **111n83**
I, 185:12, **111n84**
I, 232–34, **110n74**
II, 15:11–15, **7n49**
II, 79:6–9, **5n14**
II, 258–81, **115n106**
II, 259, **115n107**

II, 259:11, **115**
II, 262:8, **129**
II, 284:14, **117–19**
II, 294:10, **116**
II, 352:13, **118–19**
II, 408:14, **116**
II, 408–28, **115n100**
II, 409:9, **117**
II, 409:13, **116**
II, 409:15, **117**
II, 410:12, **117**
II, 411:14, **116**
II, 412:4, **117**
II, 413:5, **116**
II, 415:12, **117**
II, 420:9, **118**
II, 420:13, **115**
II, 424:3, **116–17**
II, 424:5, **115**
II, 424:6, **117**
II, 424:13, **117**
II, 469:11, **115**
II, 479:15, **117**
II, 488:7, **118**
II, 505:5, **116**
II, 546–47, **116**
II, 547:13, **116**
II, 547–48, **115n102**
II, 548:6, **116**
II, 583:4, **119**
II, 586, **10n85**
II, 586:9, **117–18**
II, 586:10, **119**
II, 586–91, **115n105**
II, 590:15, **118n116**
II, 598–605, **115n103**
II, 599:3, **119**
II, 599:5, **116 and 118**
II, 599:5–6, **119**
II, 599:8, **118**
II, 602:15, **117–18**
II, 602:16, **119**
II, 603:2, **115 and 118**
II, 603:2–3, **119**
II, 603:14, **116**
II, 603:16, **116**
II, 605:4, **117–18**
II, 605:11, **117–18**
II, 605:12, **119**
II, 605:15, **117–18**
II, 605:15–16, **119**
II, 605–6, **115n104**
II, 641:6, **117**
II, 703:3, **116**
II, 716:2, **118**
II, 738–46, **115n107**
II, 740:2, **119**
II, 740:5, **118**
II, 740:6, **119**
II, 832:3–8, **44n91**
II, 832:13–833:11, **49n3**
II, 834:16, **56n22**
II, 838:6, **75n146**
II, 838:6–839:15, **74n132**
II, 840:3–5, **74n133**
II, 840:13–15, **74n133**
II, 841:2–3, **74n132**
II, 842:9–843:6, **83n14**
II, 842:12, **84n27**
II, 842:13, **84n30**
II, 842:14, **84n31**
II, 843, **88n49**
II, 843:1, **85n34**
II, 843:2, **88n50**
II, 843:8, **88n47**
II, 843:9, **88n48**
II, 844:10, **117**
III, 111, **115n101**
III, 111:14, **115**
III, 304:1, **10n86**
III, 481:10, **59n37**
III, 481–82, **24n27**
IV, 1:8, **121–22**
IV, 31:1–13, **121n124**
IV, 43:9, **121**
IV, 50:13, **121**
IV, 53:12, **122**
IV, 54:11, **121**
IV, 54:14, **121**
IV, 54:16, **121**
IV, 54–55, **121**
IV, 55:1, **121**
IV, 66:1, **122**
IV, 196:9, **123n134**
IV, 347:13, **124nn140–41**
IV, 348–49, **124n141**
V, 7, **126n149**
V, 20:14, **128n157**
V, 20:14–15, **129n174**
V, 20:15–16, **129n179**
V, 30:14, **128n161**
V, 37:10, **127n154**
V, 37:10–11, **129n172**
V, 37:11, **129n176**
V, 49:14, **127n153**
V, 289:3, **129n171**
V, 314:8, **127n156**
V, 314:8–9, **129n173**
V, 314:9, **129n177**
V, 315:11, **128n159**
V, 316:6, **128n160**
VI, 5:6, **10n88**
VI, 6:3, **10n84**
VI, 6:6, **9n76**
VI, 7:7, **9n78**
VI, 380:5–6, **132n192**
VI, 385:3, **132n192**
VI, 386:8, **132n193**
VI, 397:3, **132n194**
VI, 462:15, **133n197**
VI, 523 (26), **133n199**
VI, 679:3, **134n204**
VI, 679:13, **134nn201–2**

www.ingramcontent.com/pod-product-compliance
Lightning Source LLC
Chambersburg PA
CBHW031708230426
43668CB00006B/148
9781589837355